90 0846771 8

UNIVERSITY OF PLYMOUTH

WITHDRAWN FROM UNIVERSITY OF PLYMOUTH LIBRARY SERVICES

KV-314-498

BEING

A Psychology of Self

Robert Wrenn

Reed Mencke

Charles Seale-Hayne Library
University of Plymouth
(01752) 588 588
LibraryandITenquiries@plymouth.ac.uk

SRA

SCIENCE RESEARCH ASSOCIATES, INC.
Chicago, Palo Alto, Toronto
Henley-on-Thames, Sydney, Paris

A Subsidiary of IBM

We wish to acknowledge the following for permission to reprint copyrighted material:

pp. 33–40, 42–43: From Peter Madison, PERSONALITY DEVELOPMENT IN COLLEGE, 1969, Addison-Wesley, Reading, Mass.

pp. 53: Reprinted from LET'S BE PEOPLE by Donald Decker. Used by permission of the author.

p. 57: Copyright © 1972 Human Behavior Magazine. Reprinted by Permission.

p. 59: Excerpted from "What it Feels Like to be a Mental Patient" in the *Arizona Daily Star*, July 16, 1972. © 1972 Arizona Daily Star. Used by permission.

pp. 85, 177: Excerpted from *Toward a Psychology of Being* (2nd ed.) by Abraham H. Maslow. © 1968 by Litton Educational Publishing, Inc. Used by permission of D. Van Nostrand Company.

pp. 93–94: Copyright 1920 by permission of Macmillan Publishing Co., Inc., renewed 1947 by Raymond Swinford Shackleton and Edward Arthur Alexander Shackleton. Permission also granted by the Trustees of the will of the late Sir A. L. L. Lucas-Tooth.

p. 95: Excerpted from "Last Thoughts of a Drowning Man" by C. Thurmond in *Journal of Abnormal and Social Psychology*, Vol. 38, 1943. Reprinted by permission.

p. 118: Copyright © 1972 by Robert E. Kavanaugh. Reprinted by permission of Nash Publishing Corporation from FACING DEATH by Dr. Robert E. Kavanaugh.

p. 127: From "Through Death's Door" by K. Goodall from TIELINE, PSYCHOLOGY TODAY MAGAZINE, October 1972. Copyright © Ziff-Davis Publishing Company. All rights reserved.

Library of Congress Cataloging in Publication Data

Wrenn, Robert L., 1933–
  Being: a psychology of self.

  Includes bibliographies and index.
  1. Personality. 2. Adjustment (Psychology)
I. Mencke, Reed A., 1939–   joint author.
II. Title.   [DNLM: 1. Personality. 2. Self concept. 3. Social adjustment. BF698 W945b]
BF698.W74   155.2′5   74–30207

ISBN 0–574–19900–4

p. 130: From "Dead on Arrival" by D. Sudnow in *Trans-Action*, November 1967. Used by permission of Trans-Action Society.

p. 131: From "Grow Old Along With Me" by B. Neugarten from PSYCHOLOGY TODAY MAGAZINE, December 1971. Copyright © Ziff-Davis Publishing Company. All rights reserved.

p. 133: From "LSD and the Anguish of Dying" by S. Cohen in Harpers, September 1965. Used by permission.

p. 141: "The Lesson of the Moth" from *archy and mehitabel* by Don Marquis. Copyright 1927 by Doubleday and Company, Inc. Reprinted by permission of the copyright holder.

pp. 146–47: Paul E. Meehl. "Law and the Fireside Inductions: Some Reflections of a Clinical Psychologist," JOURNAL OF SOCIAL ISSUES, Vol. 27, NO. 4(1971), page 68.

p. 177: From *The Pursuit of Loneliness* by Philip Slater. © Beacon Press.

p. 200: From *Future Shock* by Alvin Toffler. © 1971 Random House, Inc. Used by permission.

pp. 243, 251–52: From *Gestalt Therapy Verbatim* by F.S. Perls. © 1969 Real People Press.

pp. 254–55: Reprinted from "An Autobiographic Sketch" by Otto Loewi in *Perspectives in Biology and Medicine*, Autumn, 1960. © 1960 by The University of Chicago Press. All rights reserved. Used by permission of The University of Chicago Press.

pp. 263, 273: Reprinted by permission of Collins-Knowlton-Wing, Inc. Copyright © 1966 by Mulla Nasrudin Enterprises, Ltd. Reprinted by permission of Idries Shah and Jonathan Cape Ltd.

p. 275: From *The Natural Mind* by Andrew Weil. Used by permission of the Houghton Mifflin Company.

P. 276 (Fig. 11-2): Adapted from "The Physiology of Meditation" by Robert Keith Wallace and Herbert Benson, SCIENTIFIC AMERICAN, February, 1972. Reprinted by permission of the publisher and Robert Keith Wallace.

pp. 298–99: from "Experimentally-Induced Telepathy in Dreams: Two Studies Using EEG-REM Monitoring Techniques" by M. Uhlman, S. Krippner, and S. Feldman. In the International Journal of Parapsychology, Vol. 8, 1966, pp. 577–98. © 1966 The Parapsychology Foundation, Inc.

p. 301: Excerpted from "The Role of Neurological Items in Psychiatry" by Donald Hebb in *The Journal of Personality*, Vol. 20, 1951. Reprinted by permission.

pp. 301–02: from THE MEDIUM, THE MYSTIC, AND THE PHYSICIST by Lawrence LeShan. Copyright © 1966, 1973, 1974 by Lawrence LeShan. Reprinted by permission of The Viking Press, Inc.

© 1975, Science Research Associates, Inc. All rights reserved.
Printed in the United States of America.

This book is dedicated to six outstanding representatives of our future generation:

Todd
Kim
Scott
Susan
David
Lisa

and to eight outstanding representatives of our previous generation:

Gladys
Mac
Kathleen
Gilbert
Dorothy
Carl
Charlotte
John

UNIVERSITY OF PLYMOUTH
LIBRARY SERVICES

Item No.	9001408617
Class No.	155.25 / WRE
Contl No.	057419 9004

A culture has to get its values across to children in such simple terms that even a behavioral scientist can understand them.

Margaret Mead

Table of Contents

Preface

Having taught a course titled "The Normal Personality" for a number of years, we have come to the conclusion that there is no such thing. Terms such as *normal, personality*, and even *adjustment* require many qualifying statements to tease out whatever meaning they may have. The more precisely such terms are defined, the less interested in them the student becomes. Therefore our goal in writing this text has been to select some of the more exciting and interesting ideas and areas of research available today and to present them simply and clearly. We aim at selectivity, not comprehensiveness.

This text is divided into four parts. Part one is an introduction to some basic ideas and values that we will be looking at throughout the book. In chapter one, we will examine those psychologists in our field who have been looking at the question of how psychology can contribute to an understanding of personality. Within their lives we can see their own difficulties in separating themselves from their subject matter. In this chapter we will also present the idea that there are several ways to look at the subject of personality.

Part two covers the general topic of learning who we are. It contains three chapters that focus on different aspects of the question "Who am I?" In chapter two we will attempt to identify and accept the many selves that we are day by day. Chapter three will explore the effects of labeling people and some of the means of coping with the forces behind this. Finally, in chapter four, we will focus on personality growth, enhancement, and our potential for the "good life."

Part three delineates the basic tasks of life and discusses how we adjust to them. We will begin, in chapter five, by recognizing the basic adjustment we must face at any age to all that we have come to cherish: the adjustment to loss and death. Chapter six relates the forces that influence us as we develop beliefs and defend them. In chapter seven we attempt to relate our basic drives of sex and aggression to the culture we grow up within. In the last chapter in part three, chapter eight, we will consider our sexual (loving) and aggressive (hating) tendencies in terms of the relationships they occur within as we mature.

In part four we will look at ways of changing our lives and methods of intervening into areas that cause us concern. First, we will consider the topic of counseling and psychotherapy in chapter nine. It seems that each therapy tends to increase our awareness of a slightly different aspect of our personality: one focuses on the way our biology influences our behavior, another deals with our social environment, and a third focuses on our unconscious. Chapter ten is devoted to our dreams and how we may use them to become more aware of ourselves. In it we will also examine anxiety and relaxation as important aspects of our conscious experience. Chapter eleven discusses anxiety and its causes, as well as psychological techniques such as hypnosis, meditation, and biofeedback that we can use to learn to relax and to cope with anxiety. Finally, in chapter twelve we will look at the frontiers of human awareness. Is there any limit to what we are capable of sensing? We will discuss extrasensory perception, sensitivity to electromagnetic waves, poltergeists, and other "things that go bump in the night." Such phenomena support the view that most of us use only a small fraction of our full potentials for sensing and perceiving.

The problem of what topics to include in this book was resolved mainly by examining the interests and questions of our students. God bless them one and all. In each chapter, *conceptual material*— including theory, concepts, methods, glossary, and bibliography—is presented for intellectual enlightenment. *Personal sharing*, either of author or of student experiences, is also included in each chapter. *Exercises* for individual or class use help you to practice what we preach. With one exception, exercises are included at the end of each chapter. A general glossary is included at the back of the book. Bob Wrenn wrote chapters 1, 5, 6, 7, and 8; Reed Mencke authored chapters 2, 3, 4, 9, 10, 11, and 12.

The presence of conceptual material needs no explanation, but a word or two might be said about the value of personal sharing and exercise material in a book of this sort. For many college students, "norming in" is very difficult. Most universities or community colleges consist of quite a number of fragmented student-culture groups; the overall picture of a well-rounded "college identity" is often hard to find. Such personal sharing from our experiences and those of a wide variety of students is intended to ease your orientation by giving you operational cues about how others handle their affairs. The exercise material is intended to allow you to become more aware of what the chapter concepts "feel like" when they are applied practically.

Each chapter provides reference notations, a summary, a glossary of special terms, and a bibliography. In general, we have attempted to avoid sexist stereotypes and terminology—given, of course, the limitations of cultural reality and the English language. Reference material from such popular magazines as *Psychology Today* and *Human Behavior* was deliberately used in many instances with the hope that these magazines are more readily available and are more interesting than clinical journals.

In the final analysis, this text aims to do what every text aims to do: to give texture, to add structure, to compose (from the Latin *textus*). Our particular weave of cloth is focused more on process than on status. As you study the psychology of personality, we hope to give you alternative viewpoints in problem solving, not a party line to one school of thought. Looking at alternatives is the way we, the authors, operate as practitioners, and it is what we believe in. We must admit that although we make a strong attempt to be objective, we generally fail. The science of psychology provides few final answers for the complexities of working with people. Yes, there are useful methods and techniques and principles and laws. There is a body of knowledge. But the context in which these principles and laws are scientifically revealed is far removed from their general application.

Another point. We believe that psychology will never quite achieve its goal of prediction and control of behavior. Heresy? Perhaps. But the study of humanity is a hit-or-miss proposition. The amount of literature devoted to how psychologists get in the way of their own findings is so plentiful that we feel to handle that problem alone will take longer than our lifetimes. This is not as pessimistic as it may appear. Every field of study finds it impossible to get directly at the truth—we can get close for a moment, but it always slips away. Furthermore, we as psychologists have placed definite limitations on what we should be studying, even though we are very far from agreement even as to that. Of course, we may be on the brink of a new era in which psychology will embrace areas that heretofore were thought to be out of the mainstream of respectability, such as voluntary control of the autonomic processes and parapsychology. At any rate, although we have no inside predictions about where psychology is going, we feel it is an exciting field for the research-minded student and for the practitioner as well. As long as you can live comfortably with ambiguity, you will probably find psychology to your liking.

We are indebted to a great many people for the fact that this book was ever published. While we alone stand behind whatever criticism there may be of this text, we would like to first and foremost thank the many hundreds of students who touched and shared their lives with us. We also thank Peter Madison, friend, colleague, and inspiration to us both; Bill Thweatt, for teaching us the rudiments of TA; Vaughn Huff, for far-out ideas; Harley Christiansen, who introduced us to hypnosis; Karl Schmidt and Gary De Walt, who kept our powder dry and our guns aimed; Dick Coan, for his intellectually stimulating thoughts and procedures; David Laird, University of Arizona Librarian and his dedicated science library staff, for providing writing space, reference materials, and humane treatment; to John Schaefer, President of the University of Arizona, Dick Edwards, Vice President of the University of Arizona and Neil Bartlett, head of the psychology department of the University of Arizona, for providing support in our teaching and research efforts; Anne Roe and George Simpson, for use of the SIMROE Foundation library and for being wise and venerable models for living; Lucille Downey, for her accuracy and patience in typing both drafts of the book; Pat Billings and Nancy Yanaway, for keeping our office safe and sound. We owe you all our deep appreciation. We are especially indebted to Marcy Wrenn and Jean Mencke for just being.

Robert L. Wrenn
Reed A. Mencke

Tucson, Arizona
January, 1975

PART ONE

Introduction

In part one we are faced with a dilemma that is repeated throughout this book. The psychology of personality is the psychology of people. As we become more scientific by selecting tighter, more precise controls in our laboratories, we selectively rule out those very factors that affect us in a free environment. We move further away from the way life really is. We compound this problem by being the subjects of our subject. Of all the fields of science, none is more open to the factor of human error than is the science of personality. Yet pioneers who established the basic schools of thought in psychology have done much toward solving this dilemma. We introduce this book, then, by looking at the basic ideas and values that form a foundation for the chapters that follow.

Chapter One: A Short Overview of Psychology

"I saw one [a Heffalump] once,"
said Piglet. "At least, I think I did,"
he said. "Only perhaps it wasn't."

A. A. MILNE, *Winnie-the-Pooh*

The Fascinating Worlds of Perception

Psychology cannot be separated from the psychologists who study it. The human side of psychology reflects the richness of the varying perceptions that psychologists bring to their day-to-day work. Although our focus in this chapter will be on the three main forces in psychology in the United States today, it is the human quality of perception that makes this study so exciting. Let's turn first, then, to some general considerations that have both plagued and delighted psychologists.

SELECTING A REALITY

The "reality" we experience so vividly is created by our enormous capacity for selective attention to only those stimuli that help us to adapt to our environment. For example, we cannot see an X ray. As a matter of fact, we have never seen most of the kinds of energy available to us in the visible-light spectrum. Consider how different the world would appear if we were sensitive to all of the many varieties of light energy shown in figure 1-1. What a different world it would be!

As you can see, the narrow black band up the middle of figure 1-1 is a very small piece of the action. Buckminster Fuller, the revered architect-philosopher-lecturer, has repeatedly used the values shown in figure 1-1 during his college lecture tours to remind us that most of the forces that act and work on us are unseen, unfelt, unheard, untasted, and untouched. Not only do we fail to see the full light spectrum but also we are deaf to the full range of sound; neither do we see our own heart, bladder, kidneys, or brain cells react, grow, or die. (However, we are sometimes aware of the effects of these forces.)

Our perception and understanding of the world around and within us requires that we make sense of the direct information input we receive. Have you had the experience of naively enjoying an event and then having to question and change its meaning

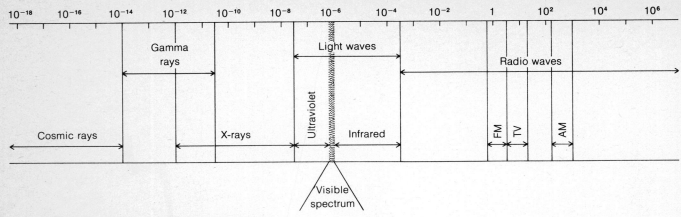

FIG. 1-1 *The electromagnetic spectrum*

to fit your perceptions of the world? Direct information input is mediated or altered depending on the values instilled in us from our parents and culture. New experiences are often interpreted in the light of old ones. For example, as a boy I was once given a sandwich that I devoured hungrily. When I learned that the meat in it was cow tongue, I blanched.

SOME COMMON ILLUSIONS

To demonstrate that we bring our past experiences with us in interpreting new data, take a look at the illusions in figures 1-2 through 1-6.

What do you see in figure 1-2? Some people see an old hag, a witch. Others see a young girl. If you allow yourself to look at it in a relaxed way, you will find that you can shift back and forth and see first one and then the other. It is practically impossible to see both patterns at the same time. In other words, we can tune in the particular reality we want to experience at a given moment, but we are limited to only one reality at a time.

After looking at these figures you are probably more skeptical of what you see and perhaps not so willing to trust one sense alone. The search for an understanding of personality is much like what you have just experienced visually. We also bring our own experiences with us in other ways to the obser-

vations we make about people. This is true whether we are students in a casual "people-watching" situation or psychologists conducting a more objective analysis of personality in the laboratory. This fact is inescapable and very frustrating for most of us if and when we become aware of it.

FIG. 1-2 *Old hag or young girl?*

FIG. 1-3 *Which figure is taller?*

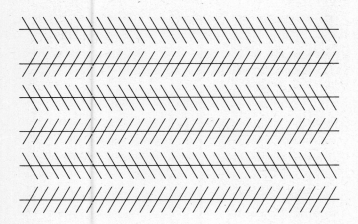

FIG. 1-4 *Are the horizontal lines parallel?*

FIG. 1-5 *Which one looks longer?*

FIG. 1-6 *How many blocks—six or seven?*

Knowing Our Limitations

Just as it is difficult to explain that you knew you should not be seeing the illusions in the figures because your mind told you they *were* illusions, it is difficult to explain why you took the time to look at them in the first place. Even when your response is "It was assigned reading" or "How else can I get through school?", the questions still remain, "Why read?" "Why get through school?" Ultimately to answer them you must offer some value of life such as "One must get ahead in this world" or "Education is personally worthwhile."

Nature, in all its beauty and wonder, has placed definite limits both on what we can know of ourselves and on what we can do about it. This is not cynicism; it's realism. For example, most of us take the responsibility of eventually convincing ourselves that we have found a good (for us) vocation, a good spouse, a good political party, a good religion (or variation thereof), a good car, and so on. Yet what kind of chance does this world give us to make such choices with any sort of objectivity? We can't directly test all the alternatives. We make these important decisions after years of selective conditioning and perceptual biasing. We can't *be* a doctor, lawyer, or Indian chief before choosing a vocation. We can't live with Susan or Robert for a few months and know what it's really like to be married. So we take a sample and satisfy ourselves that at some point along the way we have done the best we can. If we can't trust our senses for accuracy and if we are limited in what we can know and do, how should we feel about this state of affairs? What does it all add up to?

THE STRUGGLE FOR CLOSURE

I want to answer the question above. But in all honesty, I don't have *the* answer. I have *my* answer, as you have yours. Is it more valuable to paint a landscape or to photograph it? It depends, you might say, on the purpose of the act and on the desires of the one who executes the activity. It also depends on whether a person can do both. We are fortunate: we have a painter (subjective self) and a photographer (objective self) within us. These aspects of our personality work hand in hand. Now we may be able to see a little more clearly that although we look at an illusion objectively, we see it subjectively. Although we choose a career or mate objectively, we don't really operate like computers. And, although we seek and struggle for some closure or answer to the many questions of life, we don't always leave the table of knowledge satisfied.

Alan Watts, an expert on eastern and western religions, once gave a speech entitled "Divine Madness." He illustrated the dilemma of not knowing the final answers to questions by a story of a man who lost a prized horse. All the neighbors said, "Oh, how awful," to which the man's response was "Maybe." The horse returned accompanied by six wild horses and all the neighbors said, "How wonderful," to which his response was "Maybe." The next day his son tried to ride one of these bucking broncos but fell and broke his leg, and all the neighbors said, "How awful." His response was "Maybe." The next day the son was rejected for an army physical because of the broken leg and the neighbors said, "How wonderful! He won't have to go to war," to which the man responded, "Maybe." How hard it is to formulate a final answer!

SITUATIONAL LIMITATIONS ON OUR BEHAVIOR

Finally, we must acknowledge that we are trapped in another way—by our history. Some of us are trapped more than others and some parts or aspects of us are trapped more than other parts. Nevertheless, the situation we are in, the country we grew up in, and the century we live in are all aspects of our personalities.

For example, there is a tendency in our culture to attribute to boys, men, and in general the masculine nature as being (across the board) emotionally controlled, confident, self-sufficient, counteracting, independent, intrusive (Freud loves that one),

tough-minded, objective, analytic, active, rational, unyielding, and so forth. Anything feminine is generally thought of as being subjective, passive, sensitive, yielding, empathic, conservative, dependent, emotional, intuitive, tender-minded, and so forth. These labels that others deal to us often teach us how to behave in a given situation. For example, shall I leap over tall buildings at a single bound or shall I gracefully glide up the first step? Shall I tell that (*!Z#*#) off or shall I just avoid him next time he comes my way? Different situations seem to reward different behaviors. In his book *Future Shock*, Toffler points out the inappropriateness of interacting with everyone you meet in a fluid social context, such as your fellow riders in the subway or a friendly shoe salesperson. Such relationships are tentative and functional, and you tend to remain passive. But in a family or in an encounter group you jolly well better do more than sit there like a bump. To do otherwise may cost you your ego.

By now you can begin to appreciate the fact that the psychologists who have tried to make a science of behavior are no different from you or me in being vulnerable to this fascinating world of perception and bias. They were not always sure what direction to go in. But go they did. Human beings are purposive, and if no direction is apparent for what they are doing with their lives and their observations, they will find one. Three directions that psychologists have ventured along stand out more clearly than others. Before we discuss them, let's spend a moment considering how such historical forces might be treated.

A Short History of Psychology

Some general approaches to the history of psychology are outlined in *A Brief History of Psychology* (Wertheimer 1970). The chronological account of events is a most popular form. If you are hungry for sequence and detail, dip into either Boring (1950) or Murphy (1949); they do this quite well. Here you can see how the Greeks, such as Socrates, Plato, and Aristotle, laid down the assumptions and raised the sorts of questions that would later titillate the empiricists (or budding researchers) of the Renaissance era. You will probably become aware that Marco Polo was a thirteenth-century world traveler who had more to contribute to our heritage than just a name to shout in the swimming pool. Certainly the German and British philosopher-scientists before the turn of this century, such as Fechner or Galton, not only thought grand thoughts but experimented with them as well. They developed systems, methods, and number rules that helped to legitimize the field of psychology as an objective science.

A second historical approach is to describe certain schools of thought. In psychology, although many late nineteenth- and early twentieth-century schools had their roots in England, Germany, and France, they quickly became Americanized. Both the names of their prominent researchers as well as their essential thought or methodology are familiar —

The Basic Approaches to Personality Theory

We have our own theories as to why we do what we do, but many times we are confused about how we feel and behave. Psychologists have tried to establish a system of personality theories but have had similar problems in procedure. A theory is not factual; it is a guess. A good theory sets up certain rules so that we don't have to observe everything in order to study something.

In 1938, Henry Murray, a Harvard psychologist, looked at the problem of personality theory and decided that there are two sorts of personality theorists. One group are the centralists, or those who emphasize human inner workings and transformations; the other are the peripheralists, or those who emphasize physical patterns of overt behavior. To oversimplify, the peripheralist counts the number of wags of the dog's tail while the centralist wonders why it is wagging. A third, later, point of view accepts that both the centralist and the peripheralist points contribute to psychology, but attempts to assess what is applicable to humankind in both these psychologies and to go on from there. The centralist or dynamic approach we might label the first force in the history of psychology in the United States. The peripheralist or behavioral approach is the second, and the third has become known as the humanistic approach. (A fourth approach—normative-descriptive—is basically a tool and will be discussed at the end of this chapter.) Table 1.1 shows the basic characteristics of these three approaches.

DYNAMIC PSYCHOLOGY

We will take a look at each of these in turn, beginning with first: dynamic psychology.

Darwin and Freud:
Biological Adaptation and Repression

Charles Darwin (1809–1882) gave psychologists who followed him a motivation theory based on biology and adaptation. His concepts of natural

Titchener's structuralism, the Chicago and Columbia schools of functionalism, Pavlov and Watson's behaviorism, Wertheimer, Koffka, and Köhler's gestalt, Freud's psychoanalysis, and later the western forms of existentialism and humanism. Hall and Lindzey's *Theories of Personality* (1957) is classic in this approach.

A third method is the "great men" approach, or the autobiographical account of pioneers in the field. The best known work here is that edited by Carl Murchison (1932–52) and, more recently, one by Boring and Lindzey (1967).

In keeping with the selective nature of this book we will bypass most of this material and suggest that if you are interested in one or another of these approaches to a history of psychology, you should begin with one of the aforementioned texts. This text will focus more on autobiographical material and on trends that are current to much of today's interest in psychology.

TABLE 1.1

Three Forces in the History of Psychology in the United States

Approach	Spokesmen	Basic Belief	Scope
Dynamic (centralist)	Sigmund Freud Alfred Adler Carl Jung Eric Berne	"Nothing is as it seems, especially the important inner workings of human beings."	Encompasses those approaches that study inner drives, urges, and thoughts
Behavioral (peripheralist)	Ivan Pavlov John Watson B. F. Skinner Joseph Wolpe	"Since we can never know what goes on inside people, let's focus on what they do."	Encompasses those approaches that study the observable external environmental influences
Humanistic	Abraham Maslow Carl Rogers Rollo May Fritz Perls	"My feelings and behaviors are inseparable. I can do much to carve out my own existence."	Encompasses those approaches that study both dynamic and behavioral aspects of observation only as they relate to the betterment of humankind

selection and survival of the fittest affected both the dynamic and behavioral schools of thought. Darwin, the biologist-geologist, and Freud (1856–1939), the founder of psychoanalysis, had a number of special characteristics in common. As was true of a number of the early psychoanalysts, Freud deviated considerably from standard medical practice, venturing off into hypnosis and other equally exotic ideas about human function and personality to form his own theories. Darwin, also bent on a medical education, became sidetracked by his own selective observations. Both Darwin and Freud had unusual powers of observation and made what were thought of in those days as strange interpretations of what they observed. Both were exceptionally sensitive men in the best meaning of that term. Darwin thought in terms of dynamic struggles among species and Freud saw dynamic struggles taking place within individuals. Both men were conflict-oriented and observed the kinds of things that most of us would easily pass by.

Darwin and Freud could have been called neurotics (and functionally they were). Darwin became physically ill at the slightest provocation and was plagued for years by insomnia, "stomach troubles," and the like. Freud, of course, has been accused of reading into his theory many of his own preoccupations as though they were true of all people. But, as has been the case with so many other productive men and women, they worried themselves into some of the grandest and most fascinating notions about the whys of human existence we would care to come across. One need not be well of mind and body to have great and lasting thoughts.

Noting the conflicts, struggles, and projections within the personalities of such searching people as Darwin and Freud helps us realize that findings in the field of personality research, as in other research areas, are inseparable from the people who make such discoveries.

Looking at Freud with the 20/20 vision of hindsight, we can see how much his theories were influenced by his milieu. At the turn of the century the tendency was against even acknowledging that sex exists. For example, Mary R. Melendy (M.D.,

Ph.D.) wrote a book in 1901 entitled *Maiden*, *Wife*, *and Mother*: *How to Attain Health*, *Beauty*, *Happiness*. In this book she talks about masturbation as an abuse to the nervous system that will lead, if practiced with any regularity, to consumption, paralysis, and heart disease. Yes, she was serious — serious enough to advise one mother to tell her son that if he kept up the bad habit a brown spot would grow on his abdomen and eventually kill him. The good doctor then advised the mother to carry through with the threat. When the mother found her son once again asleep with his hands on his penis, she put some iodine on his stomach while he slept. The next night, while bathing him, she "discovered" the spot and said, "Look! Already it has come." The boy cried out in fear and was "cured." This, then, is the atmosphere that hung over much of the civilized world as Freud developed his theory of personality.

Perhaps the strongest part of Freud's theory is his emphasis on childhood sexuality. He found that his patients fantasized or dreamed about early seduction or intercourse experiences with a parent. Freud began to wonder about the unconscious relationships within his own family and even interpreted sexual desire for his own daughter from a dream he had about his American niece, Hella. From such evidence he came to the idea that the infantile period of life (roughly birth to six years) was a movement from one psychosexual stage to another and that preoccupation at one level could produce a neurotic trend in later life.

He called the first year of life when everything is sensed through the mouth the oral stage. The parents' investment in the child's learning "correct" bowel training culminates in an anal stage — a stage in which the child can show some control over its parents for the first time. Freud shocked his age by then postulating a phallic (or Oedipal) stage of ages three to six in which a little boy regards Dad as a rival, competitor, and potential castrator. This idea shocks our age, too, but for different rea-

son. For, conversely, according to Freud, when the little girl realizes that she lacks what boys have (namely, a penis) she blames this lack on her mother. To us, this seems to be adding injury to insult.

Basically, Freud felt that most of our reasons and motives for what we do and how we behave are hidden from us (repressed) in an effort to protect the ego or self-integrity factor we all seem to possess. At birth we are entirely self-seeking. We are constantly pursuing pleasure and avoiding pain. This illogical, amoral, unconscious striving he called the id. During the second year of life or thereabouts we begin to develop some conscious awareness that we are separable from others and can do some things to better our own condition. This reality factor Freud called the ego. Then as we absorb our parents' values and admonitions we begin to incorporate a conscience and moral sense of right and wrong, which he called the superego.

Freud's progression of stages asserted that boys identified with fathers and girls with mothers. After a somewhat dormant (homosexual) period (ages six through twelve), a child became able to achieve adulthood. Sexual and spiritual union with a young woman or man of the opposite sex and the ability to love and work and become a productive person would complete the cycle that moved the adult into marriage and parenthood.

Freud was also inspired in his theories by influences other than those of his repressive culture. Many of his insights for therapy came from his relations with colleagues and friends. For example, his relationship to a dear friend, Dr. Wilhelm Fliess of Berlin, was one of mutual respect and sharing. But as the relationship progressed Freud came to overestimate and mistrust Dr. Fliess and to attribute to him a kind of fatherly importance that put Freud on edge. When he later understood what was going on within himself he saw the therapeutic value of this "transference" phenomenon — the tendency to act toward another as though he were a father. He could begin to see himself with his own patients as both an object of transference and a subject of its influence. Such sensitivity and persistent pursuit of detail in human relationships was what made Freud a genius of his time.

Adler and Jung: Social Interest and Mystical Revelation

The inseparability of the person from the theory can be seen again in the following story about Alfred Adler (1870–1937). Adler was hosting some friends at lunch in a New York hotel. According to Orgler (1963), "Adler was relating an amusing anecdote when all at once I saw his face cloud over. He sprang up and started to push chairs aside to clear a passage for a lady. She was blind. We not only had failed to observe this but to us all her entrance had been unnoted. But Adler had seen her and acted instantly. When she had passed by Adler sat down again with us, murmuring, 'Isn't it dreadful?'" Adler placed great importance in his therapy on developing in the patient a sense of social interest.

Arguing with Freud's emphasis of sexual motivation and analytical preoccupation, Adler was disdainful of chopping people up into parts and "complexes" and instead spoke of an "individual psychology" that could treat the whole person. Adler was the second of six children. As a child he suffered from rickets, which made him physically weak and clumsy. Not surprisingly, in his theories he emphasized the role of birth order of children and the basic sense of inferiority. Adler theorized that people are born helpless and dependent and remain so during much of childhood. This inferiority is accented by physical defects and by having older and more powerful siblings or dominant parents. People, he felt, strive to gain control of themselves and others and develop different styles of accomplishing this. Many constructive socially recognized forms of achieving come from compensatory activities for these weaknesses such as leadership skills, social and athletic prowess, and the like.

Both Alfred Adler and Carl Jung (1875–1961)

provided positive psychologies and bases for a new dynamic emphasis on ego (reality) functions. In fact, Jung, who was closer to Freud than Adler, became weary of the negative, pessimistic aura that surrounded the mechanisms of Freudian thinking and altered his approach to encompass the religious and the occult.

While Freud was stressing how present behavior is determined by our past, particularly by our progression through childhood, Jung was entertaining the notion that our thoughts and expectations of the future could be sufficiently strong to alter us at any here-and-now moment in time. Not only could the future influence our present existence but also the racial or ethnic origins from our collective past could, over generations, affect our personalities. These were difficult and preposterous notions for Freud. They clearly illuminated the more limited scope of cause-and-effect relations he was able or willing to handle. Jung felt humanity was evolving into a more perfect relation to all that exists or can be imagined, and added a dash of free will that was consistent with his theological bent. He theorized that as we become older, more energy is drained away from the biological drives to the spiritual inclinations. Jung imagined a person as a delicate operation of forces that articulate and shape each other. He thought in dimensions while Freud thought in stages. The result of men and women living together through the ages gave each woman a masculine tendency (animus) and each man a feminine tendency (anima). It was therefore normal and fitting that we be able to sense the world through the qualities of both sexes.

Contemporary Theorists:
Berne's Transactional Analysis

It is easy to pick and choose at least one among the various psychoanalytic theorists that makes more sense to you than some other. It has been practically impossible to prove in any scientific way that any of these theorists had a franchise on the truth.

Some aspects of each may make sense to us as we reflect on the meaning they have on our lives.

For example, contemporary thinkers such as the late psychoanalyst Eric Berne have taken the basic stuff of Freud and woven it into our current love of gamesmanship. To Berne, the parent in each of us is akin to the superego, the adult in each of us to the ego, and the child in our relations with others is based on the id-like qualities of self-centered narcissism. For those who want a practical set of conceptual tools that can be understood in everyday terms, the transactional analysis (TA) of Berne and Harris will be a breath of fresh air. (In fact the TA explanation of human behavior will play an important part in this book.)

William James, an early twentieth-century psychologist-philosopher, once remarked that in any dialogue between two people there are six participants operating. Each of us as we appear to ourselves at the moment, each of us as we are seen by the other, and each of us as we would like to be. Perhaps once in a while these selves get together and communication improves. But does this occur as the dynamic psychologists might expect—by increasing our awareness (insight), thus achieving better control? Or should we attempt to control our environment more directly, as the behaviorists would do?

BEHAVIORAL PSYCHOLOGY

Psychology as the behaviorist views it is a purely objective experimental branch of natural science. Its theoretical goal is the prediction and control of behavior. Introspection forms no essential part of its methods . . . (Watson 1913).

Thus speaks John B. Watson, the American translator of Pavlov's conditioning concepts. The contemporary link to a more reasoned portrayal of the value of objectivity is that of B. F. Skinner (1904–). Since Skinner's views are opposed vehemently by ardent Freudians and humanists alike, we afford him a place in the center of the bed as the representative of the second great force in applied psychological thought in the United States.

B. F. Skinner: From Baby Boxes
to Communal Life

Of course, an objectivist like Skinner would not be unduly bothered by inner rumblings or pangs of superego and might take on the task of proving his point of view right at home where subjects are handy and controllable. In fact, he did. In 1945, when his daughter Deborah was approaching one year old, Skinner designed a baby box in which she was placed. The box was a glassed-in, insulated, temperature- and humidity-controlled enclosure with a ten-yard-long sheet stored on a spool at one end that could be rolled up as it was soiled. The box was soundproof to some extent and had a shade that could be drawn. At the desire of the parent the child could be taken out for cuddling and play. In an interview for *Time* magazine (September 20, 1971), Deborah, then twenty-seven, reflected on the experience to say, "I think I was a very happy baby. Most of the criticisms of the box are by people who don't understand what it was." Presumably many parents are reluctant to be the first in their neighborhood to try one, though at least 1000 of them were in use in 1971.

His own childhood probably led Skinner to believe there was a way to build a better mousetrap. Although Skinner's early life was warm and stable and free of physical punishment, he did have trouble, at times, getting his head together. He was taught to fear God and be concerned about what people might think. His grandmother on his father's side showed him glowing red-hot coals in the parlor stove to remind him of the possibilities of hell. His father took him through the county jail and treated him to a slide-discussion show about life at Sing-Sing prison. Aside from these diversions, Skinner found great enjoyment in "tinkering" and built skate scooters, wagons, rafts, and water pistols. In high school he played in a jazz band and enjoyed

writing. In 1922, at Hamilton College in New York, he decided to major in English. In 1965 I wrote to Skinner asking his permission to reprint one of his selections and asked him to comment on his college work. He replied, "In college I wanted to be a writer but soon discovered I had nothing to say. I turned to psychology as the most closely related science." His interest in writing has certainly maintained itself through such works as *Walden Two* and *Beyond Freedom and Dignity*.

To Skinner, freedom, autonomy and personal conviction are myths. The emphasis on right and wrong, guilt and shame, dread and perversity are useless and mind-befuddling notions. Instead, reward or punishment immediately after an action is what regulates a person's next approach to the situation. We seek to avoid punishment and pursue pleasure (or lack of punishment). In fact, by selectively rewarding pigeons with food for correct movements, Skinner has taught them to dance and play ping-pong. With his now famous "Skinner box," a soundproofed box with a food dispenser lever or key that any rat, pigeon, or monkey can manipulate, he has been able to test the various schedules or variations of reward and time to determine what works best to encourage learning. It was after having visited his daughter's fourth-grade arithmetic class that he devised the first teaching machine for programmed instruction, in 1954. "Why can't kids learn math like pigeons learn ping-pong?" might have been his thought.

It seems clear that Skinner and his followers have simply been more explicit about what they are up to than is true of a good number of psychologists. The power of association is a very potent force to deal with. The consequences of what we do become associated with the doing. All theorists, including such anti-behaviorists as Carl Rogers, make use of this fact. The displeasure with Skinner has come on moral and ethical grounds: the idea of deliberately ignoring consciousness is a hard pill for many to swallow.

A SHORT OVERVIEW OF PSYCHOLOGY

Since behavior, rather than internal dynamics such as thought or feeling, is the currency of behaviorists, they have become known as behavior modifiers. The simplistic but gutsy statement by Perry London (1972) may illustrate: "Actually, there were only about three principles that they [behavior modifiers] ever referred to, all of which can be reduced to one or one and a half principles — namely, that learning depends on the connections in time, space, and attention between what you do and what happens to you subsequently."

When we talk about modes of intervention in chapter nine we will discuss several examples of applied behaviorism.

Conflicting Opinions: A Vice-President and the Twin Oaks Community

In a speech in Chicago to the Farm Bureau reported in *Psychology Today* (January 1972), former vice-president Spiro Agnew unleashed his anxiety about behaviorism. The behaviorists' suggestion that the family alone may not be able to prepare young people for the world of the future and that rugged individualism may disappear from the face of the earth (if Skinner has his way), provoked the vice-president to offer the following: "You can see here that our traditional concept of the individual would disappear completely if it were left up to the behaviorists; moreover, the family would become an anachronism in the new scheme of things." An even spicier tidbit from Agnew is the following: ". . . future generations of Americans face a far bigger threat to the loss of their individualism from the sugar-coated theories of social scientists and behavioral psychologists than they do from the machines we have developed, manufactured, and can control, making life easier and more abundant for mankind." (There was no mention of political machines.)

Some of you will agree with the former vice-president and some of you won't. However, if you want some data on how communal living *a la* behaviorism works then you will want to read Kathleen Kinkade's book *A Walden Two Experiment*. Applying behavioral principles at Kinkade's Twin Oaks community did not go according to textbook plan. "We have experimented with behavior shaping at Twin Oaks, but these experiments have remained peripheral to our basic cultural planning," Kinkade explains. For example, if you lost control of your temper you might take a baseline reading of your behavior and count the number of times this occurred each day for a week. The task, then, would be to try to control and reduce the number of times this behavior occurred on a subsequent week and put the data on a graph for all to see. The reward is largely the new behavior itself. Whether from behaviorism or not, the members of Twin Oaks found that life worked out better for all concerned if there were procedures or ways of communicating that all felt were just and equitable. This may not be taking us as far from American ideals as the former vice-president seems to believe.

HUMANISTIC PSYCHOLOGY

The third and most recent force in our very recent history of psychology centers on humanistic values. Tributaries that feed this ill-defined lake are labeled *self-theory, phenomenology, gestalt,* or *existentialism.* They have in common the importance of the "inner moment": the sudden "aha" experience, the momentary feeling, and the importance of what we tell ourselves. This school of thought asserts that our basic motivation is to actualize (realize) our potential, to stop conforming blindly, and to find our own existence — our own being. We are essentially free if we take the time to listen to our guts and what they have to say about where we are at any given moment. We may then act on this knowledge with intelligence and compassion. Just so many words? Perhaps.

Abraham Maslow: Anyone Who Ever Had a Baby Couldn't be a Behaviorist

Abraham Maslow (1908–1971), who was responsible for the phrase "the third force," once said that anyone who had a baby couldn't be a behaviorist (Maslow 1968). Yet this same man earlier in his career described his introduction to Watson's behaviorism: "I had discovered J. B. Watson and I was sold on behaviorism. It was an explosion of excitement for me . . . Bertha [Maslow's wife] came to pick me up and I was dancing down Fifth Avenue with exuberance; I embarrassed her, but I was so excited about Watson's program. It was beautiful." Was this another Saul-to-Paul experience? Maslow, who was first ardent about the value of psychoanalysis, then excited about the value of behaviorism, and finally wound up in the humanist camp, would seem to be a personification of American psychology and its three basic approaches.

As was true of many of our great psychologists, Maslow grew up more comfortable around books than friends. He was isolated and unhappy. He began work at any early age selling and delivering newspapers and spent many summers working for the family barrel-manufacturing company. He married at the age of twenty, at which time he felt life began for him. He was sold on behaviorism, and as a graduate student of Harry Harlow wrote a doctoral thesis on the sexual and dominance characteristics of monkeys. Then he got into Freudian and gestalt psychology and his interest in behaviorism began to diminish. When the bombs struck Pearl Harbor on December 7, 1941, signalling the beginning of our involvement in World War II, Maslow decided to devote the rest of his life to creating a comprehensive theory of human behavior that would be useful to mankind not only in putting down war, prejudice, and hatred but also in helping mankind to better understand religion, poetry, art, and philosophy.

Unlike Freud, Maslow tried to study the most

Self-actualization

Growth Needs*

TRUTH	JUSTICE
GOODNESS	ORDER
BEAUTY	SIMPLICITY
ALIVENESS	RICHNESS
INDIVIDUALITY	PLAYFULNESS
PERFECTION	EFFORTLESSNESS
NECESSITY	SELF-SUFFICIENCY
COMPLETION	MEANINGFULNESS

SELF-ESTEEM
ESTEEM BY OTHERS

LOVE & BELONGINGNESS

Basic Needs

SAFETY AND SECURITY

AIR, WATER, FOOD, SHELTER, SLEEP, SEX

THE EXTERNAL ENVIRONMENT
PRECONDITIONS FOR NEED SATISFACTION
FREEDOM, JUSTICE, ORDERLINESS
CHALLENGE (STIMULATION)

———

*Growth needs are all of equal importance (not hierarchical).

FIG. 1-7 *Maslow's Hierarchy of Needs*

talented people to develop his ideas. (We will see more of how he went about this in chapter four. Freud built his theory on observations of sickness. This is an important distinction between how first- and third-force practitioners operate. It is of interest to note that in the area of mental health the dynamic psychologists focused on one end of the continuum and the humanists on the other, while the behaviorists were concerned with studying the averages.)

Perhaps one of the best-known aspects of Maslow's theory of human motivation is his hierarchy of basic human needs (see figure 1-7). Within this construction of basic- to higher-level needs, Maslow contended that one acts as a whole when mastering a need. In other words a *person* is hungry, not just a stomach. The most basic needs are physiological. Once these are satisfied, we can deal with the various safety or protective needs. Finally the need for love, affection, and a sense of belonging emerges.

Contemporary Theorists:
The Human Potential Movement
Frank Goble's *The Third Force* (1971), Frick's *Humanistic Psychology: Interviews with Maslow, Murphy, and Rogers* (1971), and Maddi and Costa's *Humanism in Personality: Alport, Maslow, and Murray* (1972) are recent books that delve much more than we can in this text into the lives of people such as Maslow who are shaping this area of increasing interest in psychology. The humanist movement's lack of systematic theory or of scientific methodology that is found in psychoanalysis and behaviorism leads its critics to say that it all sounds grand but, like cotton candy, is sweet and lacks substance. On the other hand, adherents of the humanistic approach believe that they haven't gotten very far with existing theories and methods and that it may be time to chuck the whole thing or parts of it in favor of a fresh look at ourselves. Who is to judge?

Many of the techniques and procedures that stem from this viewpoint are inherently radical and nontraditional. The encounter-group movement as discussed by Carl Rogers (1967), the self-disclosure values of Sidney Jourard (1971), the various pronouncements of the late Fritz Perls, and the many growth games (Lewis and Streitfield 1972) that have evolved from the human potential movement all attempt to help us drop our defenses (and in some cases, our pants) and expose the well-kept secrets and apprehensions we all live with. However, it is reasonable to conclude that these various techniques that question tradition and seek a new form for living should themselves be questioned by people who have an investment in traditional psychology.

Another Point of View:
The Normative-Descriptive Approach
Another approach, which centers on gathering good descriptions and meaningful norms of large groups, is called normative-descriptive. This approach has always been a part of psychology, since it is really more of a methodology than a theory. People who use it are concerned with identifying traits, stages, and norms. In fact, most psychological tests are based on the ideas that (1) traits such as introversion and aggressiveness can be measured with some reliability and (2) once people are measured you can make better predictions about them than you could if they had not been measured.

One aspect of the normative-descriptive approach is a statistical tool called factor analysis that is used to determine the extent to which test scores overlap with each other. For example, factor analysis can be used to tell whether a sample group of plumbers has the same expressed interests as another group of carpenters, artists, or physicians. It can also be used to determine whether other traits are associated with a given one. The technique can be applied to test scores or to expressed statements of any kind as well as to simpler behaviors (such as groups people join or acts they have committed). One use of the technique by Dorothy Adkins (1973), a well-known psychological statistician, has been to determine the basic factors in the interests of members of the American Psychological Association. This is no small task, since psychologists have very diverse interests.

If you were to conduct a factor analysis on the members of your family, fraternity, or church, you would find that there are a few basic values that bring people together and that exclude people in a group one from the other. Richard Coan (1968) had the audacity, charm, and cunning to try this approach on his own peer group — a psychology department in which he and we work (see next page.)

We, your searching authors, feel that a chapter on the search for an understanding of personality would be remiss if it did not mention how that search might be applied to ourselves. Psychologists, after all, have been called many things ranging from divine to perverse.

Coan's study (1968) pulled out a number of factors that pertain to the way psychologists define what psychology is and how they approach their own work in the field. By asking psychologists to evaluate a stand on a wide assortment of statements about values Coan determined that subjectivity and objectivity played a large part in determining their answers. More precisely, the answers they gave could be labeled, through factor analysis, as ranging from a very subjective or fluid frame of reference to a very objective or restricted one. Coan also found, among other things, that the belief in genetic determinism versus social determinism was another way to cut the pie.

Then he did an interesting thing. He plotted the two sets of factors (subjectivism versus objectivism and genetic versus social) and put each person in the psychology department (who was willing to go through this ordeal) in a spatial relationship to everyone else (see the figure).

At some level of validity the representation in figure 1-8 makes sense to at least two of us, since Reed Mencke is *D* and Bob Wrenn is *J* on the map. We have noticed that the people we seem to see the most and work most closely with are not far from us spatially. We must now confess, of course, that we are not as objective as we think we are and we must somehow reckon with *this in writing this book.*

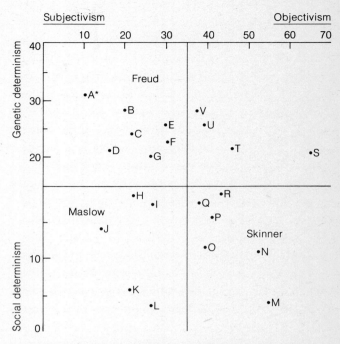

*A–V are individual psychologists in the department. We have also roughed in where the proponents of the three forces might be placed if they were to have completed Coan's questionnaire. We are less than secure in our feelings about these placements, however.

FIG. 1-8 *Scattergram of one psychology department*

Developmental Theorists: Havighurst, Erikson, Kagan, Piaget

Just as factor analysis attempts to discern what factors or influences are common among test scores, the developmentalist is concerned with common influences that affect us at different times or stages during our lives. For example, four-year olds are not concerned about dating or making it with the opposite sex, although in their current relations they are paving the way for such events. Eighth graders do not worry much about what they will become in life, although they develop some skills that they may focus on five or six years later. Since we all go through certain events at roughly the same times in our lives, some psychologists have found life stages a convenient method for organizing data. I am no exception.

I have selected four well-known developmental psychologists who all differ somewhat in their views. Although there is neither time nor space to go into each in depth, I have tried to line them up in table 1.2.

Robert Havighurst (1952), who coined the phrase "developmental task," emphasizes task or learning events (learning to walk, choosing a vocation, and so forth) and bases his labels on stages of life in which there are common tasks to overcome and achieve. Erik Erikson (1950) takes an enlightened Freudian position that might be best thought of as a psychodynamic point of view. In his system the development of interpersonal relations triggers the separation of life stages. Jerome Kagan (1969) is more of an eclectic or humanist who combines psychodynamics with behavioral psychology and is concerned mainly with the experimental results that are found in different age groups. Finally Jean Piaget (1952), the Swiss psychologist, takes a cognitive (thought-process) point of view in which he applies logical and physical frameworks to functions of the developing intellectual and moral person

It is of interest to note that, although Kagan and Piaget are most concerned with the period up to college age, all four of these psychologists have focused more on early than later life. They have also agreed that from birth to age six certain things occur that are somewhat different and unique from those that take place from six through twelve or from twelve through eighteen, and so forth. There are obvious external social influences that affect these periods, such as the fact that most children enter first grade when they are six. There are also strong internal influences that determine the construction of stages such as puberty, "the awakening of the hormones," that comes along around age twelve or so. It is understood that there is tremendous variation in what takes place within an age grouping and that these categories are flexible and can bend a year or so here and there.

TABLE 1.2
Stages of Developmental Growth

Age	Havighurst	Erikson	Kagan	Piaget
0–6	Infancy & Early Childhood (0–6)	Stages of Trust (0–1) Autonomy (1–2) Initiative (2–5)	Critical Period (0–1½) Initial Socialization (1½–3) Parent Identification (3–6)	Sensorimotor Period (0–2) Pre-operational Period (2–7)
6–12	Middle Childhood (6–12)	Stage of Industry (6–12)	Peer Group and Sibling Identity (5–10)	Concrete Operations Period (7–11)
12–18	Adolescence (12–18)	Stages of Identity (12–15) and Intimacy (15–25)	Media Identity (12–18)	Formal Operations Period (11–15)
18–30	Early Adulthood (18-30)	Stages of Intimacy (15–25) and Generativity (25–45)		
30–55	Middle Age (30–55)	Stages of Generativity (25–45) and Ego Integrity (45+)		
55+	Later Maturity (55+)			

Chapter One Summary

We selectively construct our reality, but we are unaware of much of what affects us. It is the same way for psychologists who must choose what is important to observe and what is not. Since the early 1900s there have been three main approaches to guide their observations:

1. Dynamic psychology—which looks chiefly at inner motives, thoughts, and drives
2. Behavioral psychology—which studies what people do and how they behave
3. Humanistic psychology—which borrows from the first two approaches but goes beyond them in insisting on constructive, healthy aspects of personality as opposed to pathological or median ones.

Finally, there are those psychologists who are most concerned with gathering empirical data regardless of what approach it would best fit. The normative-descriptive and developmental approaches are of this sort.

Glossary

Baseline   A procedure in which the frequency of one's activities is plotted for a period of time as a reference point to compare with whatever changes in behavior one plans to undergo.

Cynicism   The tendency to react skeptically to everything that takes place: "Have a good day— if it is a good day, which I doubt."

Existentialist   Referring to the belief that the meaning of the universe is contained within one's own existence and experience.

Neurotic   Referring to someone who is excessively inhibited, anxious, and otherwise self-occupied (we are not using this term in a medical sense but rather in the sense that most of us have experienced this state at one time or another).

Oedipal   The Freudian term for the phallic stage in which a child is attracted to the parent of the opposite sex .

Psychoanalytical   Referring to the Freudian brand of dynamic psychology.

Teleology   The belief that one's thoughts, plans, and expectations can influence one's future behavior, regardless of what sort of history one has achieved.

Exercises (*for individual and class use*)

You can work the following exercises and tasks at your own leisure. Perhaps some of these would be more enjoyable to go over with a friend. Those with an asterisk (*) should be done in consultation with your teacher or in class.

1. What experience have you gone through that was generally pleasurable or disgusting, only to have the event take on a different meaning at some later date? What do you think influenced your reversal of opinion?

2. Of the three basic approaches described in this chapter (dynamic, behavioral, humanistic), which seems to be most reasonable to you? Why?

3.* As a starter for classroom or small group discussion describe the merits, if any, or the risks, if any, of placing your child in a baby box for the first year of its life. Assuming cost of the box is no problem, what other factors would influence your decision?

4. Take a look at figure 1-8. Taking the question "How does someone learn to love or to hate someone else?" see if you can guess what individual *A* might say to *M*. What would *M* reply to *A*? Where would you place yourself on this two-dimensional chart? And your teacher?

5. Why do we know so little about people over fifty-five relative to what we know about children under six? Can you think of some reasons?

Bibliography

Adkins, D. 1973. A simpler structure of the American Psychological Association. *American Psychologist* (January): 47–54.

Barlow, N., ed. 1958. *The autobiography of Charles Darwin 1809–1882*. London: Collins.

Berne, E. 1964. *Games people play*. New York: Grove.

Boring, E. 1950. *A history of experimental psychology*. New York: Appleton.

———— and Lindzey, G. 1967. *A history of psychology in autobiography*. Vol. 5. New York: Appleton.

Coan, R. 1968. Dimensions of psychological theory. *American Psychologist* 23:715-22.

Erikson, E. 1950. *Childhood and society*. New York: Norton.

————· 1964. *Insight and responsibility*. New York: Norton.

Frick, W. 1971. *Humanistic psychology: interviews with Maslow, Murphy, and Rogers*. Columbus, Ohio: Merrill.

Goble, Frank. 1971. *The third force*. New York: Simon & Schuster.

Hall, C. and Lindzey, G. 1957. *Theories of personality*. New York: Wiley.

Harris, T. 1969. *I'm OK, you're OK*. New York: Harper.

Havighurst, R. 1952. *Developmental tasks and education*. New York: McKay.

Jourard, S. 1971. *The transparent self*. New York: Van Nostrand-Reinhold.

Kagen, J. 1969. *Personality development*. New York: Harcourt Brace Jovanovich.

Kinkade, K. 1972. *A Walden two experiment: the first five years of Twin Oaks community*. New York: Morrow.

Lewis, H. and Streitfield, H. 1972. *Growth games*. New York: Bantam.

London, P. 1972. The end of ideology in behavior modification. *American Psychologist* (October): 913.

Maddi, S. and Costa, P. 1972. *Humanism in personology: (Allport, Maslow, and Murray)*. Chicago: Aldine-Atherton.

Maslow, A. 1968. A conversation with Abraham H. Maslow. *Psychology Today* 2:55,37.

Milne, A. 1954. *Winnie the pooh*. New York: Dutton.

Murchison, C., ed. 1932–52. *History of psychology in autobiography*. 4 vols. Worcester, Mass.: Clark University Press.

Murphy, G. 1949. *Historical introduction to modern psychology*. New York: Harcourt Brace Jovanovich.

Murray, H. 1938. *Explorations in personality*. New York: Wiley.

Orgler, H. 1963. *Alfred Adler: the man and his work*. New York: Liveright.

Piaget, J. 1952. *The origins of intelligence in children*. New York: Intel. Univ. Press.

Psychology Today. 1972. Agnew's blast at behaviorism. *Psychology Today* (January).

Rogers, C. 1967. The process of the basic encounter group. In Bugental, J. F. T. (ed.). *Challenges of humanistic psychology*. New York: McGraw-Hill.

Skinner, B. 1948. *Walden two*. New York: Macmillan.

————. 1971. *Beyond freedom and dignity*. New York: Knopf.

Time. 1971. Skinner's utopia: panacea, or path to hell? *Time* (20 September).

Toffler, A. 1970 *Future shock*. New York: Bantam.

Ward, H. 1927. *Charles Darwin*. New York: Bobbs-Merrill.

Watson, J. 1913. Psychology as the behaviorist views it. *Psychological Review* 20: 158.

Wertheimer, M. 1970. *A brief history of psychology*. New York: Holt, Rinehart & Winston.

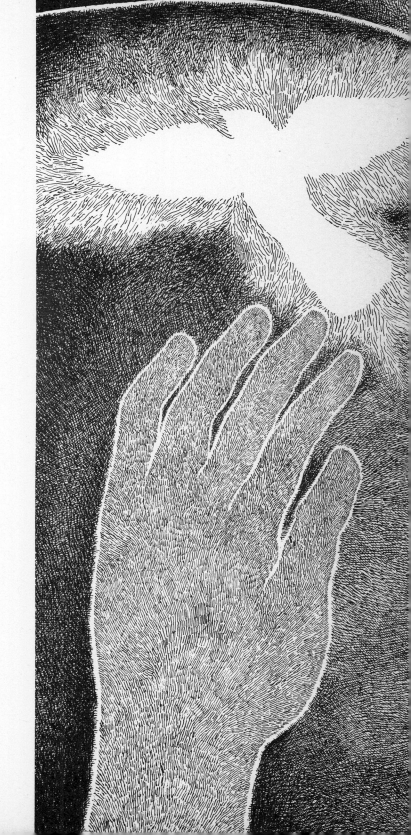

PART TWO

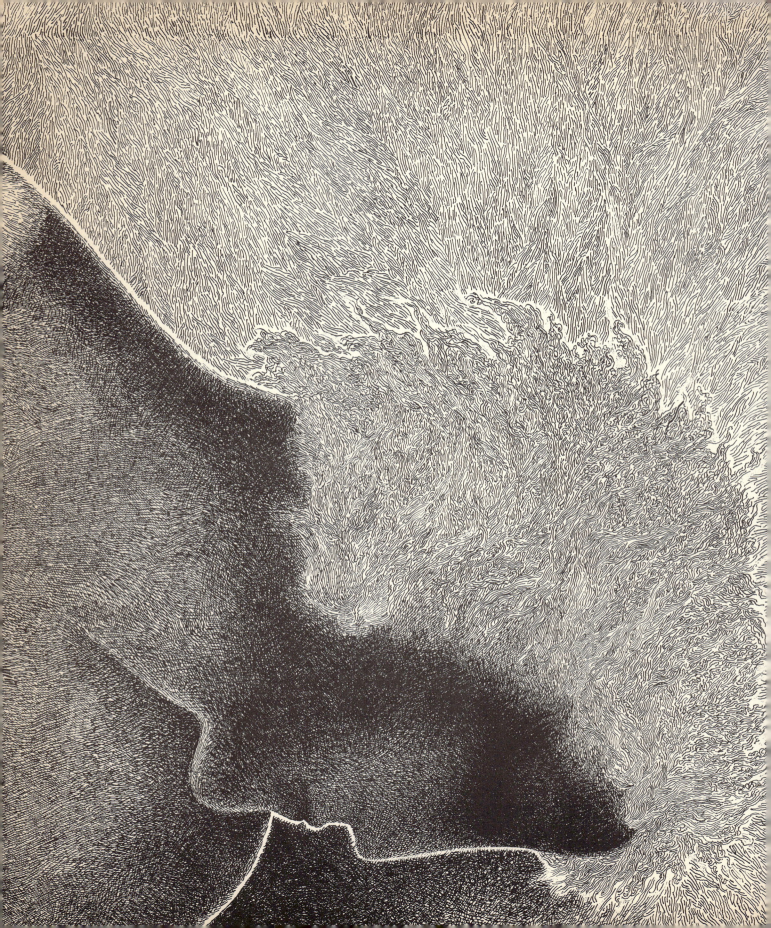

The Identity of Self

Part two covers the general topic of learning who we are. It contains three chapters that focus on different aspects of the question, "Who am I?" In chapter two we will attempt to identify and accept the many selves that we are day by day. Chapter three explores the effects of labeling people and some of the means of coping with the forces that do the labeling. Finally, in chapter four, we focus on personality growth, enhancement, and one's potential for the "good life."

Chapter Two: I Thought I Was There a Minute Ago (The Search for Self)

Who am I?
To my children I am . . . "wise
old father"
But my parents see me as "a child."

Who am I?
When I'm with my teachers
I become . . . "a student, "sort
of wild."

But who am I?
For then I join my students
Who a teacher see in me.

So who am I?
Should I be a worker as my
colleagues suggest?
Or perhaps a husband as my wife
often does protest?
It seems there are so many selves
that I can be.

Which self do you suppose is
the *real* me?

REED MENCKE

The Elusive Self: Finding Out Who We Are

Sometimes the definition we choose of who we are is too superficial. Lacking a clear picture of the essence of our inner selves, we create in our minds definitions that are concrete and objective and easily verifiable. Such descriptions may help reduce the ambiguity of not knowing who we are for a time but they ultimately result in confusion. So how do we create a valid concept of who we are? The answer is similar to the reply of a sculptor who was asked how he had made such a beautiful elephant. His answer was that he just chipped away all the marble that did not look like an elephant. For many of us, our search for a sense of who we are proceeds similarly.

As young children we tend to feel at first that we are our behavior. If we fail we are bad; if we succeed we feel good. Gradually as we mature we begin to realize that our behavior is merely a reflection of something deeper: our needs and the degree to which we are aware of them. Our needs and awareness, however, are also far from being static. For they in turn reflect all of our varied inherited tendencies and life experience. Our awareness may expand as we experience more, and, as that happens, our needs may also change. The essence of our inner selves is the thing that decides whether we will change and grow or remain trapped in our present state of awareness. But what is that essence? And how do we find it?

These two questions constitute goals for us in this chapter. We hope you will have a clearer idea of who you are after reading this. We cannot hope to tell you what your essence is; that's up to you to figure out. But we will offer some tools. The first tool is the poem, which will, we hope, stimulate some intuitive insights about who you are. The second will be transactional analysis—a way of making sense of your present motives and understanding where they come from. Third, we will provide some fairly extensive case material that demonstrates quite graphically the nature of the personal search for an identity as it occurs in college. So . . . let's start looking.

OUR THREE SELVES: CHILD, ADULT, PARENT

Who am I really? Many of us find this question very confusing. Much of the time it seems almost as though there were a whole series of *me*'s. This gets most confusing when the *me*'s seem to be talking and behaving in ways that contradict each other. A few years ago one of us asked his class to jot down "a description of a time in your life when you felt you were abnormal." Following is one student's description of such a time:

> My selfishness got particularly out of hand Friday evening, when I blew up at my husband, who is very ill right now. I felt shocked at myself in a part of me watching coldly on, even as I was yelling. I told him he didn't love me; I said all he ever did was criticize me. I think this is abnormal behavior.

While the above may strike many of you as far from abnormal behavior, the incident considerably bothered the student who wrote it. What bothered her appears to center around the fact that she found herself behaving in a way that strongly contradicted her image of herself. She was expressing anger, perhaps even hatred, towards someone she loved. Most personality theorists have observed similar contradictions in the thoughts, feelings, and behaviors of their subjects. It's as though there were several "selves" within each of us. In literature we have Stevenson's *Dr. Jekyll and Mr. Hyde*. Jekyll was a scientist, a moral man who lived by reason. Hyde lived solely for pleasure and was given to violent passions, including rape and murder. Freud described the inner conflicting selves of his patients in much the same way, as we can recall from chapter one. There was an id that lived for pleasure, a superego that was a "good guy" who incorporated all the *shoulds* and rules of society, and an ego whose function was to reach out to reality and

reconcile the needs of the id with the moral code of the superego.

One of the most useful modern expressions of this idea, which we briefly reviewed in the first chapter, of conflicting inner selves is seen in a new kind of therapy called Transactional Analysis (TA) (Berne 1964; Harris 1969). TA practitioners help their clients to become aware of three ego states: a Parent, a Child, and an Adult.

Your Parent is that part of yourself that contains all the external events that have happened to you. The Parent in you feels and behaves in the same way your mother or father or whoever raised you did. Your Parent can be critical, helping, or both.

At the same time external events are being recorded in your Parent, a second series of recordings is being made simultaneously. The second set of tapes include all of your internal responses to the input of your Parent. It is called your Child because it includes what you were when you were little. Your Child has the same feelings and ways of behaving that you had when you were very young. Your Child (self) may be natural; that is, on its own and not under the influence of your internal Parent. Or it may be "adaptive" so as to please your internal Parent.

Your Adult is the part of you that figures things out by looking at the facts. Your Adult is an observer, a computer, and a decision maker. It is capable of looking at events in your life without the prejudices of your Parent or the archaic feelings of your Child. The Adult is then capable of adding up these observations to see what needs to be changed. Your Adult can make decisions and act on them. All in all, your Adult is the key to personal change.

These three people within us (the technical term is our *ego states*) have some identifying characteristics or stock phrases. Whenever you hear a voice inside blaming you, saying "you should," or "don't," or mouthing slogans such as "You can't win," or "Children should be seen and not heard," it is very likely that your Parent is talking. Your Child is more likely to say things like "I want," "Try and make me," "I feel . . ." or just "Wow!" Your Adult tends to deal with observable facts and logic such as, "Let's see now, the most efficient way to proceed would be . . . ," or, "Now, what I hear you saying, John, is that. . . ."

With this much background in TA you should be able to unscramble the source of some of our angry student's conflicting messages. Who (which ego state) was talking when she said her husband didn't love her and that all he ever did was criticize her? Which ego state was shocked? And which was the observer watching coldly?

Becoming Aware of Ego States

In the example of the woman who lashed out at her husband, it was reasonably clear that we had a hurt Child, a Parent who was shocked, and an Adult observing the action. But applying these ideas to our own behavior can be difficult. Often we mistake the judgmental admonitions of our Parent or the fears of our Child for the genuine awareness of reality that can come only from our Adult. Who do you think is "in charge" of most of your behavior? Your natural Child? Your adaptive Child? Your Adult computer? Your critical Parent? Or is it your helping Parent?

Campous (1969) suggests that you can find out by actually observing your ego states as they are reflected in your behavior—for example, in your posture, the language you choose, your relations with others, childhood memories, and present feelings:

1. Posture—The posture of the Parent may be of the ranting, finger-shaking variety. The Child will be spontaneous, the Adult more controlled.
2. Words—The Parent prefers words such as *cute*, *bad*, *good*, *childish*, and so forth. The Child says "Gee," "Wow," "won't," and "can't." The Adult tends towards "suitable," "practical," "correct." Become aware of your choice of words in your everyday relationships with others. Do your words come from your Parent? Your Adult? Your Child?
3. Relations—Observe how others react to you. If people frequently behave like upset children when they are with you, check out your Parent. You will probably find that it is bossy and a bit know-it-all. If others seem to loosen up and enjoy themselves with you, it is likely that your Child is fun-loving and happy. If others frequently berate you and put you down, your Child may be a bit of a brat. Finally, if everyone treats you with great respect and control, your Adult is probably in charge most of the time.
4. Childhood—Recall how you and your parents spoke and behaved when you were a child. Then try to notice present instances

in which you sound as you did then or say things you used to hear your parents say.

5. Check your feelings—you will find yourself actually feeling each role. When do you feel like a Child? A Parent? An Adult?

PUTTING YOUR ADULT IN CHARGE

The P-A-C (Parent-Adult-Child) concept is a basic tool to use for becoming aware of who you really are. All three ego states have considerable potential value. But to function as fully autonomous people who have our own values and make our own decisions, we usually have to modify our Parent and Child. This modification is best handled by our Adult or more reasonable self.

The Parent is often a source of prejudice and *shoulds* that are based on archaic and outmoded data. As you become more aware of your parent, you may discover injunctions to be a particular kind of person. Such injunctions sometimes appear in the form of slogans such as, "All work and no play makes Jack a dull boy," "Work and you shall prosper," "Stay out of trouble," "Leave well enough

alone," "Look for the silver lining," and so forth. Other parental injunctions come in the form of subtle nonverbal clues that say to us: "You are a loveable person," "Don't get close," "Drop dead," or "Sex is disgusting." Frequently parents send conflicting injunctions: their words may "Work hard and succeed," while their nonverbal message is "You are a loser."

Your Child may contain old feelings that no longer fit you. For example, if your parents often ignored you, your Child may overreact when a friend forgets your birthday. If you always felt afraid of your grade-school principal, you may still react with fear with professors, bosses, or other authority figures who mean you no harm. Or, if your Child is spoiled, you may still expect others to come to your rescue and become enraged or hurt when they don't.

It is the function of your Adult to identify the parental messages that you have assimilated to decide which make sense and which you must reject. This kind of awareness, coupled with a conscious decision to change your Parent, is the first step towards full autonomy.

The goal of P-A-C analysis is simply to 1) increase awareness of the Parent and Child in each of us, and 2) to bring the Parent and the Child under the control of our Adult. When this is accomplished we are left with a new Parent that takes responsibility for its own prejudices, possesses the values that make sense in the context of our present life, and lives by injunctions that are consistent with our personal goals and supportive of our personal growth.

How does one discover one's Parent and Child and bring them under the control of the Adult? One obvious answer after reading this section is to join a TA group or work with a good TA therapist. (This possibility is discussed at length in chapter nine.) A second possibility is to undertake a self-analysis. The exercises at the end of this chapter, chapter three, and chapter nine will get you started in becoming more aware of your own Parent, Adult, and Child and how to change them. You will also find exercises that can lead to self-awareness at the end of each chapter. Those who really want to work at TA on their own will find James and Jongeward's *Born to Win* (1971) a must. Their presentation of TA concepts, examples, and exercises is very complete and interesting.

Still a third possibility is explored in the remainder of this chapter. Just going to college can have an impact on one's personality development that is as large as the changes that occur during psychotherapy. And this effect can be greatly enhanced when it is combined with the kind of self-study course that we describe in the next section.

A COURSE ABOUT YOU

Perhaps the two most universal questions that college students ask themselves are *Who am I?* and *Why am I?* The college experience often fosters confusion and concern about who we really are and whether we are really important. Large impersonal universities with complex registration procedures, computerized grading, and TV lectures attended by a thousand or more students tend to promote feelings of isolation and unimportance. And the challenges and confrontation between the values students have assimilated from parents and those they encounter in other students, in professors, and in the content of their courses is often great enough to cause severe shocks to their senses of who they are. These challenges often lead to a situation in which a student's main concerns throughout college center around finding out who he or she is.

"If we are all so curious about who we are, and psychology is supposed to help us find out, why not have a course where we study ourselves?" This was the essence of the question put to Dr. Peter Madison some years ago by one of his students. Because Peter is more open than most human beings I know, he didn't just mumble, "Hmmm . . . ahem . . . hmmm . . . well" and shuffle off to

read another volume of Freud. The idea of students studying their own personalities was challenging but rather radical in the late fifties. Psychology faculties were cautious about "giving away psychology." Nonetheless, Madison decided to try a self-study type of course the next term. Thus began one of the most interesting personal searches we will report in this book. Madison's students wrote autobiographies and kept daily journals of their emotional lives and innermost thoughts and concerns. Once a week they got together with him to see what psychology might have to offer in their search for a self. We think the case histories in Madison's book (1969) have more to say about the personal lives of college students and what it is like to search for self in college than any other source we have encountered to date. We present below the cases of Bob and Sidney (code names), abridged from Madison's book, which expose some important ways college may influence a student's sense of self.

BOB: LOOKING FOR A NEW SELF

For some students, college comes as a strong shock to their senses of who they are. When this happens they may have to literally rebuild their personalities. The rapidly changing roles the entering college freshman experiences often tend to reinforce feelings of alienation. Bob's college career illustrates this process very clearly. In high school Bob had been in essence a big fish in a small pond. He lived in a small rural community. His high school enrolled fewer than two hundred students. He was very successful in high school academics, athletics, and in his social life. He was the president of his student body, got good marks, and was able to compete successfully in athletics even at the state level.

Such high school experiences lead one to expect similar success in college. However, if such students enter a large university with very selective admission requirements they may encounter a series of failure experiences that fundamentally shake their senses of self-esteem and identity. This is precisely what happened to Bob (Madison 1969).

Freshman Year

My first impression of college didn't actually come until the end of the first week—we were so busy. I mainly remember being impressed that first week by the rate at which things came at me and the largeness of the campus. I came from a small town thirty miles away from the nearest small city. The number of students impressed me; although I was mentally prepared for a large college, I wasn't prepared for the hundreds of students. I felt somewhat subdued by the fact that there was so much talent here. I didn't feel nearly as competent as a lot of those people were. . . .

For about the first two days, I had a pretty high opinion of myself, and from then on out for the rest of the year I felt like a midget among the giants. In high school I was a big man. I came down here with the thought that there would be no problems in college, and that I had a pretty good background; when I got down here I found out that this wasn't very true, academically, socially, just all around. Right from the first I would run into people who had definite ideas about politics, and I hardly knew who the people they talked about were, and this sort of thing. It didn't seem like I knew very much: my confidence level wasn't very high.

Failure. These feelings of being less sophisticated than his classmates were compounded by the fact that Bob's old areas of greatest success—namely athletics, academics, and school politics—now became failure experiences. After three years of unsuccessfully trying to make the track team, he finally quit. He was also unable to maintain his former high grades. His freshman grades averaged C—. He described his freshman social life as non-existent: "study, study, study." He held no offices. How his self-esteem and sense of identity were affected by these experiences is exemplified in the following quotes. When asked how often he felt blue or depressed he said, "Actually, quite often, because I can't really seem to make heads or tails out of what I'm doing. It's a feeling of being lost . . . no sense of direction. For a few minutes you feel like you have got to start doing something, but when you get on something a few minutes later you want to turn around. What good are you doing when you don't know where you are going?"

Identity Shock. Bob's freshman experiences illustrate what Madison has called *identity shock.* Such a shock to one's sense of who he or she is often occurs in cases such as Bob's when a student who was high on the totem pole in high school is suddenly without close friends or family supports in a highly competitive environment where the range of talent in almost all areas is far greater than it has been. As we shall see later in this chapter, such shocks don't have to be permanent. As a matter of fact, the student who is open to experience and willing to change often shows marked growth as a result of college shock.

SIDNEY: A PERSONAL SEARCH FOR VALUES
College classes and the people one encounters in them may also lead students to question many of their former explanations of who they are and why they exist. Madison (1969) reports the experiences of Sidney, which illustrate how one's personal values, career choice, and overall sense of identity can be deeply influenced by the curriculum. Sidney was a highly motivated student. He graduated with distinction from a very prestigious college. When Sidney first arrived at college, he intended to become a doctor. When he was asked as a freshman why he preferred medicine over other careers, Sidney replied:

I shall major in the subject that interests me most. I hope to become a doctor because I believe medicine to be most compatible with the golden rule, which forms the fountainhead of my morality.

On the surface this explanation leaves the impression that Sidney is going into medicine to help others. But why, wondered Madison, did Sidney choose medicine over social work, the ministry, or other helping professions? Sidney's autobiography, written in his sophomore year, suggests some other motives were involved. He came from a thrifty Jewish family. He describes his family's hopes for his future as revolving around respectability and social and financial security. He described his parents as more aware of the importance of money as security than of the things it could buy. Their reactions to his choice of medicine were predictably positive:

My mother thought this [being a doctor] was very good. My mother would like me to be happy most of all; second, to be respected; third, to be secure, to have a good position, to have money, to have a good wife, to have a family.

The autobiography also suggests a second way in which security came to be an important motive of Sidney's:

> Another prominent motive in my background is the desire for materialistic things and for security. I am a Jew, and the harm that was done to the Jews during the Nazi reign has deeply impressed on me the horrible insecurity of it. Some scenes of the murdering of relatives were probably related to me in all their terror. This deeply impressed me and I have, like many other people of my race who grew up around this time, been imbued with not only a deep hatred of the Nazis and the German people but with a deep need for security and the deep need to put myself in a position in which I'd be invaluable, indispensable. Related to this is a deep fear for my life.

Three Sidneys. Summarizing these three conflicting motives in transactional-analysis terms may help us clarify Sidney's conflict. His Adult was truly motivated in an altruistic manner. Medicine was a logical, rational place to practice the golden rule. As is usually the case, Sidney was far more aware of the motives of his Adult than of his Parent or Child. The paragraphs in which he describes the influence of his mother's values (his Parent) and his fear of the Nazis (his Child) were written in his sophomore year after a year of heavy introspection. As we shall see, he became aware of these influences only gradually. The freshman year of college was very conducive to becoming more aware of his Parent because for the first time he was living away from home and could step back and look at his relations at home more objectively. Likewise, Sidney's Child only emerged into full consciousness as some of his old childhood fears were touched off by his reading existential literature during his freshman year. So we have three Sidneys: an altruistic Adult, a frightened Child, and a Parent whose injunctions center on the importance of security. The remainder of the case illustrates how he became more aware of the motives of his Parent and Child and how he gradually integrated them under his Adult.

Madison (1969) points out that as a freshman, Sidney became increasingly aware of the degree to which his choice of careers was motivated by his need for security. Excerpts from his diary suggest that the reading he was doing in his freshman literature course acted on these new insights like a match on an incendiary bomb:

> *September 28* — What are my moral values? How deep do they go? I have just finished reading Gide's *L'Immoraliste*. I don't think I live by the golden rule, but society smiles upon this. Is my desire for acceptance the reason for my surface moral values? I must probe deeply the question: What is right?

> *October 17* — I see how much money motivated my desire to be a doctor. Although I would enjoy liberal arts more, I will spend my life with science, probably because of money.

> *December 16* — I am going home for Christmas with horror. I feel horror at the social rejection and loneliness that is certain to engulf me at home. I am leaving college in fear. My past is suffocating me. Have I committed some crime that demands I get air, air, air?

> *January 31* — Fear of becoming a doctor haunts me. I dare not write my thoughts of my motives for medicine for fear they will bring me out of self rationalization.

> *February 7* — All my courses are playing up the spiritual crisis in modern man in search of an absolute on which to hang his life.

How did all this change really occur? Two years after Sidney's graduation, Madison asked him to make a comment on the effects of his freshman reading:

> As I read I saw it was the ideas themselves and not the form and style of literature that interested me . . . I could not admire the ideas of what I read and hold the values that I brought to college with me. In some sense it was as simple as that.

College classes and reading may open exciting, novel, and frightening avenues for consideration. What is your relation to other human beings? To God? To the universe? Such questions often occur to thoughtful students as parts of the curriculum touch their deepest childhood motives and anxieties.

Openness and Going to College

At the beginning of this chapter we asserted that the most basic essence of each of us is the thing that decides whether we will change and grow or remain trapped in the state of awareness that we have carried from childhood. Carl Rogers has described this essence as "psychological openness." The degree to which we are open to our life experiences and the inner psychological experiences that accompany them is very likely to decide how much we truly become a part of life. As we become more open we gradually come to realize the ways we are intimately related to every living creature, to our physical world, and even to the cosmos. Likewise, whether we move toward a full sense of identity in college is directly related to the degree we are open and receptive to new ideas, people, and alternative lifestyles.

Mildred Henry and Harriet Renaud of the Berkeley Center for Research in Higher Education recently interviewed (1972) a large sample of students at five small experimental colleges that claim to strongly influence their students. They found the students they interviewed tended to illustrate several identity types. Each type showed a different orientation towards openness to developing and changing their concept of who they were.

THE PSYCHICALLY FORECLOSED

The first group of students were characterized by a strong tendency to avoid personal change. They often had predetermined career goals that they clung to rigidly. They tended to avoid faculty and other students whose views might challenge theirs.

Their preference for security over growth was often reflected in a career choice based on practical issues such as how much the job would pay rather than on considerations such as whether it would fulfill their interests. One student in Henry and Renaud's sample illustrates this tendency clearly. He had never seriously considered going into any field but law:

> I decided on becoming a lawyer back in the eighth grade. I don't know how I decided on this really. But I am certain this is what I want to be. I don't feel I will dislike the law. . . . I feel it won't bore me to death and it pays adequately . . .

Asked whether he knew what it might be like to be a lawyer, he said:

> I have some phone numbers of people to call who could tell me something about it, but I haven't bothered to do this yet.

Despite this vagueness about what he was really getting into he stuck rigidly to his plans. Each year his responses to the interviewer's queries about his life plans varied only slightly in content and manner. His interest in Russian ended immediately when he decided it "wasn't relevant to law."

When asked if there were any important ways in which he would like to change in the future, he answered, "No." His basic response to challenges to his existing values appears to have been primarily one of avoidance. Asked what he found most challenging or difficult in college, he responded, "Since the faculty is less conservative than the students, you have to learn to express things in their terms, and that can be difficult." This tendency to regard any difference as a threat of conflict appears to be the major distinguishing feature of the psychologically foreclosed individual.

THE SITUATIONALLY FORECLOSED

A second group of students appear on the surface to be foreclosed to change. They also appear very rigid and closed, at least initially. But the reasons for their "closure" are different. Rather than reflecting fear of threat and anxiety about change, this group is simply lacking an exposure to information, ideas, and different lifestyles. Given this exposure, members of this group may show dramatic growth.

In the case of Bob (Madison 1969), which we introduced earlier in this chapter, the influence of other students, particularly that of a close friend whose values and background differed vastly from his, had a dramatic opening-up effect, which led to considerable change in his personality and lifestyle. Asked about his roommate, Bob said:

> He's pretty obstinate and quite dogmatic. He will not change his views, and will rarely listen to anyone else's opinion. It's interesting because a friend of mine has a mutual friend who is black. . . . One of the fellows we have is a Greek from Kenya. . . . He's a segregationist and, in some respects, a warmonger and, being a member of the minority population in Kenya, he's also an imperialist: so it makes a rather interesting situation for arguments. . . . The Greek from Kenya spends quite a bit of time in the room, and it sets up some pretty good arguments when we get this older roommate and the black and the Kenyan into arguments. I think basically it's a good situation because it helps you to make your own convictions concrete.

The end results of the identity-shock aspects of Bob's campus environment and the exposure the college provided to persons with divergent ideas and lifestyles were significant shifts in his attitudes. Views about people (which became more cynical), drinking, and sex (both of which became more accepting and less Puritanic), attitudes towards grades (as a senior he was more concerned about what he actually got out of the courses than the letter grade he received), and attitudes towards a career all changed. Perhaps most significant was the shift in Bob's life goals. Asked to describe his

The third group of students were committed to self-exploration. The term "moratorium" describes their tendency to delay final commitments to people, ideas, or lifestyles during a time of testing and exploring alternatives. This group represented the antithesis of the psychically foreclosed. They sought diverse friends, experiences, and ways of thinking actively. Their search was extensive and often led them to read widely, to seek out professors with unusual ideas, and to become intensely involved in many varied activities and projects, usually for short periods of time. They were constantly involved in introspection about their experiences, their motives, and so forth.

Sidney represents a good example of a moratorium student. Very open to his experiences and involved with trying to put them into words in his journal, Sidney actively sought out all the college had to offer. Unhampered by the fears of the psychically foreclosed, or by the limited background characteristics of the situationally foreclosed student, Sidney was able to engage the task of developing his personal identity with all of his energy. After a freshman year filled with introspection and soul searching, he used his sophomore and junior years to experiment with majors in philosophy and sociology. By the time he was a senior he was ready to make a firm commitment to a career.

In Harmony with Our Social Environment: Roles and Identities

When psychologists discuss the question *"Who am I?"* they tend to use the terms *self-concept* and *identity*. In a way both of these terms refer to the same thing: namely, the person's perception of who he or she is. *Self* refers to the things the person thinks of as "me." The content of such a self will vary, of course, for each individual, but it commonly includes one's body and physical attributes, personal qualities, ideals and values, goals, plans, and hopes. The term *identity* is useful because it

life goals as a freshman, he did so in terms reminiscent of Sidney's "security-oriented parent":

> I want security and a chance to be able to support a wife and children in a good community, to be able to give them what I consider the necessities and more. . . . I'd like to have the kind of family that can afford to have television if we want it, hi-fi if we want it, a dishwasher, and so on and so forth.

As a senior his life goals were radically changed:

> I am hesitant to say now because my ideas have changed so recently and so much. . . . Right now I want to be someone I'll be satisfied with. . . . being rich is not that important if I like what I am doing, if I am getting the most out of life, and if I have a chance to do what I want to do. I want to be able to talk freely, be independent, and not have a job where I am just a worker who takes orders all day long. I want a job in which I can use my own thoughts and initiative. . . .

THE SEARCH FOR SELF

states very clearly that the boundaries of our own personalities go a bit further than physical and psychological characteristics. Identity as it is used by most personologists refers to the fact that "I exist" not in a vacuum, but in a very particular social environment. Madison (1969) defines identity as "the sense of felt correspondence between the self and the roles he occupies in his immediate environment."

OUR ROLES AND WHY WE PLAY THEM

A role is simply a pattern of behavior that is expected of us. It is very difficult to imagine a person who has no roles. Certainly any individuals who live together tend to have some expectations of each other. This is true even in living environments purposefully designed to maximize the freedom of the individual participants. Even communes inhabited by those who seek refuge from the dehumanizing aspects of society do not offer a role-

free existence. Everyone has the role of a contributing, participating member. The way commune members are free is that they may be allowed to develop roles that are more in harmony with how they see themselves as people. They are encouraged to use their own talents rather than to pretend to be something they don't want to be. We know of no successful commune where noncontributing members are actively encouraged to remain noncontributors!

Likewise, in the encounter-group culture where the goal is a maximum of free, open, and spontaneous communication, there are still patterns of expected role behavior for members. I have a fantasy here of Albert Einstein suddenly leaping up in the middle of a nude marathon and in a voice quivering with excitement, saying, "I just saw the relationship between energy and mass." It would be a sensitive group indeed if at least one member failed to respond angrily, "Aw, come on, Al, knock off all that intellectual bullshit!" It isn't that people in encounter groups are rigid, it's just that for any group to function effectively there have to be some ground rules and expectations.

Being a college student is a role. Certain patterns of behavior are expected of students. Moreover, the patterns vary depending on who is doing the expecting. Parents often expect students to be studying hard, earning good grades, and preparing to enter a career field. The man in the street may expect all students to be wild-eyed radicals. Professors, like parents, frequently view a student as someone who studies diligently, but they are more inclined to expect the outcome of college to be deep analytical thinking and involvement with ideas rather than a good job. Although students themselves vary widely in what they consider to be their roles, they are as a group far more likely than parents, outsiders, or faculty to see those roles in terms of learning to understand and interact with other people or as developing their own personalities. Small wonder that such conflicting expectations on the part of parents, instructors, and one's own peers can result in a student's feeling pretty confused at times as to just who she or he really is.

IDENTITIES: BRINGING "ROLE" CLOSER TO "SELF"

A sense of correspondence between *self* and *roles* is most likely to occur in individuals who have clear-cut goals such as a sense of who they want to be or what they want to accomplish. Identity is a feeling that "I alone am responsible for my own life. I can control what happens to me." The case of Sidney that we discussed earlier in the chapter provides a good example. Although Sidney's identity was changing rapidly in college, the role of student suited him well. His academic talents allowed him to be highly successful in college and thus supported his self-esteem. College was an ideal place for his "moratorium" in that it allowed him to keep the door open to either a materialistically motivated career in medicine or a more humanistically motivated career in philosophy or the social sciences. Thus college was an environment uniquely suited to supporting Sidney in his search for an identity. The result was that he seldom felt alienated and could perceive a real sense of direction in his searching.

GAINING A SENSE OF IDENTITY

A sense of identity implies a sense of harmony and acceptance that begins with accepting ourselves. As we come to full awareness of the many aspects of our selves, our varied ego states, feelings, goals, and motives and as we learn to accept ourselves without feeling guilty, we gradually come to realize that we are capable of genuine closeness to others as well. Likewise, as we gain the courage to accept full responsibility of our own goals and to accept the motives from which these goals stem, we begin to develop social roles that are genuine expressions of our true feelings, goals, and motives. This sense of harmony between ourselves, our significant others, and our social roles is called a sense of identity.

Chapter Two Summary

1. *Transactional analysis.* The search for self is complicated by discovery of what appear to be conflicting selves residing within us. TA theorists refer to three selves: the Parent, the Adult, and the Child (P-A-C). P-A-C analysis provides some useful guidelines for "hearing" our own behavior more sensitively.

2. *The Parent* is a set of recordings our minds have made of all the external events that we have experienced, particularly the words and behavior of our parents.

3. *The Adult* is our computer. It is capable of evaluating the contents of our Parent and Child, deciding when they fit our present reality, and reprogramming.

4. *The Child* is the set of recordings of our inner reactions to these events, particularly those we experienced as small children.

5. The term *college shock* refers to a temporary feeling of loss of identity brought on by college experiences. The case of Bob illustrates that such shock may result in personal growth.

6. *Openness and growth.* We looked at three degrees of openness: those who are psychically closed to experience, those who are situationally closed, and those who leave themselves open to change by declaring college as a moratorium. The latter group tends to show the greatest change in college. In general, members of the first group change very little.

7. *Roles and Identity.* A role was defined as "a pattern of expected behavior." All of us have roles if we conform at all to what is expected of us. The crucial question for growth is "How well do my roles correspond to my real self?" When we feel a strong linkage between our roles and our inner selves we have a sense of identity.

Adapted Child That part of the Child ego state that shows an alteration of the natural child. Such alterations usually result from the demands and expectations of parents. The adapted Child often tends to be complying, to withdraw from others, to procrastinate, or to rebel openly.

For example: John hears his wife calling him for dinner. "Just a minute, dear," he answers. He then goes on working.

Marie has been wanting to marry Bill for the past ten years. But she can never quite get up the nerve to tell her mother she wants to leave her.

Adult ego state—our ability to reason, to evaluate situations, and to reach decisions based on present here-and-now sense data.

For example: A child of ten months who becomes able to climb on top of the TV set *at will* has developed a small Adult. When the child explores the neighborhood independently the Adult grows larger. The child sees a dog hurt in the street and decides, "Mom was right. It is dangerous to play in the street." When he or she is eighteen, the Adult decides that "Mom was wrong. Sex is OK."

Child ego state—the set of recordings of all the internal events (feelings, concepts, and so forth) that the young child experienced.

For example: a five-year-old Janie sees a sour face and feels it is her fault, thinking, "I messed up again." When she is twenty-five, her husband comes home from a bad day at the office, yells at her, and *she apologizes to him.*

Ego According to Freud, that part of the mind that is in contact with the world by means of perception, thinking, and logic. The ego's job is dealing with reality. It must mediate between the demands of the id and the prohibitions of the superego.

Id The deepest unconscious instinctual impulses. The id is out of contact with the conscious mind and with the external world. It functions solely for the pleasure and immediate gratification of the body. Because the id is only in contact with the body and has no contact with the world outside, examples are difficult to come by. The newborn infant who wets when its bladder is full and sucks when it is hungry is as close as we can get. Dr. Jekyll, Frankenstein, and the werewolves provide some good literary examples of the id coming to the fore.

Identity A sense of harmony between ourselves, our significant others, and our social roles.

Identity shock The feeling that "I don't fit in here." Identity shock is a temporary loss of one's sense of who he or she is. The cause is a dramatic change in one's interpersonal environment. Some very common identity shock situations are: coming to college, beginning a new job, moving to a new community, and getting a divorce.

Identity types Henry and Renaud's three orientations towards personal growth in college: the psychically foreclosed, the situationally foreclosed, and the moratorium student.

Moratorium student One who has an orientation towards college that emphasizes personal growth and self-exploration. Exposing oneself to many diverse experiences, friendships, activities, and ideas is the goal of the moratorium student.

Natural child That part of the Child ego state that is the impulsive, rebellious, affectionate, curious, self-centered, expressive infant in each of us.

For example: an old man gleefully licking an ice cream cone; a couple skipping down the beach hand in hand; an office worker throwing a temper tantrum because he can't have the day off.

Parent ego state The set of recorded messages from our parents, other parent figures, and other early external events. Some common Parent tapes are of the form "You should . . ." or "Don't you dare . . ."

Personologist Your authors are personologists. What we do has sometimes been defined by our more hard-headed colleagues as "trying to find out who I am by studying everyone else." We admit that there is a grain of truth in this accusation. A more formal definition is *someone who studies* *human personality*. A person-ologist's tools are limited only by his or her imagination. Some common ones are case material, therapy interviews, and personality tests.

Psychically foreclosed The identity type of the individual who invests most of his energy in keeping himself from changing. An example is the guy who always has reasons for not trying anything new that you suggest to him.

Role A pattern of behavior that is expected by ourselves and others in our interpersonal environment. Some common role patterns are "student," "father," "wife," and "firstborn child."

Self-study course One in which the subject matter is your own personality. The academic content of such a course is limited to psychological concepts that can help you understand yourself better. The "tests" are tests of your ability to apply these concepts to yourself. And the "laboratory" involves inter- and intrapersonal experiences that are designed to help you understand yourself better.

Situationally foreclosed The identity type of the individual who is unable to respond fully to new situations because of a lack of background. Some common examples are the entering freshman who was very successful in high school but is failing in a large university, the new resident of a large metropolitan city who feels overwhelmed by the diversity of life styles encountered there, and the young white

middle-class social worker beginning work in a New York ghetto.

Superego The set of values, attitudes, and morals that we have incorporated from our parents and from society (very similar to the TA concept of an internalized Parent).

Transactional Analysis A system of psychotherapy that helps us understand our personalities by analyzing and interpreting the transactions between ourselves and others. The P-A-C (Parent-Adult-Child) method of interpreting transactions, which we introduced in this chapter, is the basic tool of this form of therapy.

Exercises (*for individual and class use*)

You can do the following exercises at your leisure. Perhaps some of these would be more enjoyable with a friend. Those with an asterisk should be done in consultation with your teacher or in class.

1. *Getting to know your Parent ego state*. The goal of transactional analysis is to achieve a balance between your Parent, Adult, and Child. For your Parent and Child to work for you rather than against you, they must be under the control of your Adult. However, there are also places for the Parent and Child in your personality. Exercises 1, 2, 3, and 4 will help you get to know your Parent, Adult, and Child and to decide whether you use each to best advantage. The first question is, "Do I use my Parent ego state too frequently or inappropriately?"

- Do others accuse you of thinking for them, being bossy, being a know-it-all, or mothering them?
- Would your parents have belonged to the groups you belong to? Why or why not?
- Do your groups always depend on you to make their decisions for them?
- What is your style of leading a group—to tell others what to do, to encourage them to think for themselves, or to wait for someone else to get things started?
- Write down one thing that you still do that you copied from a parent figure.

2. Your Adult

- Do you use your Adult ego state too often or inappropriately?
- Think of a situation in the past month or so where you gathered facts and made a decision you feel is a good one.
- Do others complain that you are too rational or think too much and feel too little?
- Do you have very little time for recreation?
- Are your friends all in your own college major? Are they primarily people you study with?

- Do you tend to be continually involved in reasoning and data processing or do you allow time for parental concern or childlike playfulness with others?

3. Finally, how about your Child?

- Are you using your Child ego state too often or inappropriately?
- Do you "set yourself up" by giving others powers over you?
- Do others frequently rescue you? Give you the answer? Put you in your place?
- Are the groups you belong to primarily for fun? For attacking authorities?
- Do you constantly turn to others for approval?

4. Is there a good balance between your Parent, Adult, and Child?

- Which ego state do you use most of the time?
- When you talk to others, which ego state do you speak from most of the time?
- Which ego state do you use to greatest advantage?
- Think of a problem you have in relating to to others. Which ego state do you usually use in this situation?
- Might this situation improve if you used a different ego state?

5. *Your present life roles*. Imagine your life as a stage on which you are the star. What are the major roles you play? Who expects you to play each role? List four or five roles and think about what each really means to you. Then draw a diagram like the one in the figure on the next page that shows how much time and energy you are now investing in each role.

- Is the amount of time you invest in each role similar to the amount of energy you invest in each?
- How well do these roles fit your real interests?

- Who encourages you in each role?
- Who directs you in each role?
- Who decided you would play each part?
- How satisfied are you with what you invest of yourself in each part?

6. *Keeping a personal journal.* Perhaps you would like to make thinking about your present experiences and who you really are a major project for this semester. If so, keeping a personal journal like Bob and Sidney is a fine way of collecting your thoughts and experiences.

A good procedure for writing a journal is as follows. Find a time of the day when you are most likely to feel relaxed. Find a place where others won't interrupt you. Spend a few moments just relaxing, and then let your thoughts turn outward to the events of the day. What has happened that was personally important to you? What was the most satisfying event of the day? Describe to yourself all the feelings you had about it. What events do you feel vaguely anxious or unhappy about? What events were of a crisis nature?

Now turn inward. How do you feel here and now? Are you happy? Depressed? Relaxed? Also notice your body. Where do you experience tension? What part of your body worked hardest today? Next, turn to your breathing. Is it fast or slow? Deep or shallow?

Now try to record as much as you can of your personal experience for today. Be sure to discuss both external events and your feelings about them and the observations you have made of your internal states. Do this every night for the entire semester. From time to time, go back over what you have written. You may find some of your experiences very interesting to return to when you begin to study awareness in part three of this text.

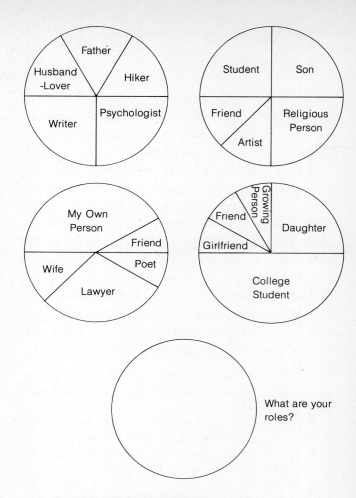

FIG. 2-1 *Typical role diagrams*

Bibliography

Berne, E. 1964. *Games people play*. New York:
Grove.

Campous, L., and McCormick, P. 1969.
*Introduce yourself to transactional analysis: a
TA primer*. Berkeley: Transactional
Publications.

Harris, T. 1969. *I'm OK, you're OK*. New York:
Harper.

Henry, M. and Renaud, H. 1972. Examined and
unexamined lives. *Research Reporter*.
Berkeley: Center for Research and
Development in Higher Education. 7:1, 5.

James, M., and Jongeward, D. 1971. *Born to win*.
Reading, Mass:Addison-Wesley.

Madison, P. 1969. *Personality development in
college*. Reading, Mass.: Addison-Wesley.

For a few minutes
Can we be people
Instead of positions?
Can I be I
And you be you
And free?
Can you judge me
And I judge you
As a person
And not as a position?
Can you react to me
And I react to you,
Without thinking
Of what you should be doing,
Because of your position,
And what I should be doing,
Because of my position?
Can people just be people
Together, and for once, escape
The boundaries of assumed correctness
Imposed by those who assume
They must react to a position
Instead of a person?
Why do people attach more importance
To position than to people?
Silly, isn't it?
Why do people attach more importance
To their positions
Than to themselves?
Sillier, isn't it?

DON DECKER

The Pain of Felt Differences: Being Different

This is a chapter about that part of ourselves that is different from others. We are all unique in some ways. Each of us has strengths and talents that set us apart from others. Some have more patience; others are better able to assert themselves; some are intelligent; others are intuitive. Each of us has something unique to offer to those who love us . . . and to those who hate us, as well.

So our differences are our gifts. We must guard them carefully. But this is not the entire story, because there is always some pain associated with being different from others. The first time I can remember "feeling different" was when my mother told me I was an adopted child. I was about four at the time. I can still hear her voice explaining that someone else was my mother, that she and Dad had waited for a very long time for a child and that they "loved me as much as if I were their own." I found all that pretty confusing at the age of four. The only thing I think I really got out of it then was that I was different somehow — not quite legitimate. I also felt a great surge of gratitude to them for taking me home with them. I knew I was loved, but I felt pain because I thought I was loved for a different reason than other people were.

Pain also occurs when our way of being different offends someone else's values or expectations. There is a human tendency to value most highly those behaviors we are familiar with. Deviant or novel behaviors are frequently overtly punished. And those who would help* all too often use the strategy of applying pressure to conform rather than taking the time to understand.

The extreme social pressure that is exerted on the deviant is the subject of the first part of this chapter. We will look at the effects of labeling a person a deviant, the punitive history of "help" for

---

*In this chapter *help* has some rather different connotations than usual. You may want to look ahead to the chapter glossary to see what some of these connotations are.

THE DEVIANT SELF

the mentally ill, and the negative aspects of parental "help." In this section we will examine two very extreme examples of techniques that may be applied to manipulate us: psychological brainwashing and the Milgram studies on obedience. Next we will visit the laboratory to observe the effect that labeling a person as deviant has on the behavior of those around him. This section ends with a look at the implications of all this for our own developing sense of who we are.

How we can cope with "the pain of felt differences" is the subject of this chapter's second section. Here we will look at case examples illustrating the process that we go through when we change the direction of our lives. We will then return to transactional analysis for an understanding of how we can make interventions in our lives that can accelerate our personal growth. Finally, we will suggest some practical guidelines for those who want to help others. So—let's find out what "help" is all about.

DEVIANTS AS SCAPEGOATS

Often a person who is deviant becomes a scapegoat. For example, when I was a child I suffered from rheumatic fever, which made it impossible for me to attend school for two and a half years. Because I was in bed much of the time, I became weak, clumsy, and obese. When I returned to school in the fifth grade I immediately became the class scapegoat. I was teased relentlessly because of my weight, consistently rejected when we chose up sides for athletic events, and was frequently the victim of class bullies. I feel this experience sensitized me to situations in which deviant persons become scapegoats just because they are different.

An objective person would of course point out that the observations I have made about deviants being scapegoats are very likely to be biased in several important ways. First is the possibility that I wasn't a scapegoat at all. I have no accurate count of the number of times that I was beaten up or teased. Nor can I produce a set of norms on how often other children in my class were teased or beaten. The whole thing could just reflect my own hypersensitivity at a time when I felt particularly vulnerable.

Even assuming I was a scapegoat, it is impossible to know why. I could have been mistreated just because I was different from my classmates (weaker and fatter). Another factor was that I lacked aggressive skills and hence was a pushover. Or maybe I did things that encouraged others in my class to mistreat me, thereby confirming my own expectation of being attacked: recall that I've already admitted to some early feelings that I felt "different" from others. As we pointed out in chapter one, psychologists are biased observers.

The same may be said of most people's observations of their own lives. This is why social psychologists prefer to check out their hunches in a laboratory experiment rather than trust to intuition. In the lab it is possible to control what goes on. Then (if you control the right things) you can say with somewhat more certainty that your hunch was correct.

Anthony Doob (you guessed it, a social psychologist) had the same idea about deviants being scapegoats that I had. Being objective, he did a controlled study instead of just trusting his intuition (Doob 1971). First of all he measured observable behavior rather than relying on personal reports. One behavior he measured was the number of electric shocks people would give to a subject who was clumsy. To insure that whatever results occurred were due solely to people's *impressions* that a subject was deviant, he used a stooge who behaved the same throughout the experiment. Doob impressed half of the subjects that the stooge was normal and the others that he was deviant by telling the first half that the stooge had scored "about average" on a personality test. The other half, whom Doob wanted to believe that the subject was deviant, were told that they had scored "very low."

This technique had the advantages of insuring that the stooge's personal characteristics, such as "lack of skills" or "being an obnoxious kid," would be averaged out of the results.)

The subjects had been asked to participate in a perception experiment involving a very elaborate piece of apparatus. The experimenter left the subjects in the room with the apparatus. One subject (actually the stooge) broke the equipment, making it impossible for the members of the group to earn the five dollars they thought they were going to get for participating. Then all the subjects were offered the opportunity of giving electric shocks to the stooge. When they thought the clumsy subject was deviant, they gave him more shocks than when they thought he was normal.

Doob's study helps to establish that discovering someone is different from ourselves may be used as an excuse for punishment. At such times just labeling a person as "different" is all it takes. One doesn't even need to know in what way. Doob also discovered some interesting effects of a person's being told she or he is deviant. We will return to these results later, but first let's look at the implications of this tendency on our helping institutions, including the American family.

HELPING (?) DEVIANTS

The tendency to punish those who are deviant even carries over into those situations where we are committed to help. Throughout the centuries, there has been much talk about helping the deviant. In the past, deviance was often labeled *sin* or *possession*. "Help" consisted of beating, burning at the stake, and imprisonment.

DEVIANCE AS MENTAL ILLNESS

Today we often refer to deviance as mental illness. This has led us to talk at one level about care and treatment for the deviant. However, sometimes such humane-sounding words continue to be a rationalization for rejecting and punishing. Thomas

Szasz, a psychiatrist, has attacked the danger of such semantics in mental-illness-related terminology (Kiester 1972):

> If you give a person's pattern of behavior a label and call it a "sickness," that justifies your placing the person in a hospital and treating him for his "illness." Suppose you are old and poor, as most people diagnosed mentally ill are. You begin to behave in a manner that offends your children. They have you examined by a psychiatrist and he says you are "sick" with a "senile psychosis" and locks you up, when in fact your problem is nothing more than children who don't want you.

Is the mental health professional really an executioner in disguise? We don't think so. Most of those in our profession are sincerely dedicated to helping others. And there are state hospitals where the environment is genuinely supportive and humane. Experiments such as those described are certainly signs of awareness and change. So is the fact that Szasz's critique is routinely taught in most modern training programs in clinical psychology.

But there is a problem. Our history of helping by punishing still has its impact. Those who seek professional counseling should be sure they understand what their counselor means when she or he says, "May I help you?" Certainly professional helpers have a greater responsibility to understand themselves and how they feel towards those they help. We think their potential clients have a right to know what these feelings are. In chapter nine we will discuss the various modes of professional help that are available.

But the confusion of help with punishment is not limited to laboratory subjects and mental health professionals. We must also deal with it in our roles as friends and parents.

The Negative Aspects of Parental Help
THE PREJUDICED-PARENT EGO STATE
Our Parent ego state may be filled with prejudiced ideas. When this is so, we inflict our standards of behavior on others. These may be based on opinion rather than fact. For example:

"Girls shouldn't wear pants."
"Boys should cut their hair short."
"Girls shouldn't be aggressive."
"Boys shouldn't express love."
"Kids should be seen and not heard."
"Adults shouldn't be silly."

James and Jongeward (1971) refer to such tapes as our prejudiced-Parent ego state. Very often when we label someone a deviant we are acting like our prejudiced Parent. For example:

"Anyone who does that *must* be crazy."
"What a *sick* thing to do."
"The way that guy dresses is *disgusting*."

Many of us have in our Parent ego state a rule that says in one form or another, "Children must be made to behave." So we punish them to "help"

them grow. Most parents are warm, supportive, or protective on some occasions and punitive, moralizing, or unresponsive on others. But some parents consistently try to be "helpful" by sending out critical destructive messages:

"The trouble with you, Johnny, is that you're lazy."

"Nancy, this room looks like a pig sty!"

"The way Joe is going he will probably fail fourth grade." (Said to another parent while Joe listens intently)

"Shut up, Martha!"

Critical messages do need to be delivered to children at times. Johnny may be defeating himself or the family by avoiding responsibility. Rooms resembling Nancy's may make life uncomfortable for other family members, particularly if "that room" is the living room rather than her bedroom. Sometimes a child like Joe is in danger of failing and must be made aware that a problem exists. And parents do need some quiet time in which to tune into themselves without the presence of their children.

Our objection is not with the surface content of such messages but rather with the manner in which they are delivered. All of them go beyond the helpful stage of identifying or clarifying a problem. All employ punishment and name calling. Johnny is called "lazy." It is implied that Nancy is a "pig," Joe is a "failure," and Martha is discounted as a sort of subperson unworthy of being listened to. As we shall see in this chapter, labeling an individual this way often tends to result in his behaving as though the label were correct. Thus telling Johnny he is lazy may result in his becoming more so. Likewise Nancy may fulfill her parents' prophecy by becoming messier, and Joe may be more prone to fail after having a displeased parent predict failure.

A second aspect of such messages is that they all contain a *should*. Every child needs some shoulds to protect him from harm and to convey

What It Feels Like to be a Mental Patient (McDaniel 1972)

Twenty-nine employees at a state mental hospital were selected at random to be "patients" in a mock ward. Another twenty-one were selected to staff the ward. Observers took notes and filmed the proceedings.

The "patients" went through regular admitting procedures and were given showers and issued ill-fitted clothing. They were searched and all personal belongings were confiscated. They ate in a dining room with actual mental patients.

The "staff" treated the "patients" just as they would treat patients in their wards. They gave tokens as rewards and took away tokens as punishment.

Interviews afterward showed the experience was realistic and often frightening. A questionnaire filled out by participants also demonstrated its realism. The experiment showed mental hospitals can cause people to react in ways that are considered abnormal.

The observers said the "patients":
—Sat together but did not react to each other
—Lied and cheated to get what they needed
—Complained of having no place to be alone
—Moved about constantly to reassure themselves that "everything is OK because I can feel something happening"

A questionnaire answered by the "patients" after the experiment showed that seventy-five percent did not feel they were being treated as real people.

All said they especially felt a lack of freedom. Eighty-nine percent said they felt at times that they were being deprived of their identity, and ninety-three percent said they felt as though they were in prison.

Frank Fetters, a worker who was a "patient," said afterward: "I felt like an animal being kept in a barn; I didn't go to sleep until very late in the morning; and I didn't sleep very well."

He said his behavior toward patients changed immediately.

"I was the coach-type," Fetters said, explaining that he was authoritarian and "hollered a lot" trying to control patients.

"I don't think I've screamed at a patient since I got back," he said. And now, no matter how ridiculous the patient's request, he said, he has tried to honor it.

Steve Piser, a "patient" who escaped several times during the experiment, told an interviewer he did it because "things just got a little intense." For him, "the atmosphere changed from hospital to jail."

Once Piser was put into restraints for his recalcitrance.

Altogether he found participation in the experiment "a pretty humiliating experience."

that "Mom and Dad care about me." But a parent who constantly criticizes and loads a child up with literally thousands of *should*s leaves the child with the choice of either giving up thinking independently or openly rebelling.

James and Jongeward (1971) cite as an example a client who complained he could never enjoy anything. Whenever he picked up a book he immediately began to hear Parent tapes saying, "Work before pleasure." His Child naturally wanted to enjoy itself, but he felt too guilty to relax and would soon put down the book and go back to work cleaning the garage.

Other Parent tapes have no message at all other than a punitive one:

"You do what I say and like it."

"Shut up! Don't ask me another stupid question."

"Here's something to really cry about." (Hits child)

Such messages seldom accomplish any goal of the parent's except to hurt. They result in the child becoming either 1) overly conforming, 2) withdrawing, or 3) procrastinating.

The conforming child simply gives up feeling, thinking, sensing, and being creative. He or she lives just to please others or to get by.

Other children withdraw from punishment. They learn to satisfy their needs through fantasy. Some common fantasies of the child who withdraws are: being a super hero with x-ray vision and unlimited powers, being rescued by a prince in shining armor, becoming sick and being taken care of by others, or becoming a beautiful or handsome person.

Still others respond by becoming procrastinators. It doesn't pay to get involved in work if parents are never satisfied. If a child's parent is critical, then completing a task just leads to criticism for not doing it well enough, or more jobs, or more parental demands, or more frustration. When every effort leads to frustration the child may respond by

putting off getting started. Procrastination may become a life style.

Finally, as we saw in chapter two, such messages tend to become internalized. This means that the way our parents behaved towards us when we needed help will tend to become the techniques we apply to others. For example, when I was a boy my father's usual response to me when I fell and hurt myself was to laugh and tease, "Did you hurt the sidewalk, Reed?" I always felt angry and hurt by this response and vowed I would never tease my children when they were hurt. I believe strongly that to do this denies children's feelings and discounts their right to express them. Nonetheless I frequently catch myself starting to tease. Sometimes I even use his exact words! I can control this, but I almost always have to stop and turn off the tape. Such modeling of parental techniques of "helping" is very common. For example, an overly critical teacher may point out unimportant flaws just as his parents did with him, or a woman may assume the exact hands-on-hips posture that her mother used when scolding her.

A good question to ask yourself in situations where you find yourself being overly critical of others is, "How did father (or mother, or any other of your parent figures) handle this situation?" "Is it possible that I am modeling a response of theirs that is not appropriate?" Another good question to ask yourself is, "How did I feel when they did this to me?" It isn't uncommon to find ourselves doing something with our children, friends, or spouse that we vowed we would never do. My teasing is one example. Some others are:

Betty's response to her father's complaints about a messy room was to become even more messy. But now as a mother she uses the same technique to get her daughter Susie to clean her room.

Jack's dad always punished and scolded him for his driving. It never did any good. Jack would say under his breath "I'll show him," and

drove all the faster. But now Jack does these same things to his son Bob. And with the same result.

Sally's mother always backed down when it came time to discipline Sally. Instead of setting limits she simply said, "You kids are impossible! I don't know what to do with you." When Sally's father got home he would become enraged. Sally vowed not to manipulate her kids and husband this way. But now she often does. She says, "Somehow I just can't bring myself to punish the kids. I really don't know how."

THE NURTURANT-PARENT EGO STATE

Some parents consistently send messages that are nurturant (James and Jongeward 1971). Some nurturant-Parent tapes are:

"I'll rub it for you where it hurts."

"Hey, that's OK. Anyone can make that mistake."

"I love you."

The fact that James and Jongeward use the term *nurturant* to describe this ego state reveals their bias that such messages are usually genuinely helpful and conducive to growth in the recipient. We agree. Support and warmth from those we are close to is something that all of us can use. But there are times when behaving like a nurturant Parent is inappropriate or even destructive.

Nurturant parents are sometimes guilty of being overly protective and oversolicitous. These dangers also apply to "helpers" who always come on as nurturant Parents as well—for example, a counselor who constantly tells clients they don't have any problems or a doctor who never tells patients when they are dying.

Perhaps the most important thing that anyone who wants to help others can do is to become as aware as possible of the contents of her or his prejudiced- and nurturant-Parent ego states. And one of the most important of these tapes says, "Do as you're told—it's for your own good."

THE DEVIANT SELF

Psychological Brainwashing

A very extreme example of how our belief in ourselves may be attacked and weakened is the technique of psychological brainwashing. Fortunately, most of us will never have to undergo such conditions of stress. However, there are certain procedures that survivors of prison camps tell us have literally saved their lives. Edward Hunter, who has spent thirty years studying how people defend against prison conditions, identifies the following techniques for weakening a person's resistance.

Purpose

1. To develop self-concern; to make the victim dependent on the interrogator and erase group support
2. To fix attention on the immediate discomforts
3. To weaken the mental and physical ability to resist
4. To foster compliant behavior and expectations of "no way out of this"
5. To hinder adjustment to privation
6. To emphasize the futility of resistance
7. To reduce the prisoner to animal-level concerns
8. To further develop compliance

Techniques

1. Solitary confinement; complete isolation, semi-isolation, or group isolation
2. Physical isolation, prolonged interrogation, or forcing written answers to questions
3. Semi-starvation, exposure to the elements, exploitation of wounds, sleep deprivation, prolonged constraint, prolonged interrogation, or forced writing
4. Threats of death, nonrepatriation, punishment as a war criminal, or endless isolation; threats against family; changing living quarters and interrogators without explanation
5. Alternating rewards and punishments with occasional favors, fluctuating interrogator's attitudes, making special promises, giving rewards for partial compliance, and
6. Techniques for convincing the prisoner, "We know all about you" and saying his friends have "come around"
7. Preventing personal hygiene; providing filthy surroundings; giving demeaning punishment, insults and taunts; denying privacy
8. Forcing writing, enforcing rules, and upping the ante for compliance to demands

THE IDENTITY OF SELF

Developing a Self-Concept of "Deviant"

Given the tendency for society to "help" its deviants by isolating them, removing their personal rights, and being generally punitive, several predictions can be made about what a person will do when he or she is made to feel deviant.

1. A person who feels deviant should tend to be worried about the treatment she or he will receive from nondeviants.
2. He or she will try to avoid mistreatment in a variety of ways. The deviant could: a) avoid contact with nondeviants, b) try to please nondeviants (that is, try to be a "good guy"), or c) try to conceal the deviance from others.

AN EXPERIMENT IN DEVIANCE

Anthony Doob decided to test out these ideas in a second series of experiments (1971). Again he decided to manipulate the feeling of deviance rather than working with people who were judged to be deviant. This allowed him to look at the effect of feeling deviant all by itself. For example, one of the symptoms of schizophrenia is withdrawal from others. Thus if Doob chose schizophrenics as subjects, it almost goes without saying that they would avoid contact with nondeviants. But whether such a result would be attributable to "being schizophrenic" or "feeling deviant" would have been up for grabs.

So Doob decided to make people who were normal feel deviant. There were a lot of ways he might have accomplished this. He could have made a Madison Avenue executive wear business clothes to the beach or he could have gotten people to wear their shoes on the wrong feet for one week. Any list of fraternity pranks is rich in suggestions. You can scan your list of embarrassing moments for further ideas.

Doob, being a psychologist, was familiar with the embarrassment that many people experience when they find their scores on a personality inventory are particularly extreme (high or low). So he

got some people to take some personality tests. When they were finished, he explained that he could show them where their scores were in relation to a standardized population of 1000 others who had taken the tests. "Unfortunately," he added, "I can't tell you what your scores mean until the experiment has ended."

But Doob was being sneaky. People didn't get back their real results at all. Doob had made up the profiles before they ever took the tests. He decided ahead of time (by means of a table of random numbers) that some people would be made to feel deviant. To these people he handed out profiles that showed extremely high and low scores on all the scales. To the remaining subjects (those he wanted to feel like "my fellow Americans") he gave profiles that showed their scores to be at or near the center of the distribution (see figure 3-1).

Feeling Deviant

Several such tests were administered. Surprisingly, the people in the experiments appeared to be very convinced that the results were representative of what they were really like. They were easily taken in by what an authoritative test had to say about them. Often after the first test, those who were labeled "deviants" would laugh a little and ask for more information. As the series of tests continued with consistently deviant results, many subjects began to show worry and concern about their scores. The tests seemed to have the same effect that the psychiatrist's "Hmm . . . very interesting" can have.

Sticking Together

Doob now had his subjects feeling deviant without their really knowing what was supposed to be wrong

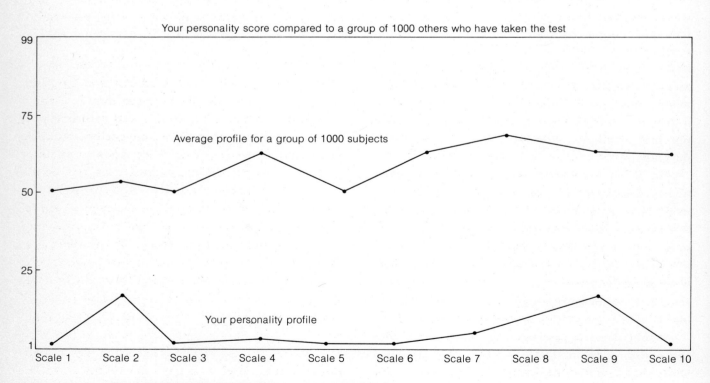

Your personality score compared to a group of 1000 others who have taken the test

FIG. 3-1 *Sample of the feedback Doob provided to "deviants"*

with them. Having gotten this far, he performed some further tests. First, would birds of a feather flock together? To see if this would be true when a feeling of deviance was manipulated, Doob asked his subjects to choose three partners they would like to be with for an experiment in cooperative problem solving. They made their choice from a sheet containing the scores of twenty-five subjects who had taken the tests. Two findings emerged. Birds of a feather did flock together. Deviants tended to chose more often those whose scores were at the bottom of the scale (close to theirs) than did the normals (averaging 2.00 extreme choices and .91 extreme choices, respectively.)

Secondly, it turned out that deviants also chose more people above the median than did nondeviants, suggesting perhaps that weird birds like other weird birds because of their weirdness *per se* rather than merely because they are similar. Normals, in contrast, chose people primarily on the basis of perceived similarity.

Concealing Deviance

Doob also wanted to know if people labeled "deviant" would try to conceal their deviance from others. What would the difference be between someone who was obviously deviant, say a person with two noses, and a person who is less obviously deviant, like someone with eleven toes? In this experiment test scores were announced publicly to one group and privately to another. The expectation was that, like homosexuals who avoid discussing sex and light-skinned blacks who pass as whites, the deviants would attempt to avoid detection. Subjects were asked to indicate their preference for working alone or in groups on a one- to six-point scale, where six was the highest possible preference for working alone. Subjects with undisclosed deviance tended to prefer working alone, while known deviants and nondeviants were more eager for the company of others like themselves.

Good Guys

When you feel a bit freaky or deviant, one way to feel better is to assume the role of super good guy. This results in other people liking you and is a way of avoiding the punishment deviants often receive. Doob studied this phenomenon in still another experiment. After receiving phony test results that implied that they were either normal or deviant personalities, subjects were left alone together for a short time. One subject (another stooge) got up and asked a nonstooge subject if he or she were willing to write some letters about preserving the redwoods. If the subject agreed, the stooge went on to try to get her or him to write as many as fifty letters. As predicted, subjects who thought they were deviant tried to be good guys. They wrote twice as many letters as those who had been described as normal by the phony test. It also made a difference whether the stooge was labeled deviant or normal. Deviants complied more to requests from a stooge they thought was normal. Nondeviants were more helpful when the stooge was identified as deviant.

IMPLICATIONS: THE WHEEL OF "KOOKINESS"
Doob's study provides one model of how a person may become mentally ill. Suppose that as a child you began to feel a bit strange and someone you trusted (your mother, perhaps) suggested you were acting strangely also. One thing leads to another and. . . . Doob's results suggest that this could happen to anyone. You don't really have to be deviant. All it takes is for someone else you believe in to say you are. Doob has clearly demonstrated our vulnerability in this respect. If he could get college students to feel deviant simply by giving them phony test results, consider how much more the young child is vulnerable to being called a "brute" or "stupid" or "weird." Much of the time such feedback is not accurate at all. Often it is simply the projection of a parent who failed to find purpose in life and is blaming this on the child. Or it may be the outpourings of a teacher who hates to

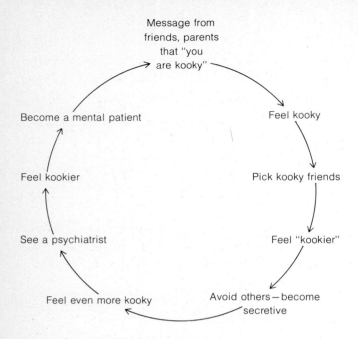

Message from
friends, parents
that "you
are kooky"

Feel kooky

Become a mental patient

Pick kooky friends

Feel kookier

Feel "kookier"

See a psychiatrist

Feel even more kooky

Avoid others — become
secretive

FIG. 3-2   *The Wheel of kookiness*

teach and has never dared to admit it, or it may come from a friend who needs to build up his or her self-concept and feelings of worth by attacking others.

Actually it makes no difference whether the feedback is valid or invalid. The important thing is whether you come to believe it. If you do, a vicious cycle begins. If you begin to feel deviant you may begin to select and choose friends who have also been labeled as deviant. And once you do this you have some more reasons for feeling badly about yourself: "I hang around with strange people; therefore I am strange." Or you begin to go to great lengths to hide your strangeness from others. But in so doing the problem just gets worse. People only laugh at an ostrich who buries its head in the sand, and when people laugh you feel more deviant. Thus a never-ending cycle similar to that in figure 3-2 is begun. If the cycle continues long enough you may end up in a psychiatrist's office. Hopefully the cycle

should end at this point. But it may not. Just seeing a psychiatrist is admitting that something is radically wrong, and this may result in greater feelings of deviance and hence more deviant behavior. Eventually it may lead the psychiatrist to commit you to an institution. Once in the institution, the orderlies regard you as weird and avoid you, and you are given medication that may make you feel even more strange.

Intervening with Yourself

Thus far we have focused on the ways our self-image can be negatively influenced by others such as parents, friends, and professional helpers. But what can we do to intervene in our own lives? How do I change how I feel about myself? And how can I help myself and others who I care about to grow?

CAN I BELIEVE IN MYSELF?

Be yourself. Especially do not feign affection.
Neither be cynical about love, for in the face of
    all aridity and disenchantment
It is as perennial as the grass.
Take kindly the counsel of the years,
Gracefully surrendering the things of youth.
Nurture strength of spirit to shield you in sudden
    misfortune,
But do not distress yourself with imaginings.
Many fears are born of fatigue and loneliness,
    beyond a wholesome discipline.
Be gentle with yourself.

In short, "Be cool." But how can a person be cool in a hot environment? In one of our classes we asked our students to report anonymously an incident in which they felt they had lost their cool. The student's response on page 68 begins with the realization that she can't go on as she is. She literally has to change. Notice how she goes through a time of really struggling with herself before she can admit this to herself. Such a struggle is often the prelude to growth.

THE IDENTITY OF SELF

Obeying Orders

The following experiment by Stanley Milgram* (1963) emphasizes the universal social power of the person in the white lab coat and how this may lead to punishment of those who are deviant.

Milgram wanted to see how far an authority figure could go in getting people to punish others. More specifically, he wanted to see how much electric shock a subject would be willing to give another person simply because he was ordered to do so. Subjects for the study were recruited on the pretext that they were needed for a learning experiment. On arriving at the laboratory a subject met another subject (really a stooge) and the experimenter. The experimenter was a dignified and intelligent-looking person of about thirty who always wore a white lab coat. The subjects were told that one of them was to serve as a teacher and the other as a learner in a study on the effects of punishment on learning. A rigged drawing was then held, which always resulted in the stooge being assigned the role of learner and the subject the role of teacher. The subject was then shown the stooge being strapped into an apparatus resembling an electric chair. Following this, the subject was taken into an adjoining room and shown a very impressive shock-generating apparatus consisting of a realistic-looking instrument panel containing thirty switches. Each switch was clearly labeled with a voltage designation ranging from fifteen to 450 volts. Verbal designations were also provided at various points for "mild shock," "strong

shock," and so forth, to a final reading of "Danger: severe shock." Two switches after this point were simply labeled "XXX." The subject was then instructed to begin training the stooge to memorize a list of words. Every time the stooge made a mistake she or he was to get a shock. Furthermore, the level of shock was to be increased by fifteen volts after every error.

The experience began, and the stooge started making mistakes. At the 300-volt level the stooge pounded on the wall demanding to be let out and refusing to participate further in the experiment.

How far would people go in obeying orders? To Milgram's surprise, twenty-six out of forty subjects went all the way to 450 volts. No one stopped before 300 volts (the point where the stooge beat on the wall).

Most subjects appeared to believe the situation was for real. Many were extremely anxious and tense as they went through the experience. Some broke down under the strain of deciding whether to follow orders or to refuse to go on.

Milgram's study has been replicated many times with many interesting themes and variations. It illustrates particularly well the degree to which most of us can be influenced by a direct order from someone identified as an authority figure. Our definition of how to "help" has almost always come from respected authorities: priests, doctors, psychologists. And we nave almost always believed.

---

*Some readers may question the ethics of Stanley Milgram's work. Does a researcher have the right to subject people to so much emotional stress without their consent? This concern has been shared by psychologists as well. For example, in August 1974 the National Institute for Mental Health included the following as guidelines for conducting psychological experiments:

"Describe and assess any potential risk—physical, psychological, social, legal or other—and assess the likelihood and seriousness of such risks. If methods of research create potential risks, describe other methods, if any, that were considered and why they will not be used.

Describe consent procedures to be followed, including how and where informed consent will be obtained.

Describe procedures (including confidentiality safeguards) for protecting against or minimizing potential risks and an assessment of their likely effectiveness."

I was unable to accept the fact that the man I loved was destroying me. I knew I had changed and I hated myself. I then avoided everyone except my fiance. I quit attending classes, I slept all day and stayed up until the sunrise. I don't know where the nights went. I made up a perfect world to live in where I spent many hours fantasizing a perfect life. I found that when I had to be with other people I could communicate with them when necessary and then withdraw to my perfect inner world. Then one day I finally realized that this life wasn't quite right. I had no friends and I desperately wanted some. My fiance wasn't enough company for me. I realized that I couldn't live my life for only one person. So I found enough strength to break my engagement. It wasn't easy but I'm beginning to be my old self once again. I don't hate myself anymore and I have regained some of my old friends and made some new ones. I still have some fear of people but it really is lessening with time. I know now that it is wrong to try to be something or someone other than who you are because if you can't accept yourself then you may never be at peace with the world. I feel like I had a real fight inside me and the wrong side was winning for quite sometime.

Seligman (1973) writes that, in his opinion, one of the most important beliefs a person can have of himself is that he is not helpless. In his studies he strapped dogs into a harness so that they could not move and then gave them a traumatic shock (not physically damaging). Later when these dogs were put into a nonrestraining shock situation they simply sat down on the job—they gave up trying to escape—while the dogs not previously restrained busily hustled themselves out of the shock compartment. One interpretation here is that in the belief (assuming dogs can believe) of complete lack of hope or of control over things, a "nothing-will-help"

hypothesis sets in. Seligman goes even further to say, "Rewards as well as punishments that come independently of one's own effort can be depressing." Success and positive beliefs about oneself follow on the heels of responses that produce results. Perhaps the opposite is also true; appropriate responses follow on the heels of positive self-belief. I suppose whichever way it works for you will be the interpretation you will find believable. Your belief in yourself, as Rother (1971) has aptly pointed out, tends to be either that the environment controls you, or you it. Depression is a rare occurrence for those who believe they have some control over their environment.

One of the most extreme forms of negative self-belief can be found in Bruno Bettelheim's case of "Joey: A 'Mechanical Boy'" (1959). Joey's mother reports that his birth made little difference to her. She didn't wish to nurse him or even to see him. In short, she denied his humanity. He became a mere object. With this continuing hands-off treatment, Joey began to believe he was neither of any value nor any different from the dining room table—something to be cleaned and put in the corner when not in use. Early in life he became preoccupied with disassembling and assembling an electric fan. He and the fan became friends. When Bettelheim first saw Joey for treatment he was seven years old and much of the damage had been done. He believed he was a machine, and interestingly, reinforced others into treating him like one, lest he blow a fuse in their presence. He would string out his imaginary cords to an imaginary electric outlet before he would (could) eat. He insulated himself with paper napkins. Children and staff would avoid stepping on his "wires." His bed was filled with tubes and wires, which the maids would pick up off the floor and carefully return to his bed. In order to use the bathroom Joey had to clutch a vacuum tube in one hand with the other hand on the wall as a ground. In short, he felt more at home with machinery than with people. Through extensive therapy he was eventually encouraged to believe in his own humanity, but he never fully recovered a normal sense of well-being.

Discovering some things about yourself that you can genuinely appreciate is a first step towards changing the self. People tend to overlook their own assets and strengths. Most of us tend to seek out more assurance from others than we need to. Like the characters from the *Wizard of Oz*—the lion with no courage, the straw man with no brains, and the tin man with no heart—we look for a wizard to tell us that we really have the equipment we are searching for. It's just hard for us to believe that we do. Toffler (1970) talks about the New York cabbie who, in his spare time, is a rodeo rider. "How absurd!" you might say. But the group this cabbie pals around with are his friends. They share highs and lows with each other and form a sort of family atmosphere in a world that is otherwise alien. This man lives positively in the belief that he can (and he has) controlled the environment to fit his particular needs. No wizard was required. Personally, Bob Wrenn and I have found jazz bands and hiking clubs to serve a similar purpose for us, respectively.

Finally, when a person comes to the point of view that he is worth believing in, he takes action accordingly. The following letter from Sam to his father follows a pattern that frequently accompanies change. Before we can change we must acknowledge that something is wrong.

> *Dear Dad*,
> . . . I'm miserable. I'm in school and for the present it's lost all direction for me. *I'm out of focus* [our italics throughout]—out of perspective with myself. I've tried to define what's going on and it has been hard and painful doing it. School has lost its meaning. Very simple. Just no meaning at all. I'm going to classes, standing up under the pressures, forcing myself to study and get good grades. I think I must have what they call in

psychology a high achievement motivation. Can't seem to blow things midstream and let my grades fall. I'm going crazy, insane; but my grades are good. I must be doing well. Not true. Like I said, I'm miserable.

As Sam continues, he gets clearer about what is really bothering him:

> I've been speeding frantically through school, not taking any warning to slow down, because I wanted badly to make myself the best fucking Ph.D.-carrying psychologist that ever was. And you know something, Dad, I still want that as badly as ever, but have realized that it just isn't going to happen. Never. Not this way at least. And there is a good reason for it. *I've neglected something very basic, very fundamental in my conception of how to make myself the best psychologist ever. That is simply that I've neglected myself.* I've been operating under the false assumption that I could use books, and academia, and science as catalysts to turn me into what I want to be. I've got to have books, their knowledge, and academia, and all the rest, but all of that is only part of what I need if I'm ever going to be more than Mr. _____, who draws graphs plays with statistics, or even Dr. _____, who alienates as many patients as he helps.

Having become clearer about what he is not, Sam then proceeds to zero in on what he is and what he believes in:

> *I feel the time is right to start looking.* As young as I am, I need to begin to turn my attention inward and start knocking around until I find something so startling that when I see it I'll just sit down and cry for days. I'm only eighteen and already I'm polluted by values that are not my own, prejudices, and

norms that are alien to me. That is, I've never taken time to determine things like why I feel strange around a group of blacks or chicanos. Things like that are real pressing needs that need to be resolved now—before I forget how to question. Answers, Dad. That's another key. I simply don't believe a lot of the garbage that is taught in the university. And so I'll look for my own answers, and when I have them, I'll return to compare.

I'm going to finish this semester at the university, Dad. That will make me a junior with two years' credit behind me. I want to take a year off to turn my attention inward, in new directions. I want to take perception of life and turn it upside-down, inside-out, stand it on its side, look at things (myself) at new angles. To do that I feel that I've got to get away. Put myself in new situations and be attentive to myself learning to react. I'm thinking in terms of going to Europe where life will be new and alien to me, and learn to learn and experience—to open myself up. There are a thousand practical considerations involved with such an undertaking. My purpose is not to be impractical and I have thought through a lot of those things. Others have yet to be thought through. I'm aware of that. I think I can learn a lot in a year. I think I would like to come back and finish school after that time. I don't feel that a year is time enough to do all that I feel that I want/need to do. But I feel that it will give me enough new insight to carry me further in the direction I want to go.

Finally, Sam comes to see his life as his own. He takes responsibility for his decision and expresses a willingness to assume the risks that are involved:

I have about $700 saved that I am willing to use to get me under way. If you can see the value in what I want to do, then I would ask you for the use of about $500 that has been put away for my education. *If you can't see any value in any of this, Dad, let me know and I won't ask for that kind of support.*

Mostly what I'm asking for, Dad, is your understanding, your confidence, and your love. Please write to me.

> I love you both,
> *Sam*

There is often considerable pain in renouncing a life plan or acknowledging that you are in the wrong career, the wrong friendship, engaged or married to the wrong person, and so forth. When the announcement finally comes it is likely to be an explosion of feeling. The "explosive layer" is Perls' term for this stage of personal growth. Signs of the explosive layer are:

- An "Ah-ha, this is what I want to do" feeling
- A release of pent-up emotion
- A new sense of courage and belief in yourself
- A feeling that you and you alone are responsible for your destiny

Sam informed me that when he finished writing that letter he had the feeling of complete emotional exhaustion. This sort of release of feeling is very characteristic of Perls' explosive layer.

WHO IS STOPPING YOU?
It is often difficult to do what Sam did—to let ourselves be aware of constraining forces and constraining people in our lives because of the special ties we have with them. Some examples follow.

Loved Ones. Ties with loved ones are the hardest to break. It is possible to love someone who smothers you out of existence.

Parents. By and large prejudiced parents are easier to leave than nurturant ones (they provide plenty of reasons for hating them). But nurturant, well-meaning parents can literally protect you to death. All parents are hard to leave. Few children can afford to stay.

Marriage Partners. For most of us our marriage partner becomes the most important person in our lives. To acknowledge that a divorce is the only way out is one of the most difficult of life's decisions. One friend of mine spent twenty years postponing the inevitable decision. It took that many years of spending his evenings in bars plus a close brush with death for him to leave his wife.

One major reason that divorce occurs so often is that we avoid being aware of the real nature of who our marriage partner is. In TA terms we may marry our partner's Child ego state, which says "I love you," "You're really handsome," and so forth. Then, after a few years of marriage, we discover our partner's Parent ego state has values about many things that our Parent can't accept. Or our Child may marry our spouse's nurturant Parent, which says "I'll take care of you, baby." We discover too late our partner's Child also demands taking care of. One very important thing that is done in premarital counseling is to take a look at each other's Parent, Adult, and Child to see how they match up.

Jobs. What is stopping you may not be a person. Perhaps it is a job where you receive money but no sense of fulfillment.

Limited life experiences. Or maybe you feel you haven't let yourself live fully. Do you want to travel to Australia? Write a book? Climb a mountain no one else has? Build your own house? Become a potter? Get your master's degree? If so, what is the force that keeps you where you are? What are you willing to do about it?

Or is it you? There is a danger in this kind of analysis. The danger is that your saboteur may not be on the outside at all. It may be inside your own head. Some people go through life moving from one job to another, one marriage partner after another, from one friend to another, one town to another, one _____ to another.

(fill in your own blank)

YOUR SELF-DEFEATING TAPES

If you believe you can change and have succeeded in identifying your saboteur (the external forces that are keeping you where you are) change should follow naturally. But it often doesn't.

Your self-defeating tapes are those internalized tapes that result in failure if you insist on turning them on and listening to them. We have already identified many such tapes. Some come from your Parent ego state in the form of injunctions: "Don't think." "Don't feel." "Don't be too smart . . . it might scare the boys away." "Isn't she a little mother?" "You're crazy." "Stupid!"

Other self-defeating tapes come from the Child ego state: "I'm too scared to change." "If I change he won't love me." "I'll show that professor he can't talk like that to me." "Nobody cares about me."

THE DEVIANT SELF

Those who live most of their lives running tapes such as these through their head are probably on what TA therapists call a *loser script*. Loser scripts represent our unconscious decisions about how our life will go. Such scripts have themes, and each scene we write in our lives is likely to be based on the same basic theme. It is easier to observe a compulsion to live out a life theme, to fulfill a destiny. See if you can think of someone you know who is living out some theme such as the following (James and Jongeward 1971):

Losing my Mind
Missing the Boat
Commiting Suicide
Sorry for Being Alive
Being the Best
Waiting for Santa Claus
Carrying my Cross
Rescuing Others
Being a Rug for Others to Walk on
Saving for a Rainy Day
Being Miserable
Being Helpful
Trying Hard but Failing

Maybe you recognize one of these scripts as your own. According to TA theory, such themes are written into a play, act by act. The play follows this theme until *you* rewrite it.

REWRITING YOUR SCRIPT

The first step in change is to become fully aware of your life script. More specifically:

- Who do my Parent tapes tell me to be?
- What do my Child tapes tell me to feel?
- What does the objective data I get from my Adult tell me?
- What is my life script and where will it lead me? Is it a loser script or a winner script?

Perhaps after reading the last two chapters you can already answer these questions. If not, there are some exercises at the end of the chapter that may be of value.

When you are really aware of a self-defeating tape you can hear it going off like a fire bell: "There is my prejudiced Parent going off again," or, "That sounds like my adaptive Child."

Once you hear the bell you have a choice: "Do I go on listening?" or, "It's time to turn this thing off and get on with my new script."

Being clear about the consequences of listening to the tape helps. Completing the "obituary" exercises at the end of this chapter is one simple technique. Having very clear life goals also helps you stay on the track.

Helping Others

Since we have been rather critical of many "helpers" and many existing forms of "help," perhaps it is time to stick our neck out a bit and say what we think help is all about. Briefly there are four characteristics common to effective helpers. Effective helpers are:

1. Self-aware: they know who they are as people.
2. Active listeners: they can sense and respond to feelings.
3. Creative interveners: they are good at restructuring relationships and finding ways of intervening when people are playing games (at a professional level this creativity may lead to developing new therapeutic techniques).
4. Growing people: they are committed to their own personal development and are doing something about it.

BEING SELF-AWARE

One important aspect of understanding others is to have a very clear understanding of yourself. Knowing whether it is your Adult or your prejudiced Parent who is giving advice is one good example of the importance of self-awareness and understanding to those who want to help. This chapter and chapter two have provided several others; hopefully this course will provide many more.

ACTIVE LISTENING

The first thing that we all need when we are tired and hurting is a response to *our* feelings. When I feel bad I often find myself doing all sorts of strange things to get attention. Sometimes I sulk; sometimes I go around being depressed; sometimes I just hang around others and make conversation. Sometimes I do favors for people. My ulterior motive at such times is that I want someone to respond to my feelings and say "Hey, you seem kind of down. What's going on?"

The kind of listening that helps another involves focusing all of your attention on what *he or she* has to say. Because many people never develop this simple skill, we have a lot of people around who feel no one ever really pays attention to them.

- A little boy says, "Dad never seems to care about what I say."
- A wife complains that "John just sits there behind his newspaper and ignores me."
- Dad says, "I've told Jimmy a thousand times not to do that. Why won't he listen?"
- A secretary says, "Everyone else's opinion counts in this office but mine."

Counseling or therapy may have value just on this basis alone. Some of the most frequent kind of thank you's I receive for my efforts focus on my taking the time, having the skill, or making the effort to "just listen."

- "This is the first time I've ever been able to say this to anyone."
- "Everyone else has always just lectured me about this. Thanks for *hearing* what I had to say."
- "I feel better just having said that. I thought you would be shocked but you didn't seem to be."

Because listening is a skill that is so important for human growth, we will discuss it in the next chapter as a form of creative or transcendent human behavior. Creative listening is truly an art that demands the same kind of psychological preparation as creating a beautiful painting. Finding a good listener and learning to listen effectively to ourselves are two of the basic tools to change how we feel about ourselves.

MAKING CREATIVE INTERVENTIONS

Knowing yourself is a prerequisite to being helpful. So is knowing how to listen actively. But those I know whom I consider the real pros go beyond these two basic qualities. To be a potent helper you have to be able to intervene rapidly and forcefully in personal problems that your client has been working on for years. In part three we will discuss the products of many such creative therapists. Dream interpretation, behavior modification, transcendental meditation, and transactional analysis were all invented by people who possessed a genius for intervention. And such techniques work best when they are applied by a creative person.

BEING A GROWING PERSON

Just being around a person who is really growing can help you grow also. Such a person provides a model of being aware and unafraid of the self. One friend of mine in particular comes to mind as I write this. Every time I am with him I see signs of new growth. He is always eager to tell me about the "something new" in his life. He always seems to be reaching beyond his own resources . . . transcending himself. I always come away eager to challenge myself, to try something new, to encounter myself more deeply. This kind of growth is the subject of the next chapter.

Chapter Three Summary

1. *Social pressure.* We may find our greatest strengths and talents in our uniqueness. Nonetheless, to feel different is often to feel pain. Social pressure is often exerted on the person who is deviant. The pervasive human tendency to punish those who don't conform to our expectations was discussed in four important social contexts:

   a. Mental institutions
   b. Parenting techniques
   c. Brainwashing techniques
   d. Social obedience

2. *Feeling deviant as a life script.* Telling someone he or she is deviant is often a self-fulfilling prophecy. In the text this phenomenon was called the "wheel of kookiness."

3. *Coping.* How can we cope with the expectations of our parents and our negative feelings about ourselves? There is usually a three-stage process:

   a. Awareness—awareness usually begins with our openly acknowledging the obstacles to our growth. Identifying our parent types and life scripts may help us accomplish this.
   b. Impasse—A time of depression and discouragement often follows awareness, but is usually a sign that growth is about to occur.
   c. Autonomy—The impasse ends and growth begins with the realization that "I alone am responsible for my own behavior."

4. *Helping others.* There are three guidelines for effective helping:

   a. Being self-aware
   b. Active listening
   c. Being committed to one's own personal growth

Glossary

Active listening—Those behaviors that convey to another person that he or she has your full undivided attention. Behaviors that convey attention are looking directly into the eyes, leaning forward, and verbal messages that convey understanding and empathy for what is being said. This is an important ingredient in Thomas Gordon's Parent Effectiveness Training (P.E.T.) program.

Deviant Someone who is different from others in enough ways to make a difference.

Explosive stage In Perls' view, the final stage of change. It is an explosion into full awareness and expression. It tends to be accompanied by feelings of greater power over one's own life.

Help Several alternative definitions of help have been discussed in this chapter.

A Szasz-type definition of psychiatric help: "A means of social control by which people who offend others can be put away and punished."

Wrenn and Mencke: "The ability to convey a feeling of being deeply understood and accepted while simultaneously challenging another to grow to his fullest capacity. That's all there is to it."

Implosive stage The stage of growing in which we are aware of being dissatisfied but feel powerless to change. The accompanying feelings are anxiety and depression.

Loser script The kind of unconscious life plan that leads to continued failure in life experiences. Losers have programmed themselves to self-defeat. Most of our scripts have some areas in which we consistently set ourselves up to fail. Noting situations where you feel powerless, bored, or trapped may be a tipoff to the loser aspects of your script.

Nurturant-Parent ego state
Those Parent tapes that convey support, concern, or protectiveness for others for their own gain.

Phobic stage The initial stage of growing (really a stage of non-growing) in which a problem exists, but you deny its existence.

Prejudiced-Parent ego state Those Parent tapes that convey prejudiced value judgments. Example: "All boys should have short hair."

Psychological brainwashing A series of psychological techniques designed to weaken the victim's self-belief and to increase feelings of deprivation. The ultimate end product is that the person conforms, complies, and does things he or she would normally consider amoral.

Scapegoat Someone in a group who is a target for hostility that is unfair or unwarranted by his or her behavior.

Script The life play that we write for ourselves, often at an unconscious level.

Social psychologist A psychologist who studies how individuals are influenced by the groups to which they belong.

Stooge In social psychology, someone who agrees to help the experimenter by pretending. The stooge may be asked to pretend to feel differently than he or she really does, to impersonate someone, or to behave in some strange way suggested by the experimenter. Examples: In the Milgram study a stooge pretended that shocks were causing great pain. In the same study a second stooge pretended to be a scientist studying how people learn. In the Doob study a stooge pretended to be clumsy and broke some equipment.

Winner script The kind of life plan that results in frequent success and an ability to bounce back after failure. Most of us have some winner elements in our script. Some clues to our winner tendencies are to be found in situations where we are courageous, times when we feel we are in full control of our lives, instances in which we are able to be honest even when a risk is involved, and times when we feel fully aware of our feelings and completely alive.

Exercises (*for individual and class use*)

You can do the following exercises at your leisure. Perhaps some of these would be more enjoyable with a friend. Those with an asterisk should be done in consultation with your teacher or in class.

1. *Parental control techniques.* Think back to the things your parents did to you to be the way they wanted you to be.

- What did they do when they wanted to encourage you?
- How did they look when they were doing the encouraging? Try to picture their facial expressions, their gestures, movements, and postures. Did they touch you? Pat you on the back? Put their arms around you? What?
- What did they do to keep you in line?
- What did your parents do when they wanted to punish you? What words, gestures, facial expressions, and so forth do you associate with being punished?
- What limits did they set for you? Looking back, which limits seem most reasonable to you? Which seem irrational, unduly punitive, or overprotective?

2. How did you adapt to the above parental control techniques?

- Did you comply? How?
- Rebel? How?
- Withdraw? How?
- Procrastinate? How?
- Stop thinking for yourself? How?
- Which kind of adaptive mode did you use most often?
- Which of these do you use in your present life?
- How do you feel about these adaptations? Are they useful and helpful to you? Or do they harm you, keep you from succeeding, or result in your alienating others you care about?

3. *Changing your adaptations.* If you have become aware of ways of adapting to demands that you feel are harmful to you, think what would happen if you did just the opposite. Just fantasize a situation where you say *no* instead of *yes,* approach others instead of withdrawing, and so forth. The idea is to do just exactly the opposite of what you normally do. Spend several minutes on this. Then answer the following:

- As you thought of changing, what did your Parent say to you?
- What response did your Child have to this Parent tape?
- Start a dialogue between yourself and your Parent ego state. See if you can persuade your internal Parent to give you permission to change.

4.* *Epitaph.* Imagine that you are a newspaper columnist assigned to cover the death of a very important person. The person is you. How do you think your own obituary should read? Write down exactly what comes to mind. Then answer the following:

- What does this obituary say about the direction of your life? Is it a winner script? A procrastinator script? An "I'll do anything if you will like me" script? What?
- What do you think your epitaph should be?
- Is it possible that you are living up to this epitaph? How?
- Is there any way you would like to change it? How?

5. *Your childhood.* Get out your family album and look carefully at the pictures in it. Recall your life as a child.

- What did you feel like? Joyous? Scared? Sad? Free? What?
- What words do you recall about: Your looks? Your abilities? Your health? Your sexuality?

- What predictions were made about your future?
- If your father were told to sum up in one sentence what he thought of you, what would that sentence be?
- What would your mother say about you in one sentence?
- Does the way you feel about yourself now relate somehow to their evaluations of you?
- If you feel their evaluation was unfair, try to imagine a dialogue where you tell them so. What specific data do their evaluations ignore? What prejudices of theirs are revealed in their evaluations of you?
- Is there some way you are allowing your life to be programmed by such an unfair parental evaluation?

Bibliography

Bettelheim, Bruno. 1959. Joey: a "mechanical boy." *Scientific American* (March).

Doob, A. 1971. Deviance: society's side show. *Psychology Today* (October):47.

James, M. and Jongeward, D. 1971 *Born to win.* Reading, Mass.: Addison-Wesley.

Milgram, S. 1963. Behavioral study of obedience. *Journal of Abnormal Social Psychology* (March):371.

Perls, F. 1969. *Gestalt therapy verbatim.* Lafayette, Calif.: Real People Press.

Rother, Julian B. 1971. External control and internal control. *Psychology Today* (June).

Seligman, M. 1973. Fall into helplessness. *Psychology Today* (June):43–48.

Toffler, Alvin. 1970. *Future shock.* New York: Random House.

United States government. 1956. *Hearings before the permanent subcommittee on investigations of the committee on government operations, United States Senate.* Eighty-fourth Congress, second session. June 19, 20, 26, 27, 1956. Washington, D.C.: Government Printing Office.

――――. 1974. NIH guide for grants and contracts. U.S. Department of Health, Education, and Welfare 3:12.

Chapter Four: Of Yeast and Leavening (The Growing Self)

A journey of a thousand miles begins with a single step.

CHINESE PROVERB

Getting Ready to Grow: Healthy Anxiety

Life is a continuous process of transcending the person we now are and moving on. We can never stay exactly as we are without paying a price. The price for not growing is a shrinking self. This is true because the only way to avoid growth is to avoid the challenges that our lives present us. The only way to avoid such challenges is to block out of our awareness the need or the aspect of ourselves that has been challenged. This kind of blocking out is called a psychological defense. Although our defenses may do a pretty good job of protecting us from feelings of failure, they usually do so at the cost of decreased awareness of ourselves. As we continue to deny we get farther and farther out of contact with our sources of energy and our strongest motivations. Life becomes very safe but also very dull and boring. And eventually we come to feel that our inner self is unworthy of the challenges that are extended to it.

Furthermore, it is when we deny those experiences that challenge us most deeply that we stand to lose the most by hiding. A challenge can't be strong unless it hits our strongest motives. I could easily ignore a challenge to swim against Mark Spitz in the Olympic freestyle because I have very little ego involvement in my swimming. I do it for exercise only. On the other hand, I am very vulnerable and easily depressed by messages that I am failing as a parent or as a husband or as a psychologist. These roles are intimately tied to my strongest motives (my guts). I need to feel that I am growing and making progress in them. If I get a clear message that I'm not doing well as a parent, it becomes a challenge to change. If I ignore and deny the challenge, saying, for example, "Aw, it's not really important to me to have a close relationship with my son," I am pushing out of awareness a motive that is a central part of me and is based on important experiences in my childhood.

The end product of denying challenges is a world that shrinks and gets smaller and smaller.

First, we lose contact with our awareness of who we are; and then, since our awareness of others is based primarily on our awareness of our own feelings, we lose our sensitivity and understanding of others. The result is alienation. Continued denial may lead to neurosis, a condition in which more and more awareness is sacrificed for the benefits of a tight system of defenses.*

LOOKING FOR THE GOOD: FINDING A HEALTHY LIFESTYLE

Abraham Maslow is perhaps better known than any other personality theorist except Sigmund Freud. Unlike Freud, whose fascination seemed to be captured by the dark side of humankind, Maslow has been concerned throughout his career with studying the positive. When he was in graduate school he became inspired by two of his instructors, Ruth Benedict and Max Wertheimer. In their lives he saw a vision of what mankind is capable of becoming. That vision came to occupy more and more of his thinking. What fascinated him most was their motivation. Here were people who loved a challenge, who seemed to be using all of their potential and to be living fully. And, very much to his surprise, they didn't seem to be doing all these things because of a compulsive tendency or because of some deep need to achieve. The only motive he could discover was a strong drive to live fully and creatively.

At first these interests were private, more of a hobby than a professional interest. Maslow was teaching then, and he began to share some of his thoughts about "people who grow" with his students. Eventually he began to do what clinical psychologists before him would have viewed with disdain: he began a serious clinical study of normal people.

———

*Denying challenges has a healthy aspect as well as an unhealthy one. We must select our challenges carefully or we will be overwhelmed with anxiety. The importance of defense mechanisms will be discussed in chapter six.

SELF-ACTUALIZATION: LIVING CREATIVELY

Maslow was trying to understand what a healthy lifestyle is by studying the lives of people who were living in a healthy way. Since no one had researched the issue before, he decided to select his first subjects almost solely by intuition. Very early in his work he became convinced that the most basic attribute of a healthy life is a tendency to be all we are capable of—to use almost all of our talent, ability, and potential. Maslow referred to this tendency as *self-actualization* and he began to call his subjects self-actualizers (Maslow 1954).

Not too surprisingly, he found such persons to be highly creative. He states that every single self-actualized person he studied displayed a special kind of creativeness, originality, or inventiveness. But as he studied these creative persons, Maslow gained an important insight about the nature of creativity:

I soon discovered that I had, like a lot of other people, been thinking of creativeness in terms of products, and secondly, I had unconsciously confined creativeness to certain conventional areas only of human endeavor, unconsciously assuming that *any* painter, *any* poet, *any* composer was leading a creative life. Theorists, artists, scientists, inventors, writers, could be creative. Nobody else could be. . . . But these expectations were soon broken up by various of my subjects.

The bias Maslow so openly acknowledges above is clearly present in his initial selection of subjects. Early in his research his subject roster read like *Who's Who in America:* Albert Einstein, William James, Abraham Lincoln, Jane Adams, John Muir, Walt Whitman, and Henry Wadsworth Longfellow were among those whose biographies he studied.

Gradually, however, Maslow extended his studies beyond those whose talents had made them famous. He then discovered that the kind of creativity he was seeing could not be described as a product or as a special talent. For one thing, many of the world's most talented individuals were not healthy people (van Gogh is one well-known example). On the other hand, Maslow discovered that many of his self-actualized people were not famous and produced products that would never lead to professional eminence.

One woman, uneducated, poor, a full-time housewife and mother, did none of these conventionally creative things and yet was a marvelous cook, mother, wife and homemaker. With little money her home was somehow always beautiful. She was a perfect hostess. Her meals were banquets. Her taste in linens, silver, glass, crockery, and furniture was impeccable. She was in all these areas original, novel, ingenious, unexpected, inventive.

Another was a psychiatrist, a "pure" clinician who never wrote anything or created any theories or researches but who delighted in his everyday job of helping people to create themselves. This man approached each patient as if he were the only one in the world, without jargon, expectations or presuppositions, with innocence and naïvete and yet with great wisdom in a Taoistic fashion. Each patient was a unique human being and therefore a completely new problem to be understood and solved in a completely novel way.

From another man I learned that constructing a business organization could be a creative activity.

From a young athlete I learned that a perfect tackle could be as esthetic a product as a sonnet. . . .

Maslow came to see that creativity is not just a product; it is a special way of being. The self-actualizer is able to appreciate again and again the basics of life with feelings of awe, pleasure, and wonder. Any sunset may be as beautiful as the first one; any flower, even the millionth, may be breathtakingly lovely. Everyday casual living can be an esthetic experience. Actualizers also perceive reality more accurately, welcome the new and the unknown, and accept themselves and others without unnecessary guilt, shame, sadness, anxiety, or defensiveness; are unconventional, spontaneous, and natural; are strongly committed to a personally chosen mission or life task; and are autonomous and capable of meeting most of their own needs without undue dependence on others. In short, the actualizer's entire personality is geared to creative living and growing as a person. It makes no difference what occupation such a person's talents lead into; actualizers create and grow.

But what is growth? And how do we grow? In this chapter we will study the aspects of personality that appear to characterize those who grow. We have begun by looking at Maslow's studies of the creative individual; next we will examine various levels of growing experiences. Creative thinking, growing relationships, and survival experiences will be considered separately. As we shall see, all three forms of growing have certain common characteristics that we can use for our personal growth.

In a chapter devoted to growth it seems appropriate to examine in detail as wide a range as possible of instances where someone really got on with it and transcended the old way of being. We will begin by briefly examining the process of creative thinking and the untapped resources of our unconscious. Next we will look at some of the attributes of interpersonal relationships that seem to be related to personal growth. Then we will turn to some examples of individuals who have transcended most of our conceptions of the limits of human endurance and survival.

Such examples are worthy of study primarily because they provide us with models of ways of growing and examples of the basic dynamics of transcending ourselves. Transcendent thinking and creativity, transcendent human relationships, and transcendent survival experiences all have several elements in common. In the final section of the chapter we will discuss these common areas and their implications for personal growth.

Transcendent Behaviors: How Do We Know When We Have Grown?

How do we know when we have grown? The answer is deceptively simple. We grow when we transcend ourselves. Going beyond our present state of awareness into a new mode of experiencing, moving beyond our present ideas or values to a new way of thinking that allows us to understand more of life than we did before, and performing beyond what we formerly believed were our physical or mental limits are all examples of such self-transcendence.

Sidney Jourard (1968) points out the term *transcendent behavior* is a misnomer. No one can transcend his or her own potential. All we can transcend is someone's (perhaps our own) limited and inaccurate concept of that potential. Because we receive so many admonitions to be aware of our limitations, we may come to ignore our potentialities.

TRANSCENDENT THINKING: THINKING CREATIVELY
Both Freud and the behaviorists agree that there is a tremendous momentum that predisposes us towards continuing to think, and perceive, and behave (in short, *to be*) in the same way day after day. Freud viewed this inertia as an instinct coming from within the person, while behaviorists like B. F. Skinner refer to it as control from outside and use the term *reinforcement*. Maxwell Maltz (1960) describes much of our everyday awareness as a state of hypnosis: we appear to Maltz to be wandering around in a trance thinking the thoughts that have been subtly suggested to us by our parents, teachers, friends, and Sesame Street. Writers control our emotions in tear jerkers simply by presenting stimuli that we have been programmed to respond to emotionally: a family living in poverty, a fluttering American flag, a bugle playing Taps, and so forth. The analysis of Freud and the behaviorists leaves us convinced that much of our behav-

Thomas Agassiz: Dreaming and Creativity

The following example illustrates very well some of the processes that seem to operate when we think creatively. Although this example is a scientific discovery, it could just as well have been making a creative everyday joke, responding in a novel way to a friend's plea for help, selecting your clothes for the day, answering a child's question, or any other everyday creative process.

Thomas Agassiz was a talented paleontologist. For months he had been trying with no success to decipher an obscure impression of a fossil fish on an ancient stone slab. Frustrated and weary, he finally decided to forget it.

Several mornings later he awoke convinced that he had dreamed of the fish. In the dream all its features were extremely clear. However, on awakening, the vision disappeared.

Hopeful that he would now be able to decode the mystery, he resumed working on the stone the following morning. But again the problem of the fish proved insolvable.

The next night he dreamed of the fish again. But again when he awoke the memory was too blurred to be useful.

The third night he was prepared. He placed a pencil and paper beside his bed. Towards morning the fish dream recurred. At first its features were fuzzy, but gradually, like a man adjusting a microscope, he brought his dream into focus. Still half dreaming and in complete darkness, Agassiz traced the fish's features on the pad of paper.

Next morning he examined the sketch. It revealed features that were novel and rather strange. He found it difficult to believe his dream was telling the truth. He hastened to his laboratory and chiseled away the stone, using his sketch as a guide. The fossil was soon revealed. It corresponded perfectly with his dream.

Agassiz's experience (Koestler 1964) illustrates the process that occurs in almost all instances where a very difficult problem is encountered and solved. First we see him hard at work; then he hits a brick wall. No amount of intellectual force will yield the secret of the fish. He finally gives up, at least consciously. Then in his sleep the answer comes to him spontaneously in a dream.

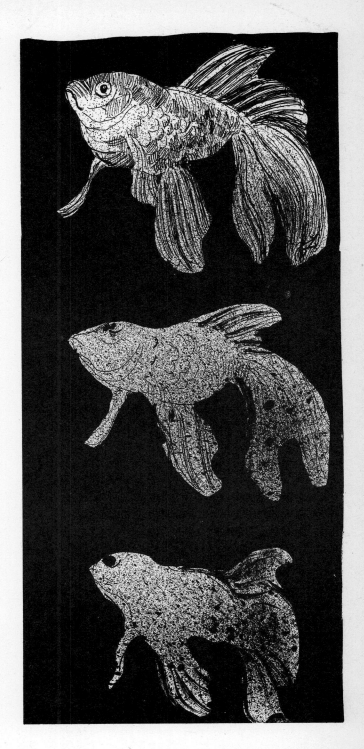

ior is in fact compulsive, conditioned, or trance-like. But to what extent is it possible to break this trance? Can we sometimes think thoughts that were never thought before? And, if so, where do they come from?

To think creatively requires an ability to break out of this "trance." Terms such as *creativity* and *inventiveness* refer to a departure from the usual. We have already seen that Maslow found novel or infrequent behaviors, thoughts, and solutions to problems to occur so frequently in his self-actualizers that he came to consider their creativity as the fundamental definition of their life-styles. It wasn't that they were all geniuses. Many of their products were neither artistic, literary, nor scientific. But their everyday responses were novel, spontaneous, and apparently not a result of rigidity, compulsiveness, or cultural conditioning.

Many examples of transcendent problem solving seem to occur during a time of *letting be*. The literature of creative genius is abundant with them. Experiences in psychotherapy also suggest that personal problems are often resolved in the same manner. The client or patient struggles and struggles, sometimes for months. Then suddenly the patient arrives in my office thanking me profusely for my help; the problem is suddenly solved! I don't know what I did, and I feel strongly that the person has finally done it alone. The patient, being totally unaware that she or he has done anything but flounder, attributes the miracle to some magical power of mine. I strongly suspect that such instances are analogous to Agassiz's dream solution. The logical, rational mind gives up and in so doing allows the person's intuition to take over. As we shall see in chapter ten, this conclusion is supported by what is currently known about the physiology of dreaming. It is also supported and suggested by techniques used to attain transcendent states of consciousness in Eastern-style meditation. Zen training, for example, requires endless concentration on a koan, which is a special kind of riddle that is absolutely impenetrable by logic. What usually occurs is that after a very long period of concentration the novice just gives up. Not infrequently the person falls asleep and begins to dream, sometimes going into a deep trance. It is only then that the solution to the koan yields itself to awareness. Again it appears that the intuitive solution becomes available only after the intellect has exhausted itself.

TRANSCENDENT HUMAN RELATIONSHIPS:
LIVING OPENLY

Occasionally all of us experience moments of deep, intense closeness to another person. At such times it is as though we two are speaking to each other from the very depth of our souls. Nothing else exists. All judgment is suspended; there is only deep understanding between us. And there is no purpose to our communication; being intimate becomes an end in itself.

Transcendent human relationships may be studied from several different perspectives. At one level the term simply refers to moments of closeness and deep communication such as those described. At a second level we can study the effects of such moments on personal growth. Clearly some relationships lead us to grow, some encourage stagnation, and unfortunately some constitute daily reminders to "be crazy," "be depressed," or even to "drop dead."

Still a third perspective is to examine the conditions that seem to facilitate relationships that nurture and support our efforts to grow. This is the approach we will take in this chapter.

While some people are exceptionally adept at concealing their need for closeness from others, neither of the writers of this book have ever encountered another human being who had no need for closeness. This (subjective) finding does not, of course, establish that such people don't exist. But it does appear to us that they are relatively rare.

The ways different individuals try to get close

growing relationships from other less transcendent exchanges. These are 1) accurate empathy, 2) an open, spontaneous, "let it be" quality, 3) self-disclosure, and 4) psychological preparation.

Empathy. Really being attended to and having one's words and the feelings that underlie them understood is a rare experience. When Johnny says, "I hate my teacher," he is likely to elicit from his mother an evaluation of him:

"You shouldn't feel that way, Johnny."
"It's your own fault for being so sassy to her."

Likewise when Sally comes in saying, "I feel so rotten. I flunked my Spanish exam," her roommate may just make a bad situation worse by giving advice or pointing out what Sally is doing wrong:

"You never study. No wonder you're failing."
"Why don't you see your teacher about it?"
"Why don't you try studying in the library more often?"

Such responses tend to freeze others up. When Sally is hurting and feeling upset she is coming out of her Child ego state. Evaluations of her behavior from her roommate's Parent only tend to make her Child feel worse. Advice accompanied by verbal and nonverbal clues that her roommate is displeased with her will have the same effect. The best response in such situations is to respond to Sally's Child feelings of hurt, frustration, and anger first and save the advice for a time when her Adult is in charge. Some good responses might be:

"Gosh, Sally, I'll bet you are feeling awful about that."
"I know you've been working like mad on Spanish. What a bad break."

or, if Sally never studies:

"It must be awfully tough trying to get yourself to work on that course when you get such low grades."

are highly varied. Some like to "let it all hang out" with most people most of the time. They share deeply with many people and may extract much satisfaction from even a very short relationship. Others may prefer less intense long-term relationships to a more intense short-term one. Still others are characterized by a need for just a few close relationships in which they share deeply with only one other person but continue this over a period of many years, possibly even a lifetime. Also, there are those who can feel close without words. Joint activities, shared work projects, hobbies, and so forth yield strong feelings of closeness and sharing for such a person, who may prefer not to disclose intense emotions or talk about personal concerns. For these individuals, shared projects may have some of the same developmental impact that highly emotional sharing experiences have for the first type.

Four basic qualities seem to distinguish true

Such responses free the other person to start being aware. They convey unconditional positive regard and a sense that "you are a capable and responsible person." And feeling capable and responsible is the first step towards growth. Blaming, on the other hand, simply leads to more bad feelings and may lead to a game of "If it weren't for you" on Sally's part—followed by a game of "I only wanted to help you" initiated by the roommate.

Unlike blaming, advice does have a contribution to make in a growing relationship. Advice that comes from your Adult, uncontaminated by your blaming Parent, can lead to genuine change and growth. There are times when we all need information and data about what we are doing, how it affects others, and so forth. And sometimes another person who perceives what is happening more accurately than we do can help us to see how we can change.

Letting Be. Often I find myself approaching others in a very needy state. At such times I am seeking *their* approval, *their* love, *their* respect, *their* sex, *their* help. But there are other moments when I come with needs fulfilled, or almost so. At such times my lack of expectations sometimes lets me see beyond surface characteristics, roles, and games. Then several different kinds of experiences may occur. Sometimes I see the beauty and uniqueness of that person more clearly than before, or I may see and even feel his or her pain through the filter of my own experience. Very often I feel a deep sense of closeness, a realization that we are, in some hard-to-describe sense, the same part of the same flux.

Abraham Maslow found the love relationships of his self-actualizers to be one of the best reflections of their actualizing personalities (Maslow 1954). The quality of letting be was the most permeating feature of actualizing love. Love, for such persons, was not a contest. There was a minimum of defensiveness and no evidence of love being a battle between the sexes. Rather, love had a quality of deep, sincere appreciation of each other's uniqueness. This appreciation was so great that it often continued and even grew stronger after forty years or more of marriage. Rediscovery of each other occurred over and over again. This quality of appreciation rather than the mutual manipulation that is so often mistaken for love implies that a transcendent relationship—be it friendship, love, or even a professional therapy relationship—is simply a vehicle that allows two people to be more fully themselves.

Figure 4-1 is an optical illusion. It may be seen in two different ways: as two people facing each other with a white background or as a vase with a black background. In a transcendent relationship both people stand out clearly, as in the first illusion. The relationship is the background; the individuality of each person is the focus.

Less healthy, dependent relationships are like the background in figure 4-1. Concern over structure and rules becomes important, and the uniqueness and individuality of the partners become the background. When a relationship is in trouble it is usually a sign that the individuality of the people involved is getting lost or ignored. Appreciating individuality can bring the people in the relationship back into perspective. The relationship itself then recedes into the background where it belongs.

Self-disclosure. Alive, growing relationships are of necessity characterized by opening up, revealing, and disclosing the self. The depth of disclosure may vary from person to person. Sometimes it involves sharing our deepest emotions and feelings. At other times it is simply letting ourselves show through in the joyous moments of a mutually shared project or experience. But it is axiomatic that to be "deeply known" or "deeply understood" one must somehow allow oneself to become transparent to others. Sidney Jourard, a clinical psychologist, has explored the implications of disclosing oneself to another person in *The Transparent Self,*

FIG. 4-1

a book that deserves to be read by anyone who is deeply interested in human relationships. Jourard considers self-disclosure to be the major key to transcendent relationships. He suggests that successful psychotherapy, nursing and healing, and good marriages are all facilitated by self-disclosure.

Jourard began his work by asking people who knew him well to describe him as they thought he was. He discovered many of his friends hardly seemed to know him at all. Perhaps you would like to repeat his experiment with close friends or loved ones to see how much of yourself you reveal to others. Jourard's work suggests that the following areas are important to cover:

1. *Attitudes and opinions*—How well does the significant other know your views about religion, sex, current political controversies, and so forth?
2. *Tastes and interests*—Can he or she accurately describe your preferences in foods, music, reading matter, movies, clothes, hobbies, gifts, and such?
3. *Work*—Can she or he describe what pres-

sures your work exerts on you, ways it bores you? The satisfactions you feel are most important? Whether you feel successful and appreciated? How you feel about the people you work with?

4. *Money* — What does the other person know of your present financial status, wages, debts, needs, and budgeting?

5. *Personality* — Can the other person describe accurately the things about yourself that you are most unhappy with? The things you feel guilty about, the things you get depressed about, how your feelings can be hurt, and so forth?

6. *Body* — Can the other person describe accurately how you feel about the major parts of your body (such as your face, eyes, nose, mouth, legs, buttocks, genitals), how you wish you looked, your present and past health concerns and physical measurements, such as height, weight, waist, and so forth?

There are several ways of looking at the results you get. First, they are an index of how much you reveal to others and how well your revelations communicate. Another way to use the feedback is to appraise yourself in terms of which of the six areas you disclose most. Jourard's data suggest that most individuals disclose more of their attitudes, tastes, and work, and less about their money, personalities, and bodies. Which areas are you most open about? In which areas would you like to try being more disclosing?

Preparation. It might be inferred from our discussion of the element of spontaneity and letting be that we think transcendent moments in a relationship just happen. Although closeness and understanding cannot be manipulated or forced they are far more likely to happen when one is psychologically prepared for them.

Those of us with busy lifestyles and much on our minds need brief moments of commitment before we rejoin those who are important to us.

An Experiment in Preparing to Love

Giving and loving take considerable energy. We can prepare to give by relaxing our minds and bodies and quietly committing ourselves to live fully with the person to whom we are about to relate. An interesting experiment that you may want to try for yourself is to spend a few minutes quietly contemplating your relationship with a friend or loved one before you get together. Think how you would be with this person today if you knew that tomorrow one or both of you would die. As you contemplate the person in your mind try to get as deep a feeling of empathy as you possibly can. What is that person thinking and feeling right now? What may be troubling her or him? What may have happened to that person during the day, and how do you suppose he or she will feel about it? Finally, spend a few minutes thinking over the following:

- What do I need from this individual?
- Do my needs sometimes blind me to the other's needs? How?
- How do I currently discourage this person from being himself or herself?
- How may I find new ways to encourage this person?

When we feel overwhelmed with our personal problems, physically exhausted, and tense from overwork, our relationships are bound to suffer. It is very easy at such times to ignore, take for granted, or even take our suppressed anger out on those we are closest to. Behavioristically oriented marriage counselors encourage their clients to actively structure their environment to nurture (reinforce) their loving, caring responses. Providing quiet surroundings, a fifteen-minute nap before husband and wife meet at the dinner table, or expressing the day's pent-up aggression on a pillow or a punching bag are techniques often suggested by behavioral marriage counselors for allowing a potentially healthy relationship to survive and flourish.

In 1914 Sir Earnest Shackleton and an expedition of twenty-seven men set out to cross Antarctica (Shackleton 1920). Before the expedition got under way, however, its boat was crushed by an ice floe and sank along with all but three months' worth of food and supplies. Stranded with only the ship's lifeboats, the expedition was forced to remain camped on the ice floe for three months. They slept and worked in below-zero weather, often soaked to the skin and starving as well. At first they were able to shoot penguins for meat, but later these migrated. Their food supplies dwindled until finally they began to shoot and eat their dogs. Then, with the nearest land 120 miles away, the party set out across the frozen sea in three lifeboats. After enduring a gale, sitting soaked in a wind-swept boat for days at a time in below-zero temperatures, and going forty-eight hours with no water at all, they finally arrived at a remote island. Here they were safe from the possibility of being crushed by ice or drowned in the sea but were still eight hundred miles from the nearest human being. Leaving the weakest of his party behind, Shackleton and five others set out in the largest of the lifeboats across the eight-hundred-mile stretch of open water that separated them from the nearest civilized outpost. Arriving in South Georgia (U.S.S.R.) after surviving heavy gales, freezing weather, and days of intense thirst, Shackleton found himself stranded on the wrong side of the island, separated from rescue by an impenetrable mountain range covered with steep glaciers. With only a couple of biscuits for food and a fifty-foot length of rope that had been abused by the weather for over a year, Shackleton proceeded to tackle this final obstacle. He and his party made the trip in two days, stopping only to eat (they had no sleeping bags). The following was Shackleton's reaction when they finally spotted the whaling station from two thousand feet above. The

words are words of triumph:

> *6:00* A.M. *May 18, 1914*—Whilst Worsley and Crean were digging a hole for the lamp and starting the cooker I climbed a ridge above us, cutting steps with the adze, in order to secure an extended view of the country below. At 6:30 A.M. I thought I heard the sound of a steam whistle. I dared not be certain, but I knew that the men at the whaling station would be called from their beds about that time. Descending to the camp I told the others, and in intense excitement we watched the chronometer for seven o'clock, when the whalers would be summoned to work. Right to the minute the steam whistle came to us, borne clearly on the wind across the intervening miles of rock and snow. Never had any one of us heard sweeter music. It was the first sound created by an outside human agency that had come to our ears since we left Stromness Bay in

1914. That whistle told us that men were living near, that ships were ready, and that within a few hours we should be on our way back to Elephant Island to the rescue of the men waiting there under the watch and ward of Wild. It was a moment hard to describe. Pain and ache, boat journeys, marches, hunger, and fatigue seemed to belong to the limbo of forgotten things, and there remained only the perfect contentment that comes of work accomplished.

The transcendent qualities of Shackleton's adventures are obvious. Each of the four tasks he encountered were, by anyone's reckoning, "impossible adventures." No sane person would ever have freely chosen to undertake them. Surviving on an ice pack in sub-zero temperatures is a feat that has claimed many lives. Shackleton managed it with totally inadequate equipment and wet, starving men. Likewise, his ocean voyage was "impossible." The second ocean voyage crossed the Drake Passage where winds are often of hurricane intensity, 150 to 200 miles an hour. The waves in this area are legendary among sailors. Their length from crest to crest is often a mile and they sometimes are higher than ninety feet in height. Moreover, Shackleton and his expedition had to brave this sea for hours at a time, completely exposed to the wind and with very limited navigation instruments. When they slept it was in the water-filled hold of the boat.

Finally, their mountain climb was impossible. No one had crossed the interior of South Georgia Bay in the seventy-five years it had been occupied prior to Shackleton's ascent. It was 1955, thirty-nine years later, before a second attempt was made. Shackleton made the crossing without sleep, without shelter, and with only a fifty-foot strand of rope to aid in the difficult ascent.

Transcendent survival experiences such as Shackleton's have much to teach us about surviving life crises. Three related themes may be found in such experiences: 1) a high level of commitment and life-supporting values, 2) self-confidence, and 3) adequate preparation and mastery of relevant skills.

Commitment. Shackleton was totally committed to the task of getting his expedition out. His journal entries show amazingly few instances of self-pity, blame, or despair. Often after sixteen-hour days of extremely demanding work he would spend much of the night planning in meticulous detail exactly how he would carry out his objective for the next day. He felt an enormous amount of responsibility for his crew. Some people would have sat up all night worrying. But Shackleton invested his anxiety in mapping out positive actions that he could take if particular disasters occurred. He seldom allowed his attention to be diverted from his major goals by fear.

A similar degree of commitment is observable in instances of transcendent survival varying from survival of supposedly incurable illnesses and POW experiences. Jourard (1971) reports instances of strong commitment in patients who survived "incurable" and "inoperable" cancer, and Frankel (1959) describes the commitment of POW's who survived the Nazi concentration camps by finding meaning and purpose in their pain-filled lives.

Self-confidence. Shackleton had many difficult decisions to make and many of them turned out to be wrong. Often he and his crew invested weeks of work exploring an escape route only to meet with failure. Shackleton never doubted he would survive; he vigorously attacked the tendencies toward feelings of hopelessness in his expedition. Only once in the face of the 800-mile sea voyage did he appear shaky about his chances of success, and even then he actively sought the support of his ablest navigator, who assured him that all was well.

Preparation. Shackleton's confidence in himself was well founded. He had behind him a wealth of experience. He had in a sense been preparing for his ordeal for half a lifetime. Maxwell Maltz, in *Psychocybernetics* (1960), points out that crisis-coping skills are best acquired in situations when one isn't under pressure. Champion athletes often rehearse exactly how they will compete. Gene

A Drowning Man

Most accounts of survival experiences focus almost entirely on the description of the environmental challenges that the hero faced and ignore almost completely the inner struggle. Thurmond's *Last Thoughts of a Drowning Man* (1943) is a notable exception. We turn to it for clues as to the nature of the battle that Shackleton and each of his men must have faced with their inner selves. The subject of Thurmond's study was Don, a nineteen-year-old Oregon State College student, who was swept out to sea by a powerful undertow. Don was in the water four hours before he managed to swim to shore. After being found on the beach, he was taken to a friend's cottage where he went into delirium and verbalized a detailed account of what he had experienced and thought about during the catastrophe. His words, recorded by Charles Thurmond, provide a rare description of the inner struggle with hopelessness, apathy, and despair that survivors of disaster experience.

During the first hour after being swept out to sea Don's thoughts were taken up primarily with fears of the physical danger and attempts to bolster his courage. Then he began to anticipate the possibility of death:

Your nineteen years are going to be over quick—you are not going to know what life is about . . . kiss them goodbye . . . only thing smacks you is a wave. . . .

Mother—she'll go crazy—what will she do when she finds out?—she is not well enough to stand it. . . .

As the ordeal continued Don frequently lost his sense of identity and even suffered momentary amnesia. This continued for almost eight hours after the rescue. It may best be understood as a form of psychological defense designed to minimize threat of impending death. (See also chapter five, pp. 114). That this is so strongly suggested in the following paragraph where thoughts of death frequently punctuate his expressions of amnesia and identity loss:

I can't remember back any more—what's happening to your mind—what's your name?—How'll they know your folks?—why worry about that when you are out in the ocean?—I always said I would be buried at sea—you always wanted to be buried at sea—here's your chance—I hope you never wash up on the beach—If your mother should find you—the birds'll pick your eyes out—that's fine . . . you'll go a long ways—I hope I don't wash up on the beach—I saw a guy do that once—you know what he looked like—one leg was gone—crabs ate the eyes out of his head—he fell off the jetty—you might as well shake hands with yourself—this is the last time you'll have both of them—why don't people sit by the fire and talk like this more often—I hope a fish doesn't grab you—I wonder if there are fish on the bottom that are saying, "paddle your own canoe"—you can't hand the paddle to the guy in the back—you've got to paddle your own canoe—get a granddaughter and lose a son—what will my folks think?—she looks like you, Mother says—you've been awfully ornery—this'll finish it sure.

Don's disordered mental condition is reminiscent of the acute psychotic episodes that Silverman (1970) suggests may lead to psychological growth. It is a full exposition of many of his deepest fears of death. Later Don even had to wrestle with his tendencies towards suicide. Throughout his verbalizations there is a vivid picture of his healthy adaptive self struggling with death wishes and thoughts, attempting to suppress and deny them even at the price of his own sense of identity.

Tunney, the boxer, prepared for the fight in which he defeated Jack Dempsey by buying all the old films of Dempsey's previous fights. He literally memorized all of Dempsey's moves. Then he practiced in front of a mirror, imagining each move Dempsey would make and practicing his counter-moves until they were automatic.

Similar survival strategies are used by college students who are expert examination survivors, public speakers, Olympic stars, and by many others whose success depends on their abilities to cope with their own anxieties.

Some Common Denominators of Growing Experiences

Several factors are often present when people grow. A strong challenge, anxiety, or impasse; a sense of wonderment or awe; preparation; and a time of letting be are all elements that we have often seen in the examples of transcendent behavior in this chapter. Please note that we say "often," not "always." We think these factors are facilitating conditions for growth but some, such as self-confidence, are obviously by products as well. (You will discover a marked similarity between these factors and those presented in our discussion of creative problem solving on page 86). Growth, as we view it, is a process of creatively solving one's problems as they occur.

THE CHALLENGE AND COMMITMENT

In every instance of transcendent functioning we have studied there has been an element of strong challenge. Koestler (1964) in his discussion of creativity devotes an entire chapter to what he calls the night journey. This journey, a very common theme in the mythology of most civilizations, begins when the hero is forced to realize the triviality or shallowness of his or her life style. Sometimes, as in the case of Sidney described in chapter two, this insight comes very slowly as the result of a long series of related developmental events. Often it occurs in a sudden catastrophic manner, as when Jonah was swallowed by the whale in the Old Testament. Bob's plunge into college (chapter two), Shackleton's shipwreck, close encounters with death (see chapter five), and the initial impact of an LSD experience (chapters five and nine) are further examples of such catastrophes.

THE INNER STRUGGLE: ANXIETY AND IMPASSE

Following this initial challenge, the night journey begins. In literature it is usually symbolized by some kind of a descent, such as Dante's descent into Hell, Jesus' burial in the garden of Gethsemane, Orpheus's visit to the underworld, or Jonah's agonies inside the whale. In real life the descent usually involves a period of mental anguish and anxiety such as that experienced by Don the drowning man and Sidney in his search for values in literature. This night journey is called many names, depending on who you happen to read. In literature it is sometimes called the *death-rebirth theme,* pointing out that such anxiety is a healthy symptom of growth rather than evidence of pathology. The gestalt therapist Fritz Perls calls it the *impasse*, referring to the fact that much of the anxiety and depression we see at this point is due to the person's clinging to old habits and perceptions and being reluctant to fully embrace the new way of being that the catastrophe has forced upon him or her. The case of Sidney provided a clear description of how the journey into night or death and the accompanying impasse and anxiety really feels: "My past seems to have died. I stand alone before my life-to-come, full of doubts and fears of inadequacy."

THE SENSE OF WONDERMENT AND AWE

A feeling of total fascination with some problem, place, thing, or person is almost always present when people transcend themselves. Maslow found that his self-actualizers were characterized very strongly by such feelings of wonderment and awe. Likewise Maslow himself was so fascinated with

Ruth Benedict as a person that he spent the next thirty years studying self-actualizing people. Louis Agassiz was completely preoccupied with the problem presented to him by his fossil fish, so much so that when he tried to put the problem aside, his unconscious mind continued to work on it in a dream. Shackleton was fascinated with the challenge of the South Pole; Maslow's self-actualized housewife was continuously appreciating and working on the esthetic properties of her home.

All of these examples support the contention that to transcend ourselves we must first learn the art of becoming fascinated, appreciative, and deeply involved. We will return to this topic in chapter eleven.

PREPARATION

Abraham Lincoln's advice, "Study and prepare and someday you shall succeed" once moved me so deeply that I overcame my fear of failing academically and applied for a doctoral program in psychology. Long years of preparation may be found associated with most examples of transcendent behavior. In this chapter the importance of preparation was perhaps most apparent in our examples of scientific discovery and survival. However, I doubt that any amount of dreaming I might do would yield the shape of Agassiz's fossil fish. I simply lack the impressions of a mind focused on fossils for twenty years. Likewise, while Shackleton's adventure is a story of supreme courage and cool judgment, it is also the story of a man who had in a sense been training for survival for years. He was an expert whose judgment and courage were based on many previous expeditions. On the surface it might seem questionable that much preparation is involved in our relationships with others. But we have seen that on closer analysis, loving requires continuous appreciation, commitment, and dedication. To come to fully appreciate another human being is a task that requires a lifetime of dedication at best.

LETTING BE

We have seen that creative ideas are very likely to occur in our dreams and that strong motives and needs tend to distort our perceptions and blind us to those we love. It is at those times when we have struggled long and hard with a problem and have finally given up and stepped back for a breath of air—during a time of quiet such as a trip to the mountains or after a good night's sleep—that our break-through finally comes. Knowing when to let go, when to lose control, and when to relax is a very important key to growing. It is as though by relaxing the attention of our logical conscious mind we allow the attention of our intuitive unconscious mind to focus.

Most artists and musicians are well aware of this. I once had as a teacher a fine concert pianist. He never performed a piece that was freshly learned. Instead he always practiced for several months until he knew the piece perfectly. Then he put it aside for a few months more. Finally he would return to it, brush it up, and perform it. The letting-be time, he informed me, was a crucial secret to transcendent concert performances. Anyone who has ever mastered any skill has undoubtedly experienced plateaus, or times when no amount of continued work would produce further improvement. At such times letting be is often the key to a breakthrough. We will return to this topic in chapters ten and eleven. Chapter ten deals with our dreams and fantasies and how they may be used to help us grow. Chapter eleven covers meditation, biofeedback, self-hypnosis, and other techniques that may enhance your ability to "let be" when you want to.

EXERCISE: TRANSCENDING YOURSELF

Try to recall an instance when you transcended yourself—that is, when you moved beyond your own concept of who you were. Close your eyes and let yourself remember it vividly in all details. How exactly did you feel? How was this experience related to your past? Was the stage set in some way by your earlier experiences? And how did it relate to your future? Has it or could it continue to influence you in some way?

After a period of enjoying recalling your experience, you may want to let your mind travel to consider other experiences.

Chapter Four Summary

Personal growth is usually accompanied by some anxiety. Despite this, many of us choose to grow rather than face the consequences of staying the same. But what is growth? And what is a growing person?

1. *Self-actualization.* The self-actualizer is more than anything else a person who brings his or her creative energy to each daily situation.

2. *Transcendent behavior.* Growth means going beyond what we are accustomed to thinking we are capable of.

3. *Transcendent thinking.* To think creatively is essentially to break out of the patterned ways of experiencing that were conditioned by our culture, our parents, and our past experiences.

4. *Transcendent relationships.* This refers to those rare moments when two individuals experience a sense of deep intimacy or communication. Some relationships send a clear message to "Drop dead." Many more encourage stagnation. A very few are transcendent and provide strong support to "be everything you are capable of." There are four characteristics of such transcendent relationships:

   a. Empathy
   b. Letting be
   c. Self-disclosure
   d. Preparation

5. *Transcendent surival experiences.* The factors that appear most correlated with surviving in a hostile environment appear to be:

   a. Commitment
   b. Self-confidence
   c. Preparation

6. *General characteristics of transcendent experience.* Transcendent experiences have five common elements:

a. A sense of fascination with the problem, person, or survival task
b. Preparation—A prolonged period of study and work to master an academic area, a marriage, or a physical challenge, for example
c. Challenge—A major, perhaps even catastrophic, event that may precipitate the growing experience
d. A period of struggle
e. Letting be—A "letting go" of previous constraints that makes struggle turn into a moment of transcendence

Koan A special kind of riddle that is used as an object of meditation in Zen. A koan is absolutely insoluble by logic and can only be solved by intuition. Try to imagine, for example, the sound of one hand clapping.

Letting be A special form of attentive inattention common to many varieties of transcendent experiencing. The process of letting be is characterized by physical relaxation and giving up logical or conscious problem solving. It appears related to bursts of intuition such as Thomas Agassiz's dream of the fish.

Neurosis The label for those psychological disorders in which a person becomes overly defensive to the point that he or she makes poor adaptions to the environment. Morbid, excessive fears, extreme anxiety, and overreaction to everyday stress are among the behaviors mental health workers associate with neurosis. Because such symptoms occur in healthy individuals as well as neurotics it is advisable to leave diagnosis up to your friendly neighborhood psychiatrist.

Preparation The blood-sweat-and-tears aspect of transcendent experiencing. It may involve difficult academic work, devotion and commitment to a loved one, or years of developing practical knowledge and coping skills, depending on what the area one wants to be transcendent in.

Psychological defenses A series of mechanisms we all use to avoid being unduly threatened or overwhelmed by our life experiencing. Rationalizing our mistakes and blocking our awareness to threatening inputs are two common garden varieties of defense. For example:

> "I would have studied for the exam but I don't like my teacher."
> "You didn't really mean to hurt me, did you, Johnny?" (Right after Johnny hits me with a baseball bat.)

Self-actualization "Being all I am capable of." Self-actualizers live creatively and use their own unique potentials fully, not because they have to but because they love to live fully.

Self-disclosure Allowing others to know us fully by opening up and revealing our thoughts and deeper feelings.

Transcendent behavior Moving beyond the concept that others or we ourselves have of our limitations. Examples of transcendent behavior are intuitive, creative solutions to seemingly insoluble problems, relationships in which both individuals grow to be more than they were before, and survival in the face of insurmountable obstacles.

Exercises (*for individual and class use*)

You can do the following exercises and tasks at your leisure. Perhaps some of these would be more enjoyable with a friend. Those with an asterisk should be done in consultation with your teacher or in class.

1. *Living creatively.* Creative behavior means doing something that is novel, intuitive, and in some way enhances your life. Try doing something novel:

■ Break up your everyday pattern of living. If you *always* get up at 6:00 A.M. sharp, try setting your alarm for 3:00 A.M. one day and 9:00 A.M. the next. What happens? What might be good or bad about changing your schedule for getting up?

■ If you always avoid strangers, try role playing an extrovert for one day. Walk up to every new person you can find and try to strike up a conversation. What happens? Does the result surprise you in any way?

■ Try changing your usual mode of dressing. If you always wear bright, hip clothes, try a gray suit for one day. Or if you usually dress very carefully, loosen up. Wear jeans, go barefoot, try not combing your hair, and so forth. Whatever you normally wear, try changing it radically. Then notice how you feel in your new costume. What do you like about it? Dislike about it? Does your reaction surprise you? How about other people? Do they respond differently to you? How?

■ If you are always punctual, try relaxing and arriving whenever you feel like it for one day. If you are always late, make yourself arrive five minutes early for each of your commitments. What happens to your day?

■ Or change any of the other hundreds of habits you possess *for just one day:* Your hobbies—try a new activity, the place you study, the way you eat, or how much sleep you get. Is it possible that any of these changes could enhance your lifestyle?

2. Think of some area of your life in which you really want to grow. Perhaps it will be a friendship or a love relationship. Or maybe it's a life situation in which you want to really excel. Whatever it is, take a moment or two to get this area into "mental focus." Then consider the following exercises:

■ How can you challenge yourself to grow in this area? What can you read? Who can you talk to? What situations might you put yourself into that will pose a challenge? Recall that a challenging situation is usually new in some way. And any real challenge is likely to be at least mildly anxiety-producing. List five or ten things you could do to challenge yourself in this area.

■ *Preparation.* What concrete steps can you take to get ready to go? List three things you could do before 3:00 P.M. tomorrow afternoon that would prepare you to grow.

Now that you are prepared, it's time to "let it be." Consider whether you are using your potential: Can you relax physically and mentally when you need to? Are you always uptight? Do you make use of dreams, fantasy, reverie, or free association in this area?

In chapters ten and eleven we will return to the art of letting be.

■ *Impasse.* Maybe you feel you are on a night journey or at an impasse in this area. Chapter two identified ways we get into impasses and gave exercises for getting out of them.

■ *Sense of wonderment and awe.* Often we fail to appreciate people, places, or jobs. The way to appreciate is to shift our attention. Meditating on the things that are important to us is one way to develop awareness. Let yourself really see what is going on: Choose a simple object or situation to examine. Allow your body and mind to relax. Take a few deep breaths. Then really look at the picture or object you have chosen. What do you see? What do you feel? Now refocus. Look at your object or situation from a different perspective. Now what do you see? See how many different perspectives you can employ in looking at it.

3. *Your growing environment*. Consider the environment that you and those you live with create for each other. How much support is there for each of you to grow and transcend?

- *Support for accepting new challenges*. When someone wants to try something new, what reaction do you usually give them? "Great, let's do it." "Go ahead if you want to, but count me out." "I'll be glad to babysit while you do that." "That sounds crazy!" "That sounds dangerous." "Let's look at the possibilities. How can we approach this one?"

  Do you sometimes challenge and confront each other? Do some people get more support than others for growing? Who gets it? Who doesn't?
- *Support for coping with the night journey*. When the pressure is on, do others seem to care? Do they listen? Can they really help? Is your home a refuge or an insane asylum?
- *Support for becoming fascinated, appreciative, and deeply involved*. Do you really enjoy the projects each other is involved in? Can you share your interests with each other? Is there time to play and meditate, or is it like living in a factory or a subway station?
- *Support for preparation*. Is each individual allowed time to work on things in which he or she is interested? Is there a quiet place where each can work? A place for noisy projects? Do you encourage each other in your work?
- *Letting be*. Is it possible to just relax in your home? Would you describe each individual as tense? Relaxed? Worried? Preoccupied?
- *Restructuring*. Think of some changes you would like to make in your growing environment. Discuss your proposal with your "family." What do they think about your idea? can it be implemented?

Bibliography

Frankel, V. 1959. *From death camp to existentialism*. Boston: Beacon.

Jourard, S. 1968. *Disclosing man to himself*. Princeton: Van Nostrand.

_____. 1971. *The transparent self*. New York: Van Nostrand.

Koestler, A. 1964. *The act of creation*. New York: Macmillan.

Maltz, M. 1960. *Psychocybernetics*. Englewood Cliffs, N.J.: Prentice-Hall.

Maslow, A. 1954. *Motivation and personality*. New York: Harper.

_____. 1968. *Toward a psychology of being*. New York: Van Nostrand.

Shackleton, D. 1920. *South*. New York: Macmillan.

Silverman, J. 1970. When schizophrenia helps. *Psychology Today* (September) 62–65.

Thurmond, C. 1943. Last thoughts before drowning. *Journal of Abnormal and Social Psychology* 38:165–84.

PART THREE

Coping with Basic Life Tasks

Part two focused on some aspects of the question, "Who am I?" We went through the search for self-identity, the effects of labeling, the need to personally grow and savor the "good life," and the forces that psychologists have been influenced by in their search through these very questions.

In part three we stop for a moment and consider the basic tasks of adjustment we all must face. We begin, in chapter five, by recognizing the basic adjustment we must face to all that we have come to cherish at any age: the adjustment to loss and death. Chapter six relates the forces that influence us as we develop beliefs and defend them. In chapter seven we attempt to relate our basic drives of sex and aggression to the culture we grow up within. In the last chapter in part three, chapter eight, we will consider our sexual (loving) and aggressive (hating) tendencies in terms of the relationships they occur within as we mature.

Chapter Five: In the Midst of Life (On Death and Dying)

Why did Sally put her father in the refrigerator?
Because she wanted a cold pop.

CHILDREN'S JOKE

What is your first reaction to the children's "joke" —laughter or irritation? Feelings about death run deep and are often denied to our awareness or held in such awe or fear as to make this a touchy area to discuss. The French moralist La Rochefoucauld once observed, "One can no more look steadily at death than at the sun." This chapter will explore the attitudes and feelings we have about death and loss and will expose us to what little is known about the subject.

On the Fear of Death

Modern technology, by and large, spares us from having to experience death at close range nowadays. However, in the rural society of the early 1900s the dying person died at home. The family was present, and the ceremony and reception of people to witness the final rites also often took place at home. The body was rarely prettied up. But in our age of specialization, signs of impending death are promptly attended to by hurrying the dying person off in an ambulance to the intensive care ward or to a specialty ward where he or she may receive medical attention (not necessarily psychological attention). The person may die completely alone; there may be no family members present. The body is taken to a mortuary and duly processed, preferably cremated, and that is the end of it.

This series of events, although efficient and in many ways rational, keeps us from experiencing what was often experienced in earlier times and gives the young person less of a basis for countering her or his own natural fear of death in any real way. In fact, the fear and disdain of death are often reduced by the structure of loved ones around one before and after death is legally declared. A most remarkable and courageous example of one such possibility was what Ruth Hoffman, a fifty-seven-year-old woman who was dying of bone cancer, did. She threw a party for her family and friends. In fact, she decided to make it an open house. So from her bed in Sequoia Hospital, in Redwood City, California, she gathered all she loved around her. After the party she was ready to die.

In short, the psychology of the event, which by definition does not have to be rational, and most often is not, is fully as important as the efficiency and speedy medical and mortuary care the specialists have to offer. Structuring the situation with familiar people and events often helps to reduce the tension and fear of death and allows people (including the dying one) to be themselves more readily since they have some idea what the structure of the situation will allow. (In fact, support for those who grieve is a good preventative against suicide.)

Fear is inherent in anything we hold dear (from material possessions to people) because some day we will lose it. Only the very young, who have no symbolic comprehension of life, are fearless in the face of death. Fear of death or loss is probably learned and is very difficult to recognize. Religions are of comfort to some in promising that we can reunite with those we lose. In many cultures material goods have been stowed away with the burial of the deceased for use in another life. Still, many of us are not convinced. What's it all about? What happens to us when we die? Is it a decomposition of body matter, period? Is that all?

No one knows, of course. We believe, but do not know. Perhaps it's just as well, since it's probably more beneficial to believe in something pleasant if there's no way of knowing anyway. But fear is also a natural consequence of ignorance, and since we can never know death and must be to some extent ignorant of it, we will always have some fear of it.

In his treatise on the uses of fear, Gabriel Fielding (1962), a physician, offers several examples of how fear is disguised. One example is that of a little boy who had been reassured over and over again that his trip to the hospital to have his tonsils out would be nothing but rocking horses and ice cream. The boy remarked, "Then why is it so nasty to have your tonsils out?" When the doctor admitted it was painful, the boy asked to hear the worst of it and was told the worst would be when he woke up. The doctor continued, "The pain sits in your throat and stops you from thinking anything at all." The boy's fear melted away when the structure and expectations were out in the open, and he said, "Well, I'll remember that and when that first morning is actually happening I'll say to myself, 'I'm in it now. This is the really worst part, and it'll soon be over and then I won't be frightened any more.'" His fear was at least well handled, if not dissipated, and he had the encouraging promise of hope.

A more typical way of handling fear of loss is given by Doris.* The following was written several years after she graduated from college.

Probably the most personally significant event that happened to me that year was discovering that I had a tumor on my leg. All of a sudden it was there and it seemed rather big. The doctor was very pessimistic; he felt it could well be malignant. I think his philosophy was that you tell people what the worst could be so that they are not so shocked if they have to go through it. But I don't think he counted on naturally pessimistic people like me. Surgery was scheduled a week away, and during that week I felt that I was going to die. Picking up a magazine and seeing a big spread on cancer or hearing about some young woman who had leukemia only reinforced my sureness. I was so tense and my chest so tight that it was difficult to breathe. Ted [her husband] was no help. He took it lightly, feeling that everything was going to be all right. I don't think he realized the stark fear I was living with. I was very superstitious about it. I felt that the ugliness and hostility I'd

---

*Doris grew up in a small town in the Southwest. Her background could best be described as middle class.

been living with the last months had caused it. I guess I still believe that. I finally talked to someone, a friend. One of the saddest things I felt was that after all the bad times Ted and I had been through together, I wouldn't be around for the good times. And I hated the idea of being in the hospital, of being poked and prodded and sliced up, of being a thing rather than a person. That went against my pride. Talking it out helped a lot. We also got very drunk with Julie the night before; in fact I spent half the night vomiting in the back yard. It seemed somehow cathartic. Going in for out-patient surgery while you're hung over seemed to be easier.

It was all right; it wasn't malignant. I felt like I was reborn. I hadn't felt such zest for life in a long time. I had a new lease on life and I was determined to make better use of it.

COMMON ATTITUDES TOWARD DEATH AND DYING

Although fear is a natural reaction to the fact of death, the insensitivity, false assurance, and panic are attempts on our part to handle the unknown. The subtlety of the denial process can be inferred by making observations when defenses are down. By denial we mean a lack of conscious awareness of what or why we are doing what we do. Anthony (1940) asked a sample of children to complete a series of brief story themes, without suggesting how they were to end. Roughly half the children introduced references to death. Similarly, I assumed in teaching a personality course to freshman and sophomore college students that I would have great difficulty in evoking any discussion from the class on the subject of death. On the contrary, this has always been one of the best vehicles for class discussion I have found—even better, some semesters, than discussions about sex.

DEATH AND SOCIETY: DEATH AS A SOCIAL DISEASE

Does our society put more emphasis in IQ and class standing than on teaching sensitivity and the management of suffering? Are medical students admired for research and lab work to the extent that they later find themselves at a loss for words when a patient asks a simple question? How can science and technology increase the weapons of mass destruction without resolving the effect of their existence on our minds? The "life-after-death" notion is becoming less universal and machines and computers that prolong physical life are increasing in number. How can we deal with all this except through denial, restlessness, distrust, and free-floating anger? We seem to be on our own when it comes to answering these questions; society provides few answers. We will return to these questions at the end of the chapter when we talk in more detail about euthanasia, LSD therapy, and the extension of life beyond presently known or accepted limits.

The Stages of Death

The dying person, if given sufficient notice, and the survivors, at any rate, often go through a series of psychological processes in order to ready themselves for death or, in the case of survivors, to get back to normal living. In her book *On Death and Dying* Elisabeth Kübler Ross spends a great deal of time elaborating these stages, which we will briefly discuss here.

STAGE ONE: DENIAL AND ISOLATION

The fact is that one out of one dies. The belief is that there is one exception—"me." The shock of being told you are about to die is the most difficult thing you will ever be asked to believe. It is also very difficult for ministers and especially doctors to tell a person his or her time is up. Would you be able to tell someone she or he was about to die or would you find some excuse to postpone the news? One woman described by Weisman (1972) suffered from cancer of the bowel. She dreaded her doctor's daily visits, but realized they were hard on him also. He was awkward and unable to say anything helpful to her. So, to make the doctor feel better, she minimized her complaints, spoke optimistically, and helped foster denial in him. In fact, her doctor's inability to face death probably prolonged her life as she had someone to be concerned about besides herself. Quite a switch, wouldn't you say?

Some people will blame a mixup in X rays to reassure themselves that they can't possibly be dying. Others will seek out further consultation as a means of satisfying their disbelief, even when the evidence appears conclusive. Since denial functions as a buffer to shock, in such cases temporary denial probably has positive value. This denial, according to Ross, appears with decreasing frequency as death approaches. It should be understood as a normal and healthy reaction; well-meaning persons should not counter the dying one's denial of impending death by insisting that he or she is "being defensive." An example of such denial is given by

Attitudes Toward Death

Shneidman (1971), a well-known thanatologist (expert on death), found that his survey of *Psychology Today* readers on their attitudes toward death reaped a return sample of 30,000. (When he made a similar sample of attitudes toward sexual practice the number of returns was only a little over 20,000.) Some of the answers (attitudes) from the survey Shneidman conducted are listed below. The sample, as any magazine sample would be, is biased. The "typical" respondent is in her twenties, single, female, Caucasian, protestant, a college graduate, living in the Midwest, coming from a small family, and in good health. With that bias in mind here are some of the attitudes expressed:

1. About half the sample recalled death discussed in their family when they were children, and about half did not.
2. A large proportion believed that psychological factors can influence or even cause death.
3. Grandparents and animals were most of the sample's first personal involvement with death, and this generally occurred before the age of ten.
4. As children, half of the sample learned a heaven-and-hell concept of death.
5. Almost half shared some sort of belief in life after death.
6. Almost all of the sample felt that religion played some role in their attitudes toward death.
7. Almost all the sample would not choose to die young (before the onset of old age) and would choose a quick, quiet, dignified death.
8. The major reason given for sacrificing one's own life was "for a loved one."
9. Over half indicated there had been a time in their life when they wanted to die (with no indication of the seriousness of that wish).
10. Only twenty-two percent would choose burial of their own bodies, if it were up to them.

a college student who was told that his father had died. In the following he describes his reaction:

The Death of Joe's Father

In my own experience, the death of my father was quite a trauma, not only for me, but for my mother and sister too. My family and I were waiting outside his hospital room, and since he had only been sick for two days, we were quite unprepared for any news of death. There were three doctors and two nurses working on him, and it was mutually agreed that whatever illness he had contracted was extremely serious. When the head doctor finally came out and told us that they had done everything possible but my father had died, I was engulfed in a series of successive reactions. The first reaction was a state of shock, and I just could not believe that what I had heard was true. My next reaction was that I was not really experiencing this on this particular day, and that I must be dreaming. My final reaction became an accusation of negligence, and that the hospital staff had made some gross mistake which they would pay a heavy price for committing. (I feel compelled to insert the fact that this was not the case.) Then the doctor suggested that we go in and see my father's remains for a few minutes, and since my mother had sheltered me as a child from viewing "dead people," I hesitated. Upon the necessary prompting from my mother, I decided to go in and see for myself. I could not believe my eyes. I could not believe that this empty shell of a man had once been my father. It was so cold-looking, so still; it reminded me of looking at an empty frame where once a beautiful picture had been encased.

STAGE TWO: ANGER

"Why me?" As reality begins to sink in, the dying person begins to defend with various forms of anger and resentment. Again, what could be more natural? It is inconceivable to believe that people who have necessarily spent a lifetime in an effort to pull things together, to construct an identity, to gather from life what treasures they can would not be upset when told that they will be separated from all they have worked for and enjoyed. Anger is a natural consequence. Dying people often become very "bitchy." Nothing you do will suit them. In fact, they may create some anger in you and debate and fights may ensue if you are not mindful of the underlying motive.

It should be stressed that the unfolding of these stages of reaction is not a neat "now-you-see-it, now-you-don't" sort of phenomenon. The emotions, as we have indicated previously, often merge and defy any attempt to categorize them. A good example of how the various feelings combine can be seen in the case of Doris, who, once again, gives us her experience in the death of her grandfather at a time when she was a high school freshman.

The Death of Doris's Grandfather

I suppose the most significant thing that happened this year was the death of my grandfather. We had found out the year before that he had cancer, that he was not going to live, and the rest of it was a long, painful, and ugly way to die. I see no dignity in death, just the animal man giving up life, only sometimes it is simpler than other times. Over a period of eight or nine months my grandfather was in and out of the hospital, more and more in as time passed. His mind was good until the last couple of months, maybe less—so up until that time it wasn't as hard to visit with him because we could laugh and talk. I'd sit on the bed with him. My brother was especially close to him, and had been since he was a little kid. (Have just been staring at the typewriter for about half an hour.) As my grandfather got worse, as his mind and body wasted and decayed and died, *I found myself withdrawing* [our italics throughout] more and more from the situation, staring on in wonder, observing the death of a man and the movements of the people around him. I can remember myself *observing it all as an onlooker*, not especially thinking about it, just observing, not actively feeling it. The end of everything seems interminably long. *I wanted him to die*, to end his agony. He was no longer the man whom I had called Gramps and laughed when I kissed him because his moustache tickled me or would sit in his chair smoking his pipe or would make a big deal of eating breakfast with me because my grandmother would fix us pancakes with real maple syrup from Vermont. This man was blotting out these other memories with an ugly death that he didn't want but quietly endured. I guess there was a dignity in my grandfather's death after all. When he went into the hospital the last time my brother and *I didn't go out to visit him any more.* Oh, I remember that our minister was really great to my whole family at this time, especially to my grandfather. We had become friends with him over the couple of years that we had been going to that church and liked him very much. He thought a great deal of my grandfather and used to spend quite a bit of time with him talking about any number of things. When my grandfather finally died, my brother and I were at home, watching a movie on TV. The phone rang, my brother answered it, hung up, looked at me and told me that he had died. We just looked at each other, then at the TV, not saying much of anything. In a couple of minutes my brother got up and turned the TV off and started to cry, going off to his bedroom. I just sat there for awhile and then *I started to laugh.* I ran to the bathroom and looked in the mirror and was still laughing. I could hear my brother's muffled sobs from his bedroom. *I went into my own room and tried to cry into my pillow, but nothing came, not even laughter* any more.

The next few days were bad. We spent most of the time with my aunt and grandmother. People from church and friends were very good to us, would bring meals over to the house. We kids went one night to the funeral home, which was one of the most horrible experiences of my life. There were a lot of people there, friends I guess. My sister cried, my brother looked sternly sad. I just sat on a couch, vigil of the dead or something. *I knew my grandfather was in that goddam box in the corner, but I didn't want to go look.* Finally I did. My impressions were of masses of white silky material, my grandfather's hands folded, his face filled out with cotton, I supposed, to disguise the remnants of his illness, and a thin line of glue under his eyes and between his lips. *What the hell.* I went into the rest room and tried to cry, but I

couldn't. I went outside and sat on the curb until someone took me home. The funeral itself was short and simple with a memorial service that night. They played Mozart because my grandfather liked him and because he was my grandfather's ancestor. It was in September and still hot. Sometimes we kept the cooler on at night. Once during all of this I asked them to turn it off because the noise bothered me, *scared me.* Another night, I think the day my grandfather was buried, I asked them to put it on even though it wasn't that hot; I needed *noise.*

Doris finds herself playing the same range of emotions the dying person usually encounters. As we have said, it is a normal reaction for those close to the dying person to go through a similar series of reactions from a vicarious point of view. We might take an educated guess that Doris's difficulty in crying at various times was the layer of unrecognized anger that characterized her behavior in other situations as well. One can no more cry when in an angry state than be anxious when relaxed.

STAGE THREE: BARGAINING
This stage is less important in that it generally represents an attitude the patient has with his God more than with those around him. It's the "Dear God, I'll do anything you ask; just give me another chance" stage. In the bargaining stage one may set a challenge for oneself in the hope that the day of final judgment can be postponed. This may be the psychological moment when people, at varying degrees of awareness, set timetables for their own death. It is well documented that the dying patient will gather strength to be alive for an important event such as a birthday, or for a certain person to arrive at the bedside, or for a certain financial transaction to occur, and then, feeling that all is well and that he can afford to give in, does so and dies. If you are interested in data on this subject see Tanur (1972).

acceptance, often with a sense of security and quiescence, will emerge. The family of someone who has suddenly died may take months or as much as a year to reach this stage of acceptance, and even then flashbacks will occur for years. In fact, hallucinations and apparitions are not uncommon for those who have experienced a great loss. The phantom-limb phenomenon, in which a person cannot accept the fact of the loss of a limb for some time, is fairly well known. The amputee often makes movements and gestures as though the limb were still there and often insists that he or she can "feel" the missing arm or leg. What is not as well known is that the same phenomenon can occur when a spouse, child, or some other significant person is lost to one through death. These reappearing ghosts, or images, whether in the head or outward projections, are a part of adjustment and grief and do not necessarily indicate psychosis.

Ross describes the stage of acceptance as a quiet time, very often one in which communication is nonverbal. Holding hands or just being present may be the most one can accomplish. Robert Kavanaugh (1972) summarizes this stage quite well in the following quote:

> Once it becomes clear to a person that death is inevitable, two important problems need facing if death is to occur with any degree of serenity for all concerned. First, the dying person needs to receive permission to pass away from every important person he will leave behind. Only then can the patient begin to deal with his second problem, *the need to voluntarily let go of every person and possession he holds dear* [our italics]. Both problems deserve careful consideration, since therein lies the crux of dignified and peaceful dying.

This is not necessarily a happy stage, but rather a stage in which one finds peace, where all issues have been settled and where death is welcome. Not everyone reaches this stage, because people react to death with the same personalities they had when they were well. If a person has been able to accept

STAGE FOUR: DEPRESSION

As time goes on and reality sinks in, it is natural for the dying person to slump into a deep depression. She or he has been fighting through denial, anger, and bargaining and if no reward is apparent, the futility of it all begins to settle in. The only emotion left is exhaustion and depression—the submission to an inevitable fact. Our initial reaction to people who are depressed by their impending death is to try to cheer them up, to give them encouragement and hope. This is probably more for our own needs than for theirs. It is far better to just be there, silent, when a person is at this stage, ready to respond if a sign is given that she or he would like you to.

STAGE FIVE: ACCEPTANCE

Assuming again that death is not sudden and that the person has had time to adjust, the final stage of

very little of life, she or he may also have trouble accepting death. A hard-headed fighter may fight to the end and never reach the stage of acceptance. However, most people do come to this point, whether in terms of their own death or that of someone close to them.

I had a student one semester who wrote such a poignant story of dealing with death that I would like to include it here. Her reactions to the death of her son run the gamut of emotions, ending in her final acceptance of the tragedy she experienced.

The Death of Clark

I am thirty-two years old. My minor is psychology. After high school I went to college for one year. Then two years ago I started back again, taking seven to eleven units each semester. I am married. My husband has done quite well and we are fortunate to have many of the "extras." This is the second marriage for both of us and we are very happy.

I have four children from my first marriage, ages twelve to seven (my first baby, born seven weeks premature, died at five weeks old). I have four stepchildren, ages ten to seventeen, who visit us on weekends and vacations and I have our four-and-a-half-year-old Betsy and two-month-old Amy. And I am Clark's mother. Clark died last May. He was two years old.

It is difficult to tell Clark's story in a short paragraph or even to choose the right words. He was born in November 1971. He was delivered early due to an Rh problem and had a complete transfusion. Having survived the first week, Clark developed into a healthy, happy baby . . . a normal baby, although "normal" seems like an insignificant label for Clark. "Special" seems to fit him better.

Last May 15th I decided was to be Clark's day. Classes were over for me except for one final. Clark and I spent the day doing the things a toddler enjoys. We went to the car wash, had lunch with Daddy, and went to the grocery store. At the store I bought him some animal cookies but I said no to the pinwheel he wanted because he already had the cookies and the pinwheel could be dangerous.

Late that afternoon Clark inhaled charcoal starter from a scout "Buddy Burner" that the older children had left in the yard. We had him in the hospital in fifteen minutes but there was nothing anyone could do. He died at noon the next day.

During the agonizing hours at the hospital we were allowed to help care for Clark. By midnight I realized there was no hope. If by any miracle Clark had lived, he would have suffered severe brain damage. The next morning our doctor suggested we go home for a while and talk to our children. I knew they would keep Clark "alive" until we returned. Shortly after we got back to the hospital he died.

My husband Bob and I felt it was important to ourselves and to our children to handle Clark's death and the funeral in our own way. We planned a short, private graveside service and asked for donations to the hospital instead of flowers. We know hundreds of people and didn't want them at the funeral nor did we want a lot of money wasted on flowers. We wanted our children with us and we did not want a lot of people running in and out of our house. We met with some static with several relatives and we were sorry to have to offend them. Traditions and customs are hard to change but we held tight and are glad we did.

During those days and those that followed, I remember telling myself to "hang on" and not to become "unglued." Crying was okay and necessary but I had to keep some control of myself. I refused tranquilizers and sleeping pills from a number of people. I didn't need them anyway. Life must go on, they say, and my physics final was scheduled for the day after the funeral. Bob called the professor to see what I could do. I had made my mind up to take the final on schedule rather than take an incomplete until fall. I didn't feel it was wrong to think about school at this time, but I sensed that some people thought I was wrong or that I was trying to escape reality by being so concerned about a final. But I was lucky. I had an *A* average so I got an *A* without taking the final.

The next week was the worst time of all. The first time in twelve years all the children were in school and there was no baby at home. I had no classes and nothing to do around the house. I could have kept Betsy out of preschool but that wouldn't have been good for her. The only thing I had to do was a sociology correspondence course that now seemed dull and depressing. I couldn't bring myself to work on it, although before I had worked on it without difficulty. Now I began to notice that I categorize things as to "before" or "after" Clark's death and that many things appeared quite differently after than before. Bob was going through the same thing and we spent a lot of time together. Nothing we should have been doing seemed too important and it was hard to realize that Clark was really gone. We had planned a trip to Canada for several months and we decided it would be good for us to go. But it was not the same exciting place we had known before. We were miserable and we left after two days. Later I realized we wouldn't have enjoyed ourselves anywhere then.

For Betsy's birthday in June I looked in every toy store in town for something special for her. Finally I found a beautiful doll house and we planned a big party. I was trying to raise our spirits with a big party and lots of presents. In a way I was making up for all the presents I would never buy for Clark.

Three of the older children were gone most of the summer. I was relieved that they were going. Two of them had been involved in Clark's accident and they felt guilty. I knew we had to make them understand it was an accident and that we didn't blame them but how could we? It is one thing to forgive a child for breaking a lamp or even burning the house down but a tragedy like this is hard to smooth over. Especially when the children knew they were careless. I found I was just doing the routine things with them without really talking to them. I just did not want to discuss it and I hoped time would help, which it has.

A vacation that summer had no appeal to us without Clark so we decided to work all summer. Bob had a special model home to work on and I enrolled for ten units of chemistry. We did get away together for several weekends and really had a good time.

The first day in summer school I saw a friend from physics. She asked me why I hadn't taken the final and I told her. She was so shocked that she turned away without saying a word. I felt miserable for having upset her. The sadness I felt then was more for her than for Clark. I hoped I didn't run into anyone else that day and I wondered how to handle the situation the next time. There is no easy way to tell someone your baby died.

Chemistry presented a challenge. The first exam was very hard and when I couldn't answer one of the questions I almost started to cry. I felt panicky and all the sadness of the past weeks seemed to overwhelm me. I knew I had never reacted this way before so I told myself that crying and walking out couldn't help and that I had to figure out a way to handle this. I revived an old habit, biting the inside of my lip when I am upset—you can't cry if you're biting your lip. I finished my exam and the rest of the summer with two *A*'s and an almost pierced lip.

The first few weeks of summer school I

stayed in the classroom during the breaks. This way I avoided any conversations where the subject of Clark might come up. Later I joined several of my classmates during the breaks. They were either married or near my age. Telling them about Clark came easier than I expected and they were understanding and not shocked.

Over the summer we were concerned about Betsy. Often she cried about Clark and she wanted to sleep in our bed. We didn't give in, although at times we wanted to. She told us Clark talked to her at night. It was hard to handle these things. Before I had found the children's problems not too difficult to solve but now my emotions and my common sense were suggesting different reactions to Betsy. Sometimes I cried with her and sometimes I comforted her.

I felt very sad about Clark. I thought of him often and every few days I would feel very depressed and I would cry awhile. As time passed I was aware that these times were further apart but the depression seemed deeper although it didn't last very long. Sometimes I really wondered how I would make it. I knew time would help as it had when my first baby died but Clark had been with us so much longer. It was helpful to me to think of others who had lost children and to remind myself that Bob and I had each other and the other children. This sounds like "old stuff" but it works. The baby buried next to Clark and a week before him was supposedly beaten to death by his stepfather. His mother told me the baby was badly bruised because he had fallen out of his crib many times. It makes me feel better knowing that Clark had such a happy life compared to this poor baby. But the pinwheel I didn't buy. This really bothers me. Clark didn't fuss when I said no but I still wish I had bought it. Seeing pinwheels in the store still makes me bite my lip

and all summer I kept a pinwheel near Clark's grave.

In August we reached a big decision. We wanted another baby and we had to decide whether to have a baby or to adopt one. Blood tests told us what we already knew—with one or more transfusions we had a fifty percent chance of having a healthy baby. With Clark I had found that an Rh pregnancy is psychologically difficult. Your own healthy body is fighting against the baby and there is nothing you can do. I didn't think I could handle this now, waiting seven or eight months not knowing the outcome. So we decided to adopt a baby. Our friend, an obstetrician, told us the next baby would be ours. We were excited and glad to have taken the first step.

Fall came before we knew it and the children were back in school. I took eleven units

ON DEATH AND DYING

and finished up the sociology course. One day in pharmacy class my heart sank to see Clark was a statistic—one of twenty-three poison deaths in the state in the past eight months. I couldn't help thinking how insignificant this made Clark and the other twenty-two—just numbers. I bit my lip and somehow managed to sit through the rest of the lecture.

One time I got involved where I never would have before. A woman came out of a store holding her child (under two years old) upside down and hitting him on the head. She was yelling at him about minding and he was screaming. People were staring and I walked up to her and told her to stop. When she told me it was none of my business I replied that it was because there are laws against beating children. She was furious and told me that when I had kids I would realize that you had to beat them sometimes. For some reason I didn't tell her that I had children but I told her I was taking her license number which I did. She appeared scared then and I hope she realized the seriousness of what she was doing.

The fall passed quickly. Thanksgiving brought the good news that a baby was on the way. At this point everything looked brighter. Christmas turned out much happier than I had anticipated. I was afraid I wouldn't have much Christmas spirit but I was too busy to think much about it. Moments of depression were less frequent and not so deep. Occasionally a day or two went by that I hadn't thought about Clark. I considered this a good sign. I found I could not remember how well Clark walked or what words he could say. And other things like that. This was surprising to me and a little sad, but I accepted it as natural.

After New Year's and finals, I started preparing for the new baby. I was reluctant to buy too much until the baby arrived—just in case. In my psychology class came the opportunity to write this paper. Often I had thought about writing down my thoughts and experiences since we lost Clark. I felt it would be helpful to me and maybe even to others. After I decided to write this, it took months before I actually started it. I often "wrote" parts of it in my mind but it was a big step to start the first words. Then I could hardly stop.

February 20th Amy was born. We were thrilled to tears, literally. We brought her home when she was three days old. A beautiful baby and very good.

Now it has been almost a year since Clark died. I look back and see many things have changed. Relationships with friends slipped for a while but are now getting better. We declined many invitations, especially those that included children. To see others with all their children, especially babies, was very hard. When we did get together I was very quiet in contrast to my before-Clark days. I found most conversations dull and often trivial. Going to the University had always set me a little apart from most of our friends and now Clark's death has widened the gap. They felt I was different, and I am. A close friend wonders why I have changed. Twice recently she has seen something in the house to remind her of Clark; once several of his pictures and once a favorite toy of his. Both times she was very shaken and she told me how upsetting it was to her. I could only think how very often these things happen to me, almost every day— a red wagon, babies near Clark's age, a toy monkey, and many pinwheels. No wonder I have changed.

Bob and I are closer. After losing Clark we had become very dependent on each other but we learned that you can't lean on someone else entirely. We have helped each other over the rough spots and we are now able to accept what has happened to us.

After Clark died I became more protective towards Betsy. I worried about her getting hurt. I think the protectiveness was needed by both of us then but now we are pretty much back to normal.

Things that once seemed important to me are not so important now. I am more appreciative of many things now, especially my family and life itself. Before when I might have gotten into a hassle over something, I now realize that usually it isn't worth it. I have learned a lot about myself. I am more aware of what things tend to unnerve me and how to handle or avoid them. I know it was better for me to keep busy than to sit back and feel sorry for myself. I have accepted Clark's death.

Looking back, I realize that all these feelings are a necessary part of what the books call successful mourning. I will never be the same nor do I want to be. Clark brought much happiness into our lives and he will always be a part of us. We have come a long way in the past year and we will make it now because we have a lot going for us.

Educating Children About Death

As we do with sex, we shield children from those experiences that would teach them directly about handling feelings when death occurs. (It is my feeling that once we can begin to be honest about teaching sex in the schools we will have paved the way for the second big taboo: death.) Straightforward answers to children's questions about death are rare. We tend to protect rather than inform. "Where will poor Rex, our beloved dog, go now that he has died?" "He will go to doggie heaven up in the sky where there are other doggies to play with and there are lots of trees and bones." It's enough to make you wish you could go there too, if only to watch.

Nagy (1948) sought to answer empirically the question of how children view death. Her conclusions were that children under the age of five often view it as a reversible process. That is, you can be dead one minute and alive the next. While playing cowboys and Indians, a child may dramatically "bite the dust," only to be resurrected a minute later for another shot. From the ages of five to nine, death seems more real to the child, but is still held at a distance. For example, at this age death is often personified as a "bogey man" or similar character who carries people away. (It is interesting that this is also the concept of death held by various primitive civilizations. The Hopi Indians draw a line between the burial site and the village in an effort to keep the dead in their place and to prevent them from haunting the living.) According to Nagy, after the age of nine, children begin to view death as maturely as most adults. The Swiss psychologist Jean Piaget also asserts that the concepts of life and death change as children grow older. Of course, the more a child is exposed to sensitively handled personal experiences with death, the more mature he or she will become about the subject.

V. A. Suzhomlinskii, a Russian teacher and scientist, encourages parents to let children experience death as a natural reaction to the facts of life. He emphasizes that one's own humanity is related to the humanity of others—to that of one's father, mother, sisters, brothers, and grandparents. Therefore, he urges, the young child should be exposed to the sufferings of life as well as the joys. "One of the most painfully difficult things in education is to teach the child the labor of love."

Dr. Wolfenstein, a psychiatrist at the Albert Einstein College of Medicine, is reported by Fishman (1968) to offer the following guidelines to the surviving parent who must educate and handle the children.

1. The parent who takes principal care of the children should not monopolize them, so that someone else could care for them in the event of that parent's death.

2. What is told a child about death is less important than a comfortable communication about whatever questions are raised.
3. Don't evade the issue. If a parent is dying or has just died, the child should be told without delay—and with feeling.
4. Don't be shocked if your child sounds callous ("Can I have Daddy's guitar?"). He or she doesn't intend disrespect.
5. Let your child talk about the dead mother or father if *the child* brings it up. At first the child may idealize the deceased parent and later become more reasonable about him or her. Respond to the feelings, not the facts.
6. Be alert for a drop in schoolwork. If the child's attitude of "there's no use" persists, seek professional help.
7. If possible, try not to withdraw in your grief so as to put up a good front.
8. Stay in the same house for a while after the death, if at all possible financially.

There is a tendency, as Hetherington (1973) has pointed out, for boys and girls to grow up feeling awkward or uncomfortable with people of the same sex as a parent who died when the child was younger. It is therefore helpful for the child to have a variety of people of all ages and of both sexes to interact with.

Probably more relevant to your present situation are two accounts by college students of their attitudes toward loss or death. The situations they describe are probably typical of a college population.

I had been engaged for two years and suddenly I lost [him]. It was a terrible blow and very difficult to overcome. Months managed to slip by and I thought I had finally conquered the pain when my parents came back home. Never once did they offer a lending ear for me to express how I felt; all I got was words of wisdom and little sayings like, "There's other fish in the sea." It didn't take long to become fed up with such talk, and after a while I found myself breaking up whenever I received such words of wisdom, especially when I would lose some-

thing or someone close to me. At times I was so fed up with the dating bit, and life in general, that I'd become superdepressed and begin to cry. Always it traced back to my losing my guy. I'd go down in the shed down on our property and spend hours sitting in there crying and honestly thinking I couldn't stand it much longer. I felt as though I'd soon have a nervous breakdown but I'd continue and continue. At times I'd shout out or some dumb thing to relax myself. This kept up for three weeks. And then suddenly I stopped it. I don't know why. It just stopped.

Another woman had very mixed feelings toward a father who left the family when she was ten, never to return. She had told a boy friend once that she had received a telegram that her father had died—a lie she gave him in order to break their date that night. A counselor once told her in college, "Bury your father and divorce your mother" as an attempt to get her to realize the preoccupation she had with her parents. The following description is one of seeing her dying father after twelve years' absence.

We had been married for a year when we received news of my father. He was in a hospital in Minnesota, in an advanced stage of disease. After the initial shock and a few days of depression, I knew I had to see him. I only hoped he would remember me. My sister met my husband, my brother, and I at the hospital, and she introduced me to my father—this man I had not seen for twelve years, but who had played a role in my development despite his absence. If it had not been for his eyes, I would not have known him. My memory of my father did not match this man. This man was thin, short, balding, had lost the caps to his teeth, and shifted anxiously from foot to foot. When I saw the look of recognition in his eyes, I hugged him. In somewhat a disorganized manner, he said he was sorry that he had left us, that he missed us, and that he had always loved us even when he was gone. And he said he was so proud to have such a pretty daughter. I cried in his arms then, and some of the hurt melted, never to return. And the hate was gone. This pitiful shell that was once a man did not deserve any of the resentment that I had held for years. But neither can I now love him. The only connecting lines between my father and me are blood lines. Even if I get to know him, in the next meeting the entire relationship would have to be reestablished. My brother sees him often and can testify to that. I do not want to see him again. I do not want to watch him become more senile and become a vegetable and die. I do not feel as if it would serve any purpose. I think of him often, and sometimes lie awake at night and cry, trying to dispel the deep sadness that I feel now. But now it is much easier to cope with. The simple things that used to distress me: filling out applications, and not knowing whether to circle living or deceased, and having an answer when people ask where does your father live. And those few things that he said to me were things that I always wanted to believe, and now can. I know that I might have the same feeling, a grief over something within reach but never fully clasped, even if he hadn't left. Having missed that important relationship, I more fully realize the importance of the parent-child relationship. He really taught me a lot. When my husband and I have children, I will remember what I have learned the hard way, and I have the highest hopes that all our lives will be better for it.

To Almost Die

In our own fantasies we have probably wondered what it would be like to die and return to tell the world the real truth about death. (I can recall at various times in fantasy or daydream setting myself up as "THE FIRST PERSON TO TELL ALL" and having my testimony reported in scientific journals.) The next best source we have at present in learning about death is the testimony of those who have undergone brief death and returned—those who have almost died. This is certainly a far cry from learning about death firsthand, but most of us don't want to volunteer as subjects for that experiment.

Alvin Toffler, who wrote the controversial book *Future Shock,* describes research by Drs. Holmes and Rahe based on a concept by Dr. Wolff that change itself is a very important variable in understanding human behavior. They developed a Life-Change Units Scale to measure how much change an individual experienced. (We could certainly consider "coming close to death" as a unit for the scale.) The death of a parent, a divorce, a move, a marriage, a vacation trip, or the loss of an eye are examples of stress events. The amount of changes per unit of time is also an important variable. The researchers determined that most people agree about what life experiences are most stressful, and death of a loved spouse ranks number one (see table 8.1).

They conclude that alterations in lifestyle affect one's health. The U.S. Navy tested this scale by asking sailors to fill out a questionnaire covering the preceding year's life changes. The sailors then took a six-month sea duty cruise. On their return, a computer analysis of the follow-up data came up with a direct correlation between the amounts of previous recent change and the sailors' degrees of health on the cruise. This line of reasoning is consistent with data on death rates being higher for widows and widowers during the first year after loss of a spouse. Change, of whatever sort, appears to carry a psychological and physiological price tag with it.

If that is the case, what might we expect of the effect of the change that survivors of Hiroshima experienced when an atomic bomb killed thousands in an instant? Robert Lifton, in his study of the survivors of Hiroshima (1967), interviewed a sample from their midst in 1962. What happens to people in an environment permeated by death? The people of Hiroshima were completely surprised when the bomb hit. They had only a few moments before they heard the all-clear signal. The sudden change in environment was an important point here. Try to imagine it, if you can. One minute everything was fine and the next everything had changed. Lifton describes the first reaction as "psychic closing-off." This is related to the defense mechanisms of denial

TABLE 8.1

The Stress of Adjusting to Change

Events	Scale of Impact
Death of spouse	100
Divorce	73
Marital separation	65
Jail term	63
Death of close family member	63
Personal injury or illness	53
Marriage	50
Fired at work	47
Marital reconciliation	45
Retirement	45
Change in health of family member	44
Pregnancy	40
Sex difficulties	39
Gain of new family member	39
Business readjustment	39
Change in financial state	38
Death of close friend	37
Change to different line of work	36
Change in number of arguments with spouse	35
Mortgage over $10,000	31
Foreclosure of mortgage or loan	30
Change in responsibilities at work	29
Son or daughter leaving home	29
Trouble with in-laws	29
Outstanding personal achievement	28
Wife begins or stops work	26
Begin or end school	26
Change in living conditions	25
Revision of personal habits	24
Trouble with boss	23
Change in work hours or conditions	20
Change in residence	20
Change in schools	20
Change in reaction	19
Change in church activities	19
Change in social activities	18
Mortgage or loan less than $10,000	17
Change in sleeping habits	16
Change in number of family get-togethers	15
Change in eating habits	15
Vacation	13
Christmas	12
Minor violations of the law	11

and isolation and to the behavioral state of apathy: "If I feel nothing, then death is not taking place." This reaction has apparent survival value. Then, in time, came the feelings of pity and self-condemnation: "Why did I survive?" Then came the fear of contamination through witnessing others as well as yourself suffering secondary reactions (bleeding, nausea, ulcerations, and so forth). Following this, even years later, emerged concern with the possibilities of radiation disease and questions of whether this "taint of death" was passed on to one's children (which generally was not the case). Lifton distinguished what he felt were certain attitudes this group evidenced over the seventeen years between the disaster and his interviews:

1. The need for a sense of immortality; a need to transcend biological life
2. The need for a sense of connection and relatedness; the dislike of the threat of total severance from all that one knows
3. Death as a test of the meaning of life; the importance of how one dies and lives and for what purpose
4. Death as a test of life's sense of movement; the threat of nonmovement as distinguishing life from death

More contemporary phenomena that also contain the element of suddenness are auto or airplane crashes. During the Christmas season of 1972 a Miami-bound jet crashed in the Everglades. The survivors of this disaster felt the same psychic closing-off or emotional numbness. Many of them shortly after the crash engaged in completely irrelevant behaviors (*Time* 1973). Some of them recall talking to each other about what they did for a living, or singing Christmas carols, or walking to places they could not recall later. Guilt because of having survived and various forms of psychic denial seem to be normal reactions to this sort of event in many cases.

It is of interest to note that the stages of dying enumerated by Ross also seem to occur in the brief moments when one expects sudden death. Goodall

(1972) reports that Russell Noyes, Jr., a psychiatrist at the University of Iowa College of Medicine, has found in his studies of those who have nearly died that in such situations the initial reaction is resistance. There is at first a violent struggle that gives way to a conflict between fighting and surrender (similar to the stage of anger). Then there is a review of one's personal past and an acceptance of the way things are (similar to the stage of acceptance). It appears that the mind or ego splits from the body, perhaps in an attempt to establish some anchor point or simply to cut off all awareness of the situation. Noyes comments that the process may be similar to the out-of-the-body experiences described by parapsychologists. Finally there occurs a transcendence or mystical state in which the person does not know where he or she is and seems to be totally divorced from reality. In this same report (Goodall 1972) Albert Heim, a Zurich geology professor, describes his seventy-foot fall from a mountainside as follows:

> What I felt in five to ten seconds could not be described in ten times that length of time. Mental activity became enormous, rising to a hundred-fold velocity. I saw my whole past life take place in many images, as though on a stage at some distance from me. I saw myself as the chief character in the performance. Everything was transfigured as though by a heavenly light and everything was beautiful without grief, without anxiety, and without pain. The memory of very tragic experiences I had had was clear but not saddening. I felt no conflict or strife; conflict had been transmuted into love. Elevated and harmonious thoughts dominated and united the individual images, and, like magnificent music, a divine calm swept through my soul. I became ever more surrounded by a splendid blue heaven with delicate roseate and violet cloudlets.

The extent to which denial of reality will take us is also reported by a medical doctor who has studied the behavior of patients undergoing surgical

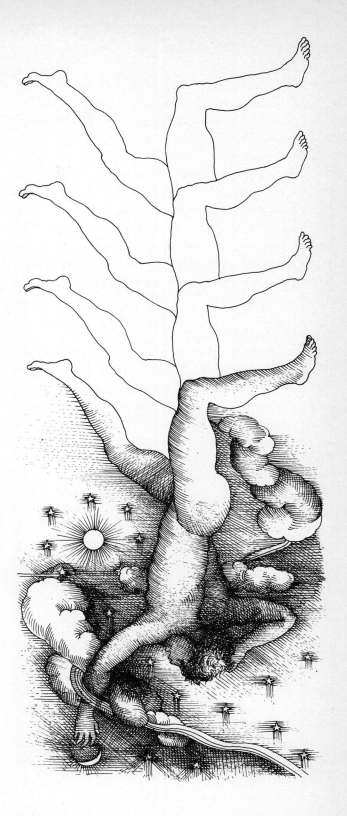

operation where threat of death is possible. Dr. Richard Blacher (1972) studied twelve of the most normal patients out of 300 postoperative open-heart surgery patients over a nine-month period at Mount Sinai Hospital in New York City. Eight of these model patients did just fine until a few days after the operation, when "reality" began to hit them. Then they got the shakes. They had repressed the reality and associated anxiety of the situation until the ordeal was over and then the anxiety came back in full force. Any of you who has been in a "trauma" where you found yourself managing only to fall apart when the stress was over, will probably recognize this as a normal series of events that frequently occurs in such cases.

Suicide: Who and Why?

In 1897 Emile Durkheim published his classic *Le Suicide*. He dismissed the prevailing theory of external social influences and suggested that a major factor that motivates one to take his own life is his or her relation to the social group. In the final analysis that conclusion still holds today. The lack of self-acceptance, as often judged by how others see us, the feelings of alienation, the desire to decrease the suffering of others, and the inability to meet standards, are all tied to the act of suicide.

According to Welu (1972) the feeling that "no one cares" is a powerful precipitating factor toward suicide. The irony of this attitude is that it is a self-fulfilling prophecy. The person who is convinced that no one cares gives up any interest in others who, in turn, give up whatever interest they have had in him or her. Finding lack of interest from others, the person becomes convinced that she or he was right in the first place. Of course, it is forgotten that this collision course was set up that way to begin with. The reaction of disgust from those who must deal with the unsuccessful suicide confirms the person's feeling that no one cares. Such comments as, "Why didn't you put the gun to your head and do the job right?" or, quite phlegmati-

cally, "Next time, make the cut deeper" are examples. (However, these samples are most likely not the rule.)

It has been established that while women attempt more suicides, men are more successful by about three to one (Jackson 1954). The reason generally given is that our society has encouraged women to be more dramatic and histrionic. Thus many of their suicide attempts are more cries for help than serious undertakings of self-destruction.

Seiden (1966) conducted a study of twenty-three students who had committed suicide at the University of California (Berkeley) between 1952 and 1961. The approach he used was to take a comparison group from the entire student body on which to judge the subset of student suicides. For example, if four of the twenty-three students were foreign students, he compared that ratio with the total number of foreign students to the total number of students. Since this is one of the more careful studies, methodologically, it is worthwhile to cite some of Seiden's findings:

1. There were numerous warnings in almost every case.
2. Prior to their suicides, a disproportionately large number of these students were involved in psychiatric treatment.
3. Concern over studies, unusual physical complaints, and difficulties with personal relationships were the main categories of conflict.
4. Compared to the student population at large, the suicide population was older and contained greater proportions of graduate students, language majors, and foreign students.
5. The undergraduate suicides had better academic records than their classmates.
6. The peak danger period was the beginning of the school term, not midterm or the end of the semester.

It is not safe to generalize from this study to your own situation, but there is one generality that stands out, which you have probably already deduced. In various ways the suicide group was marginal to the system it was in. Putting it another way, the suiciding students, in substantial ways, felt different and were different. They were more often than not part of a minority and were trying, in ultimately self-defeating ways, to be recognized as acceptable.

The following verbatim reactions are from students who presented some of the typical feelings of those who made or considered an attempt to self-destruct. All three of these students are still alive. All three are women.

It was a period of prolonged depression—the entire world seemed to be one ugly mass of humanity. I hated everyone, but mostly myself. I didn't want to live; suicidal thoughts crossed my mind endlessly. I still don't understand how it all began; nothing was really wrong with my life, I had good grades, lots of friends, and went out a lot. Sometimes I could hide my feelings, but most of the time people could tell something was very wrong. I didn't want to get up—every day seemed like an eternity to live. If I had to live it over again, I don't think I could make it. I don't know how it ended, all I know is that it lasted for months—months that seemed endless.

I guess that the time I considered myself to have acted very abnormally was the time I tried to commit suicide. As I look back on the episode I can see how abnormal and how irrationally I acted, but at that time I really felt that death was the only solution to my overwhelming problems. I had been in a very depressed state ever since my boyfriend had been killed in a car accident a few months before. Many times I tried to rid myself of this haunting feeling, but my loneliness and fear of the future without him sort of dimmed my rationality. I don't believe my suicidal tendencies would have come through though without the help of a minor frustration at school. As it turned out we were all getting awards for yearbook work, but the editor decided that I didn't deserve one. And that so to speak, blew my fuse. All I believed was that no one cared about me and nobody would ever care if I died. So I went home, these feelings of insecurity, hate and helplessness eating at me. I didn't know what to do. Then I decided that at this point in my life that no matter how awful it sounded, that suicide was the only answer. In desperation and without thinking of the consequences, I quickly finished twenty-five or so pills of some type, then the first shocks of what I had done registered and suddenly I knew that wasn't the answer to anything and I screamed for help.

I had come to Arizona for many reasons, primarily to get away from home and to play tennis, and for the latter reasons one of the first people that I met in Arizona was the president of the tennis team. This person was Sarah. I can't remember what it was that impressed me most about her—maybe it was her New York sophistication—maybe it was her attitude, but it wasn't very long before I realized that I really wanted her to be my friend. During the first month and a half I could tell my same old feelings of depression and discouragement with myself were returning, and it was at this point that I began to feel the overshadowing doubt about my friendship with Sarah. The fact that she was three years older than I and that she was from an entirely different type of environment didn't necessarily mean that we couldn't be friends, but that was what I began to base my doubts on. I began to write her letters. The first ones were the usual—I don't want to be a bother to you anymore, I'm not good enough to be your friend, I wish I was, and I'll leave you alone. I could feel my depression getting deeper as I wrote the letters. I was now in one of the deepest depressions I had been in for a long time, and as my mood got worse, the letters began to show it. Now I was writing things like— I have realized that I'm not good enough to be your friend and now I realize that I'm not good enough for anyone, and if I'm no good to anyone then what use is it to live. I've come to the conclusion that everyone would be much better off if I weren't around, and the best way not to be around is to be dead. And so the letters went. I was getting scared, because I knew that if I thought about suicide long enough I could talk myself into it. Down deep I knew that suicide was not the way out—I had tried it once. But I didn't have too much longer to wait for an answer to my pleas for security. Sarah, I could tell, was getting scared too. She tried to talk to me, and our conversations cheered me for a while, but then I would drop into the same old mood. I knew she accepted me by the way she talked to me, although she wouldn't come right out and say it. She tried to show herself through other means. Finally, I wrote one last note and at the end I said—Good-bye, Sarah. But before I had a chance to do anything I received a note from her saying—Judy, I want to see you right away! I went to see her, and for the first time whatever good feeling she had for me came to the surface and she begged me to go and see one of the psychologists at the school. I didn't want to at first, but after seeing just how much she wanted to help me, I said yes. As I found before, I got some help, and slowly I came out of my depression. With my acceptance of her offer for help, our relationship stabilized and began to grow anew. Although Sarah has never come right out and said "Yes, I accept you as a friend and I need you as a friend," she shows it through her actions, and though every now and then I can feel the doubt begin to creep up on me, I am sure that Sarah is one of my true and lasting friends, and I know that I will always care for her and that she will always care about me.

The question remains whether under any condition suicide is morally correct. With the negative stigma that still hovers over the act, suicide is certainly punitive to those left behind who must painstakingly justify their own behavior in relation to the suicide. We will talk more about this moral issue in our discussion of mercy killing.

Growing Old and Facing Death

When the phrase, "Today is the first day of the rest of your life," first attracted attention, it had a very positive ring to it. However, the aging person may counter, "Yeah, what there is left of it!"

The premium placed on youth in our culture does not make things easier. The older person may

actually develop feelings of guilt in the same way as the survivors of Hiroshima and the airplane crash: "With all these young people being squeezed together into less and less space, what am I still alive for?" The guilt is usually but not always, dissipated by the rationalization that "it was meant to be."

Reports (*Human Behavior* 1972) indicate that during the last decade (the 1960s) the ratio of old to young has increased by sixteen percent, and in 1970 there was estimated to be thirty-five people over sixty-five years of age for every one hundred people under age fifteen. Whatever the figures may portend, they do not indicate that aging and care for the aging will be less of a problem in the future.

There are numerous prejudices in our society that older people must cope with. Professional people, including doctors, may view the aged as "not pulling their own weight any more" or of being "less responsive to rehabilitation"—both statements being facts that have turned to value judgments. Sudnow (1967) exposes us to an even more subtle and devastating form of prejudice found in the treatment of old people brought to an emergency hospital room as suspected DOA (dead on arrival) victims. For example:

Two persons in similar physical condition may be differentially designated dead or not. For example, a young child was brought into the emergency room with no registering heartbeat, respirations, or pulse—the standard "signs of death"—and was, through a rather dramatic stimulation procedure involving the coordinated work of a large team of doctors and nurses, revived for a period of eleven hours. On the same evening, shortly after the child's arrival, an elderly person who presented the same physical signs, with—as one physician later stated in conversation—no discernible differences from the child in skin color, warmth, etc., arrived in the emergency room and was almost immediately pronounced dead, with no attempts at stimulation instituted.

People also often confuse the symptoms of mental

and physical disease with those of old age, and some mentally healthy old people whose behavior resembles that of the mentally ill are shuttled off to mental hospitals to await death (Markson 1971).

Bernice Neugarten (1971) comes to the aid of the elderly and indicates (correctly, I think) that since much of the research on the aged is done by people who are treating "the poor, the lonely, and the isolated," there is a bias against the elderly in most samples. She continues:

> Studies of large and representative samples of older persons are now appearing, however, and they go far toward exploding some of our outmoded images. For example, old persons do not become isolated and neglected by their families, although both generations prefer separate households. Old persons are not dumped into mental hospitals by cruel or indifferent children. They are not necessarily lonely or desolate if they live alone. Few of them ever show overt signs of mental deterioration or senility, and only a small proportion ever become mentally ill. For those who do, psychological and psychiatric treatment is by no means futile.

Whatever the case may be, older people tend to be increasingly preoccupied with death, if for no other reason than the awareness that their peers are dying. Cicero, a Roman orator of note, observed that 1) withdrawal from employment, 2) impaired physical vigor, 3) reduction of sensual pleasure, and 4) preoccupation with death contribute to the problems the older citizen must cope with. At the same time, there may be much to look forward to, in spite of these changes, if others are there to talk to and to listen.

Who Should Survive — and How?

There is a growing sentiment that, under certain circumstances, it is appropriate and moral to kill — out of mercy. Euthanasia (from the Greek, meaning "a good death"), or mercy killing, as it is often referred to, is contraindicated by the physician's Hippocratic oath, which states, "I will neither give a deadly drug to anybody, if asked for, nor will I make a suggestion to this effect."

Twenty-five or thirty years ago the doctors who treated dying patients could make few decisions. They simply prescribed what was available and let nature take its course. The subtleties involved today as to when someone is being helped or harmed are most intriguing. Is giving a fatal dose of a normally beneficial drug the same as giving a fatal dose of a known harmful drug? Is not doing something positive for the patient the same as doing something harmful? If there are ten patients and five heart-lung machines to sustain life, on what basis do you choose those who will live? By age? Status? Sex? The simple-minded notion that doctors and others should not play God is irrelevant at this point since by doing *something* or *nothing* lives will continue or stop. More than seventy percent of deaths occur in hospitals or nursing homes (*Time* 1973). This demands that nonfamily members be involved in some way in decisions that lead toward the sustaining of life or the encouraging of death.

As it now stands, the matter is often left to the doctor; the family often defers to his or her judgment, and that judgment is often far from objective. However, this is not necessarily bad. In the words of Dr. Kessler, associate dean of Northwestern University Medical School, as quoted in *Time*, July 6, 1973:

> There's no single rule you can apply. For me it is always an intensely personal, highly emotional, largely unconscious, quasi-religious battle. I have never said to myself in cold analytic fashion, "Here are the factors, this is the way they add up, so now I'm going to pull the plug." Yet I and most doctors I know have acted in ways which would possibly shorten certain illnesses — without ever verbalizing it to ourselves or anyone else.

Few are aware that Sigmund Freud was probably given "passive" euthanasia. At the age of eighty-three, after undergoing thirty-three operations over sixteen years for cancer of the jaw, his doctor gave him two centigrams of morphine and repeated the dose in twelve hours. Freud lapsed into a coma and died.

In contrast, on December 26, 1972, the thirty-third president of the United States, Harry S Truman, died. Listen to how *he* was cared for (as reported in *Time*, January 8, 1973). In the initial phase of Truman's last illness he was given antibiotics for rales (difficult breathing) to reduce infection in the lungs. On about December 6 he was given oxygen and antibiotics, "pressor" drugs to normalize blood pressure, and CO_2 to balance blood chemistry. A tube was inserted through his nose and throat for breathing and eating. He was given a liquid preparation containing amino acids, proteins, and vitamins. To encourage kidney function, special amino acids were flown from California to Kansas City. He then slipped into a coma and died a few days later. During these twenty or so days, a constant vigil was kept to sustain Truman's life. Now the questions. Was it worth it to Truman? To the country? Does one's status in the community affect his treatment? Should it? Would you want this treatment in a similar situation? And the answers?

According to a Harris Poll (Harris Survey 1973) sixty-two percent of the public feel the doctor should be allowed (in terminally ill patients) to carry out the patient's will that life not be extended, but only thirty-seven percent feel the doctor should be allowed to carry out the patient's will that life be ended. The difference, if there is one, in not extending life and in ending life is probably the crux of an issue that will surely be with us for some time.

LSD THERAPY FOR THE DYING

The use of lysergic acid diethylamide (LSD) in the treatment of the dying is clearly one of the more interesting possibilities in facilitating the dignity of death. In 1938 a biochemist in Switzerland, Dr. Albert Hofmann, synthesized LSD, a derivative of the ergot fungus. It was not until the early 1960s that anyone had considered the effects of LSD in the treatment of the dying. Now it appears to definitely facilitate reducing pain and accepting death and is being increasingly researched, in particular with cancer patients.

A pilot study, including case histories and an extensive bibliography on the use of LSD for the dying can be found in Richards, et al. (1972). Although Richards' experiment was not controlled, it gives great encouragement to those of us who may someday face a drawn-out terminal illness. Much of what we have described previously as stages or conditions to be met in order to face death with a sense of dignity are seemingly facilitated by the controlled use of this drug. Briefly, LSD takes the patient's mind off his or her illness. It helps patients to transcend their preoccupation with death and gives them a new perspective. It also gives relief from pain for periods of weeks or months following a single administration of from 200 to 500 micrograms.

Sheehan, of the Menniger School of Psychiatry in Topeka, Kansas, states (1972) that LSD seems to keep the patient from concentrating on any one sensation. The meaning of pain seems to change. Ego boundaries fade, and because the patient no longer feels intense attachment to the body, he or she can better accept the transition from life to death.

A nurse described by Sidney Cohen (1965) contracted cancer of the rectum at the age of forty-five. She was divorced, had no children, and, except for one sister, no relatives. Her skin had turned a deep yellow-green and her face and arms were emaciated and wrinkled. Her abdomen and legs were distended with fluid. She knew what her enlarged liver, her jaundice, the bone pain, and the swelling meant. She was in severe pain and there was no one around to give a damn. The following is an excerpt from her testimony while under LSD.

> I could die now, quietly, uncomplaining—like those early Christians in the arena who must have watched the lions eating their entrails. Will I remember any of this? And what about the pain? I suppose I'll be a baby about it again. Right now, the pain is changed. I know that when I pressed here yesterday, I had an unendurable pain. I couldn't even stand the weight of a blanket. Now I press hard—it hurts—it hurts all right—but it doesn't register as terrifying. It used to throw me and make me beg for another shot.

One patient described by Richards offered a great deal of optimism about how a person can transfer from a stage of depression to one of acceptance through the use of LSD. This patient was a fifty-year-old Jewish married woman with two children. Breast cancer had spread to her spine, ribs, and thighs. She was depressed. Neither her thirteen-year-old daughter or her eleven-year-old son knew she was dying. She resented her husband who had previously known she was dying but didn't tell her. Her mother, in her seventies, had not been informed for fear the news would shock her to death. It was a closed system. The idea was to keep up a good front. She could not talk with her husband about her condition as he would always reassure her and change the subject. The patient's mother-in-law came to the hospital to see the patient for an allotted fifteen minutes before her bridge game and would chat about trivia, then leave. The patient hated her mother-in-law's visits. Finally her husband was counseled to open up to her and the two of them reached a point where they could cry and share together. They both seemed relieved over this turn of events. Then the patient was given 300 micrograms of LSD intramuscularly. After the effects of the drug had faded, her husband, sister, mother-in-law, and a dozen friends gathered at her bedside. When the mother-in-law

bent over to give the patient a kiss, the patient grabbed her wig and tried to pull it off, to the dismay of the mother-in-law and the delight of everyone else. The patient subsequently called her daughter and son home from camp and in the presence of her husband explained her condition to the children. Finally she invited her mother to visit and explained the situation to her. Everyone who had been told rose to the occasion. For two months following her LSD session, the patient appeared to be free of depression. She spoke of death as a friend and seemed to have little fear. Six days after her readmission her children came in and said goodby to her. Her husband and sister remained with her as she entered into coma. The following afternoon she quietly died. The hospital staff commented that hers was one of the most peaceful deaths they had witnessed.

THE NEED TO EXTEND LIFE

According to Aronson (1973) there were at the time of his study eleven frozen bodies waiting for immortality—eight in California, two on Long Island, and one in New Jersey. Robert Ettinger, a Detroit physics professor, founded the cryonics movement. His theory is that if bodies are frozen at the time of death they may be thawed later when science has sufficient technology to bring them back to life and perhaps cure them of whatever disease they died of.

Since antiquity, we have fancied immortality by entombing mummies, preserving heads, and so forth. But cryonics is the most scientific approach to date. A first-class freezing capsule may cost nearly $10,000. Maintenance charges covering rent and replenishment of the freezing component, liquid nitrogen, run at least $1000 per year. Apart from the difficulties with cost (which is usually provided by life insurance) and the question of whether the body can be thawed without extensive cell damage, there are those who question the cryonics movement either on religious grounds or on the practical grounds that old people should die and make room for the young. But when it comes to life and death, who are we to question the possible future value of throwing your hat in the ring (your body in the vat)—just in case?

Even if body freezing is out of the picture as far as you are concerned, there are efforts being made about ways to retard or stop the aging process that would probably have more appeal and make more sense. By the time one reaches the age of thirty, brain cells are dying off at the rate of 100,000 per day (Davidson 1969). And that's only the beginning. The body literally begins to fold up and the contrast between young and old begins to show. Not all of us have an interest in or an ability to shell out for a Hugh Downs-type hair transplant or a Phyllis Diller facelift. But most of us would like to preserve our youthful health.

One theory of aging states that it is caused by cell death. The various cells in your body begin to die out randomly, and eventually there's not much left of the young you. Another related theory, that of the Finnish chemist John Bjorksten, is that stray protein-like molecules attach themselves to the long-chain molecules within a cell and gum it up so that the cell dies. If there are bacteria that could dissolve these cross-linkages, as Bjorksten believes, aging might be delayed. Fasting, or just eating less, is also thought to retard the aging process, since the body functions must work harder when energy is introduced to the system. Other tests that are being made concern the control of growth hormones, the use of negatively charged ions, the use of food preservatives such as BHT, the consideration of hibernation, the preservation of living brains, and so forth. Sound like plots from an old Dracula or Frankenstein movie? Who can tell?

Chapter Five Summary

Life and death, like love and hate, are inseparable. Our society smooths over fears of loss by establishing customs for thinking about the dying and the dead. Elisabeth Kubler-Ross describes five stages that are common in our adjustment to death:

1. Denial and isolation
2. Anger
3. Bargaining
4. Depression
5. Acceptance

Our society does very little to lift the veil of mystery from the topic of death. For example, children could be sensitively exposed to the idea in school, but they are not. Taking one's life as an alternative to living is generally an alien concept in our society and is indicative of the taboo nature of death. We come to appreciate the value of life as we grope for some answers to other questions, such as how to handle senior citizens in ways that will be most enhancing to them, who should survive, how we can decide that, and what the point of prolonging life is.

Glossary

Apathy A lack of feeling or emotion.

Defense A way of avoiding anxiety.

Denial A method of defense in which one refuses to admit reality.

Depression A state of sadness usually accompanied by feelings of "what's the use?"

Cryogeny the practice of body freezing soon after death. The purpose of this venture is the hope that the body may be brought back to life when science finds the way to do so.

LSD Lysergic acid diethylamide.

Parapsychology The branch of psychology that studies telepathy, clairvoyance, and psychokinesis.

Phantom-limb phenomenon
The feeling that an amputated limb is still really there. The person actually experiences pain, pressure, or temperature changes in the missing arm or leg.

Thanatology Thanatos means death and ology means the study of. Anyone who studies deadly subjects is a thanatologist. Contrary to popular belief Thanatosis is not a body odor condition.

Exercises (*for individual and class use*)

You can do the following exercises and tasks at your leisure. Perhaps some of these would be more enjoyable with a friend. Those with an asterisk should be done in consultation with your teacher or in class.

1. Draw up a will stating the conditions you prefer for the disposal of your body. Will you have a ceremony? What sort of ceremony? Will those left behind have some say in it?

2. What would you do if your doctor gave you six months to live? Try to imagine the changes, if any, you would make in your life style. Would you tell anyone? How?

3.* Describe on paper or to the class your first encounter with death. What were your feelings at the time?

4.* Role play the different stages of death. One person plays the doctor on his daily rounds; another is the patient caught within one of Ross's stages (denial, anger, bargaining, depression, acceptance).

5. If you were a fifth-grade teacher and decided to offer a unit on "death education" to your class, what activities and problems would come to mind?

6.* Did you ever consider suicide? Talk about it with someone. If you thought someone you knew was considering it, what would you look for? What would you do?

7.* Following are a number of exercises designed to help you get into your feelings regarding loss and death. The procedure for all of the following exercises is to close your eyes and listen to the group facilitator. Do not talk or ask questions. Try to follow his or her suggestion. After a few minutes' silence, open your eyes and see if you can relate your thoughts to the group.

Fantasy #1—*A Partial Loss*

Group Facilitator: "Close your eyes and imagine that some part of your internal or external body has been taken from you, except tonsils, appendixes, and other minor body parts. What part of your body do you now focus on? Try to get into what it would be like to have gone through this day thus far with that part missing."

Fantasy #2—*Real Versus Ideal Loss*

Group Facilitator: "Close your eyes and imagine that you have been allowed to choose the time, place, and circumstances surrounding your own death. Dwell a bit on these particulars. (Allow three minutes.) Now imagine how it will *really* happen. Do you see a difference?"

Fantasy #3—*Losing Someone Close*

Group Facilitator: "Close your eyes and imagine you have left this room. Someone stops you on the street and gently takes you aside and tells you that someone very close to you has just died. Who might have died? Think about your reactions to the news and what you would be feeling in the next twenty-four hours. What would you be likely to do?"

A Suggestion for Ending the Fantasy Exercises

Form a circle, standing up, with your arms around each other. Close your eyes and listen to your own body, your heart, your perspiring hands, your grounded feet, and note that you are very much alive. Feel the closeness of people on each side of you. Open your eyes and look around you. Welcome back to life!

Bibliography

Anthony, S. 1940. *The child's discovery of death.* New York: Harcourt Brace Jovanovich.

Aronson, H. 1973. The fine art of living forever. *Cosmopolitan* (January): 89–91

Blacher, R. 1972. Post-operative shakes. *Journal of the American Medical Association* 222, No. 3:305–08.

Cohen, S. 1965. LSD and the anguish of dying. *Harpers* (September): 69–78.

Davidson, R. 1969. The demise of death. *Avant Garde* (March) 52–55.

Fielding, G. 1962. The uses of fear. *Harpers* (February): 92–95.

Fishman, K. 1968. Death in the family. *New York Times Magazine* (February).

Goodall, K. 1972. Through death's door. *Psychology Today* (October): 16.

Hadas, M., ed. 1951. *The basic works of Cicero.* New York: Modern Library.

Harris Survey. *The Arizona Daily Star*, Monday, April 23, 1973, Section A, page 5.

Hetherington, E. 1973. Girls without fathers. *Psychology Today* (February): 49.

Jackson, D. 1954. Suicide. *Scientific American* (November).

Kavanaugh, R. 1972. *Facing death.* Los Angeles: Nash.

Lifton, R. 1967. On death and death symbolism: the Hiroshima disaster. In Bugental, J., ed. *Challenges of humanistic psychology.* New York: McGraw-Hill.

Markson, E. 1971. A hiding place to die. *Trans-Action* (November/December): 48–54.

Nagy, M. The child's view of death. *Journal of Genetic Psychology* 73:3–27.

Neugarten, B. 1971. Grow old along with me! The best is yet to be. *Psychology Today* (December): 45.

Richards, W., Grof, S., Goodman, L., and Kurland, A. 1972. LSD-assisted psychotherapy and the human encounter with death. *The Journal of Transpersonal Psychology* 2:121–50.

Ross, E. 1969. *On death and dying.* New York: Macmillan.

Seiden, R. 1966. Campus tragedy: a study of student suicide. *Journal of Abnormal Psychology* 71:389–99.

Sheehan, D. 1972. A review of the use of LSD for the patient near death. *Psychiatric Forum* 3, No. 1:21–23.

Shneidman, E. 1971. You and death. *Psychology Today* (June): 43.

Sudnow, D. 1967. Dead on arrival. *Trans-Action* (November): 36–43.

Tanur, J., ed. 1972. *Statistics: a guide to the unknown.* San Francisco: Holden-Day.

Time. 1973. The last illness. *Time* (January 8).

————. 1973. (January 15) 53.

————. 1973. Deciding when death is better than life. (July 6).

Toffler, A. 1970. *Future shock.* New York: Random House.

Welu, T. 1972. Psychological reactions of emergency room staff to suicide attempters. *Omega*, 2, 3:103–09.

i was talking to a moth
the other evening
he was trying to break into
an electric light bulb
and fry himself on the wires

why do you fellows
pull this stunt i asked him
because it is the conventional
thing for moths or why
if that had been an uncovered
candle instead of an electric
light bulb you would
now be a small unsightly cinder
have you no sense . . .

and before i could argue him
out of his philosophy
he went and immolated himself
on a patent cigar lighter
i do not agree with him
myself i would rather have
half the happiness and twice
the longevity

but at the same time i wish
there was something i wanted
as badly as he wanted to fry himself.

DON MARQUIS, *archy and
mehitabel*

We may catch ourselves wondering why we believe so strongly about something. Are our beliefs just a matter of conditioning? Or are there universal truths that all reasonable people will eventually come to recognize? This chapter will explore the ways we come to believe what we think is real and how we maintain and change our beliefs.

Playing with Categories: Beliefs, Attitudes, Opinions, and Faith

Psychologists, like other scientists, find themselves playing around with categories. The phrase *playing around* is used because these categories are often misinterpreted. For example, to take such well-known words as *belief, attitude, opinion,* and *faith* and distinguish among them is almost impossible. In this chapter we will attempt to deal with the meanings of these four words without expecting to define them clearly. We will start with a few ideas about distinguishing beliefs from attitudes, nonetheless. Let's look at four philosophers and psychologists who have studied the subject.

Feigl, an outstanding philosopher from the University of Minnesota (my belief), pointed out two extremes in attitudes that one might take (1969). The dogmatic attitude, in which a firmly held position is taken, is one extreme, and the extremely skeptical position, in which no point of view is ever convincing, is the other. Feigl concludes that most of us live neither by asserting that we know everything that there is to know nor by doubting everything. Therefore we live by faith or belief much of the time. One sort of belief is empirical in nature, such as, "I believe it may rain tonight," or, "Oranges are round." Another type of belief relies on faith, or on the supernatural. All religious beliefs are of this sort, since they cannot be proved or disproved by science or logic. The third meaning of the word *belief* might best be labeled commitment. It is a firm attitude that contains both personal feeling and involvement—"I believe in human equality," is an example.

Charles Peirce (1839–1914), an early American philosopher, discerned four ways of fixing belief (Ianni 1967). The first way he labels the method of tenacity. It is similar to belief by faith. This is the I-just-know-it's-true belief that someone can give no further evidence of. A second method is by appeal to authority: "Forty million Frenchmen can't be wrong," or, "Do it because Daddy says so, and he knows best." The third method is *a priori* or intuitive and is an appeal to reason rather than to shared or public experience. A fourth type of belief is based on the scientific method (deduction). All four methods or types of belief may be valid for their purposes. Bem (1970) divides beliefs into four categories: cognitive foundations [thinking], emotional foundations [feeling], behavioral foundations [doing], and social foundations [relating]. Finally Rokeach (1968) offers still another portrayal of the nature of a belief and its relation to an attitude. Figure 6-1 is based on summaries of Rokeach's and Feigl's data but is my responsibility, not theirs. By now you must be happy and content in the knowledge that you know how to categorize beliefs.

Beliefs in Authority Figures

"I've got it! The government is boss of all the governors, probably, like the president is boss of all the senators. Senators are people from all different states."

The above quote comes from Tommy, a rather bright seven-year-old second grader. He never heard of Watergate, but his beliefs are close to the public sentiment. He was one of 12,000 children in grades 2–8 from all over the United States who were sampled by Hess and Torney (1967) in early 1962. Tommy is now in his twenties. Given the fact that much has taken place in American politics since the early sixties, there are still likely to be some basic attitudes and beliefs that have continued. At least this is Hess and Torney's contention.

For example, Hess and Torney indicate the young child generally comes to believe that government is powerful, competent, benign, and infallible. This may be similar to the child's attitudes about Mom and Dad. He or she trusts them all to offer protection and help. (Of course there are exceptions: in ghettos and other strife-ridden areas where constant disappointment and disillusionment prevails, there is increased skepticism.) The child's initial relationship with governmental authority is with the president, who is seen in positive, personal terms (usually). Police, fire fighters, and doctors are also typical "good" authority figures for children. Trust and belief in authority figures become increasingly differentiated and less categorical as the child grows to adulthood.

Our institutions generally reinforce these positive, general feelings and beliefs. For example, the importance of the presidency is emphasized to the child rather than the dealing and compromise inherent in presidential maneuvering. Schools are famous for selectively teaching what is good about our country, its history, and its leaders. The rest we find out as we live.

CHANGING BELIEFS IN AUTHORITY

In the late 1940s, a group of psychologists at the University of California at Berkeley described research they had been working on in a book entitled *The Authoritarian Personality* (Adorno, et al. 1950) Partly spurred on by the atrocities of World War II and partly by the fact that two of the researchers had themselves fled Nazi Germany, the findings they uncovered indicated that there are people who are authoritarian or fascistic in their general approach to life. Such individuals are thought to be highly ethnocentric (own-group-oriented). When interviewed, they generally reported harsh, threatening parental discipline, where love was contingent on "good behavior," and were taught to be concerned with family status and what others might think of their families. Basically, these people saw the world as divided into the weak and the strong.

Although most of us may be authoritarian in some situations, we usually tend to be flexible. We are able to give in on a point here and there, and we do not insist or try to modify all situations to suit us. We are also often victims of categorical thinking but we usually do not insist on others believing exactly what we do. For example, jury decisions are often swayed by a defendant's race, sex, education, and other appeals to categorical thinking. None of us are immune.

Much of our feeling on this subject does go back, for some of us more than for others, to those authorities into whose charge we were originally placed—our parents. They, in turn, were once kids under authority. All people, everywhere, have had to grapple with how to believe parents and other authorities and how to grow up with some sense of where they stand in the nature of things.

The following anonymous student reports show a small sample of ways children change their atti-

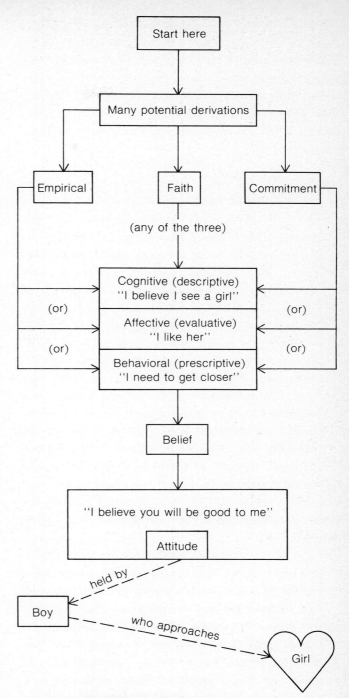

FIG. 6-1 *Analysis of a belief*
A belief can be derived empirically or by faith or can emerge as a commitment. Any of these derivations can become cognitive, affective, or behavioral, leading to an overall belief that dictates the appropriate action (attitude).

143

tudes and come to feel more confident in their own judgments of things. Even though we know nothing of the background of these students, the conditions they describe make their point. As you will see, some students stayed closer to parental thinking than others. The question this first student report raises is, "What sort of love did this mother have for her daughter?"

(Female)

As a child I had various physical illnesses. Because of this my parents spoiled me. My mother felt I was a burden to her and so, to make me feel loved, wanted, and healthy, she never said no. All through childhood and adolescence I was overindulged. I had many clothes, went on expensive vacations, had a car to use, and still no one said no. Now I am a woman very much in love with a young man. Contrary to my upbringing, he had to wait for everything he has ever wanted since he was ten. I am attempting to adjust to an adult relationship, but often find it hard, because, unlike my parents, Ron says no. I react with remarks like "You don't love me" and I pout just like a child. Behaving like this at twenty years is quite abnormal.

What would you do if you were the following girl's mother?

Six-year old girls have things set up just right when they are playing house and if a two-year old brother messes them up something has to be done. My solution was quite different than most girls'. I recalled an incident when my brother got so angry he bit me. Naturally, at that age I ran and told Mom, who sent my brother to his room to "think" about what he had done. From then on I correlated my brother's bite with getting rid of him, and it was the first thing I thought of when he messed up

my playhouse. Little brother was too young to do as I told him, so telling him to bite me wouldn't have worked; I had to bite myself. A six-year-old's jaw span is slightly wider than a two-year-old's, so I had to be careful not to open my mouth to its full extent when I bit myself to prevent Mom from finding out the truth. Mom never even questioned the teeth marks, and I was rid of my brother.

Can you see the "little boy" and "big man" identities moving back and forth in the following?

(Male)

The first I ever heard of drugs was my parents referring to heroin as dope. I really thought only slimy people did dope. Then I heard of marijuana when I was thirteen and I thought only wild people did that. When I was fifteen, I heard that a bunch of kids in our high school were smoking grass, and I was shocked and I thought they were real daring and wild. Then when I was sixteen my friends tried it, and I was appalled. I started preaching that it was wrong and that they shouldn't mess around with grass. Actually, I was just scared of a new thing, as usual. I said I had no desire to try it, that I was above it. I finally worked up the nerve to try grass and I really made it known that I had. I thought I was really cool for doing it, because only a relatively few of the kids in school smoked. This was my general attitude about smoking dope in high school. It was an ego trip.

Finally, a student goes from very strong parent-held values to very strong personal values, all in one summer! What power love hath.

(Female)

When I was in the sixth grade I saw a film against drugs. I was very impressionable and it really scared me. Although I was never in contact with any drugs, I was really upset that my folks even smoked cigarettes. This carried on to my junior year in high school. I never smoked a cigarette and I swore I'd never take any drugs. I didn't even associate with people that did anything with drugs.

That summer I met a young man whom I liked very much. He smoked grass but nothing else. This convinced me that smoking marijuana did not necessarily lead to heroin. I would let him smoke up around me but it took about a month to convince me to try it. From then on I smoke grass socially with my friends—it's no biggie.

Organized attempts to teach children virtue and morality have generally failed. Hartshorne and May's classic *Studies in Deceit* (1928) certainly supports this view. At times the harder adults try to make children good, the less successful they are. Verbal urging or discussing honesty may be helpful if it is done simply and with good timing, but the relying on verbal control to teach honesty, good citizenship, and so forth, may not often work. (Verbal control means the habit some parents have of browbeating the child verbally until she or he either acquiesces, turns the parent off, or strikes back.) Current thinking in psychotherapy today is that there are many roads that lead to town. If verbal control brings no results, try another—contingency management, for example. Contingency management is the behaviorists' term for setting up the environment so that desirable responses will come forth. Morris (1964) reports a common instance of the lack of control. He describes a mother (why is it always the mother?) who takes her son to the restaurant. The boy chews with his mouth open. She asks him to close his mouth while eating. He does for a while and then opens it again. She tells him to shut his mouth. This is an attempt at verbal control. He does, but it opens again. After a while there is screaming and wailing

and she leaves in tears. Sound familiar? Why did it build up so? In fact, the child had an allergy and his nose was plugged up, making it difficult to breathe. Why didn't Mom ask instead of tell? Why didn't Junior tell instead of sit there? We will never know.

Most law enforcers, parents, and other officials believe that they do what they do for good reasons. However, they often have as much trouble seeing our point of view as we do theirs. Also, at times we really want to believe others, although some part of us holds us back. Ulrich, Stachnik, and Stainton (1963) conducted an intriguing experiment using a psychology class of captive students. They asked the students to take some personality tests and then offered to return the results later. What the psychologists actually did was to disregard the personality test results completely and write up a standard statement they felt everyone would buy. It worked. About seventy-five percent of the students felt it was an accurate personal description of them. (Beware of psychologists. They sometimes play dirty.) Later, the students were let in on the experiment and were offered their individual interpretations. The standard description all students initially received is illustrated on the next page. Does it sound like your personality?

The context in which the test was given and returned, coupled with the need to believe, made believers of these students. The fact that the statements are general, vague, and contradictory leads us to believe the description applies to us while in fact it applies to everyone—and no one.

WHATEVER HAPPENED TO STUDENT UNREST AND THE GENERATION GAP?

Here is another example of the changing beliefs in authority from one decade to another. During the late 1960s a rash of literature appeared in popular magazines and professional journals on the topic of student activism. Many people became sudden "authorities" on the subject. (I should know; I was one.) Much of the writing tried to determine how student activists differed in background from the rest of the student body. Most studies showed student unrest to be more prevalent at the "better schools," such as Berkeley, Harvard, Columbia, and so forth. Studies indicated activists were more intelligent, more often came from "liberal" families, made better grades, and were more openminded. The older generation was shocked. Weren't these traditionally the "good guys"—the nonauthoritarians? Philip Slater (1970) summed up the differences in assumptions made by the stereotyped older and younger generations as follows:

> There are an almost infinite number of ways to differentiate between the old and new cultures. The old culture, when forced to choose, tends to give preference to property rights over personal rights, technological requirements over human needs, competition over cooperation, violence over sexuality, concentration over distribution, the producer over the consumer, means over ends, secrecy over openness, social reforms over personal expression, striving over gratification, Oedipal love over communal love, and so on. The new counterculture tends to reverse all of these priorities.

The old culture valued caution and denial of self-gratification. Things were in "good" or "poor" taste. An act or product that contained too much stimulus value was in poor taste since it might arouse some feeling that would go out of control. Things should be simple and in order. As Slater described it, "It is no accident that hostility to hippies so often focused on their olfactory humanity." The new culture is, nevertheless, a product of the old. Even the notion of dropping out has strong roots in American tradition, although the response of apathy is less related.

Speaking of Prejudice

Judging and evaluating others on the basis of some impersonal characteristic certainly reduces the ambiguity of having to think and decide our true

Everyone's Personality Description

You have a strong need for other people to like you and for them to admire you. You have a tendency to be critical of yourself. You have a great deal of unused capacity that you have not turned to your advantage. While you have some personality weaknesses, you are generally able to compensate for them. Your sexual adjustment has presented some problems for you. Disciplined and controlled on the outside, you tend to be worrisome and insecure inside. At times you have serious doubts as to whether you have made the right decision or done the right thing. You prefer a certain amount of change and variety and become dissatisfied when hemmed in by restrictions and limitations. You pride yourself as being an independent thinker and do not accept others' opinions without satisfactory proof. You have found it unwise to be too frank in revealing yourself to others. At times you are extroverted, affable, sociable, while at other times you are introverted, wary, and reserved. Some of your aspirations tend to be pretty unrealistic.

feelings about someone. We all subtly do it and deny it to our own consciences. A good example of how psychologists can fool themselves by their own biases is told by Paul Meehl (1971). Meehl, a respected clinical psychologist, tells the story of his becoming interested in the concept of punishment as a general deterrent to criminal behavior while studying and teaching in law school. His psychology colleagues were quite willing to put down legal punishment as "medieval subject matter." After all, it was outmoded and primitive to assume that punishment has any real effect on behavior. Meehl says,

> However, the same psychologist who says punishment doesn't deter relies on its deterrent effect in posting a sign in the departmental library stating that if a student removes a journal without permission, his privilege to use

the room will be suspended and his use fee not returned. This same psychologist suspends his children's TV privileges when they fight over which channel to watch; tells the truth on his income tax form (despite feeling that the government uses most of the money immorally and illegally) for fear of the legal consequences of lying; and drives his car well within the speed limit on a certain street, having been informed that the police have been conducting speed traps there.

There are many other examples of prejudice and inconsistency to choose from. For example, Klein (1972) reports a study in which fifteen adolescents with very clean driving records were cited thirty-three times (an average of over two times per person) in less than three weeks after Black Panther bumper stickers were affixed to their cars. (I've been toying with the idea of putting a "Support Your Local Police" sticker on my car.)

Prejudice stems initially from the attitudes and beliefs of our parents and family; then we get it from our peer groups and society at large. Continuing prejudice is reinforced by the "not-like-me" feeling, which is basically a type of personal-threat reaction. Teachers and counselors are often conditioned into thinking that children will more likely drop out of school if they're from a lower socioeconomic level or will do better if they're from a "better" class background. They pass their expectations on to the students, who often take this self-fulfilling prophecy to help validate the teacher's expectation! Think back on your own school career and you will probably think of times when you were encouraged or discouraged without real justification.

When it comes to racial prejudice an interesting phenomenon occurs. When a distinction is made between engaging socially with someone whose interests are similar or dissimilar to your own, people generally choose a person of either race who they feel has similar values and beliefs. But when the relationship comes close to family ties, such as

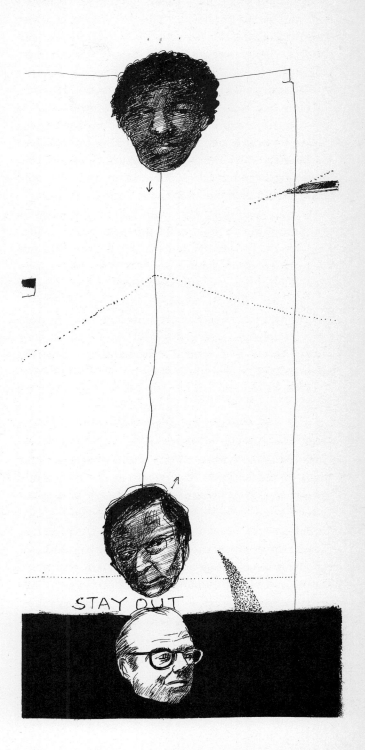

STAY OUT

the possibility that you will "date my sister" or that we will "live together," racial prejudice begins to overtake belief similarity. This is understandable, though problematic. It probably has its roots in the general threat we all feel in the "not-like-me" attitude.

Robert Coles is a remarkable man. He is a Harvard psychiatrist who has spent a great deal of time (perhaps more than any other person in our country) working with and writing about minorities. A student and friend of Erik Erikson, Coles got into psychiatry by default. He hated to stick needles into children and messed up the sutures in surgery. His teachers advised him to go into psychoanalysis to see if medicine was really the right field for him. As a result, he received his M.D. degree and left the practice of medicine to spend most of his time interviewing the poor, the migrant, and the down-trodden. In 1955 he worked with polio victims in Boston and noticed how often people who, to him, were obviously paralyzed for life would talk about getting better. The typical attitude among psychiatry or psychology in those days would have been to write these people off as operating their lives by denial, a defensive mechanism whereby the real facts of the situation are suppressed. However, Coles saw this sort of behavior as valuable in what it did for these people rather than in what it might mean to the outsider (the psychiatrist). It was this attitude and way of thinking about people that led Coles to the belief that most of the people we stereotype as misfits (sharecroppers, migrants, "poor folk" of either race) are remarkably healthy of mind and courageous of spirit. They are also more generous. Coles's theme is "antistereotype." What he is really telling us without saying it in so many words is something we already know but often forget. The more you get to know a person, the less you can think of him or her as a stereotype.

Religious Belief

Take Christ, for instance, or Satguru Maharaj Ji,

the Perfect Master, or any number of religious leaders. Those who have known these men personally and intimately tell us to believe that they can not be written off in categorical terms. True believers, like true lovers anywhere, *do* see a different person than we can see until we are within their system of beliefs. In the words of that old favorite gospel tune:

> Amazing grace, how sweet the sound
> That saved a wretch like me,
> I once was lost, but now I'm found,
> Was blind, but now I see.

The following testimonial of Peter is an example of what can happen to a regular "Joe College." One of the great mysteries of our time is the question of how someone like Peter comes to totally immerse himself in a belief system while someone else under similar life circumstances will take a course of exactly opposite action.

Peter Finds Christ*

He's a Real Nowhere Man . . . the Beatles really put into words what my life was like. After graduating from college I went to the Far East for a year of study and relaxation. That was nowhere for me. I came home in five weeks. Next, I got a job. It was a job in business. I knew that was not the answer. At the first opportunity I applied and was accepted at graduate school here in business. My thought was that during this two-year program I might continue my search, delay any major decisions in my life, and study others to see the most meaningful pursuit of life for them and if it would help me in my life.

I found what I need! I found something that fulfills and sustains me. This something has a perfect code of conduct for me. What is this answer to my needs? Quite simply it is a personal relationship with Jesus Christ, the only Son of God.

My relationship with Christ is different from anyone else's. That is because each person is a unique individual with different needs that Christ fulfills. It is surprising to see the wide variety of people in the body of Christ, yet they are compatible because of the common belief that Christ is their personal Lord. Of course, the freedom that Christ gives believers is total, if one is a slave to Him.

My problems were booze, and occasionally dope, heterosexual relations premaritally, and my ego. Let me first tackle alcohol. I was not an alcoholic by any means. The plain simple truth was that I was a weekend drunkard. Friday and Saturday nights I was never home (unless I had a visitor and I was getting her smashed). It was not the fact that I was never home that

_____
*In 1970 a student (whom we shall call Peter) asked me if he could set down in writing what the guiding belief of his life was and how it came to be.

bothered me. Rather, it was the feeling of adventure that arose in me Friday afternoons. By early Saturday morning I would be staggering home, only to do the same thing Saturday night. This perplexed me because this adventurous feeling normally changed to emptiness very early in the evening. This emptiness would occur in mixed company or with the guys. I never drank alone. My feeling of emptiness was, I believe, the catalytic agent which increased my rate of alcoholic consumption. What was it I needed? I saw the problem but what could I do about it?

Secondly, there were girls. Now do not get the wrong idea. I enjoyed sexual intercourse and the physical closeness. The area that disturbed me was my *attitude* toward girls. Women were merely objects. I could care less about their heads; I wanted their bodies. I always made it a point to refrain from saying things that were not true. I would not use "lines" because I felt it would attach them to me (making for a painful separation) or I would hate myself for the lies. Only once did I force myself on a girl—I was not happy about that either. Thus, though I knew many guys who felt like I did concerning girls, I was not happy about my relationship (outside of the sexual indulgence) with girls. How could I get into their heads and still dig on their bodies?

My last major problem was my ego. Most people who knew me considered me stable. I think most of the time this was true, but there were times when I was disappointed in my ego eruptions. These eruptions were not, to my knowledge, obnoxious bragging statements. Rather, I would call them "casting for a compliment." This disturbed me because I should not need ego building. I was already aware of some of my strengths, though I was not aware of my weaknesses.

I should have known that loneliness was

what was bugging me, but I thank God I accepted Christ as my Saviour before figuring my own way out of the loneliness I felt. Christ has done a major overhaul in my life, not only in the three areas I have presented, but also in many other areas. I have made no conscious effort at solving these problems. All I have done is listen to Christ in my heart. His results are impressive.

Similar impressive results occur from Yoga, Zen, meditation, and various other approaches. There are, reportedly (Steiner 1973) three times as many professional astrologers in the United States as there are physicists and chemists. Are people like Peter totally "flipped out"? Is there any reason you can give for religious belief? Or for belief in one point of view, like astrology? Is there any way to disprove the value of this approach? Why would you want to?

Religious belief serves three distinct functions, or needs. The *personal* function helps people cure disease, secure food, and receive comfort when a crisis hits; it offers guidelines for personal action, often through prayer. Second is the *divine* function, which satisfies our yearning to relate to some force or knowledge outside of us that may have the answers to unanswerable questions and may have the grace to deliver us. The third function is *social* in nature; from it has evolved a code of ethics and a system of morals. During this century there has been an increasingly discernible shift in the emphasis of religion from the divine to the social and personal. This indicates that as the public and political environment shifts (in our case toward increased technology and lack of concern for people), religion attempts to provide a balance for the totality of the human enterprise. It is very hard to write on this topic without taking sides and blowing my credibility as a portrayer of alternatives. But people, including writers, "go blind" very quickly when it comes to religion and politics. Everyone

tends to become a little more dogmatic—and some *quite* a little more—when discussing these subjects. So I will try to be done with some of that need by quoting William James (1915), an early American philosopher and psychologist, who says it the way I would like to have said it:

> The individual's religion may be egotistic, and those private realities which it keeps in touch with may be narrow enough; but at any rate it always remains infinitely less hollow and abstract, as far as it goes, than a science which prides itself on taking no account of anything private at all.

It's a matter of where to put your faith, and that is not open to logical scrutiny.

H. G. MacPherson, a physicist, attempted (1969) to examine science and what it has taught us as a means of uncovering what the basis for religion may be. Science, he claims, has taught us to doubt whatever can't be proved through the senses. If a scientist prays, it is not with an expectation of physical intervention, but as a personally therapeutic act. Scientists have great conflicts with such concepts as heaven, hell, and the origin of life because either such areas have not been explored or science has too little data to measure them. MacPherson concedes that science can probably never answer the problem of infinite regress—the process of discovering what began the beginning of the universe. The scientist is also stumped as to why the laws of nature are as they are and are not otherwise.

Conscious awareness is another topic that is beyond the realm of science. Science can deal with the setting in which awareness exists. It can even manipulate it, by manipulating the environment. But the quality of and reason for awareness is a mystery as yet unresolved, if indeed it can ever be. The enjoyment of a "good" symphony or a poem is an example.

A botanist by the name of Arndt (1964) solved some of the problem of what it means to have re-

ligious belief by throwing out theology and defining religion as a "commitment to the highest ideal of the good life for all." This begs the question of whether this good life for all can be atheistic. He assumes it can. Many more points of view could be brought up at this juncture, and we could easily work up a frenzy of frustration over the simple fact that religious belief is a matter of faith and any real attempt to analyze it is doomed to fail.

Finally, Rokeach (1965) brings us back to the point of view of the social scientist who accepts as a fundamental paradox that religious people often have learned little in terms of their manifest behavior from their religion. In fact Rokeach offers evidence that on the average, churchgoers (who may be distinguishable from religious people) have more prejudices than nonchurchgoers. (Of course churchgoing is a very broad category and these figures did not include the church of Satan.) One of the more

interesting findings from Rokeach's studies is the ranking that goes on among the believers. Ask a group of Catholics to rank the other denominations in terms of similarity to their beliefs and the list will very likely go in this order: Episcopalian, Lutheran, Presbyterian, Methodist, Baptist. A Baptist may simply reverse the order, while a Presbyterian's ranking may be quite different. Probably the most intriguing question from the psychologist's point of view is how to separate the religious inputs or influences (the independent variables), from wherever they may come, from the behavior (dependent variables) of religious people.

The Changing Beliefs of One Bright Student

Andrea was referred to me by her counselor while a high school student and I have kept in contact with her through the years. I have come to change my beliefs about her and she hers about the world. Let me first of all reprint the letter I first sent to her counselor, which shows my attitudes toward Andrea at that time. (By the way, this letter tells you as much about me as it does about Andrea.)

Confidential

Dear _____:

This is to report that a referral by you for the purpose of psychological consultation was seen by me for interviews and testing on four separate dates from _____ to _____.

The psychological picture this student presented to me was contradictory and, therefore, extremely difficult to diagnose. While describing herself to be in excellent physical health and doing satisfactory academic work, there are numerous references to her personal and social existence that indicate withdrawal to fantasy and an inability to relate to others, particularly to peers.

Miss _____ presents herself as attractive and well groomed, but mousy and austere in manner. She has read widely in

BELIEF AND DEFENSE

psychology and enjoys labeling herself in an attempt to shock and impress the interviewer. She feels that many of the most bizarre symptoms found in books on abnormal psychology pertain to her. She is a great intellectualizer and hides most of her feelings behind this facade of esoteric terminology. It appeared to be exciting to her to be able to talk confidentially with a psychologist, and my relationship with her very likely provided her fantasy life with ill-founded feelings of importance. In short, she craves attention from accepting adult models and will talk and react in ways to capture the attention of adults. She asked me if I would be her counselor when she comes to the university. I said I would.

She describes her own family life as intolerable. Since she appears unable to relate to either parent well, especially her father, she adds nothing to the integrity of the family. She describes her typical day as one of going to school from 6 A.M. to noon, then going home and staying in her room playing records, writing poetry, and studying. She has no close friends but receives phone calls from one or two acquaintances occasionally. She seldom, if ever, initiates any relationship. She feels there is no one in the family who loves her or cares about her. She states that her parents argue often and loudly and at times she says her father would use his belt on her. Her mother is described as very emotional. These parent models are an important cue, I feel, as to why she has suppressed her own feelings and affect. She likes things at home to be quiet and peaceful and has insured this state, to some extent, by retreating to her own room and to satisfying fantasies. She is very anxious to leave home permanently when she graduates from high school. She has intuitively chosen a college major, archeology, that has

the psychological advantage of keeping her from close interpersonal relations.

Psychological testing revealed a great deal of information, but all of it indirect. Here again it was not clear to what extent the tests were being used by Andrea to convince herself or the interviewer that she is unstable. The F scale on the MMPI was extremely high, rendering the rest of the test invalid. The F scale is either a measure of carelessness in taking the exam or a cry for help by divulging more symptomatology than is likely to exist. I suspect the latter. Certain cards from the TAT were administered and almost without exception they pictured people in situations where they become insane, suicidal, or alienated from others. The one card she refused to talk about concerned a boy-girl situation with apparent sexual overtones. It is of interest here that in a previous interview she stated that she would never marry and plans to always remain a virgin. I see this as another example of her tendency to turn resentment and hostility inward, presenting us with a cold and detached personality picture that helps her from becoming involved with others.

On the surface Andrea portrays the syndrome of incipient simple schizophrenia but the fact that she is doing adequate work in school, has no somatic symptomatology, and does relate to others and the outside world, albeit on her own terms, connotes a more schizoid character at the present time. While she describes that on occasion she hears voices, they are not voices that request any action on her part, and while she describes at times that her soul leaves her body and appears in some other form (she claims belief in astrology and reincarnation) these seem to all take place at night while going to sleep and may be an attempt on her part to seek attention. However, Andrea is at a point in life where these states of mind should be periodically evaluated since she may firm up a more schizoid or a more psychotic disposition if she is subjected to trauma. If grades start to slip, or if eating and sleeping habits begin to change, someone should be in a position of noticing these facts and reevaluating her situation. College, and living away from home, should be stabilizing forces for Andrea. Since she is channeling many of her anxieties into achievement modes (poetry, archeology) she may find like-minded peers in these areas at college that are not readily available in high school. However, it is unlikely that Andrea will ever be completely "normal" as we usually think of the word, even with extensive therapy or counseling.

The above remarks are based on a small sample of interviews and tests and should be viewed as a tentative appraisal. If I may be of further help, please feel free to call on me.

Sincerely,

Robert L. Wrenn, Ph.D.
Counseling Psychologist

After one year of college in which her grades were excellent but friendships and personal relations were a little uneasy, Andrea fell in with a group of Jesus freaks. That fall I got a letter from her indicating she was in the process of finding herself. In this letter she says, "I'm in _____ now, living for Christ. I'm very happy because for once, I know who I am. There is so much love to be found amongst my spiritual brothers and sisters. They would be willing to lay down their lives for me and I for them."

This attitude contrasts markedly, of course, from what it was a year ago when she would hide away in her room with agonizing thoughts that "no one cares."

To make a long story short, her missionary plans never materialized. Andrea went on to a small college in the East and visited and wrote me from time to time. I could see the old rigidity and dogmatic thinking loosening as each year went by. Andrea graduated from college and married (recall that in high school she vowed to remain a virgin forever) and now has plans for graduate study in psychology.

The changes in attitudes and in behavior that occurred in Andrea over the short period of five years that I knew her are too numerous to detail here. Were you to have met Andrea in high school, to see her today you would wonder what kind of strong interventions could possibly have changed a person so in such a short time. We might even have hesitated or advised against her getting mixed up with a bunch of wild-eyed Jesus freaks as being of little value for anyone even in her right mind. As it turns out, they were probably a potent force for good in her life. Andrea is, in my opinion, not unlike many college students who find these particular years of their life chaotic, off balance, and full of jumps, swings, and recurring self-doubts in their beliefs and attitudes. It is impressive how much change can take place at the ripe old age of nineteen or even twenty.

The Dynamics of Defending Beliefs

Up to this point we have discussed beliefs as they develop, change, and mature. For the rest of the chapter we will look at the ways beliefs can come into conflict, how we may defend or maintain beliefs, and some strategies for changing them.

WHEN BELIEFS CONFLICT

Solomon Asch is one of a number of social psychologists who has given us a great deal of evidence, perhaps more than we need, to indicate the way the group "helps" us to resolve conflicts of belief through group pressure. The general experimental design for showing the influence others have on us

and found an old truck and we thought it might be abandoned. The gas tank was dry and there were spider webs in the cab, but everything else was intact. All of a sudden one guy threw a rock at the windshield and cracked it and then we all went crazy. We threw bricks through all of the windows, we dented in the doors and the roof of the cab, and ripped the hood off and pulled wires out of the engine. The strange thing was the spirit that prevailed—the feelings and expressions that seemed really strange. It was the first and last time that anyone of us had committed such a strong act of vandalism.

It is unlikely that any one of these students would have done so alone.

What sorts of belief conflicts did the returning veteran from Vietnam have to deal with? Some of their common conflicts centered on questions such as "Who can I trust?", "Why can't I forget?", "Why the recurring guilt?" Some tried to keep active so they wouldn't remember; others drowned their sorrows. Some just ended it all. The continuing conflicts—the shame and guilt of being alive—may take years to resolve. Shatan (1973) writes rather convincingly on this subject and quotes a colleague to say:

> When society hails warriors as heroes, they receive absolution from a grateful nation for the necessary killings and the atrocities committed by them. But today's veterans return unheralded and unwanted to an ambivalent nation.

The nation was responsible for getting these soldiers into battle, but who is to help them get out of it mentally? Hopefully, it may eventually become clear to the government that the responsibility of helping these veterans resolve their conflicts goes beyond any program the Veterans Administration might initiate and affects us all, sooner or later.

DEFENDING OURSELVES IN CONFLICT

You can think of many more examples of how conflicts in belief occur. But how is it that people find

is to prepare a group of stooges who act as if they believe one way while one real subject wrestles with what she or he really believes. Asch (1955) asked students to judge which of several standard lines were relatively longer or shorter. About a third of the subjects believed in what the stooges said (which was false) and disbelieved their own eyes. They may even have begun to *see* the shorter line as longer after a while. Reality is elusive.

A more realistic example outside the laboratory is given by the following student.*

> Three years ago I spent five days in a cabin by a river with four of my friends. We had no adult supervision and the closest cabin was a mile away, so we were pretty much on our own. On the third day we were there, we went exploring

---

*The student was attempting to describe a time in his life when he felt he was behaving abnormally. He recalled that this incident made no sense to him at the time.

it so difficult to change their attitudes and beliefs? How do people defend points of view that to us seem untenable?

One explanation is given by the Soviet scientist E. N. Sokolov in terms of his orientation response model (Toffler 1970). He suggests that new, incoming stimuli try to match up with existing information stored in our brain cells. Novel information coming to us sets up a confusion, disbelief, or orientation response. If the information matches with previously stored information, the cortex activates our reticular system (consciousness) with instructions that "all is well." Perhaps in this mechanism there is some survival value that may even carry over to the area of thinking and believing.

Aronson (1973) makes it very clear that we deceive ourselves continually and that one purpose of this is to keep our thinking system in comfort and to reduce tension. A classic example of such behavior is told in a book by Leon Festinger, et al., entitled *When Prophecy Fails*. A woman claimed to have received word from the planet Clarion that her city would be destroyed by a flood on December 21. Soon a small group of believers began to gather and isolate themselves from the rest of the world. These believers got the word that a spaceship from Clarion would descend and save them from destruction at midnight on December 21. Midnight arrived and no ship appeared. At first they felt despair and embarrassment—perhaps confusion is a better term. Then the prophet had a new vision: "The city has been spared because of the trust and faith of you who believed." Tension was gone, everyone felt better, and the believers turned into zealots. Festinger's theory of cognitive dissonance describes this process as one in which the two inconsistent ideas or beliefs were working their way toward conflict-free resolution. In other words, the conflict of ideas that the world would end and that the spaceship had not arrived was resolved by a new idea that these two seemingly conflicting ideas were really compatible after all. In the same way, a heavy

smoker tapers down, quits smoking, or talks about "enjoying life while you can." The conflict and tension cannot exist for long. One author believes that a way out for some of us when threatened is to seek an authority to believe in, regardless of what that authority may have to say (Sales 1972). This might go some distance in explaining how a Hitler can command such obedience at times when a country is definitely under threat for survival.

A more current example of the strength of faith and the appeal to authority occurred in Barstow, California in August 1973, and hit newspapers all over the country. Lawrence and Alice Parker took their son to a faith healer in their Assembly of God church. The eleven-year-old boy had diabetes. The parents believed the faith healer cured him through God's help, and they took away his insulin. Four days later the boy died. Were they remorseful? No, they were simply waiting for the boy to be resurrected from the dead "whole and without disease," as God had promised them. The father was disappointed that his son didn't rise at Sunday services but was satisfied that, "God is letting it go this far so He can receive the most glory from this when Wesley comes back." Like the lady who expected the spaceship, the next step is either to believe that they do see their son rise from the dead (although there will likely be no witnesses) or to believe that God has more special plans for him. The last thing they will believe is that God has failed them. Meanwhile the district attorney's office is reviewing the case for possible criminal action.

Most of us could be described (although probably inaccurately) as one sort of person or another. To type someone is to lose her or him for the sake of convenience and efficiency. Such a variety of types come to mind—"He's a loner," "She's a go-getter," "He rubs people the wrong way," "She's cute," "He's plastic," and on and on, ad nauseum. Carl Jung and Karen Horney, to name just two, have developed much of their theories about people in relation to types. Although this is not a discourse on typologies, we do have tendencies as authors to think along the dimensions of object-subject, active-passive, inner-outer, and so forth. This is a kind of type-like thinking and one that presumably is unavoidable if descriptions are to be made at all.

Types can also be regarded as defenses against threat. The cynic, the optimist, the "yes" person, the manipulator, all accent a certain mode that we engage in from time to time. For example, defensive postures often take place in organizations. A "good" administrator has a remarkable talent for staying out of trouble. He or she may "go by the book" so that all situations will be covered and any possible blame can be directed back to "the manual, on page fifteen, says. . . ." The executive may also be adept at credit grabbing or may organize everything so tightly that there is little margin for error. There may be a complete lack of creative and artistic talent displayed as a result of these defenses. Such defenses are not necessarily "bad" (although they may be bad for the company); there are ways of reaching the prescribed goal of success with one's company or with one's ego. One author, in what I would consider a cynical vein, gives us ten strategies for avoiding any autonomous decision making whatsoever. (Kaufmann 1973). The decidophobe who fears making decisions can use these strategies.

1. Taking up religion
2. Following the status quo
3. Forming an allegiance to a movement
4. Forming an allegiance to a school of thought
5. Reading your own meaning into what an authority says (exegetical thinking)
6. Choosing between black and white alternatives (Manichaeanism)
7. Assuming logic will dictate values (moral rationalism)
8. Being absorbed in minute distinctions (pedantry)
9. Having faith in the future
10. Taking up marriage

Sally Felker, a college counselor, has similarly offered professional counselors a number of things they can say when they don't know what they're doing (1972). For example, when asked a question, the counselor may respond, "What do *you* think the answer is?" thereby getting off the hook. Alternatives to this are, "I see you have devoted a lot of thought to this issue. Let me get your views first," or, "I've spent a good deal of time thinking about that question; let's see if your opinions are similar to mine." Another situation Felker presents is that of when the counselor's mind has wandered or when he or she has been dozing off and suddenly the student asks, "And what do you think of that idea?" Of course the counselor never heard the idea, so a good defense is to say, "I'm not sure I'm clear on what you've said" or, "You've really covered it quite well; I have nothing to add." As a counselor, the idea of admitting that your knowledge is limited or that you just fell asleep would probably not allow you to remain comfortable with your ego. It would certainly help your counseling, however. I've even heard some of these defenses in class after putting someone to sleep with my lecture.

FREUD'S CLASSIC MECHANISMS OF DEFENSE

Late in life, Sigmund Freud and afterwards his daughter Anna defined and refined some of the better known and more commonly understood ego defense mechanisms. Freud's underlying philosophy was that much of our time is spent in defense of our precious egos and that anything that would cast us in a poor light should and would be denied or blocked from our consciousnesses by defensive maneuvers. George Mahl (1971) has discussed these points quite extensively in his book on the subject. Since it is not our purpose here to reward Freud unduly for his ability to distinguish the various psychological defenses, a summation of the basic defenses, their purposes, and a brief example of each is provided in table 6.1.

Finally, a lot of impulses never become routine

TABLE 6.1
Freud's Defense Mechanisms

Defense	Description	Example
Denial	By withdrawing our attention from painful or potentially annoying stimuli we can avoid, by denial, the problem of having to cope with a difficult issue.	A woman goes to a party with her steady. He ignores her and takes up with another woman. She drinks and smokes more than usual. When he drops her off at the end of the evening she says she had a very nice time—and means it.
Identification	Losing ourselves in the personality of someone else can be another form of escape.	A man grows a beard, right after his father dies. He believes he is doing it just for kicks. As it later turns out he had been deeply moved during the last days of his father's life to see his beardless father develop a set of whiskers.
Ego restriction	When a person gives up on something before really giving it a good try it can be a form of ego restriction.	Sally makes excellent grades in college. She spends so much time studying she has little time for men. As the years go on she becomes more and more convinced that the academic life is for her, and the hell with men.
Repression	The most common of all the defenses, repression is evidenced in forgetting important names and events or in not reacting when a situation requires a certain response.	Harold is sitting in church. During a prayer the thought of a girlfriend doing obscene things to him occurs but is quickly replaced with thoughts of home and work. Had the original thought lingered to the point of arousing Harold, he may have made an attempt to deliberately change the content of his thought. This more controlled effort is called *suppression*.
Projection	Attributing your thoughts, feelings, and motives to others are forms of projection	Pete likes to climb mountains and finds John has a similar interest. One night as they are camping out John stands up in front of the campfire, reaches inside his pants, scratches his groin, and smiles at Pete. Pete takes this as a homosexual come-on—when in fact John just itched and, being embarrassed, smiled.
Reaction formation	Guarding against a strong feeling being exposed is sometimes put in check by acting opposite to the way you feel.	A young person who has become quite bitter and cynical about people is sweet and admiring of others when with them socially. The horny minister who lectures excessively on the evils of sex is another example.
Negation	Expressing a repressed thought in its negative form makes it more palatable to our consciousness.	Someone shouts, "Who's angry? I'm not angry."
Isolation	Separating feeling from thought or thought from feeling makes reality less painful.	Tom is talking with Carl when suddenly he thinks of breaking Carl's arm. The thought flashes in and out of Tom's mind but he does nothing because he feels nothing.

TABLE 6.1   (cont'd)

Defense	Description	Example
Intellectualization	Intellectualization is a form of isolation that places an exaggerated emphasis on thought.	Mary has just witnessed a gory automobile accident and a few minutes later is describing it to a friend in a highly abstract logical manner. Also, people who come for counseling and then lecture to the counselor about all they've read about their problem are intellectualizing.
Undoing	If you've hurt someone's feelings or have gone farther emotionally than you feel comfortable going, you may find yourself trying to "undo" by making up to the person or becoming more aloof.	Bob, in a moment of rage, slaps his girlfriend across the face. They are both dumbfounded. He then spends the next week making up to her with assurances, presents, and a very agreeing personality.
Rationalization	Rationalization basically consists of thinking up good reasons for going dumb things.	Jim has a big chemistry exam tomorrow. Some of the guys stop by and say, "How about going out for a beer?" Jim decides he'll probably do O.K. on the exam and leaves with the guys.
Regression	Slipping back into old familiar, secure, and less mature forms of behavior are forms of regression.	In the extreme, temper tantrums, thumb sucking, bedwetting, and doll playing are examples. More normally, college students away from home for the first prolonged period of time learn to shift for themselves and develop maturity. The temptation when at home for Christmas vacation is to sit back and let Mom do all the work. That's regressive.
Sublimation and Compensation	These are often called "normal" defenses in that whatever the original need or motive that is being channeled, the result is recognized by society as constructive and good.	Examples of sublimation include the sadistic-oriented young person who cut off the tails of dogs as a child but later becomes a surgeon—or the person who, deprived of a family, becomes a loving, doting teacher of other people's children. An example of compensating for a weakness by outdoing oneself comes from a college student who told me that at fourteen he was just under five feet tall and had a speech defect caused by the loss of the tip of his tongue. He excelled at athletics by going out for all sports and practicing constantly. As he grew taller he felt even more normal; eventually the speech defect cleared up. He learned it was not caused by the loss of the tip of his tongue.

BELIEF AND DEFENSE

to the extent of requiring a defense because they are momentary and are worked out before they ever appear in our behavior. We are often testing limits in our heads, which may seem crazy at the time but is usually a way of coming to terms with the consequences of reality. Some examples follow; they are taken from anonymous reports from students who felt these were times in their lives when they were acting abnormally.

> Although I have never done it—sometimes, while I'm driving along a curving road I wonder as I approach a curve what would really happen if I didn't turn the wheel with the road and just went straight.

> The time I felt I was acting abnormally was one day when I was in the kitchen with my mother and I was holding a letter opener which is shaped like a knife. I wanted to see what it would be like to stab her with it, or possibly kill her. If I had been mad at her or disliked her for some reason the action might be understood, but she had done nothing to make me angry and I have always been extremely close to her. Because I can find no reason for even wanting to have done this, I feel I was acting in an abnormal manner.

> One night when I was still in high school, when everyone in the house was asleep, when my mother had gotten drunk as usual, I went to the kitchen to get something to eat. On my way, I passed through the front room, where my mother had fallen asleep watching TV. The cigarette she had been smoking had fallen onto the chair's cushion and burnt a hole. The fire had just started to spread to the chair's arm and her dress. For a moment I wanted her to be burned completely, but I didn't have the stomach for it; afterwards I wished that I did have the guts to let her burn.

> One evening while studying in my dorm room I was overcome with all of the frustrations that had been building up inside me. Instead of repressing my feelings, I became obsessed with the idea that I would feel better if I went outside and screamed—as loud as I could—and I did. It worked fantastically!

CHANGING OUR ATTITUDES AND BELIEFS

In discussing strategies of attitude change under normal conditions, Bandura (1969) offers three general approaches. The first he calls *belief-oriented* because it relies on the person's being exposed to new information through persuasion. If the "seller" is believable or respected, the message becomes more acceptable. The success of such communications relies mainly on becoming convinced of various rewarding or punishing consequences. For example, a certain hair preparation will make you irresistible to the opposite sex ("Just a little dab will do ya") while at the same time, "Only you can prevent forest fires." This, concludes Bandura, is a rather weak procedure for changing attitudes. It's amazing how much of our time as parents or teachers is spent on this approach.

Another approach is called *affect-oriented* because it attempts to change people's beliefs or attitudes by associating positive- or negative-arousing cues with the object of the attitude. For example, the ad with the voluptuous woman draped over the new car is meant to persuade via sexual arousal. Bandura argues that one aspect of this form of attitude change, which he calls *modeling*, can be quite effective. The modeling procedure is one in which a respected person teaches you what attitudes to hold by demonstrating what he or she believes. For example, an effective teacher can change attitudes by presenting himself as a model students may want to emulate.

Finally, the approach that Bandura lists last and feels is most efficient he terms *behavior-oriented*. This approach manipulates behavior more directly. Skillful management of incentives and use of a person's present behavior (rather than his thoughts or beliefs) to achieve modifications are the techniques of the behavior-oriented approach. An example is altering a person's smoking behavior by manipulating the consequences of smoking rather than by persuading him or her of the evils of smoking. Once the person stopped smoking, a change in attitude toward it would be expected.

Chapter Six Summary

Beliefs, attitudes, opinions, and faith are difficult to distinguish among. Sometimes such predispositions toward action are based on hard fact; more likely they are not. Children develop ideas about authority and power that they generalize in terms of such institutions as politics or the church. For most of us the tendency to be authoritarian is heavily tempered by the situation we are in. Organized attempts to teach morality by telling children what is right and wrong have generally failed. Demonstrating what is virtuous by introducing believable models works better.

Each generation creates its own set of beliefs partially rooted in those of the past and partially in the hopes of the next generation. An antistereotype process develops as one becomes more exposed to the person whose beliefs are questioned. Religious beliefs serve personal, spiritual, and social functions in our culture and are based on unarguable faith. We have many ways of defending beliefs that we cherish.

Glossary

A priori Drawn from principles regarded as self-evident and assumed to be true.

Delusion A belief that is not shared by others. For example: A man is walking about Times Square, snapping his fingers continuously. Another fellow notices this strange behavior and asks him why. "It's to keep the lions away," he says. "But there are no lions here," insists the questioner. "You see," says the first man, "it works." The first man has a delusion.

Dependent variable The behavior or effect one is looking for in an experiment. For example, in a test of whether smokers can quit, the number of smokers who quit is the dependent variable.

Faith Belief in something that cannot be proven empirically. For example: Two nuns were driving along the road when their car ran out of gas. The younger of the two decided to hike back the mile to a gas station they had just passed. To save time from returning to the gas station, they looked around the car for a receptacle and found a beat-up old porcelain urinal in the trunk. The nun walked to the station, had the urinal filled with gas, and returned to the car. A truck driver happened along, and priding himself on being a good Catholic, stopped to assist the two nuns. When he saw what they were doing, he exclaimed, "Boy, that's what I call faith."

Independent variable The treatment or manipulation made by the experimenter in an experiment. For example, in a test of whether smokers can quit, the treatment designed to make them give up smoking is the independent variable.

Exercises *(for individual and class use)*

You can do the following exercises and tasks at your leisure. Perhaps some of these would be more enjoyable with a friend. Those with an asterisk (*) should be done in consultation with your teacher or in class.

1. Four men were on a boat in shark-infested waters. Pete was washed overboard. Jim prepared to jump in to save him, but Bob and Frank restrained him saying, "One dead man is enough; you'll never make it." They all agreed the chances appeared to be fifty-fifty for anyone to emerge alive in those waters. Jim suddenly tore himself away, jumped in, and successfully rescued Pete. Which do you believe was the more moral decision?

2. Have some fun in a small group (and learn something about your own prejudices). The following exercise was developed by Dr. Richard Bear, University of Northern Colorado.

Who Should Survive? (a group project)

The following fifteen persons are in a bomb shelter after an atomic attack. They are the only humans left alive on the earth. It will take two weeks for the external radiation level to drop to a safe survival level. The food and supplies in the shelter can barely sustain seven persons for two weeks. In brief, only seven persons can survive. It is the task of your group to decide the seven persons who will survive. The group decision must not only be a consensus but also must be unanimous.

1. Dr. Dana—39, white, no religious affiliation. Ph.D. in history, college professor; good health. Married, one child (Bobby). Active and enjoys politics.
2. Mrs. Dana—38, white, Jewish. M.A. in psychology, counselor in mental health clinic; good health. Married, one child (Bobby). Active in community.
3. Bobby Dana—10, white, Jewish. Has attended special education classes for four years. Mentally retarded, IQ 70. Good health; enjoys pets.
4. Mrs. Garcia—33, Spanish-American, Roman Catholic. Sixth-grade education, cocktail waitress, prostitute; good health. Married at 16, divorced at 18, abandoned as a child, in foster home as a youth. Attacked by foster father at age 12, ran away from home, returned to reformatory, stayed till 16. One child, 3 weeks old (Jean).
5. Jean Garcia—3 weeks old, Spanish-American, good health, a nursing infant.
6. Mrs. Evans—32, black, protestant. M.A. in elementary education, teacher; good health. Divorced, one child (Mary). Cited as outstanding teacher; enjoys working with children.
7. Mary Evans—8, black, protestant, third grade. Good health; excellent student.
8. John Jacobs—13, white, protestant, eighth grade, honor student, very active—broad interests; good health. Father is Baptist minister.
9. Mr. Newton—25, black, claims to be an atheist, started last year of medical school but was suspended; good health. Homosexual activity, seems bitter concerning racial problems, wears hippie clothes.
10. Mrs. Clark—28, black, protestant. College graduate, engineering, electronics engineer; good health. Married, no children. Enjoys outdoor sports and stereo equipment, grew up in ghetto.

11. Sister Mary Kathleen—27, white, nun, college graduate, English major; good health. Grew up in upper-middle-class neighborhood, father a businessman.

12. Mr. Blake—51, white, Mormon, high school graduate, mechanic; good health. Married, four children (not with him), enjoys outdoors and working in his shops.

13. Miss Takigawa—21, Japanese, protestant. College senior, nursing major; good health. Enjoys outdoor sports, likes people.

14. Father Franz—37, white, Catholic, college plus seminary; priest, active in civil rights, criticized for liberal voice; good health. Former college athlete.

15. Dr. Gonzales—66, Spanish-American, Catholic, medical doctor, general practitioner. Has had two heart attacks in past five years, but continues to practice.

3.* Jot down a few of the things you believe are really important to you on slips of paper. Don't include people's names, but write down the relationship, such as, "My dog" or "My father." If you are in a small group, toss these all together and have someone redistribute them so that each of you receives someone else's (if you get your own back, don't say anything until later). Then read the slips one by one while the group tries to guess who they belong to.

4. Write a paragraph or two describing your feelings on one of the following topics:

    a. Free love
    b. Abortion
    c. Capital punishment
    d. ESP

Now that you have written your statement, decide to what extent your beliefs were grounded in empirical fact, faith, or personal commitment to a standard.

5. What defense mechanism do you use most? Why?

Bibliography

Adorno, T., et al. 1950. The *authoritarian personality*. New York: Harper.

Arndt, C. 1964. A biological concept of religion. *The Humanist*. 5:135–38.

Aronson, E. 1973. The rationalizing animal. *Psychology Today* (May).

Asch, S. 1955. Opinions and social pressure. *Scientific American* (November).

Bandura, A. 1969. *Principles of behavior modification*. New York: Holt, Rinehart & Winston.

Bem, D. 1970. *Beliefs, attitudes, and human affairs*. Belmont, Calif.: Brooks/Cole.

Feigl, Herbert. 1969. Ethics, religion, and scientific humanism. In Kurtz, P., ed. *Moral problems in contemporary society*. Englewood Cliffs, N. J.: Prentice-Hall.

Felker, S. 1972. How to feel comfortable when you don't know what you're doing. *Personnel and Guidance Journal* 50:683–86.

Festinger, L., Riecken, H., and Schachter, S. 1956. *When prophecy fails*. Minneapolis: University of Minnesota Press.

Hartshorne, H. and May, M. 1928. *Studies in the nature of character. I. Studies in deceit*. New York: Macmillan.

Hess, R. and Torney, J. 1967. *The development of political attitudes in children*. New York: Aldine.

Ianni, F. 1967. *Culture, system, and behavior*. Chicago: Science Research Associates.

James, W. 1915. *The varieties of religious experience: a study of human nature*. New York: McKay.

Kaufmann, W. 1973. *Without guilt and justice: from decidophobia to autonomy*. New York: Wyden.

Klein, D. 1972. Adolescent driving as deviant behavior. *Journal of Safety Research*, 4:98–105.

MacPherson, H. 1969. What would a scientific religion be like? *Saturday Review* (August 2).

Mahl, G. 1971. *Psychological conflict and defense*. New York: Harcourt Brace Jovanovich.

Meehl, P. 1971. Law and the fireside inductions: some reflections of a clinical psychologist. *The Journal of Social Issues* 27:68

Morris, J. 1964. Failure in teaching virtue. *The Humanist* 4:102–06.

Psychology Today. 1973. Interview with Steiner. *Psychology Today* (February).

Rokeach, M. 1965. Paradoxes of religious belief. *Transaction* (January/February).

———. 1968. *Beliefs, attitudes, and values*. San Francisco: Jossey-Bass.

Sales, S. 1972. Authoritarianism. *Psychology Today* (November).

Shatan, C. 1973. How do we turn off the guilt? *Human Behavior* (February).

Slater, P. 1970. *The pursuit of loneliness*. New York: Beacon.

Toffler, A. 1970. *Future shock*. New York: Random House.

Ulrich, R., Stachnik, J. and Stainton, N. 1963. Student acceptance of generalized personality interpretations. *Psychological Reports* 13:831–34.

Chapter Seven: **Familiarity Breeds (Aggression and Sexuality)**

. . . it is not surprising that in many species fighting is intense only during the mating season. Physiological studies also point to a close connection between sexual and aggressive behavior.

ROGER N. JOHNSON, *Aggression in Man and Animals*

The gingham dog went 'bow-wow-wow!'
    And the calico cat replied, 'Mee-ow!'
The air was littered, an hour or so,
    With bits of gingham and calico.

EUGENE FIELD, *"The Duel"*

What we hope to make clear in this chapter and the next is that familiarity can breed content as well as contempt; it can foster love as well as hate. Within this chapter our focus will be on the general nature of our own sexual and aggressive tendencies as they are shaped by the circumstances of our lives.

On the Threat of Ikness

From 1964 to 1967 the anthropologist Colin Turnbull lived with an African tribe known as the Ik. He studied the conditions placed on this former migrating, hunting, and gathering people that brought them to give up their usual way of life. When national borders that they were forbidden to cross were established and hunting lands were closed off, the Ik had to change their basic lifestyle. In order to survive, they began to abandon their former cooperative, loving ways and turned to an each-man-woman-and-child-for-himself philosophy. This was observed in their physical as well as their social environment. According to Turnbull, the fact that these people changed philosophies in less than three generations raises questions about human nature and the qualities of life upon which Western civilization was founded. We might well wonder what we would do and what ethics we would use if we were down to our last crumb of bread or if our own living territory were truly threatened. On what basis can we separate loving and hating behaviors and say that one is more natural than the other?

Looking even more closely, evidence to date indicates that there are important biological and situational determinants, as well as important interactions among these conditions, that influence us to become sexual as well as loving and to become aggressive as well as hateful—often to the same object. The distinction we are making between sex and love is simply one of the closeness and intimacy involved in the relationship. Sex can be less personal than love, and it can be an expression of love. The same holds for aggression–hate. Aggression can be less personal than hate, and it can be an ex-

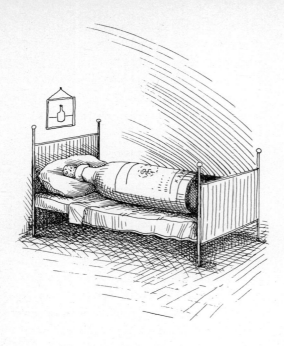

the curious set of paradoxes we present to our-selves. For example, it is acceptable to resent and be angry at someone who is alive; it is less accept-able after the person is dead. This is especially true of our feelings toward parents, grandparents, and world leaders. Though not acceptable, it is at least common to be loving and sweet to your clients and affiliates at work and then to come home and hassle your family. As a graduate student at Ohio State University I took a course in criminology where I learned of the "B & B" concept of homicide. That is, with the exception of vehicular manslaughter, more murders are committed in bedrooms and bars than anywhere else. This fact startled me at the time. Why bedrooms and bars? Could it be because very important close-to-the-core feelings and per-sonal revelations occur there? The sexual and aggressive aspects of love and hate not only seem here to stay but also appear inseparable. Let us look closer at these phenomena.

pression of hate. In reading this chapter and the next, we would like you to think of these distinctions and our basic division between love (sex) and hate (aggression). We will cover the more biological and culture-bound aspects of sex and aggression in this chapter. In the next we will discuss love-hate relationships that develop over the course of our lives more in depth.

Why Love AND Hate?

Most of us have been brought up with the under-standing that it is more blessed to love than to hate. It is also more appropriate to be sexual than to be aggressive. In fact, we may feel quite badly if we de-velop anger, hostility, or death wishes toward those whom we know we love. Yet, physiologically speak-ing, the states of arousal to love and to hate are re-markably similar. Is there really a difference, then, between loving and hating and between sex and aggression? The answer is *yes* and *no* because of

THE CONDITION OF AROUSAL

Stanley Schachter, a social psychologist, devel-oped (1964) a theory of emotion that may help to explain some of the seeming contradiction of how feelings of love and hate become intertwined and confusing. The two sides of emotion, according to Schachter, are 1) the physiological state of arousal, such as increased breathing and heart-beat rate, and 2) the meaning, labeling, or cog-nitive "sense" the person gives to the state he or she is in. Maybe this theory would also help to explain the alternating weeping and smiling behav-ior of someone who is deeply aroused but has not determined the right label for the feeling. "I'm so happy I could cry," makes no logical sense but is a very important, relevant statement, psychologically. The person is simply acknowledging that she or he is aroused. "Don't worry too much about the semantics involved," we might add. The feeling is what is important.

Another theory is based on a more intuitive approach and is usually attributed to those who have a dynamic point of view about human behavior (Freud, et al.). It maintains that intimacy of any sort is potentially threatening as well as soothing to the ego and that this intimacy establishes itself through the vehicle of parental reward and punishment—for example, "Mommy loves good boys and clobbers them when they're bad." This can create great ambivalence in your feelings toward those who are close to you.

Ideas on the origins of arousal

One proposal is that the tendency to be aggressive is determined by our genes at birth and that certain situations will trigger aggressive behavior. Another is that we learn to be aggressive through watching the rewards and punishments of those around us. A third idea has been proposed by K. E. Moyer (1973). He feels the brain contains inborn neural systems that react in the presence of particular stimuli to produce aggressiveness. The various factors and determinants of what "causes" a person to become aroused to sex or aggression seem to form a hierarchy. Thus a chemical, a hormone, a gene, or a brain structure would be at one end; the reinforcements of culture and people would be at the other. Very likely, the elements would interact to determine what behavior would occur in a given situation.

Man and Beast

It may be that some lessons can be learned from the animal world. Louis S. B. Leakey, the late world-renowned archeologist, concludes (1972) that early humans (*Homo sapiens, Homo habilis*) were like animals themselves and were neither aggressive nor violent toward each other. N. Tinbergen (1968) indicates there are scientists who, through animal study and observation, feel aggression is instinctual and is triggered by external cues—a

curious meld of heredity and environment. And when an organism is aroused, it is almost certain that nonverbal cues of aggression (such as angry facial expressions) communicate more reliably what someone is feeling and meaning than does speech.

Another ethologist, Irenäus Eibl-Eibsfeldt, observes (1961) that fights between animals of the same species almost never end in death and rarely cause serious injury to either combatant because of the ritual that must precede the attack. Thus aggressiveness, she goes on to say, seems to have been used for "spacing out" the individuals within a species—providing more elbow room. Perhaps, then, the violence we see in ourselves is in fact a reaction to physical overcrowding. Of course, we are anthropomorphizing the motives involved, but it is very possible that some share of behavior *is* determined by innate mechanisms of control. For example, Konrad Lorenz has pointed out that when a victim throws himself defenseless at his enemy's feet there is a normal human inhibition to stop the fight (Eibl-Eibesfeldt 1961). However, as Tinbergen intimated, dropping napalm on foreign villages gives little room for ceremony, ritual, or face-saving dialogue.

A psychological point of view that applies to people and offers an integrated framework for viewing sex and aggression is that of Albert Bandura (1973). His approach is based on social learning theory. Social learning theory is, in turn, based upon the expectations of reward one has of the environment. The fact that we learn to fight on the playground, not in church, and love in the bedroom, not in public, is an important one that we use throughout our lives. In other words, the environment controls us to a certain extent, and we are more likely to behave sexually or aggressively (lovingly or hatefully) when we read the appropriate cues from our environment.

Bandura also emphasizes that cognitive activity (thinking) plays an important part in helping us interpret the consequences of a certain reaction. We may learn to be aggressive by watching how others do it and noticing the consequences. We use our thinking processes to a much greater extent in both the bedroom and the bar than most how-to manuals indicate. This puts an added feature into the analysis of human love and hate that cannot be gleaned from animal research.

ON OUR DIMINISHING TERRITORY

In the previous section we mentioned the strong drive animals have to maintain and defend their territorial niches. Yet we cannot assume that whatever animals do, humans will do (see Freedman 1971). For example, John Calhoun and others conducted a study (1962) in which they placed rats in an area and watched them multiply. As the space became more dense, social behavior broke down: males became either more aggressive or more passive, females built sloppier nests, and infant mortal-

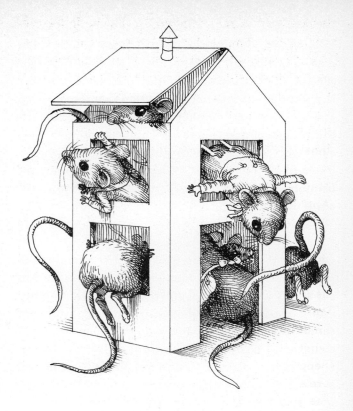

ity rose. To suggest from these results that people would succumb in like manner to spatial alterations in their environment is perhaps invalid. However, most of us are a little uneasy about being crowded.

A relatively new area of research that tries to explain how personal space affects human behavior is called *proxemics*. Lassen (1973) found that the space between the therapist and the patient can make a difference in the kind of communication that takes place. In an initial psychiatric interview, a distance as close as three feet seems to inhibit the patient from becoming personal, while a distance of nine feet away makes a patient more anxious. These conclusions were drawn on the basis of interview reactions of the patients as well as speech disturbance ratings made during the interview.

Smith and Haythorn (1972) placed pairs of men, some of whom were judged personally compatible and others not, in a 6 × 9 × 8-foot room for twenty-one days. Irritation began to build, and among the compatibles it took the form of scape-goating onto whatever *things* were available, such as the light fixtures, the chemical toilet, the furniture, and the daily questionnaire slid beneath the door. Three-man groups in $7 \times 12 \times 14$-foot rooms indicated that there was somewhat less strain on those involved. But when the three-man groups were later placed in a $6 \times 9 \times 8$-foot room, their hostility level exceeded that of the two-man pairs. Apparently we do not appreciate receiving less space than we are accustomed to.

Social Problems and the Use of Space

The question of how the space we are in influences us is not confined just to the single-room situation. An intriguing interplay between structures and emotions affects us socially also. For example, what is the American home meant to be for the people in it? How do we handle our space when we are afraid? When we are angry? How do we relate to the physical and psychological structures of such institutions as prisons and wars? A brief glance at some of these questions might tell us something about how the environment shapes our sexual and aggressive tendencies.

Closeness, Love and Fear

It is interesting how closely associated the basic human emotions—love, fear, anger, and depression—really are. In both the animal and human arena there is one known reaction to the insecurities and fears of the world: we fight to spread out but we come together when afraid. In one experiment (Feshbach and Feshbach 1963) boys aged nine through twelve were listening to ghost stories at a Halloween party campfire. Bowing to the behaviorist's love of figures, it was concluded that fear leads to closeness by determining the diameter of the campfire ring to be eleven feet before the ghost stories began and three feet by the time the last grisly story had been told. There is a great deal

more psychological research (Schachter 1959) that indicates that people have stronger desires to affiliate when they are fearful than when they are not.

Keeping the Space We Have: Population Control

The idea of birth control is not new, but the necessity for it is perhaps more pressing today than in the past. A very well done Birth Control Handbook (Cherniak and Feingold 1971) (so well done, in fact, that leading universities banned it from campus) notes that by 1917 sixteen American states had passed compulsory sterilization laws for thirty-four categories of people. Between 1907 and 1963, 63,678 people had been sterilized by court order. Today the emphasis is more on the individual's choice, and voluntary abortions around the world each year number somewhat more than thirty million. Rather than legal procedures, as in the past, today incentives in the form of models are

people to control their own destinies and being honest with them about their alternatives.

Social Situations that Encourage Hatred

An experiment that points to the conclusion that certain social situations bring out the worst in us is the Stanford prisoner experiment conducted by Philip Zimbardo (1972). In an attempt to understand psychologically what it means to be a prisoner or prison guard, a prison was simulated and all the procedures of prison life were realistically planned. Seventy college student volunteers who answered an ad in a Palo Alto paper to be research subjects for fifteen dollars a day were screened and tested. About twenty-four who qualified as "normal" (as judged by placing between the fortieth and sixtieth percentiles on various personality tests) were then used as subjects. Half were arbitrarily designated as guards and half as prisoners. The guards made their own rules for maintaining law and order. The prisoners were unexpectedly picked up at their homes by city police (to simulate reality) searched, handcuffed, fingerprinted, and booked. They were then stripped, deloused, put into uniforms, given numbers, and put in a cell with two others. The plan was to study their behavior for two weeks. After six days the experiment was terminated because of what Zimbardo describes as events that were "frightening": "We were horrified because we saw some boys (guards) treat others as if they were despicable animals, taking pleasure in cruelty, while other boys (prisoners) became servile, dehumanized robots. . . ." Three prisoners were released after a few days because of hysterical crying, confused thinking, and severe depression. The most intriguing part of the experiment from our point of view is that these college students who had volunteered for an experiment were so programmed into believing they were prisoners, not college students, that they forgot that at any point in time they could have just forfeited their daily pay and quit the experi-

being used. A King Vitamin cereal ad pictures one child at the breakfast table; a Ford Pinto ad shows two parents in the front seat and two children in the rear. Money, a prominent secondary reinforcement, as well as coupons, stamps, medals, and so forth, are also powerful incentives. Certain groups, such as church societies, can also be influential in shaping positive attitudes and actions about birth control. Other reinforcing schemes are being dreamed of. As an example, an ingenious idea mentioned by Dr. Dewey Lipe: "Suppose, for example, that every time someone purchased a contraceptive device he received a token that could then be inserted into a machine. The machine would then offer a chance prize such as. . . ." Placing birth control on a gambling basis where the house wins may not be a bad idea. What this all adds up to is making it easy for

ment. The slip from reality to fantasy was so convincing that all but three were willing to forfeit all the money they had earned if only they could be paroled. Thus they were begging for mercy when they could have simply walked out.

In reflecting on the Zimbardo study and the Milgram study on obedience that we discussed in chapter three, we may note that while we carry around in our own heads the notion that we are essentially fair, just, humane, and understanding, in reality we can be made to do just about anything when we are put into psychologically compelling situations. Fortunately, we don't have to test this assumption to know that each of us has some breaking point within some context or another. Most of Zimbardo's "normal" college subjects and most of Milgram's noncollege subjects either lost a sense of reality and perspective or administered cruelty to others. The implications are vast and include My Lai, San Quentin, Attica, Watergate, Nazi Germany, child battering, and in milder forms, child–parent relationships.

It may be the impression at this point that parents (as authorities) are the root of all evil. Not so. "The flame that melts the wax hardens the steel," as the saying goes. The more generalized cultural values of the system or society in which children grow up can make an influence in either direction. Consider, for example, the children growing up in riot-torn Northern Ireland. In *Children in Conflict* psychiatrist Morris Fraser distinguishes those children who are violence-disturbed from those who learn the system and appear to thrive on it. One such lad is eleven-year-old Bernard.

When Dr. Fraser asked Bernard about a typical day in his life, Bernard spoke of how his friends make petrol bombs, gather stones, and construct other ingenious devices to use in street fights against the invading army troops. Fraser countered that he read in the press claims that boys were being paid by older men to throw stones. Bernard laughed,

"If they were paying, the whole street would be out. But they'd be wasting their money, because we do it for nothing." From a realistic point of view we would say Bernard is well adjusted—but, we must add, there must be better systems for kids to grow up in.

Midchapter Summary
In studying the similarities between the behavior of humans and animals, ethologists have indicated that love and sex and hate and aggression are constantly intertwined. The state of physical arousal is similar for both love and hate; only the context tends to define which is which. The contexts or environments we move within offer various forms of physical structure to our life space. These structures limit or accelerate our love-hate movements. When

we are afraid we tend to huddle together; when we overpopulate we look for ways to keep the space we have. The structures of such institutions as prisons and wars can also affect how we behave with others.

Growing up Female and Male: Social Factors

Let's look at a specific instance of how environment influences sex by asking the question, "What's it like to grow up male or female in our culture?"

There is a vast amount of literature available, which we will not go into here, telling us how much and how early the environment informs little boys and girls that they are different, how they are different, and how they should get into their sexual roles and stay there. As Bettelheim (1962) describes the young girl's childhood, "For fifteen years or more she is officially encouraged to compete with boys in the schoolroom, to develop her mind and her initiative, to be second to none . . . and then our curious system insists she 'fall in love' with a potential husband: she is in fact expected to love giving up what she may have loved until then . . ."

The expectations of the parents toward the children are also sex-linked. A good example of this can be seen through the eyes of Doris, who describes something of her relationship with her father when she was in high school. She wrote the following description when she was a junior in college.

Doris

I had always gotten along well with my parents, and this relationship continued and improved. I felt very close to both of them, especially my mother. Except that I just remembered having some horrible arguments with my father and being terribly hostile towards him. I guess that we had some good times together, and we'd often go for rides together — Sunday morning rides out to the foothills, especially in the spring, became a tradition. I think that basically I have the same awful temper that my father had, getting angry about petty things, *but in the environment where I grew up, which emphasized placating and taking care of the male, I learned to suppress my anger* [our italics throughout], to rarely express it. About two sentences ago I said something about having arguments with my father. This is not quite true. My hostility was expressed in disapproving and aloof looks at things my father would do, like eating runny eggs in the morning, which I found nauseating, or kicking my bed at night because my father's snoring kept me awake. I guess my looks were very grating, really got to my father. He'd start yelling, yelling at me, but mostly crying to my mother about me or what I was doing or how persecuted he was. I was a pain, but my father was childish. I hated to see him like this, but my conscious or unconscious actions would drive him to it, and I would be disgusted with him when he did it. Funny, it's really hard for me to recall anything specific. *I remember being resentful that I could never even express my own point of view, that I always had to submit.* There must have been times when I was definitely in the right because I remember being especially resentful of the fact that my father never apologized to me for anything, and I thought that there were times that he as a person should apologize to me as a person, and that being his daughter should not mean that I would always be subjugated. I developed a definite aversion to ever apologizing, not only to my father, but to anyone. I just hated to say "I'm sorry." I could express regret in other ways, but could not verbalize it. Another thing that really bugged me about my father was some of his Victorian ideas. *Like it was perfectly all right for the men in my family to run around in their underwear and no one thought anything of it, but my father would yell if I didn't wear a bathrobe, even over my pajamas.* I could not understand or accept this. I can remember one time I was alone in the house when I was a senior. I had my pajamas on — shortie pajamas or something —

when I heard my parents' car drive up; I knew it was theirs. The door was locked so I went to open it, thought I was doing them a favor. I didn't show myself to the world, so to speak, but my father immediately started yelling at me, but more to my mother about how many times he'd told me not to run around like that. *That was another thing I hated: my father would yell about me to my mother as I stood there and always refer to me as "she" or "her" and I would feel like yelling back, "Yell at me, or at least call me by name when I'm in the room."* Never did though. *I went crying into my bedroom* and my mother came in to talk to me. I kept on crying and saying that it wasn't right, it wasn't fair, that I had only meant to do a nice thing for them, was all ready to be bright when they came in. *My mother agreed, but this male superiority business meant that we "must understand" and that it's better not to make waves.* This sort of relationship with my father continued. I guess it would still continue if I lived at home. We get along really well at times, and we do some nice things together. Going for rides is just part of our relationship, enjoying early mornings together, talking, maybe having some coffee and doughnuts together. But this other stuff is hard to live with. I can remember that one time I was changing my clothes when my father walked into my bedroom. He got very embarrassed and walked out muttering some things. I just laughed about it, not a derisive laugh, just thought it was funny. But I wonder what kind of subtle feelings about myself I picked up growing up with this.

The fact that growing boys also pay a price in having to squelch their more tender feelings and in having to be able to "be strong" is well described by Herb Goldberg (1973). The male child has more women than men to model his behavior from, beginning with the very early years of life. Yet he is a

"sissy" if he acts effeminate. Men don't go to others (such as counselors) as readily as women for help with personal problems because of the notion our culture has given them that a man who is a man can damn well take care of himself. Also, each sexual encounter is, for the male, a test of his masculinity— like shooting down ducks in the penny arcade. Women have much less worry about their homosexuality than men for this very reason and for the reason that men, generally, are taught to be less emotional. In our society, women can kiss women, and men can kiss women, but (in general, in this day and age) shame on the man who kisses another man.

SEXUAL DISCRIMINATION

The examples of discrimination against both sexes are legion. You can cite many examples from your own life. But a most intriguing example of discrimination occurs within our courts. In an article by

Nagel and Weitzman (1972) about the double standard of justice, we learn that husbands collect more, on the average, when suing their wives for lack of affection (loss of consortium) than do the wives when suing husbands. There are more than eleven times as many lawsuits by husbands for loss of their wives' services than vice versa. Male plaintiffs are rewarded by larger amounts of money. In the sample studied in this article, urogenital injury suits were scrutinized. Now if you want to be secure in your feeling that there are sex differences, this will take you to the source: The average male plaintiff (suer) who wins a urogenital injury case collects $31,966, while the average female collects $11,385. At least it is perfectly clear that a penis is more important for your day in court than a vagina. And, of course, these sex differences carry over equally to other legal areas such as child support litigation and jury selection. Add to this the fact that if a mother stays home against her choice until her child is fourteen, she can stand to "lose" $59,000 (by not working) if she is a high school graduate, $82,000 if she is a college graduate, and $103,000 if she holds an advanced degree.

It's a curious phenomenon, or paradox if you will, that while legal and other social procedures seem to put women down, there is a tremendous preoccupation with the female in our society and with the female body to the extent that the male is actually the one who is most often hidden from view. This is obvious, for example, in movies such as *The Last Tango in Paris* where the female form is viewed from every angle while the audience must content themselves with fantasies about Marlon Brando's physique. (And I'm sure he would have been willing to disrobe, were it in the script.)

In one commune (Twin Oaks), modeled some-what after the commune in Skinner's book *Walden II*, the effect of society's sexual conditioning process was quite clear (Kinkade 1972). One might expect a communal living group to be more open to each other as people and to be able to slough off the prejudices of everyday life, but this was apparently difficult for the group members. Twin Oaks men preferred women who weren't sexually aggressive, who smiled and waited to be approached, who let the men do the talking, and who had long hair and *Playboy* centerfold bodies. "The one redeeming factor," author Kinkade explained, "is that the longer a member lives at Twin Oaks, the less his or her physical appearance matters." This would appear reasonable from the point of view that a here-and-now social norm has a strong effect on changing previously learned attitudes. Newton (1971) feels in the long run women have it all over men anyway because they (women) can enjoy two-person sexual contacts in three separate functions: coitus, parturition, and lactation, while males can perform reproductive contacts only through inter-course. Physiologically speaking, it is quite clear that throughout the animal kingdom, women are capable of more sensual experience per unit time than men. So where does that leave penis envy? Back in the courts, presumably.

Another aspect of growing up female that is still a battle to be won concerns the woman's con-trol of her own body and its functions. Much of what we have discussed implies this concern, but the most explicit and controversial topic in this regard is a woman's right to abort a fetus. There is much feeling (guilt, anger, and compassion) involved in both the right-to-life movement as well as in the pro-abortion movement, hinging as it does on the unanswerable questions of "When does life begin?" and "When should it be ended?" Does a fetus belong to the mother as a part of her body to be removed, at her request, with as little question as though it were her appendix? Or does society have the right to put a halt to abortion? Even with the Supreme Court ruling of 1973 to strike down anti-abortion laws, there will be many who feel the question has not been resolved. While there is no psychologically painless way to cope with an un-wanted pregnancy, there is some evidence, according to psychiatrist Carol Nadelson of the Pregnancy Counseling Service in Boston, that giving a child up for adoption is more traumatic for the mother than going through with an abortion. In fact, you can find as many authorities who say that abortion helps a woman's mental health as there are those who say it doesn't. But amidst all this speculation the one certainty about growing up female is that it's not easy—but it is getting better as women are beginning to see they have a right to more control over their minds and bodies than history has heretofore afforded them.

GETTING SOME PERSPECTIVE

Finally, I would like to point out, as did Maslow in the preface to his *Motivation and Personality*, that the American culture characteristically asks us to take our blessings for granted and expects us to move on to greater achievements. Women's liberation notwithstanding, girls growing up still have fantasies of family, home, and lover, by and large, even though their thoughts are less rule-bound than those of their elders. In the words of Maslow,

> the fact of the matter is that no matter how much one longs for a home or for a baby or for a lover, sooner or later one can become sated with these blessings, will take them for granted, and will start to feel restless. . . .

The mistake, Maslow feels, is for a woman to regard her home, baby, or husband as a fake or trap that should be discarded when actually she may wish to hang on to everything she has—and ask for more. We may want to take a close look at our family structure and determine what there is in it that is valuable to us and what there is that keeps us from growing and developing as individuals.

LIKING YOUR BODY

Those who are aware of their bodies at all know that they both love and hate certain physical aspects of the body. Because many of these aspects are omitted from everyday conversation, they seem

even more important than perhaps they should be. Thus we often find, in ourselves and everybody else, great confusion as to what all the equipment is for, how to use it, and who to trust talking about it with or showing it to. As one little boy put it, "We come from seeds just like vegetables; that's why they call us human beans." Just try to get a sex education program going in a public school and see how all the repressed juices and most fearful apprehensions of the world come oozing out under the banner of propriety. The anatomy must be taught in cool and objective tones. That's no putdown—we all have our areas of apprehension. But why is it that what is so common and everyday as the body and its uses can create so much anxiety?

The answer is deceptively simple and is understood by all good phenomenologists, existentialists, and cosmeticians. The body defines the hidden from the public, the "me" from the "you," and, further, it expresses our feelings about ourselves in relation to others. In one of Gordon Alport's books he used two examples to demonstrate the sanctity of our body feelings. If you scratch your hand and it begins to bleed a little, might you automatically lick it? Would you lick someone else's hand in a similar situation? Check your feelings here. If you spit into a glass of water, could you be induced to drink it? If someone else did likewise, would it be more difficult to drink? (Anyone who enjoys French kissing will have trouble rationalizing that one.) As Seymour Fisher argued in *Body Consciousness*, about the only time there appears to be a legitimate occasion to scrutinize your own body is when you are ill. If you are well you are supposed to deny that you have a body. Alfred Adler, in his theory of personality, spent some time in emphasizing the effect of organ inferiority and of body deprivations in general on the growing personality. People are sensitive about their bodies and they show this in the way they use them to communicate.

In a survey of body image conducted by Berscheid, et al. (1973) 62,000 people completed a questionnaire that was included in a magazine they subscribed to. Look into this article if you are interested; it contains a wealth of detail on how people feel about their bodies. In general most people sampled seemed to feel better about themselves when they were pleased with the way they looked. Men wanted muscular chests and women wanted slim waists, but, surprisingly, the people in this sample were relatively unconcerned with penis or breast size.

The human potential movement and the gestalt practitioners in particular focus much of their energy in helping people get in tune with the inner body messages that society has, over the years, asked them to tune out. The idea has even been advanced (Fisher 1973) that much of racial prejudice stems from the fear of any human body that departs from our own appearance—the "not-me" phenomenon. Given the fact that we are taught in very subtle and circumscribed ways about what to think of our bodies, what to do (and not do) with them, and, most devastatingly, how to interpret them, how is it that our species has survived? The one answer that outshines them all is that sex is pleasurable. Of course, you don't need to study psychology to know that. We all know it. We have just learned to keep that knowledge in check, principally through guilt. However, sex at its best is shared, and in sharing we move beyond pure body sensations into much more basic feelings concerning self-esteem, security, respect, cosmic oneness, and the like.

Chapter Seven Summary

Strong biological as well as cultural forces affect our drives of sex and aggression. Environmental reinforcement, the intimacy of the physical structure we are in, and the kinds of authorities over us all have strong effects on the form that our sexual and aggressive behaviors may take.

As we grow to be men and women our parents teach us what behavior is appropriate. But the message does not stop there. The kind of family and friends we have or the kind of job we land depends on how well we play our sex roles, or in some cases, how poorly. Many of the communications we send to others are through body language. In turn, body language depends on our self-esteem and how we relate to our physical selves.

Glossary

Anthropomorphizing Reading human emotions into the motives of nonhumans. For example, telling someone his pet dogs looks lonely.

Ethology The study of biology as it relates to behavior, particularly in relation to how animals and humans evolve and survive.

Eugenics The study of ways we can improve the hereditary qualities of the human race.

Existentialist Someone who believes that our existence can never be well explained by science and that we can at any moment change our way of life, in spite of our present habits.

Phenomenologist Someone who believes that behavior is determined by the world-as-we-see-it.

Proxemics The study of space and its effect on behavior (*proximal* and *proximity* are other forms of the word, meaning *close or near*).

Secondary reinforcement Rewards or punishments that do not depend on a physiological response such as hunger or thirst but mediate behavior with great gusto (money is a good example).

Territorial niche The physical area one believes is one's own. To an ant it is his hill; to a person it is his or her home.

Urogenital Pertaining to the organs of the genital region.

Exercises   (for individual and class use)

You can do the following exercises and tasks at your leisure. Perhaps some of these would be more enjoyable with a friend. Those with an asterisk should be done in consultation with your teacher or in class.

1.* Jot down questions or reactions to any of the student descriptions you have just read that you felt were very much your feelings too. Your comments could be offered to your teacher anonymously for general class discussion or you could share them with a small group from your class on a more personal basis.

2.   What is your theory about why love and hate are such similar emotional states? Can you give examples from your own life to back it up? (Any of you who cares to jot his or her theory down and mail it to one of the authors of this text will be blessed in our prayers from here on.)

3.   Map out a set of incentives or procedures that might prove effective in helping people keep family size down.

4.   (A woman from the class can volunteer for this one.) Pretend you are interested in making a small wooden shelf for storing some of your belongings. You go down to a lumber store and describe what you want to a male clerk. Any man from the class who knows how a male lumber store clerk would act in this situation should volunteer for that role. What is the woman made to feel like? For variation, a woman can pretend to take her car to a garage and talk to a male mechanic. What are the feelings there? Why?

5.   A male can go through #4 above by pretending he is going to a fabric store to buy materials from a female clerk to make a sports jacket. How does a female fabric store clerk's behavior differ from the male lumber store clerk's?

6.* Ever take an inner fantasy trip through your own body? Have someone from your class or your teacher talk you through it. Close your eyes and mouth. Have someone begin to suggest to you to climb into the top of your head and look around a bit. Then very slowly, move down past your eyes, nose, and so on, down to your toes, naming all the vital organs on the way down. Note any area of your body where you find pleasurable or anxious sensations. You might discuss your reactions to this experiment if there is enough trust in the group you're with.

Bibliography

Bandura, A. 1973. *Aggression: a social learning analysis*. New York: Prentice-Hall.

Berscheid, E., et al. 1973. Body image. *Psychology Today* (November):119–31.

Bettelheim, B. 1962. Growing up female. *Harpers* October:121.

Calhoun, J. 1962. Population density and social pathology. *Scientific American* 206:139–50.

Cherniak, D. and Feingold, A., eds. 1971. *Birth control handbook*. Montreal: Journal Offset.

Eibl-Eibesfeldt, I. 1961. The fighting behavior of animals. *Scientific American* (December):2.

Feshbach, S. and Feshbach, N. 1963. Influence of the stimulus object upon the complementary and supplementary projection of fear. *Journal of Abnormal and Social Psychology* 66:498–502.

Fisher, S. 1973. *Body consciousness*. Englewood Cliffs, N.J.: Prentice-Hall.

Fraser, M. 1973. *Children in conflict*. New York: Doubleday.

Freedman, J. 1971. The crowd: maybe not so madding after all. *Psychology Today*. September:60.

Goldberg, H. 1973. Men's lib. *Human Behavior* (April):73–77.

Kinkade, K. 1972. *A Walden Two experiment: the first five years of Twin Oaks community*. New York: Morrow.

Lassen, C. 1973. Effect of proximity on anxiety and communication in the initial psychiatric interview. *Journal of Abnormal Psychology* 18:3, 220–32.

Leakey, L. and Ardrey, R. 1972. Man, the killer. *Psychology Today* (September):73.

Lipe, D. 1971. Incentives, fertility control, and research. *American Psychologist* 26:624.

Maslow, A. 1970. *Motivation and personality*. New York: Harper & Row.

Milgram, S. 1963. Behavioral study of obedience. *Journal of Abnormal and Social psychology* 67:371–78.

Moyer, K. 1973. The physiology of violence. *Psychology Today* (July):35 ff.

Nagel, S. and Weitzman, L. 1973. Double standard of American justice. *Society* 9:18.

Newton, N. 1971. Sensuous woman. *Psychology Today* (July):68.

Schacter, S. 1959. *The psychology of affiliation*. Palo Alto: Stanford University Press.

———. 1964. The interaction of cognitive and physiological determinants of emotional state, in Berkowitz, L., ed., *Advances in experimental social psychology*. New York: Academic Press.

Smith, S. and Haythorn, W. 1973. Effects of compatibility, crowding, group size and leadership seniority on stress, anxiety, hostility, and annoyance in isolated groups. *Journal of Personality and Social Psychology* 22:67–69.

Tinbergen, N. 1968. On war and peace in animals and man. *Science* 28:1411–16.

Turnbull, C. 1972. *The mountain people*. New York: Simon & Schuster.

Zimbardo, P. 1972. Pathology of imprisonment. *Society* 9:4.

Chapter Eight: Zeroing In (Love–Hate Relationships)

Run for the sun
Run for the sun
Run for the sun
And don't
Ever
Fall behind.
For if you do
The icicle forming
At your toes
May
Slip into your
Mind.
And then
    to your
Heart.
And the only way to
Let your
Heart be warm
Again
Is by having
Someone else
Pretty special
Melt the icicle
Melt the icicle.
And in this world, baby,
I wish you luck.
So
Run for the sun.

LISA WRENN, *high school sophomore* (1972)

Without contraries there is no progression.
Attraction and Repulsion, Reason
and Energy, Love and Hate, are
necessary to human existence.

WILLIAM BLAKE, *The Marriage of
Heaven and Hell*

All theories of personality, some more directly than others, emphasize the importance of relationships between people. Those around us excite us, scare us, depress us, love us, hate us, and care for us—and we them. This chapter will attempt to zero in on the interpersonal relations we are all familiar with as well as some that may not be so familiar. From birth to death our feelings about ourselves affect the ways we relate to others; their reactions to us in turn tell us about ourselves. We use the terms *love* and *hate* in this chapter because they are the strongest feelings—and the most personal. We are involved with them from birth to death.

Loving, Hating, and Growing Up

People who love come to trust each other. They lower their defenses. They touch and hug and entwine. As they develop and grow, they learn to care and share so that love becomes reciprocal—a two-way relationship. But closeness also often causes a loss of perspective, so that sometimes we expect too much and receive too little. At other times we may throw the trust that has grown back in the face of our loved one because we are hurt or because we want to defend our self-esteem. This is a hateful thing to do, though quite understandable. It is *because* people mean so much to each other that we both love and hate.

In this context hate may be defined as the reaction to a hurt or a loss, or a lowering of self-esteem in the eyes of the loved one. While momentary, it is intricately tied to the relationship of love. Who is there who has not hated his or her parents at one time or another, yet can honestly say, "I love them very much"? This is less a paradox than it appears to be.

During the early 1900s psychologists began to study and observe the mother-child relationship intensely. The quality of this relationship was thought to be the basis for the development of love and trust in the growing child. However, it was not until the 1960s that researchers like Maslow and

Harlow openly spoke about *love*-research as such. But even in spite of the excellent work of Kinsey, Masters and Johnson, and others, the quality of the love-hate relationship is beyond scientific or objective analysis. Keep this in mind as you read on.

Since we alter the way we approach or reject people around us as we go through life, it is perhaps appropriate to look at love-hate relationships in terms of what happens to both parent and child at each of our several stages of development. You remember that at the end of the first chapter we mentioned the developmental theories of Havighurst, Erikson, Kagan, and Piaget as examples of the normative-descriptive approach in psychology. These theorists will appear here from time to time also.

In this chapter we will discuss love-hate relationships in terms of the following life stages:

The First Six Years
Middle Childhood (ages 6–12)
Adolescence (ages 12–18)
Early Adulthood (ages 18–30)
Middle Age (ages 30–55)
Later Maturity and Old Age

Each section will begin with some description of what is happening to a person at this stage both in terms of the love-hate relationships she or he may be experiencing as well as from the point of view of others close to that person. Then we will discuss one or more of the developmental theories as it applies to that age group. Following this, we will examine a topic from the viewpoint of parent and child that demonstrates an aspect of the love-hate relationship that could occur at that age. You will see from these examples the difficulty of separating love from hate and parent from child. Since these stages are somewhat arbitrary at best, you will find that some of the material overlaps from one stage to another. Under *The First Six Years* the topic will be child abuse; for the *Middle Childhood* section it is open and closed family relations; for *Adolescence* it is a discussion of the loving and liking scales; for

Early Adulthood it is loneliness, marriage and its consequences, marriage fights, and divorce. In the last two sections (*Middle Age* and *Later Maturity and Old Age*), we will look at briefer topics pertinent to those age groups.

As you read through this chapter ask yourself, "What quality of relationship would have encouraged or discouraged what is being described here?" If you keep this question in your mind as you read, your notion of what is included in love and hate will expand by the time you finish the chapter—scout's honor.

The First Six Years

BIOLOGICAL AND SOCIAL DEVELOPMENT

The newborn is capable of seeing, hearing, smelling (and how), and is sensitive to touch, pain, and change in position. The fourth month of life brings on the smile, which, however, occurs randomly at this age and is not necessarily an indication of happiness, as we like to think. Signs of anxiety to the unfamiliar can be detected during months six through twelve. Kagan (1969) cites a number of studies to validate this claim.

Piaget (1952) described the fact that infants explore the world with their mouths and hands, thus paving the way for eventually being able to differentiate between what is them and what is "out there." For example, if a ball is placed beneath a blanket, the five-month-old child will act as though the ball no longer exists. At eight months the child will lift the blanket to look for the ball. This is the beginning of the creation of a world view. This phase of sensorimotor play is the cornerstone for later elaborating beliefs, attitudes, and values about oneself in relation to the environment.

One interesting phenomenon that takes place during the first year or two of life and then becomes less important as the child grows older is the interplay between the development of the body and the learning opportunities available. It is possible for a child to be given "too much too soon" or "too little too late." Fortunately, the human organism is very resilient at this age and, except for extreme deprivation or trauma, can overcome most of the errors committed against it.

During the second year of life the attitudes that surround the retention or expulsion of urine and feces become associated with the budding ability of self-control. Without dwelling on the extent to which mastery of this event determines personality development, it is certainly clear that it is an important part of the infant's daily life and relationships. Shame, doubt, and guilt are natural consequences of states of feeling attached to the elimination process.

During the second and third year the child learns what society prizes and what it punishes—such as the inhibition of undesirable behaviors (aggression, dependency, tantrums, and bedwetting) and the display of desirable ones (cleanliness, ambition, and love). Desire for parental acceptance and avoidance of punishment are the main socializing mechanisms at this age. The consistency with which rewards and punishments are doled out has an important effect on how anxious the child becomes. Children are constantly testing rules and limits, and could—if they could verbalize—tell you more about their parents than the parents think. Unlabeled feelings within the child come to be associated with values of himself as "good" or "bad." These understandings then begin to regulate the way the child works and plays with others.

From ages three to six the child generally begins to move more toward identifying with father (if he's available) and with brothers and sisters. Mother slips a little into the background. If sex typing is encouraged, the little boy will probably want to hammer nails, drive cars, and play at those things he feels implement his boyness; little girls will probably put on aprons, play dolls, and do whatever they feel will implement their girlness. This process is one of identification of the child with the parent. It's the "my-Pop's-better-than-your-Pop" age. The

child tends to imitate the person he perceives is most similar to him. For example, if a teacher rewards a child for studiousness but the parents show no interest, the child is likely to become less studious. It should be remembered that the modeling effect goes on throughout one's life and is not limited to children. For example, a number of people watched the Billie Jean King versus Bobby Riggs tennis match in September 1973 and rooted for Billie Jean. Her victory was theirs. This sort of behavior reflects the way a sibling will stick up for his sister or brother when an outsider attacks.

As the three- to six-year-old develops (introjects) behaviors from adults and older siblings, he or she also adopts many of the standards they live by. For example, losing a game or not staying in the lines when coloring can cause a temper tantrum because of the discrepancy between what the child feels are the correct standards and the actual poor performance.

Along with the development of a rudimentary language and the ability to use symbolic imagery, the child at this age begins to change from egocentrism to altruism. This change comes slowly; many of us as adults are still fighting this battle. In a delightful article entitled, "Piglet, Pooh and Piaget," Dorothy Singer (1972) compares the similarity of Piaget's observations of children and the stories of A. A. Milne, who claims neither to have been interested in children's behavior nor to have observed it in any detail. The two come to similar results. In Piaget's system, prelogical reasoning appears from ages four through seven, when the child takes on imaginary companions and invests a lot of time in make-believe routines.

Children develop notions about their environment that become more realistic with age. For example, in studying the principle of conservation of mass, weight, and volume, Piaget noticed that four-year-olds know that two balls of clay are equal. But when before their eyes, one ball is made into a long roll, the four-year-old says that it has *more* clay than the other ball. In other words, children at this age are continually restructuring their environment in an attempt to make sense of it. And the process continues for years to come.

During the latter part of the first six years of life a third stage occurs, according to Erikson (1950). The development of a conscience that helps to regulate what is fair play for the child also determines the extent to which she or he feels free to initiate activities, to be evasive, to be open with others, to wait for authority to speak out, and so forth. The child is particularly mindful of consistencies and checks up on the parents (if allowed to) to make sure they are following the same rules the child is and whether those rules can be bent. Children at this stage also ask lots of questions, partly to determine the omnipotence of their parents and partly to determine the limits of conditions that affect them.

BECOMING AGGRESSIVE
Many years ago, Watson (1919) noted that the natural reaction of an infant when held down (frustrated in his movements) is rage. Freud (1930) went on to say, "Men are not gentle, friendly creatures wishing for love who simply defend themselves if they are attacked; a powerful measure of desire for aggression has to be reckoned as part of their instinctual endowment." The "frustration-aggression hypothesis" (Dollard 1939) holds that a natural response to being frustrated is to aggress. Rosenzweig (1934) divides reactions to frustration into three categories: extra-punitive, in which anger is directed outward toward others (blaming); impunitive, in which the frustration is ignored or denied; and intro-punitive, in which anger is turned inward and we tend to blame ourselves for any and all upsetting events. Studies like those conducted by Bandura and Walters (1963) indicate that children behave aggressively when they have observed an aggressive model. Other studies, such as those cited in Sears, et al. (1957), indicate the powerful effects

of parental models on children's subsequent behavior. When children are grown, they often discover that some of the things they do are like the ways their parents behaved. This reciprocity makes it difficult to talk about the child's behavior without looking at the situation from the parents' point of view. Let's take a case in point of how love and hate work together in an area that has received a good deal of attention recently—child battering.

AS THE TWIG IS BENT: CHILD ABUSE
Dr. C. Henry Kempe, a physician who coined the term "the battered child syndrome" in 1962, has stated, "One of our key concepts is that love and hate go together, and it is possible to have the tenderest, warmest feelings toward a baby one minute and be extremely angry at it the next" (1971). For example, a young mother, pregnant with her second child, remembers lying in bed around 2:00 A.M. listening to the baby cry in the next room. She recalls a feeling of hate at that moment for the child, who woke her out of a sound sleep. It had been a long day of frustrations. She felt negative feelings begin to build up. She went to the kitchen and heated a bottle of milk in a pan of boiling water. She then set the bottle aside, took the pan of scalding hot water, stood over the crib, and poured the water over the baby. The baby's screams changed to shrieks. The father got out of bed and found the baby writhing in the crib and the mother standing by, pan in hand, expressionless, eyes blank (Wheeler 1972). In this case there was a critical point of no return where the parent failed to recognize the buildup of hatred for the child and was unable, at that point or before, to make an alternate move. Guilt apparently holds the anger back until it erupts into violence.

It is thought that the child abuser comes to believe, generally through the way he or she has been raised (through parental modeling), that children exist in order to satisfy parental needs. Very often the chronic abuser believes the way to be a good

chronically abused children by observing their compliant manner. These children are *too* "good." They seldom denounce the abuser; they keep their mouths shut; they don't cry when a sensitive area is touched by the physician. As we noticed in the Milgram and Zimbardo studies, this sort of blind obedience and compliance to authority is not really as difficult to shape as it may appear at first sight.

Middle Childhood (ages 6–12)
DEVELOPING "PERSONALITY": SIBLINGS AND SKILLS

Having survived the first six years, the child moves into the stage of middle-to-late childhood. Establishing personal standards for living becomes more important during these years. A certain hardening of the personality features (lifestyle, if you will) that is predictive of what to expect of the child as an adolescent takes place during these years. Defenses against anxiety, motives for affiliation and mastery, and so forth, have been pretty well roughed out by this time. Of course, the school situation and the demands it makes will help polarize the child into active or passive kinds of behavior.

The peer group (especially peers of the same sex) is important for two reasons at this stage. First, peers encourage each other to rebel, vent hostility, be aggressive, explore sex, and do all the things the adult community says "no" to. Secondly, they help each other evaluate themselves and their skill attainments. Children's self-concepts are influenced and shaped by their buddies.

There is a tendency for "restrictive" parents to produce passive children and for "permissive" parents to produce active children, but a number of factors—such as economic background, number of siblings, and so forth—moderate this trend.

There is also some truth in the statement that firstborn children come away from the home experience as junior parents, especially if there

parent is to beat the child to submission. In children under two years about one in every four fractures brought to a hospital is due to battering. Between 50,000 and 100,000 children are battered every year in the United States.

Since many abusing parents were abused themselves as children, an antidote for helping such parents is to teach them other ways to be "good" parents than the ways they learned as children. Parents Anonymous groups, based on the same idea as Alcoholics Anonymous but with the slightly changed credo, "I will go from one day to the next without striking my child," encourage all parents to acknowledge the child-beating tendencies within them. Senator Mondale, D-Minnesota, has proposed a bill that would establish a number of provisions to help monitor the area of child abuse. At present there is no federal money being spent on the problem.

Experienced medical people can usually detect

are younger siblings. Parents usually try harder with (demand more from) the firstborn and tend to leave that child with more anxiety about her or his acceptance. By the time parents have raised a child or two, they are either less hopeful of their influence or less anxious about it and usually restrict the other children less.

Firstborn children are expected to achieve, and they tend to give themselves high achievement standards. Since there have been no older sibling models to follow, they often model their behavior after their parents' and are given and accept more responsibility sooner than their siblings. Although these are not hard and fast laws of conduct, they have held up in research trends, especially when there is a four- to ten-year separation in age between the firstborn and the later children. It is also often harder for firstborn to express their true feelings, especially to adults, and when they do, guilt often ensues. There are also advantages to being first, of course. Firstborn do achieve many good things for themselves and are often quite successful at whatever they undertake. Koch (1956) has studied the effect of siblings on each other in a study of 384 families. If you are interested in the effect of birth order on personality, it is a good study to read. In another study, Bossard and Ball (1955) felt they had discovered three role identities that helped to characterize what effect birth order tends to produce. They characterize the firstborn as the responsible child, the second as the sociable, well-liked child, and the youngest as the spoiled child. (It would be unwise, however, for you to draw conclusions about your own situation on the basis of such general terms as *responsible*, *sociable*, and *spoiled*.)

The child of this age group (six through twelve) learns to win recognition by producing things. Erikson asserts that children of this age mainly concern themselves with the development of pre-worker skills. If the child often becomes discouraged or "fails" at developing a skill at this age (be it music, art, sports, and so forth), it can affect his or her later relationships. This is an important time for the child to find something she or he can do well and enjoy. In fact, the effects of relationships at home that have been affecting the child during the first six years can be seen more clearly at this time. Whether a family is basically open or closed in its relation to children is important during this period. All the members of a family can affect each other to such an extent that we cannot look at development at this age only from the child's point of view. Let us look for a moment at what an open or closed family can mean.

ALLOWING THE CHILD TO GROW:
OPEN AND CLOSED FAMILY RELATIONS

In their book *Open Marriage* the O'Neills mention the concept of closed marriage as well. A closed marriage can have a profound effect on both parents and children. In the closed marriage *she* (the wife) does the cooking and housework, *he* (the husband) carries the laundry to and from the laundromat, and they both monitor each other's friends. They socialize as a couple, watch over each other's needs for privacy, compromise each other's individuality, and "grow together." The same wife who regards her husband's time at home as belonging to her by contract is likely to howl, "My God, he's driving me crazy. I can't wait for him to get back to work." He can hardly wait himself.

Maslow (1954) found that in the growth-oriented families he studied, a number of salient characteristics existed:

1. Each person was respected as an independent entity.
2. Members did not seek to control or use each other for their own gain.
3. Jealousy was absent.
4. Both adults were regarded as equal partners.
5. Children were allowed a fundamental dignity.

Virginia Satir, a noted family therapist, talks of the family as an open or a closed system of relationships (1967). In her excellent book *People Making* she describes the various roles family members may put on for size. Quite often there is someone at home (or different people at different times) who takes the *Blamer* role, saying things like, "Why did you do that?" or, "I think you ought to. . . ." There may also be a *Placater* who smooths over all the differences between people and says things like, "It's not so bad," or "I'll try harder next time." Also in view may be an *Avoider*, who somehow is never around when important family things are going on. The Avoider's famous cry is "What?" Finally, the *Computer* may be there to take in the information and spit out the results. With no show of feelings, he or she usually says "What's really happening here is . . .".

Of course, we can spot these roles in ourselves. We may ask, "If I really do that a lot, what effect does it have on the rest of my family?" Before you begin to feel guilty about the awful effect you have had on your family—with the realization that you can't appreciably change it—let's look at how families operate. As you look at these methods, ask yourself if there are different times in your family when one of them might bring better results than another:

1. *The Edict Method*—a parent uses authority and simply says, "This is the way it's going to be."
2. *The Voting Method*—everyone gets a vote and the majority wins.
3. *The Adventure Method*—everyone states his or her point of view and these are all tested against "reality" to see what's possible.
4. *The Expediency Method*—whoever is available gets stuck with the work or the decision.

Can you spot the method your family most often uses? If so, you may be able to try a different approach.

Adolescence (Ages 12–18)

SOCIAL NEEDS AND SOCIAL DEMANDS

More emphasis is made at this time to work with others for a common purpose. Altruism strengthens. Sex attraction becomes a dominant force. Girls usually begin shaving their legs, washing their hair daily, and worrying about braces and acne. Physically and socially they mature more rapidly than boys. Boys usually also start to groom themselves and dress up. Intellectual needs give way to social ones. Interests become selective and are often unrelated to the school curriculum. Small cliques are often created and, particularly in high school, may become variously labeled as *high rollers*, *jocks*, *greasers*, *cowboys*, or the many "freak" groups that come and go. Friendship groups of two, three, and four become quite common. Group approval reigns supreme. Although almost all external details are regulated by the group, the inner life of the teenager is often quite individualistic. There is usually a great deal of questioning about how much of this inner life to reveal and to whom.

Ambivalence is the key word. Twelve- to eighteen-year-olds want very much to be totally responsible for themselves but can't always hack it. (Who can?) Parents and society tend to ignore or condescend, which is like pouring salt on an open wound. Structure is a better remedy. All parties to this conflict need to structure (spell out) things more clearly so that compromises can be offered. Then, at least if they don't agree, they won't feel guilty about their own behavior.

In an excellent article, Warren Boroson (1969) makes a number of statements about the plight of the adolescent in our society. They all boil down to the fact that our society has not found a productive or honorable place for young people to be. The adolescent is at his or her peak of energy, physical well-being, mental stamina, and sexual drive, and where can it go? What vehicle does society offer? Because this question is difficult to answer, it is often put squarely on adolescents to figure out themselves. That's not such a bad thing—except the alternatives are usually not fully open; hence the bind.

Erik Erikson spoke to this problem in 1950, when he postulated his theory of life stages. At that time our country was prospering and content. His statements, with minor modifications, seem even more to the point today.

Ego identity, as Erikson termed the process, must in some way overtake role diffusion for the adolescent. There is more diffusion or falling away of the traditional roles today than at any point in history, he said. "Falling in love," for example, is an attempt at identity and stability epitomized in the practice of "going steady." An intelligent society (democracy) cannot afford to leave matters of legislation and general policy to "insiders and bosses." Erikson's plea over twenty years ago was to

> . . . give absolute priority over precedent and circumstance, convention and privilege, to the one effort which can keep a democratic country healthy; the effort to "summon forth the potential intelligence of the younger generation."

BECOMING INTIMATE: FINDING ONE'S IDENTITY

What is greater on this earth than the ability to love someone else intimately? Many people can and do; love should not be so elevated as to seem out of our grasp. Intimacy is the high point in all the previous identifications a person has achieved and transcends any particular previous identity. It may not come in this stage (adolescence), but if it does not occur in the next, it probably never will. The adolescent's inability to attempt or achieve intimacy often leads to personal isolation and an iconoclastic style of life. Adolescence and early adulthood is an important time for finding one's identity, and sex is a natural vehicle in this exploration.

BECOMING INTIMATE: PLAYING LOVE GAMES

As a result of Eric Berne's book *Games People Play*, there has been a renewed focus on gamesmanship and on one-upsmanship styles of relating. Most people bring their characteristic styles of relating with them to the dating or mating situation. It is difficult for them to know if they're playing games or if what they do is really the way they usually are. Games of any sort generally appeal more to the task-oriented than to the person-oriented individual. For that reason there are mixed feelings about the use of games.

One popular love game that often prevails nowadays is that "woman wants relationship and man wants sex." So to get the man, the woman provides. A more subtle aspect of this duality is that a man generally has lower expectations of his date than she does of him, and consequently, men tend to fall in love more quickly but less reliably than women (Coombs and Kenkel 1966).

Shostrom (1972) puts the basic emphasis of lovingness into a developmental context somewhat as follows:

1. *Affection* (ages 1–6)—a parent's feeling for a child
2. *Friendship* (ages 6–12)—the feeling between good buddies
3. *Eros* (ages 13–21)—the feelings in a romance; they may include inquisitiveness, jealousy, exclusiveness, carnal desire, and feeling spaced out
4. *Empathy* (ages 21+)—a deep feeling and concern for another person

This does not mean that one must be twenty-one to have a deep feeling and concern for another. Rather, it is a rough guide to the general stages of one's love relationships that can eventually develop to include affection, friendship, eros, and empathy.

We previously said that love could not be analyzed objectively, but what if someone were to try? Someone did. His name is Zick Rubin and he is a Harvard psychologist.

LOVE-HATE RELATIONSHIPS

THE LOVING AND LIKING SCALES

In his book on this subject Zick Rubin (1973) sets out to devise a measure (predictor) of love. Well, that is a bit grandiose, and Rubin (*not* to be confused with the *"Everything You Wanted to Know About Sex but Were Afraid to Ask"* man) knew it. As would any well-trained researcher, Rubin chose to omit some aspects of what we call "love" from his study. Love that exists between children and parents, close friends, and worshippers and God was excluded; the focus was on that special "romantic" love that exists between unmarried persons of the opposite sex. The first step, as Rubin saw it, was to establish a scale for evaluating love. He made up about eighty items that reflected aspects of one person's attitudes toward a particular other person, such as "How much fun is _____ to be with?" and had friends and acquaintances sort these items into "liking" and "loving" sets, based on their own interpretation of what these categories meant to them. Seventy of these items were submitted to a new sample, and the results were subjected to factor analysis in order to separate the loving from the liking scales. The next step was to test the scales out in the context of ongoing dating relationships. During the academic year 1968–69 Rubin advertised, and with an inducement of a small amount of money, was able to get a sample of 182 dating couples who were students at the University of Michigan. About twenty percent of them were engaged; fifty-two percent of the women and twenty-nine percent of the men lived in dormitories; thirty-one percent of the women and sixty percent of the men lived in their own apartments; ten percent belonged to a fraternity. The sample was fifty percent Protestant, seventeen percent Catholic, and twenty-five percent Jewish. Each partner filled out the love and liking scales independent of the other. When the results were in, there were some interesting findings:

1. Men were less able to differentiate their liking attitudes from their loving ones toward their female friends than women were for their male friends. Women seemed more discriminating in this regard.

2. Average love scores of men for their girlfriends and women for their boyfriends were identical.

3. Women liked their male friends significantly more than they were liked in return. This result is at least in part due to such sex-biased items as "Would you vote for your partner in an election?" or "Would you recommend your partner for a responsible job?" These questions are somewhat slanted toward the male world.

4. Outside of the dating relationships men were no more likeable than women.

5. Dating relationships tended to emphasize role and status stereotypes. Traditional male-female relations were fortified.

6. Women tend to love their female friends more than men love their male friends.

A further check on the validity of these scales was to correlate the love-scale scores with a known behavior that occurs between people who are on intimate terms—increased eye contact. Rubin invited the couples to take part in a laboratory experiment. While the two partners sat across the table from each other waiting for the experiment to begin, two researchers observed them through a one-way mirror. Whenever the man looked at the woman's face (and vice versa) a clock recorder was activated. A third clock recorder was pushed when both partners were eyeing each other simultaneously. The results were confirming. "Strong lovers," as measured by the love scale, made significantly more simultaneous eye contacts with each other than "weak lovers." The giveaway here was not the amount of eye contact, but whether the partners tended to look at each other at the same time—an important distinction. Further, this strong or weak eye contact took place only with the lover and not when lovers were with other people.

Rubin attempted to obtain two other measures to strengthen the network of variables that seem to tie in with love. Both attempts failed, but I will include them here for the same reason he did: "Like people in most other walks of life, psychological researchers prefer to advertise their successes and play down their failures. I include them (the failures) here, nevertheless, because they illustrate a familiar aspect of every researcher's journey."

The first hypothesis was that when lovers are together, time goes by more quickly. The second hypothesis was that high love scorers should exhibit more "caring" or helping behaviors toward their lovers than low scorers. No difference between high and low scorers was noted on these two questions.

Looking at his data further, Rubin noted some other similarities between the strong lovers:

1. There was better than chance correlation (.51) of similarity on the dimension of liberal versus traditional, social, and political attitudes.
2. Sixty-two percent of the "strong" couples were of the same religion or nonreligion.

Six months later a follow-up questionnaire was sent to the 182 couples. Only three couples could not be reached by follow-up requests. One or both partners out of 179 couples responded. By this time, twenty-nine couples had broken up. By noting which of these couples felt their relationship had grown in intensity, Rubin discovered an interesting correlation. In the initial questionnaire a "romanticism scale" was used with such items as "A person should marry whomever he loves regardless of social position" or, even better, "As long as they at least love one another, two people should have no difficulty getting along together in marriage." This is an aspect of the "love is blind" notion. Interestingly, a high romanticism scale score predicted progress toward a more intense relationship, as seen through the eyes of the lovers.

A most interesting side effect probably took place as a result of this experiment. This is the effect, sometimes called the Hawthorne Effect, that the experiment or intervention itself has as it helps or hinders the thing being studied. One of the problems all social psychologists face is the extent to which what they are doing as experimenters will bias the results. As it turns out, Dr. Rubin served as a premarital counselor "in absentia." The many unsolicited comments from the couples at the six-month follow-up indicated that working in his research project helped to cement the relationship for them.

Early Adulthood (ages 18–30)
MAKING BASIC LIFE DECISIONS

This may be a lonely stage. Young adults are usually "between families" during part of this time. They are often on their own for the first time or living with someone who may or may not be particularly supportive. A number of events take place in this stage and major decisions are made for which little or no training has been given—for example, buying a house, deciding on marriage, or having a child. Havighurst (1952) notes that the move at this age is from an age-graded society to a status-graded one. In other words, although age and class in school identified status in high school or college, now job or position throws one into the company of others both older and younger. Other decisions that Havighurst enumerates at this stage include choosing whether to become a doctor, a dentist, a lawyer, a housewife, and the like. For women, there may be questions of when to quit a job for a pregnancy, whether to have an abortion, whether to nurse, and when to resume work or school. In addition, a widowed or divorced person generally questions the value of becoming available once again and often must run the gamut of making basic decisions all over again.

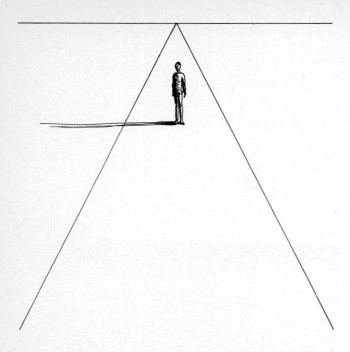

DEALING WITH LONELINESS

Loneliness does not come from having no people about me, but from being unable to communicate the things that seem important to oneself, or from holding certain views which others find inadmissible.

—*C. G. Jung*

There are those, who, for a variety of reasons, tend to develop loneliness as a lifestyle. These people very often don't listen when you talk to them. They are busy in their fantasies or in figuring what to say next. They stay inside themselves, yet they wish there were some face-saving way to be better received and responded to. We've all been there. I worked with one such person over a period of four years. On one occasion (knowing she enjoyed writing) I asked her to jot down an answer to the question, "Who am I?" She wrote a ten-page single-spaced letter and attached three poems.

She was really into herself. Of course, there are many lonely people who find themselves, day-in, day-out, moving counter to many in-groups of the system they must live in—the old, the divorced, the nonwhite, the gay. Such is the case of Judy. The following are excerpts from this young woman's response to "Who am I?" Can you detect signs of this person's loneliness? What would you counsel her to do?

The Case of Judy*

I am a brown-eyed, brown-haired 5'7" girl twenty years old. I am slim, pretty, and near-sighted without contacts.

I love to read and write most of all, but I also like people, swimming, roller skating, and miniature golfing, and the indescribable delight of pure beauty. Plus the joy of dancing.

The one thing in the world I really want to be is a wife-homemaker-mother. But first I need to fall in love, be loved, and get married. And since I've set my requirements pretty high and exact, it'll be a while before I find a man to love—I think. For, you see, I want a man who is tall, slim, strong, and at least presentable-looking—a head taller, sort of like my father. Also I want a man who is a little smarter than I am and would win fifty percent of our arguments. Yet, also, I want a partnership based on mutual respect, admiration, and love. I want a man who is intellectual, but has a very good sense of humor—enough to understand mine and know when I'm joking and not. I also want a man with a career like engineering, physics, teaching, or theoretical math. But I guess most of all I just want a man who loves me as deeply as I love him and will accept me as I am.

Meanwhile I've got a temporary career in mind: airline stewardess. I'm old enough now and besides it'd take me away from home. That's the part I'd love because right now I just don't feel like living at home and "fitting into

---

*Judy, an only child, was a loner who felt awkward around people. Most of her time as a student was spent reading non-assigned books and articles. She eventually flunked out of school.

the household pattern," where I'm graciously supposed to do what I'm told when I'm told. I just don't feel free, even if I can date any boy I want to, come in around twelve or one o'clock, go to any retreats and meetings or churches. Plus any number of other things — within reason of course (which is the way I go anyhow). This may seem like a lot of nice, uninterfering freedom, but I still don't feel free enough to do what I want to do — reading and writing. I must admit I get a fair amount done, yet somehow just when I'm in the middle of it, the dishes have to be put away or the table set. Not great burdens in themselves, but somewhere, somebody's timing is off, even if it's partly mine. I really don't belong at home any more, and I think soon it'll be the right time to move out and be on my own. It won't be the same as my two years of college days, for there'll be a job and bills, and so forth, but there'll be less pressure and perhaps I'll be one step further in my quest for self-knowledge and maturity 'cause I've still got some more growing to do.

This comes from the fact I'm still such a bundle of cross-betweens. I'm physically at midpoint between my parents, plus the fact I have my mother's sociability and dominance and my father's quietness and his own opinions.

I'm not completely the well-turned nice girl, yet I never will be the girl who smokes, drinks, swears, and plays with sex with equal abandon. This is simply my choice I've made as I've grown up some, and it's been reaffirmed by two girls I've known who were rebelling in the wrong way and direction. Plus the fact that I've been singed by some sex that was the fault of my own overeager wish for affection. And now I'm not going to do anything much until I get married (I hope it's soon!) because I know I still want to give affection and have sex anyhow, and I'm afraid I might go too far and I don't want to because I want to stay a virgin until I'm

married; therefore I'll end up with almost too much control. If only somewhere along the way I could strike a balance between things before I get much more frustrated.

Furthermore, I'm just beginning to really be interested in people, so there's still enough times when I couldn't care less or I callously kick someone completely out of my life for one reason of self-preservation or another. Also I'm still rather contented with a pile of books and a ream of paper and a pen. But if I just work at it long enough, time will improve me. Besides, I've a very giving nature under my protective covering and if only I could find something to channel this into it'd help.

On the other hand there is that hard protective covering that was formed because of childhood hurts I still sometimes remember vividly and because I always felt a little different from my friends and never felt completely "in" all the way through high school. And it's still hard to get over the feeling that the world doesn't seem to have very many people who I could understand or feel comfortable with. Also I was a "late bloomer" who almost never dated in high school and not much more in college. Somehow I encountered more kids that dated early, and that was just one more thing that made me feel lonely. Plus the fact I've never really wanted to follow any of the fads in dress. Also, reading has always been my refuge, relief, delight, hope, love, and promise that I withdraw to. It's a vicious circle. I also happened to go to a private girl's school from eighth grade through eleventh. Although it was very good academically, it set me apart further from the only group I was ever somewhat a part of, my church youth group.

Furthermore, it was as soon as I became a teenager that my revolt began. Since I didn't see any sense in revolting by dressing differently or running with the wrong crowd, I revolted by almost never getting better than C's, although I'm capable of A's and B's. I also found that I forgot or couldn't hear my mother's demands of any sort. These were the only ways I knew of rebelling, though the second was subconscious and still is. In fact I didn't stop at one or two years of it. I did a thoroughgoing job of it right up to the present. Of course, it's backfired in some ways: my parents are never sure if they can trust me or believe me about grades or the promise that I'll do better this time (I'm not sure whether I've exhausted this belief quite yet or not). And of course it'll make me (seem) more childish to them in some ways. The only things I've ever done well on are aptitude, potentiality, and ability tests like National Merit Scholarship tests or College Boards. So, if I tried I could do it; maybe I will yet.

But I need goals for trying, and so far I haven't found anything sufficiently good to do it. I love linguistics and writing, yet I haven't figured out a way to use them in a major or for a job. I like the idea of being a speech therapist, or a social worker, but I don't think I'm dedicated enough yet to be either—and if you're not dedicated it isn't right to go into that sort of career. I'm interested in Hebrew and Israel, yet they fall into the same category as linguistics. Sometimes I wonder if I set up interests and then knock them down because I'm afraid of or don't want a career in them or because I'm still a naturally vacillating youth who can't make up her mind, because all the world is so interesting.

The "I'm-never-sure-which" feeling is always cropping up because I haven't any guide to what's normal and whether I am at all, because in the majority the kids I've known for the last eight years have had somewhat different values and likes and dislikes from me and all I've known is a feeling of differentness—sometimes queenly, sometimes lonely. And while my parents are more or less like me and understand and are understandable and have shown and given standards, ideals, goals, morals, and so forth, there still is also a difference I can't bridge. I guess this is all because I just haven't met enough people anywhere near like me with problems anywhere near like mine. That sounds egotistical even to me but it seems the only way I can get a better guideline until I'm surer of myself and more interested in other people in spite of complete differences.

If reading this case makes you feel frustrated or angry, that is probably a healthy reaction. Judy does frustrate herself (and those who try to help her) beyond any doubt. She responds to slights and hurts by covering up and vowing never to venture out "there" again. She escapes to reading and writing and, in fact, spent two years in college constantly reading but seldom doing her classroom assignments. Judy sets up an interest area and then knocks it down before she's tried it. She wants a protector and stabilizer in a man. In fact, she has trouble differentiating her perceptions of "God" and "future husband." But the real giveaway is her statement, "I'm never sure what I'm feeling." The cure for Judy is to become aware of her feelings and to channel her desperation, frustration, hostility, and anger into something (someone) who can move her on the road to self-fulfillment. This, in fact, she was able to achieve a few years later.

Let's go back for a minute to the task that we associate with this particular stage of development—marriage—and focus a bit on some alternatives.

Marriage and Its Consequences

"One of the simplest explanations for the persistence of marriage," according to the O'Neills (1972) ". . . lies in man's innate need for structure." An equally cynical statement that marriage has become a habit might be proffered. If we look beyond the borders of our country and our century, we can see that some form of marriage has been part of human life for many centuries. Historically, the reasons for family life have typically been three-fold: 1) preservation of the species, 2) economic sub-sistence, and 3) education of the young. All three of these reasons are now under fire and none hold the strength of purpose they once did. The patriarchal system of marriage of the Judeo-Christian tradition is tied in with stable male-female, mother-father roles and expectations. This, too, is being vehe-mently questioned.

When women "work" in this country it is usually outside the family—a change from the ideal of Mom as housewife whose rewards were sufficient in just maintaining a home. Wrenn (1973) adds that role sharing between husband and wife and the shrink-age of the extended family are other indications of change. Yet almost half of all American females who marry do so before the age of twenty-one, in spite of the disillusionment one hears about the sacred institution.

Experimenting with Marriage

Is marriage "the real thing"? To what extent are people experimenting with group marriage, couple swaps, communal living, polygamy, sequential marriage, and various nonmarriage arrangements? And to what extent do they work? These questions are about as difficult to answer (more difficult, really) as the question of whether existing mar-riages are working out as planned, for two reasons. Invasion of privacy laws prevent social scientists from voyeuring their way into certain areas of life to gather data. Secondly, how would you judge a working system if you saw one? By sending out married researchers?

Robert Rimmer, author of *The Harrad Experi-ment*, talked about his latest novel *Thursday, My Love* in an interview in which various types of romantic unions were discussed (Rimmer 1972). He predicted the increase of socially approved group marriages, bigamous marriages, and open-end marriages in which each partner has a relationship

outside the marriage. There's a strong sentiment among those who favor monogamous marriage that "there are enough problems in relationships between two people — why compound the problem by adding more?" Certainly a group becomes more complex as it becomes larger, and increasing numbers tends to intimidate individuals.

People who hope to solve their communication problems by creating new group structures probably won't. But, a nagging thought — if structure is important to people and if a shaky structure is anxiety-provoking, then perhaps it doesn't matter what form marriage ends up in if we can just all agree what the form should be. The question that now occurs is that the economic motives for the established family may turn back upon us and force the family to add more people under the same roof to meet inflation-produced costs. Perhaps the old form of extended nuclear family will, because of economics, turn into that of an extended multigroup family.

The possessive quality of many of today's marriage agreements is certainly another obstacle to changing systems. Can a person really share someone whom he or she loves deeply without debilitating jealousy? What are the consequences? Perhaps we can talk of the value of "free love" but personally cringe at the consequences.

In his book *Future Shock* Alvin Toffler talks about the possibility of parent professional units being available in the future. Such "families" would take on new "units" as old ones graduated. He suggests that newspapers of the future might carry an ad as follows:

Why let parenthood tie you down? Let us raise your infant into a responsible, successful adult. Class A pro-family offers: father, age 39, mother, 36, grandmother, 67. Uncle and aunt, age 30, live in, hold part-time local employment. Four-child-unit has opening for one, age 6–8. Regulated diet exceeds government standards. All adults certified in child development and management. Bio-parents permitted frequent visits. Telephone contact allowed. Child may spend summer vacation with bio-parents. Religion, art, music encouraged by special arrangement. Five-year contract, minimum. Write for further details.

What do you think?

Marriage Fights: Fighting Fair

We haven't forgotten about the hate aspect of marriage. As was indicated earlier, many of the categories we are used to thinking within are products of habit. These two chapters on love and hate are as difficult to structure on paper as they are in life, so perhaps we should not try too hard to force a pattern. Marriage, family relations, and the prejudices thereof certainly relate not only to how we develop as individuals but also to the way newlyweds look at their roles in marriage. Even though we have learned from the Milgram and Zimbardo studies (1963,1972) that it is relatively easy for most people to hurt someone, we don't like to think of ourselves as so "childish" as to hurt the ones we love. Couples who do not fight may be among those few who have really got things together. More likely, however, is the possibility that they just do not care about each other any more.

Fighting in a marriage can be a way to clear the air and a prelude to constructive communication *if* the fighting follows certain rules. How can you impose rules on yourself when you are so angry that all you really want to do is smash things or toss people around? Remember the young mother who poured hot water on her baby? Rules are only a beginning. The real answer is to keep resentment down by solving little problems as they come up and not "gunnysacking" them, as George Bach terms it. In their book *The Intimate Enemy*, Bach and Peter Wyden indicate that one of the rules of fair fighting is to keep the focus of the fight on current affairs. When you "gunnysack" your problems you slip all your petty resentments into an imaginary gunny-

sack with, "Oh well, it's not that important to go into now." Then when you're mad enough to fight, you bring out all the goodies from your gunnysack with, "How you [the other person] lost something of mine two weeks ago," or, "How about last year? You did the very same thing," or, "You're just like your mother," and so forth.

Another rule is to be as honest about your feelings as possible. Without launching out on a blaming campaign, can you tell the other person the way you feel? Further, a most important point in both loving and fighting is *not* to try to win. In the same way that the surest way to sexual unhappiness is to have to have an orgasm lest you suffer humiliation and defeat, the surest way to ruin a good fight is to have to win. George Krupp (1970) a marriage therapist of some twenty years, suggests that the way we fight is more important in its consequences to us than what we fight about. For example, in a married

couples' group Krupp ran, one woman indicated that in her marriage there was screaming, yelling, and vulgar name-calling. When asked to talk about the last such incident she could remember like that, she said, "Let me think about it." Eventually it became clear to her that she approached most of her fights with her husband in the same evasive and nonspecific manner as she did when she said, "Let me think about it"—really a more important point in itself than being able to recall whatever the last fight *was* about. One of the men in the group brought up the fact that after eight years of marriage he and his wife were headed for divorce. Why? After first implicating his parents as rejecting him the question was raised, "What has this got to do with your wife?" He then described his wife as cold and distant like his mother. But when she was asked, "Are you a cold cookie like his mother?" she rejoined, "No. I'm a hot potato." Basic to their relationship was the fact that her expectations came from her parents, who were warm, physically demonstrative people. She brought this expectation to the marriage and initially showered her husband with affection. He, coming from a cold, aloof set of parents, didn't know how to accept it. The upshot of the situation was that he had turned her off and then could say, "She's a cold cookie, like my mother." This self-fulfilling prophecy is very common. One person becomes the victim of a set-up job and the other may not even be aware that he or she is projecting personal inadequacies.

There are many reasons to fight in a marriage, but the surest way to fight dirty is to hold back. Some couples may have to begin by writing notes to each other or setting up tape recorders to get a perspective on what they are doing to each other. If there is any love in the marriage, they'll eventually be able to communicate directly and become aware of those issues that can and cannot be resolved. When each person can truly accept the other's way of expressing love and hate, then the reality begins to sink in that one *can* love someone and not have to change them.

Divorce

As a friend once said, "Humor is a funny thing." It depends on incongruity for its effect. I have just this minute returned from a wedding to sit down and ponder some thoughts on divorce. It's a little difficult to jump right into the topic at this point in time. This is because the myth of wedded bliss and happiness ever after can't even be fantasized these days when the divorce rates are looked at. The odds of staying married are approaching one in two. When this is coupled with the fact that eighty percent of those who are divorced remarry (Wrenn 1973), we have a sequential marriage pattern that breaks the one-person-for-life fantasy in half.

When efforts at communication have failed or when "the love is gone" from the relationship, divorce may be a very good move. In fact, if feelings are gone and the effort is too tiring, the sooner the divorce occurs the better. Yet psychologically the same phenomena occur to people in divorce as they do in any other loss situation. Inwardly the person contemplating or experiencing divorce feels less than whole. This is expressed through anger, depression, or denial. There is a tendency to blame ourselves just as we do when someone close to us dies. "Maybe I haven't done enough" is the haunting fear. "Was it really my fault?" is a recurring echo. There is also a tendency to blame the other person and to find that one has just no more feeling left for him or her.

A network of relationship complexities begins to develop for the divorced person and all those with whom he or she associates. Friends may not be as sure any more who of the couple to invite over and, in fact, may resolve the ambiguity by dropping them both. Children may cling harder to or fight harder with the parent into whose custody they are delivered. Either parent may suddenly begin behaving in the same way toward the child (or children) and

seek new satisfactions or vent new frustrations, to the detriment of the child. Whatever the relationships turn out to be, the divorced person has to withstand a great deal of change at a time when resistance is down.

This is definitely a time for the divorced person to take stock of what is going on inside. Since she or he is probably already doing this it is usually a good idea to seek out a third party (not a potential mate, though) who might offer some perspective. Someone the person can trust is the best choice—a good friend, pastor, psychological counselor, close relative. The important thing to do is to begin feeling good about oneself again, and that is something that *can* be achieved with help.

Middle Age (ages 30–55)

ACHIEVING YOUR GOALS

Over the hill? I suppose this is the place to mention that Galileo summarized his life's work at sixty-eight, Tolstoy wrote a book on art at sixty-seven, and George Bernard Shaw wrote some great plays in his seventies. However, the various decisions that were made in one's twenties do take their toll. During the thirties divorces are high, careers are derailed, and accidents and suicides occur with great frequency. There's also a positive side to report. The Grant Study (*Human Behavior* 1973), begun some thirty-five years ago, has followed up a group of 267 college sophomore men who are now pushing sixty. The researchers report that the men reported to be the happiest with their lot tended to pursue intimacy with a woman first and a career second. Ninety percent had achieved a stable marriage before thirty and had stayed married, at least into their fifties. Men tended to hustle hard at their careers between twenty-five and thirty-five (remember this is the 1930s). When in their forties these men took closer stock of their past; some switched jobs and marriage partners, and most became more concerned about their children, (a little late, maybe). One man was reported to summarize the group's experience when he said, "At twenty to thirty I think I learned how to get along with my wife. From thirty to forty I learned how to be a success at the job. And at forty to fifty I worried less about myself and more about the children." Perhaps the most important finding of the study was that while the so-called mid-life crisis of reappraisal at age forty affected quite a few, it didn't appear to portend decay. In fact, many found a more comfortable style to live in.

Aside from the differing expectations one finds in a generation gap, middle age can be a time when increased closeness is achieved between parents and children. Often tasks can be shared and good times can be had if parents relax their guards and teenagers become less grim at home, or vice versa.

After we enter middle age, we may find that our parents depend on us a little more at this stage. This is not necessarily a disaster, since a more equal relationship often occurs after the knowledge that neither party really has to do the parent-child bit any more. In some societies the older generation retain power and property until they die; in others power and property are passed onto the middle-aged generation, which looks after the older one. And some societies leave their older members to care for themselves and to go quietly off alone and die. Our society has bits of all these alternatives.

COPING WITH WHAT YOU'VE BECOME

The final stage in Erickson's system occurs in middle age. If the previous stages have passed with some degree of satisfaction, the middle-aged person will basically feel good about where she or he is at. There is usually a mid-life crisis of feeling caught between things that can't be changed (the past) and little time or energy to change in any basic way (the future). Despair follows on the heels of the person who feels there is no way of integrating the ego at this time. Disgust may be the symptom of despair. Trust, the first stage, comes back on itself. Erikson puts it as follows:

. . . it seems possible to further paraphrase the relation of adult integrity (stage 8) and infantile trust (stage 1) by saying that healthy children will not fear life if their parents have integrity enough not to fear death.

Later Maturity and Old Age

In the words of that great American cynic, H. L. Mencken, "No show is so good that it should last forever." It *is* lasting, longer, however, since more than ten percent of our population is over sixty-five.

Kastenbaum (1971) conducted an intriguing experiment in which he took one characteristic of old age—slowness of movement—and simulated it in a group of college students. The students were required to learn to perform certain tasks. As soon as they had learned the procedures, they were speeded up to twice the normal rate. The way they solved problems was thought to be predictive of how they might handle "speed" situations forty years later. Some became impulsive, some became passive and withdrew, while others stuck to a routine whether it worked or not. Thus, it may be possible to see ourselves now as we will become and to prepare ourselves to make some changes.

Weight gain, decrease in muscle strength, falling hair, wrinkled skin, bending posture, weakening sight, taste, and hearing—these, and more, are all gradual effects of age. The cells build up poisons they can't discard and the self-repair of body parts slows down. Half of those over fifty die of some heart complication. Half who live past seventy-five will have to adapt to invalidism.

The death of a spouse can be very rough on the surviving partner. Men tend to die slightly earlier than women: by their late sixties and early seventies as many married women are widows as are not. If the relationship was very close and the survivor "lived for" the deceased spouse, there may be no more point in existence. Whether to live alone in the old home, move to an apartment or rooming house, move in with siblings or children, or move into a planned retirement home is a monumental decision to have to face alone. Yet there are those who take this on as a new adventure and brighten the souls of all around them.

In closing out the chapter I'd like to mention an old friend. He is eighty-six years old and has always delighted me by his wit, enthusiasm, and iconoclastic mind. Sidney Pressey, a psychologist, is still publishing as vigorously as he did in his thirties. Two years ago his wife, Alice, died. They had been living in an institution for old people in Columbus, Ohio. Pressey has argued for years of the value in the old counseling the old. In a recent article (1972) he described this as a "major neglected need opportunity." The opportunity also holds for young adults and the middle-aged to rub elbows with the senior citizens at these residence institutions, if done with soul and not condescendingly. Sid counsels the old where he lives. Perhaps I will too some day.

A Study of 70–79 Year Olds

Bernice Neugarten, who has studied the personality attributes of over 2000 aging people, recently (1971) described her study of persons aged seventy to seventy-nine. Psychological test data and home interviews were conducted over a seven-year period. Through factor analysis, she found four major personality types among this sample. The majority of the seventy-year-olds were in good psychological shape for their age. These were called the *integrated*. Some of them were engaged in a wide variety of activities; they were called the reorganizers. Another subgroup (the focused) carried on only a few activities. A third subgroup did not seem to be really involved in any single compelling activity (the disengaged). But all of the above were satisfied with themselves in general.

The second of the four major personality dimensions was labeled the *defended*. These were the fighters who maintained tight control over their impulses. These were the "I'll work until I drop" people. They had worked hard all their lives and it had paid off. Why should they stop now? Others focused on their health, spending hours shopping for just the right foods, talking constantly of their health and, in general, being cautious in all that they undertook.

The third group Neugarten described as the *passive dependent*. Some had, through love or guilt, encouraged others to pay daily visits or to take care of them in a number of ways. Some were apathetic and received help from those who took pity on them.

Finally there was a small group that could legitimately be described as the *disintegrated*. They were disorganized, had gross psychological dysfunctions, and required help to maintain their lives.

The fact that seventy-five percent of this 2000-person sample were satisfied with their post-retirement lives dispels a common myth in this country that once one hits seventy all is lost.

Chapter Eight Summary

In spite of excellent objective research on sex practices, the analysis of love is beyond the tools of science. It is because people come to mean so much to each other that love can be frustrated and turn to anger or hate.

Love and hate relationships evolve as we grow and take on different meanings at each of several stages. These can be summarized as follows:

1. The first six years—Trust, autonomy, and initiative, all of which affect love relationships, are developed.
2. Middle childhood (ages 6-12)—personal standards (ethics) develop; and peer involvement opens the way for a meaningful love relationship later.
3. Adolescence (ages 12-18)—Identity and intimacy interact; the adolescent tests limits of love and hate.
4. Early adulthood (ages 18-30)—The individual's role usually changes from family member to lover; the need to make it on one's own becomes paramount.
5. Middle age (ages 30-55)—Security in how and who to love becomes firm.
6. Later maturity and old age—Emotions of love and hate can still be strong, but are tempered by failing health and energy.

Glossary

Ambivalence Attraction toward something and repulsion from it at the same time. Example: "Gee, maybe you're right, but . . ." Not recommended as a life style.

Animism Attributing life to inanimate objects or forces.

Identification Becoming so much a part of someone else that one is unaware that he or she is like the other person.

Introjection The process of identifying.

Prelogical reasoning Piaget's term for the irrational associations in conceptual thought that are observed in children and, occasionally, in politicians, parents, and teachers (in that order).

Sensorimotor Referring to eye-hand, ear-leg, mouth-finger, nose-arm coordination, or any hook-up between your senses and another functioning part of your body.

Exercises *(For individual and class use)*

You can do the following exercises and tasks at your leisure. Perhaps some of these would be more enjoyable with a friend. Those with an asterisk (*) should be done in consultation with your teacher or in class.

1*. Take time to become relaxed and silent. If you are in a small group or with your loved one, alter the questions below to fit the context you are in. Then try to answer any or all of the questions below and share your answers in some detail with the one or ones you are with. Answer these questions voluntarily. Say "I pass" if you are not ready to share.

> A. What has been the most loving moment in my life (in our relationship)?
>
> B. How can I be more loving to others (to you)?
>
> C. How can others give more love to me (how can you)?
>
> D. What can I do to love myself more?

2. Develop a "family" (or use your own if all agree). Take the roles of Father, Mother, Susie, Johnie, and so forth. Have someone be a Blamer and find everything that comes up is someone else's fault. Someone else be a "smoother-over" type who tries to keep conflict at low key. Someone be an Avoider and never really attend to what is going on. Someone else may want to be the Computer. Pick a topic (buying a new car, where to spend your vacation, or some such) and see what happens. You may want others to sit around as observers to react to the whole performance later. Be creative in these roles and concentrate. Then exchange roles and try again. Discuss what happened afterwards.

3*. Tell the group, to whatever extent you feel comfortable in doing so, what parental qualities of your parents you find in yourself. Which of these qualities (behaviors) do you like and which don't you like?

4*. Try simulating a feeling of loneliness. Then share with the group or to yourself what you did with your body to achieve that feeling. How did you sit? How much of the environment became excluded? How? What did you do with your eyes? Why?

5. What sort of marriage arrangement or living arrangement do you see as possible for you? Who would you need to check this out with, if anyone? What are the advantages and disadvantages of the sort of arrangement you want?

6. Try to improvise a constructive fight between a husband and wife. What rules would be important to follow? Choose a topic to argue about (for example, one partner resenting something about the other) and have volunteers play the parts. Then discuss the outcome.

7. What do you think of Rubin's research? Pretty weak in methodology? How would you attempt to engineer a study on some aspect of the love or hate relationship? Perhaps you could rough out a design for extra credit in the course.

8. What changes, if any, might you expect in our society if all sixteen-year-olds were allowed to vote, drink, marry, pay taxes, and so forth? Perhaps this could be discussed in class.

Bibliography

Bach, G. and Wyden, P. 1969. *The intimate enemy*. New York: Morrow.

Bandura, A. and Walters, R. 1963. *Social learning and personality development*. New York: Holt, Rinehart & Winston.

Berkowitz, L. 1973. The case for bottling up rage. *Psychology Today* (July): 24–31.

Boroson, W. 1969. In defense of adolescents. *Avant Garde* (November): 20–25.

Bossard, J. and Ball, E. 1955. Personality roles in the large family. *Child Development* 26:71–78.

Coombs, R. and Kenkel, W. 1966. Sex differences in dating aspirations and satisfaction with computer-selected partners. *Journal of Marriage and the Family* 28:62–66.

Dollard, J., et al. 1939. *Frustration and aggression*. New Haven: Yale.

Erikson, E. 1950. *Childhood and society*. New York: Norton.

Freud, S. 1930. *Civilization and its discontents*. London: Hogarth.

Havighurst, R. 1952. *Developmental tasks and education*. New York: McKay.

Human Behavior. 1973. The new stages of man. *Human Behavior* July: 35.

Kagan, J. 1969. *Personality development*. New York: Harcourt Brace Jovanovich.

Kastenbaum, R. 1971. Age: getting there ahead of time. *Psychology Today* (December) 53 ff.

Kempe, C. 1911. Pediatric implications of the battered baby syndrome. *Archives of Disease in Childhood*.

Koch, H. 1956. Some emotional attitudes of the young child in relation to characteristics of his siblings. *Child Development* 27:393–426.

Krupp, G. 1970. Can fighting make a good marriage better? *Redbook* (February): 63.

Maslow, A. 1956. *Motivation and personality*. New York: Harper & Row.

Neugarten, B. 1971. Grow old along with me. The best is yet to be. *Psychology Today* (December): 45 ff.

O'Neill, N. and O'Neill, G. 1972. *Open marriage*. New York: Avon.

Piaget, J. 1952. *The origins of intelligence in children*. New York: International Univ. Press.

Pressey, S. 1972. Major neglected need opportunity: old age counseling. *Journal of Counseling Psychology* 19:362–66.

Rimmer, R. 1972. "Do you, Mary, and June, and Beverly, and Ruth, take these men. . . ." *Psychology Today* (January):57.

Rosenzweig, S. 1934. Types of reaction to frustration. *Journal of Abnormal and Social Psychology*. 29:298–300.

Rubin, Z. 1973. *Liking and loving*. New York: Holt, Rinehart & Winston.

Satir, V. 1967. *Conjoint family therapy*. Palo Alto, Calif.: Science and Behavior Books.

———. 1972. *People making*. Palo Alto, Calif.: Science and Behavior books.

Sears, R., Maccoby, E. and Levin, H. 1957. *Patterns of child rearing*. New York: Harper.

Shostrom, E. 1972. Love, the human encounter. In Otto, H., ed. *Love today*. New York: Association Press.

Singer, D. 1972. Piglet, Pooh and Piaget. *Psychology Today* (June).

Toffler, A. 1971. *Future shock*. New York: Bantam.

Watson, J. 1919. *Psychology from the standpoint of a behaviorist*. Philadelphia: J. B. Lippincott.

Wheeler, J. 1973. All the baby did was cry—and it nearly cost her life. *Arizona Daily Star*, April 22, 1973.

Wrenn, C. 1973. *The world of the contemporary counselor*. Boston: Houghton-Mifflin.

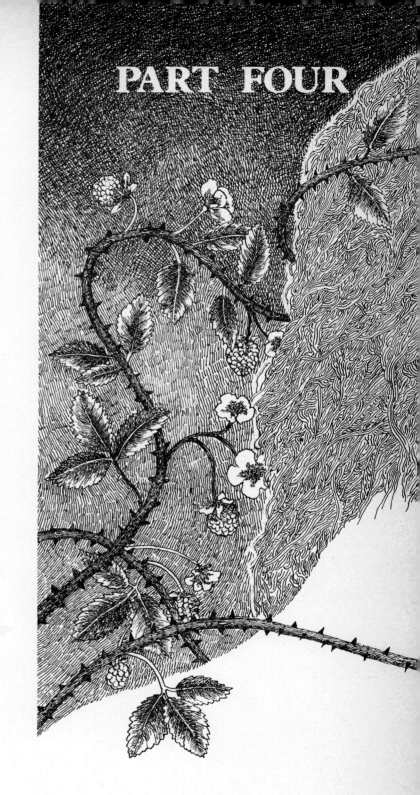

PART FOUR

Human Awareness

Part one was devoted to the factors that have influenced psychologists as they study human personality. Part two focused on the basic question, "Who am I?" We examined how we develop a sense of identity and the factors that facilitate and hinder personal growth. Underlying these sections was the basic conviction that developing a keen understanding of ourselves is the single most fundamental issue in successful living.

Part three extended the question *Who am I?* to several important areas of human adjustment: the way we adjust to the prospect of death, our personal beliefs, our sexual-aggressive natures, and our loving-hating relationships with others.

In part four we return to the theme of human awareness. First we will consider the topic of counseling and psychotherapy. Chapter nine discusses the major kinds of psychotherapy. It seems that each therapy tends to increase our awareness of a slightly different aspect of our personality. One focuses on the way biology influences our behavior, another deals with our social environment, and a third focuses on our unconscious. Chapter ten is devoted to our dreams and how we may use them to become more aware of ourselves. Anxiety and relaxation are very important aspects of our conscious experience. In chapter eleven we will discuss anxiety and its causes, as well as psychological techniques such as hypnosis, meditation, and biofeedback, which can be used to learn to relax and to cope with anxiety. Finally, in chapter twelve we will look at the frontiers of human awareness. Is there any limit to what we are capable of sensing? Extrasensory perception, sensitivity to electromagnetic waves, poltergeists, and other "things that go bump in the night" will be discussed. Such phenomena support the view that most of us use only a fraction of our potential for sensing and perceiving.

Every person experiencing his own solitude longs for union with another.

ROLLO MAY

Counseling for Personal Growth and Awareness

Most of us could use the services of a professional counselor at some time or other. I am often asked if counselors ever get discouraged and seek outside help. To this I can only reply that as I write this I am attending weekly counseling sessions to help me become a more effective parent. Another counselor I know is in marital counseling, and almost everyone on our staff seems to be participating in some sort of growth group or other awareness-raising experience. Counselors do have problems in coping and growing, and, like our clients, we do sometimes get frustrated enough to go do something about it.

Usually for a professional to be of assistance you, the counselee, must be aware that something is wrong. A problem exists, but you feel either unsure of what needs to be done or have been unsuccessful in your own attempts to intervene. Some frequent statements by clients who seek counseling:

- I feel terrible but I don't really understand what is the matter.
- I've tried everything I can think of, but nothing seems to work.
- I feel trapped. I can't see any way out of this situation.
- I feel frustrated that I'm not using my full potential.

A common theme in these and other statements is a feeling of being helpless (at least temporarily) to cope with or change some aspect of one's life. Sometimes the problem involves only one small area (such as, "I want to lose weight"). At other times the problem may involve dissatisfaction with an entire life style. All of use have problems; having problems does not differentiate those who seek help from those who do not. Instead, the common denominator among those who seek help appears to be a strong desire to change and, in general, a feeling of frustration with the results of their own efforts (Frank 1972).

But suppose I do want professional help. What kind of help is available? How do I decide which kind of help is best for me? And where do I go to get it? These are the questions we will deal with in this chapter.

57 Varieties of Help: The Bewildering World of Psychotherapy

To even begin to describe the many kinds of professional psychological help that are available would require a book in itself. Searching for professional help has become almost a hobby for some. Providing professional help is getting to be one of our major industries. One recent symposium listed twenty-two allegedly new and innovative approaches to psychotherapy. Suppose you or I decided we wanted to get some professional help. Where would we go?

For most people seeking help, the choice is not very complicated. Many who enter psychotherapy are given only one alternative. The most common way people in the community enter therapy is via an initial contact with a physician or minister who then recommends a therapist. Typically in such instances the professional will suggest one or two professionals he or she has heard good reports about rather than barrage the client with all possible alternatives. Likewise, in a university counseling center most of our initial contacts occur when a student reads that our services are available in a catalog or brochure, or because she or he has heard from a friend that Dr. so and so "helped me a lot, and I think he could help you too."

Actually the array of alternative forms of help is far greater than most seekers are likely to realize. If you live in a large metropolitan area such as Los Angeles or New York and were to make a comprehensive study of all the different forms of available psychological assistance available to you, you would be confronted with an array of alternatives similar to that in figure 9-1. And the choice is important. Considering the fact that going through therapy

FIG. 9-1. *Types of therapy*

may involve a complete revision of one's personal values and lifestyle, it may be said that your choice of therapist may be as important as your choice of marriage partner.

SOME QUESTIONS ABOUT HELP
If the choice is so important, how does one go about making it? We would suggest that anyone seeking a therapist (or simply knowledge about therapy) might begin his or her personal search by asking how a potential helper would answer the following three questions:

1. Why does this helper think that people come for help? Does this therapist's assumptions about why I am here make sense to me?
2. What is the nature of the help this person is willing to give? Does this kind of help seem relevant to the way I see my problem?

3. What kind of a person will this helper be with me? Will such a relationship be helpful to me?

These three questions are highly related. Helper's views of why people seek them are very likely to influence the kinds of help they offer and the kinds of people they try to be in the therapeutic relationship. This in turn will probably influence their beliefs about clients' needs and the help they are willing to give. Finally, the range of formal techniques and skills therapists have may limit their view of the clients' needs and influence what personality aspects they are willing to make visible.

WHAT "HELP" MEANS

While it is probably true that the motivations that lead a given individual to seek help are highly unique, there are some broader views of the matter that characterize different therapists and schools of therapy. Table 9.1 shows a sample of some of the more common views therapists hold about why people come to see them.

Although most therapists are flexible enough to view the needs of each of their clients as very unique and very individual, it is also true that many therapists tend to adhere rather strongly to one or more of the assumptions shown in the table about "the real reason" clients come to them.

The first view is essentially a medical one. "Help" involves treating a mental condition or illness. Drugs may be administered. Careful diagnosis of the underlying causes of the problem must precede treatment.

The second view has already been discussed in chapter one. There we referred to it as the second force in psychology—behaviorism. Behavior therapy is founded on the assumption that our behavior is controlled by external stimuli. "Help" to a behaviorist involves analyzing and changing our overt behavior.

The third view was discussed in chapter one as the first force in psychology—or dynamic psychol-

TABLE 9.1

What Helpers Think About Help and Helping

"People come to see me because . . ."	Help Means:	Helper's Role	Historical Origins
1. "They are mentally ill."	Diagnosing and attacking the "illness" that underlies them	"Doctor" or diagnostician	Medicine
2. "Their present behavior is maladaptive."	Changing their behavior	Expert on the psychology of learning, teacher and behavior shaper	Behavioral psychology
3. "They lack insight and understanding of their inner dynamics."	Stimulating self-understanding and exploration	Personality analysis expert	Dynamic psychology
4. "They seek personal growth and actualization of their full potentiality."	Freeing them to be fully themselves	Growth facilitator, model of a growing person	Humanistic psychology

ogy. "Help" to a dynamic psychologist means helping a person see and understand his or her own unconscious dynamics and motivation.

The fourth view was called the third force in psychology—humanistic psychology. "Help" to a humanist means helping the person to grow and to use more fully her or his inborn potential.

These conflicting assumptions about why people seek help are, of course, also operational definitions of what really constitutes help. For example, if I think your problem is an illness, I will offer treatment. Or if I think your basic problem is the way you behave, I will focus all my attention on helping you change your behavior and will view your interest in talking about how you feel as a side issue important primarily as a means of rapport. On the other hand, if I see your problem as lack of self-understanding, I will be suspicious of surface changes in your behavior unless they are accompanied by evidence of deep insight. But if I think you need to become more aware of your feelings, I may view such "insights" as a game and discourage you from wasting our time with them.

FINDING HELP

But you (the client) also have some assumptions about what needs to be changed and how you can be helped. If our assumptions don't match, we will be working at cross purposes.

As you read the following case presentation you might find it fun to project yourself into a helper role. How do each of the fussy eater's views of what would help fit with your own assumptions? Later we will describe how the medical, behavioral, dynamic, and humanistic therapist might react to the fussy eater's ideas about herself.

Representative Theories and Therapies	Founders of Faith (Famous Historical Figures)
Theory of evolution	Charles Darwin
Germ theory of illness	Louis Pasteur
Electroshock therapy	Ugo Cerletti
Mental illness taxonomy	Emil Krapelin
Behavior therapy	B. F. Skinner
	Joseph Wolpe
	Albert Bandura
Freudian psychoanalysis	Sigmund Freud
Jungian psychoanalysis	Carl Jung
Adlerian psychoanalysis	Alfred Adler
Sullivanian psychoanalysis	Harry Stack Sullivan
Transactional analysis	Eric Berne
Rogerian therapy	Carl Rogers
Gestalt therapy	Fritz Perls
Existential therapy	Rollo May

A Fussy Eater

I am a nineteen-year-old sophomore who plans to go on for a business degree, probably in finance. I come from a family of five children and I am the second eldest. My parents own their own dry cleaning business in a small town in Colorado. I live in Detroit with three other girls, including one of my sisters. We all attend college together. I consider myself a stable person but I have a "thing" about food. For instance, I have never in my life eaten such common foods as tomatoes, onions, or peaches.

It becomes very embarrassing. For example, when I first visited Colorado it was my fourteenth birthday and the dear old woman who was working for my father, with whom we stayed, surprised me with a beautiful strawberry shortcake made from scratch. Naturally straw-berries were on my blacklist and though I tried, I could not bring myself to eat more than a bite of the cake she had labored so much over. I will never forget the embarrassment and pain I felt as a result of hurting her feelings.

I have often wondered what could have happened, perhaps in my past, to have created this situation. I have considered my early mealtime disciplining as a potential beginning point.

Another idea I have had as to the origin of my problem is that it may really be in the stars. Having been born in May makes me a Taurus. From what reading I have done and evaluations I have gathered from my friends I seem to be a true Taurus in all aspects. "Down to earth" and "not prone to be adventuresome" seem to fit my personality, especially in the area of eating habits. As far as food is concerned, most Tauruses would prefer a hamburger over lobster thermidor any day.

The developmental aspect of my problem is fairly interesting. It began by my first refusing to eat certain foods. Sometimes I refused simply because of the appearance of the food and sometimes because of its smell or texture. Before long I found that I had begun to generalize in that I would refuse to eat anything that looked or smelled like an earlier rejected food. I also generalized in the sense that I wouldn't eat anything new. Finally I discovered that I had begun to specialize. I often distinctively recall odors of foods, so distinctively, in fact, that along with the odor I can even vividly imagine the taste of the food, often a food that I have not previously experienced. Another aspect of this specialization is the fact that while I do not eat tomatoes, I do eat ketchup and tomato soup. While I will not eat raw onions, I do eat onion rings.

This problem carries with it some psycho-logical effects. One of these effects is expecta-

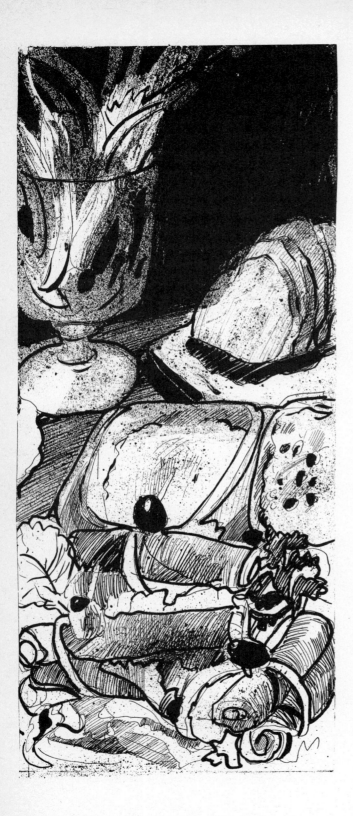

tions. This arises whenever I eat in another person's home. I cannot help but give some thought to the meal that will be served and how I should handle the situation.

My problem has stayed pretty much the same for a long time now. I think this is because there have been retarding forces that have hindered any solution of it. One of these retarding forces is that I have now grown so accustomed to the remarks and expectations of others that I often find myself responding to these expectations rather than to my own judgments. For example, I have many times chosen not to eat a certain casserole because I was warned in advance as to its contents by such comments as, "You won't want to eat this because it has onions in it." Another obstacle could be the fact that often I am stubborn and whenever I feel that I am being pressured too much to do something I will refuse to do it just because of the force involved.

Occasionally I do think about what I could possibly do to resolve this problem. One idea that I have had is to completely repress all my old ideas concerning food. Though I am fairly sure that this would probably help to eliminate the problem or at least greatly reduce it, this method would be extremely difficult if not impossible since I have carried these food taboos since early childhood.

Another possibility would be to pick up a little extra courage somewhere, enough so that I could motivate myself to at least sample "new" foods and try not to be too influenced by my old conceptions of the particular food. I can recall two cases in which this method worked. Once while dining at a restaurant with my family, my father ordered lobster for me. Though at first reluctant to even attempt to eat the creature, I was able to overcome my fear and found to my surprise that I actually like it, and since that time lobster has become one of my favorite meals. Another time my mother made me try an artichoke, and again to my surprise I found that I not only could tolerate it but enjoyed it as well. These cases are rare though, and as yet have not changed the present state of my problem very much.

A third idea has been indirectly suggested to me by my parents. In the past they have often jokingly threatened of someday putting me on a deserted island with only the foods that I do not eat. Though I feel quite sure that they would never go to this extreme, this could possibly be the method that would work best. For it seems that when in the past I have run into difficulty there always seemed to be enough food present that I could find something that I could eat.

I feel now that in the final analysis my problem will probably not change very much. As long as I am fortunate enough to have such a wide variety of food to choose from, there seems to be no reason why I must eat those foods that I am not able to and do not enjoy. Though I shall no doubt always have some difficulty when I find myself in situations where I haven't much of a choice in the matter, I seem to have managed in the past and probably will continue to do so.

It is evident that our fussy eater has thought quite a bit about her problem. And she has some clear ideas about what will and will not help her. Suppose she went to a professional therapist. Would he or she agree with her assessment of what is wrong? And what would be done to help her?

The answers depend, of course, on who she sees. As we pointed out in table 9.1, there are four rather different kinds of therapy. A psychiatrist might focus on the medical aspects of her problem, a behavioral therapist on changing her behavior, a dynamic psychologist on understanding the unconscious factors involved, and a humanistic or existential counselor would probably try to get her

to increase her own awareness of what she is doing and to learn about her inner motivations.

What Really Happens in Therapy

But this is all talk and can't begin to convey what really happens in therapy. To make it a bit less abstract we will have to use our (and your) imagination. We have chosen four representative therapies for discussion in this chapter. Our goal is to provide some idea of what each therapy has to offer. Each section is prefaced by a statement of what practitioners of that therapy feel is the basic problem. We will sketch out the basic concepts and techniques of one representative of each therapy. Finally we will develop a fantasy of what would actually happen if the fussy eater decided to enter therapy with that kind of therapist. This procedure is followed for the medical, behavioral, transactional analysis, and gestalt views. Let's begin, as many therapy clients do, with a visit to the family doctor.

"PEOPLE COME TO ME BECAUSE THEY ARE ILL": A MEDICAL APPROACH

Some helpers tend to assume their "patients" are suffering from symptoms that, taken together, are indicative of an underlying illness. Not too surprisingly, this view of those who enter their offices is most likely to be encountered among physicians, psychiatrists, psychologists, and social workers who either work in or were trained in a hospital setting. Since we have spent part of chapter two critiquing some instances in which we feel the concept of mental illness has been misused, this section will be devoted to some instances where we feel the mental illness concept is very applicable and very useful. Such examples occur primarily in instances where some kind of psychological problem occurs as a result of genetic defects, physical illness, or trauma. One such instance is phenylketonuria, a form of mental retardation that is caused by genetically produced imbalances in protein structure. This problem is now routinely diagnosed by testing the urine of infants and supplementing the diets of those afflicted with the needed proteins. A second example that is fairly common is acute brain trauma such as may be caused by an automobile accident. Although physical traumas may produce problems that are clearly psychological, (such as hallucinations, fits of rage, depression, and so forth), they are caused by physical illness and can frequently be cured by purely medical techniques such as drug therapy or surgery.

Depression and moodiness also sometimes reflect a problem that is more medical than psychological. Depression associated with menopause or the menstrual cycle can sometimes be treated by changing the balance of hormones. Other depressions turn out to be due primarily to physical exhaustion and loss of sleep, improper use of drugs, and so forth.

Finally, in cases of frigidity and inability to conceive, there are a series of possible medical causes that are correctable. Painful intercourse may be caused by clitoral and vaginal infections, enlargement of the small glands around the vagina, or torn uterine ligaments (Belliveau and Richter 1970). This does not imply that all sexual problems are really medical in nature. By far the majority are psychological. Nonetheless, a medical examination by a physician who is an expert sexologist can be very helpful in detecting such cases.

What sort of assistance might our fussy eater receive in a medical setting? Since the medical model begins with diagnosis, both medical and psychological testing might be appropriate. Medical testing could establish that her fussy eating reflects some metabolic imbalance that causes her to reject certain foods. A psychiatric interview and psychological testing might also be conducted to identify possible mental pathology that might underlie her eating problems. Following this preliminary evaluation, a treatment plan would be spelled out that might include appropriate medication and diet in combination with whatever form of psychotherapy seemed to be indicated.

Although a medical approach might be useful, its application to the fussy eater's problem has its limitations. She has no physical complaints, no depression. What she complains of most directly is one specific behavior—eating. So let's see what a behavioral therapy approach might have to offer.

"THE REAL PROBLEM IS THAT YOUR BEHAVIOR IS GETTING YOU IN TROUBLE": A BEHAVIORIAL APPROACH

Many therapists tend to dislike the implication of the medical model that a patient's problem is rooted in some kind of mental pathology. They tend to feel their patients come to them not because they are ill, but rather because their behavior is either harmful to themselves or to others, or so deviant from prevailing social norms as to be socially unacceptable (Bandura 1969). They view all such behavior as a learned means of coping with environmental demands. Since the behavior is learned, it is best modified by applying techniques based on laboratory-tested principles of learning, such as the reinforcement and modeling of desirable behaviors and the extinction or punishment of undesirable actions. Behaviorists are willing to deal with symptoms because they feel the behavioral sympton is their patient's real problem.

Suppose our fussy eater were to turn to a counselor who was a behaviorist. What would he or she think of her problem? How would a behaviorist try to intervene?

Learning. One of the fussy eater's explanations implies that her problem is one of learning:

The developmental aspect of my problem is fairly interesting. It began by my first refusing to eat certain foods. . . . Before long I found that I had begun to generalize in that I would refuse to eat anything that looked or smelled like an earlier rejected food.

Behavior counselors would agree: the problem is a learning process, not a disease. A behavioral analysis might or might not support her conviction that the learning process is one of generalization. But no true behaviorist would question that it is a learning process rather than a "disease," "lack of motivation," "the stars," and so forth.

Contingencies. A behaviorist would then proceed to study carefully the external consequences of her behavior. If a pattern of behavior exists it is because certain consequences follow and maintain it. In short, she has picky eating habits because certain external events occur that reinforce her behavior.

But what are these contingencies? That is, what external events result in her picky eating? On the surface her behavior is a bit confusing. What pos-

sible gain can there be in a behavior that embarrasses her, leads to hurting the feelings of people she feels affection for, and results in punishment and disapproval from her father?

She hints at several possibilities in her own account. She notes that it all began "with my refusing to eat certain foods." A behavioral counselor would immediately ask, "What consequence would maintain such a behavior in a small child?"

One of the most powerful controlling contingencies for any small child is attention from Mom or Dad. A baby's need for fondling and handling is almost as strong as its need for food. The infant will go to almost any length to get such attention. So a crucial question that comes up immediately is "What did Dad or Mom do when she refused to eat?"

Her own explanation here suggests that her father's reaction was to "threaten her" and keep her at the table. Could it be that her fussy eating was originally a technique to get attention from her father? This explanation may sound far-fetched. But laboratory research with pigeons has demonstrated that just such contingencies do control behavior. If a pigeon is deprived of food it may continue to peck at a dish even though all previous pecks have resulted in shock. All that is needed to maintain its pecking is an occasional food pellet. Likewise, a child deprived of affection and contact (which it may need as much as food) will continually risk punishment and disapproval just for the contact this provides with a parent.

Adults may do the same. Several years ago at a symposium I attended, Leonard Uhlman (a behavioral counselor) described a problem of behavioral control he had been consulted about at a state hospital: Jake (code name) was a patient who caused the attending staff a great deal of anxiety. He was often physically combative and frequently disrupted the ward routine by hoarding sheets in his room. He would sneak into other patients' rooms

A Story of Courage . . . Self-modification on a Quadraplegic Ward (Goldiamond 1973)

Israel Goldiamond is a well-known behavioral counselor. He has been using behavior modification concepts to help others for many years. One particular approach that he pioneered was called *self-control training.* This is an approach in which the client is taught to analyze and modify his or her own behavior with limited supervision by a therapist. Prior to 1970 Goldiamond was running a clinic on self-control for hospital patients in a physical rehabilitation program. It was in the midst of this work that a tragic accident resulted in his becoming his own patient.

An automobile wreck caused a spinal injury that put him in the hospital for nearly eight months. When he awoke from surgery, Goldiamond realized that he was in the same position as the hospital patients whom he had been a behavior therapist for at the University of Chicago. He decided to take his own prescription; that is, to apply the same principles of behavior analysis and self-control to himself that he had used with other disabled patients in his clinical practice.

The patients in his self-control clinic had to keep daily logs of their behaviors. Goldiamond imposed this same requirement on himself. He kept a careful record of his physical capabilities and his daily progress in them. He made a series of progress graphs. In addition, he recorded muscle movements, medications, surgery, X rays, and described in detail the observations of the exercises he imposed on himself.

Goldiamond's data keeping also included his emotional states. He observed and carefully recorded when he felt elated, when he felt irritable, depressed, and so forth. And he recorded the external events that appeared to be controlling these emotions. In most instances he noted that these controlling events were very easy to identify. But in one instance they were not. Then his meticulous records turned out to be extraordinarily useful.

Several months after the accident Goldiamond began to have considerable difficulty sleeping. Every two hours during the night the attendants had to roll him over to prevent the formation of ulcers. For some time this procedure did not interfere with his sleep pattern. Then suddenly for no apparent reason he began to have difficulty sleeping. The first night he missed two hours of sleep, the next night four; then he was awake for six. Soon he was unable to sleep at all.

What was the problem? Goldiamond's nurse attributed it to mounting anxiety. She wanted to know what he was thinking about. "Are you worried?" she asked. "What about?"

Goldiamond agreed with his nurse. He was worried. And his thoughts were often unpleasant. He was worried about his inability to sleep. And lying in a hospital bed is an unpleasant experience. But a behaviorist does not buy the idea that emotions cause behavior. *External contingencies cause both the behavior and the concommitant emotion.* This was the principle Goldiamond had taught his outpatients in the self-control clinic. Now he applied it to himself. Convinced that some environmental factor was causing his sleeplessness, he studied his graphs and charts carefully.

What he found was a reduction in dosage of tranquilizers. By returning himself to his original dosage and reducing intake by small amounts each day he was able to kick the tranquilizers without any further sleep problems.

Careful record keeping often reveals such unexpected contingencies that control our behavior. Without such records and a contingency analysis of emotions, Goldiamond might very well have overlooked the medication problem. In that case he might have delved into past anxieties or simply tried to accept the presence of his symptoms.

Goldiamond extended his contingency-analysis approach to other hospital situations. External contingencies seemed to dictate who got well and who did not. There were identifiable behaviors associated with getting better, such as, participating in the physical therapy programs, taking medications, and so forth. Goldiamond noted that the frequency of such behaviors depended on whether a critical contingency existed to reinforce them. In his own case the critical contingency was resumption of his professional life. He interviewed a grant committee while flat on his back, taught a graduate seminar lying on his side, took on a new client in a weight-control program and generally managed to continue his professional life while still in the hospital. His eagerness to get back to his work supported and reinforced him to behave like an ideal patient. This in turn resulted in a very rapid recovery.

Others who got well had similar contingencies to support their behavior. One young patient was a quadraplegic. Administrators at his college offered to build ramps so that he could attend classes again. He began immediately to rehabilitate himself. He learned to type with splints, began a correspondence course, and ultimately returned to school.

Likewise, when patients failed to achieve normal progress it was frequently because such a critical contingency was lacking. Such instances were, according to Goldiamond, "puzzling" to the staff. The staff had the techniques to help them get better. Patients should want to get better. Patients who "didn't want to get better" were sometimes rediagnosed with psychiatric labels such as "depressed" or "neurotically hostile."

Such labels, Goldiamond pointed out, obscure the real problem—namely, the lack of consequences important enough to the patients to act as reinforcers for trying to rehabilitate themselves.

How did Goldiamond reward himself for keeping going? He describes how he coped with the physical pain he incurred from sitting in his wheelchair. Here he observes that the way you describe the pain is important. If you say, "The pain stops me from working," the consequence will be sympathy and support from others. But if you say, "The reason I am not working is because the reinforcers that support working are lacking in my present environment," then you focus on changing the contingencies that support work before they break down completely. So he carefully arranged contingencies that would support his working. Much to the surprise of his doctors, he never experienced the depression that had come to be expected of a new quadraplegic.

It would appear that it is possible to be your own behavior analyst. By keeping accurate records of your own behavior and external events, by analyzing the relations among them, and by assuming personal responsibility for controlling yourself by changing undesirable environmental contingencies, any reasonable individual can greatly improve his or her ability to cope.

and steal their sheets, hiding them in unlikely places in his own room. Moreover, if attendants attempted to reclaim the sheets he became violent. Uhlman quickly established that there were a very clear set of contingencies that supported this patient's hoarding and combative behavior. The maintaining contingency, he discovered, was attention from the staff.

Every time the patient was discovered hoarding sheets he was immediately descended upon by an attendant demanding that they be returned. If he refused, an argument would evolve, and might continue for a half hour or more. The more Jake persisted, the more attention he got. If he were very hard to convince, the head nurse or even a psychiatrist might appear. And if he got combative he might (on a good day!) manage to get the entire staff involved in his problem.

How could Jake's behavior be modified? Dr. Uhlman suggested that the staff remove the reinforcing contingency by ignoring (and thereby extinguishing) Jake's hoarding behavior. He was explicitly given permission to take all the sheets he wanted. The staff stopped confronting him and left him alone with his sheets.

What do you suppose happened? First he began to hoard all the more. He took sheets from all the other patients' beds and raided the linen closet. The attendants did nothing except to replace the sheets he had taken from other patients. The stack of linen in his room began to grow. Soon there was very little space left in his room. Still the attendants did nothing. The stack of linen grew to the point that the bed had to be removed from his room. At this point the consequences stopped being positive for Jake. He was no longer getting attention. Furthermore, he had worked himself out of his own room. He had to sleep on the floor in the hall. And all he had to show for his efforts was a pile of dirty sheets. Anyone who thinks mental patients are irrational will be surprised at what he did next. One day he simply walked up to the nursing station and said, "O.K., you win". He helped the attendants clean up his room. From that time on the other patients' sheets were their own.

Given all this, it seems entirely plausible that our fussy eater's father systematically reinforced her by lecturing to her, spending time attending to her eating, and getting upset (and thereby communicating to her that she was getting to him). Moreover, there is some evidence that others in her life are still maintaining her fussy eating in the same way. She says her friends often expect her to be picky and even call certain foods to her attention. And sometimes, like her father, they pressure her to be more accepting of foods. Such pressure still maintains rather than extinguishes her picky eating:

> Whenever I feel I am being pressured too much to do something I will refuse to do it just because of the force involved.

Data. But enough of generalities. No reliable behavior analyst would attempt to intervene on the basis of a client's own introspections. A behavioral counselor does have hunches about clients' behaviors during the initial interview. But he or she is first and foremost a scientist. Like any good scientist, the behavior analyst checks hunches out by collecting data and directly observing the cause-effect relationships that the hunches suggest.

Our fussy eater would probably be asked to keep a careful record of her eating behavior. What specific foods does she reject? How frequently does this behavior occur? This is called the *base rate*. In what situations does she reject food? What are the consequences that occur most frequently when she rejects food?

She might be asked to record her behavior and its consequence in a chart such as that shown in figure 9-2. This chart suggests a number of contingencies that may be maintaining fussy eating. These may include the consequence of having another fight with her, "getting to" others, keeping

Date: Monday, April 18

Record each instance where you were offered food, where it occurred, how you responded, and what happened immediately afterward:

Situation	Place	Your Response	What Happened
Breakfast: cereal with strawberries on it, toast and coffee	University cafeteria (was alone)	Ate everything.	Didn't like the strawberries, but I ate them anyway.
Morning break: Carla (a friend) offered me a glass of tomato juice.	University cafeteria	I said "No."	She kept insisting I try the juice. The more she insisted, the madder I got.
Lunch: Mother wanted me to try her tomato preserves.	At home	I said "No" at first. Then I ate a little, but just gagged.	We had a long talk about this and Mom eventually apologized for being pushy.
Mom asked if I wanted a snack.	Home	I said OK and asked for a glass of milk.	She got me a glass of milk, which I drank and enjoyed.
Supper: was eating out with my boy friend. He wanted me to try a new meat sauce.	Restaurant	I wouldn't try it because it smelled like tomatoes.	He teased me about this, but I wouldn't give in.

FIG. 9-2 *A one-day sample of the fussy eater's behavior diary*

interaction going, and so forth. Clearly other people are involved, since all rejections occur in the presence of others and she eats some of these same foods when by herself. If she went to a behavioral counselor, keeping such records and analyzing them with her therapist would occupy much of her time early in treatment.

What sort of techniques might a behavioral counselor suggest to change her behavior? First, of course, is the possibility of changing the consequences that maintain the behavior. If attention and conflict with others maintains the behavior, instructing others to ignore this form of attention-getting may be an answer.

Creating new contingencies is another possibility. She might agree with her therapist to make eating the part of each meal she likes contingent on eating foods she ordinarily refuses. Or she might design some other new contingency relationship for herself. There is no reason to allow ourselves to continue being controlled by any contingency once we recognize what it is.

Stimulus control. The essence of this technique is to decrease the number of environmental stimuli that support her fussy eating. Clearly the people she chose to eat with constitute one such stimulus. She may discover that fussy eating tends to occur more often in the presence of certain people. Eating with someone else is a good way to alter this aspect of her stimulus situation.

Another stimulus control possibility is to designate some special time and place where she will agree to try some new foods. At first this might be only once a week and only one food at a time. Gradually as she is reinforced by the discovery that certain foods are appealing to her, she might be encouraged by her therapist to increase the number of such occasions per week.

Stimulus control could also be used to help her learn to like new foods that she formerly found aversive. Disguising flavors by combining the disliked favorite with another food that she enjoys is one such possibility. This is essentially the technique my wife used to get me to like asparagus. I used to dislike asparagus but have always loved cheese and sour cream. She served me asparagus with cheese or cream sauces over a period of several months. And it worked. I now can eat asparagus by itself. And I like it!

The behavioral process described above may look very straightforward and simple. But there is often a hitch to its success. Most of our apparently undesirable behavior is also buying us something we want. Sometimes an apparently simple habit like fussy eating reflects a deeper pattern of behaving, relating to others, and manipulating our environment. In this instance a professional behavioral therapist who is sensitive to such patterns may be needed. Or we may turn to a representative of the "first force" in psychology: a dynamic therapist.

"It is impossible to make any real changes in your life until you understand your own inner dynamics": A Dynamic (TA) Approach

This assumption is shared by therapists whose thinking has been influenced by Freud's ideas about the unconscious and the lasting importance of early childhood experience. Freudian, Jungian, Adlerian, and other psychoanalytic forms are the most widely known classical approaches to understanding the self. Thomas Harris, one of several creators of the transactional analysis approach to therapy, provides a modern version of the dynamic school of psychology (Harris 1969). If you were to join one of Harris's groups you would be told your problems center basically around your relationships with others, which are in turn based on how you felt about yourself and the way your parents treated you as a child. This feeling as it carries over into adult life is what Harris calls your Child. It involves how you feel about others as well as about yourself. Harris finds that those who come to him tend to feel they are "not OK." Not-OK feelings

	I'm OK	I'm not OK
You're OK	I'm OK, you're OK is a "get-on-with" winner's position	I'm not OK, you're OK is a "get-away-from" feeling of depression and a tendency to withdraw, run away, and destroy oneself
You're not OK	I'm OK, you're not OK is a "get-rid-of" feeling of distrust for others' positions	I'm not OK, you're not OK is a "get-nowhere" or "loser" position

FIG. 9-3 *Basic existential positions*

result in spending large amounts of time avoiding being intimate with others in genuine loving relationships. Common ways of avoiding intimacy are to invest most of your time withdrawing or in superficial rituals (such as "Hi, how are ya?"), in activities or projects, in "past timing" (such as bull sessions and gossiping), or in playing games like "Now I've Got You," "Kick Me," and so forth.

The ways you avoid real intimacy with others all reflect what transactional therapists describe as a lifescript. Your lifescript is the series of decisions that you made very early in life (typically between the ages of three and seven). One develops a lifescript on the basis of one's existential position. The four possible positions that may be adopted and their results are shown in figure 9-3. Only by unlocking the origins of the lifescript can the patient be freed to ignore the injunctions of the internalized parent and to rewrite the lifescripts based on who she or he wants to be.

Eric Berne, the founder of TA, felt that his clients came to see him for two reasons, neither of which put their lifescripts in jeopardy. First their Adult (ego state) came to find out how to be more comfortable living in the present lifescript. When a client is really having problems, such a therapy goal may translate into "How do I live comfortably while bashing my head against a brick wall?" The second reason comes from the client's Child. It involves keeping the script going or even enhancing it by getting the counselor to play games that fulfill the client's script. Because of this belief, TA therapists view their first task as being aware of their clients' attempts to try to get them to play games.

Perhaps the most common game that counselors and clients play is "Why don't you — Yes but." It goes something like this:

Client: I'm so sick of flunking all my courses.

Counselor: Why don't you spend more time studying?

Client: Yes, but it's too noisy in my dorm to study.

Counselor: Why don't you study in the library?

Client: Yes, but I get bored there.

Counselor: Maybe it would help if you studied with a friend.

Client: Yes, but none of my friends like to study in the library.

This kind of an exchange may continue until the counselor either gives up or catches on to the game. This game can be played by more than one player. It is also played at cocktail parties or anywhere else that groups of people gather. It is particularly prevalent in poorly handled unstructured encounter groups, where it may continue *ad infinitum*.

Like a bridge game, "Why don't you — Yes but" requires someone to open the bidding. One person (North) may open by presenting a problem or asking for advice. East, West, and South keep the game going by offering solutions. "Why don't you . . . ?" Each of these receives a "Yes, but . . ." from North. If North is adept at the game, he or she may stand off the entire group indefinitely. When everyone gives up, North wins.

The confusing thing about this game is the motivation involved. Why does North initiate such a

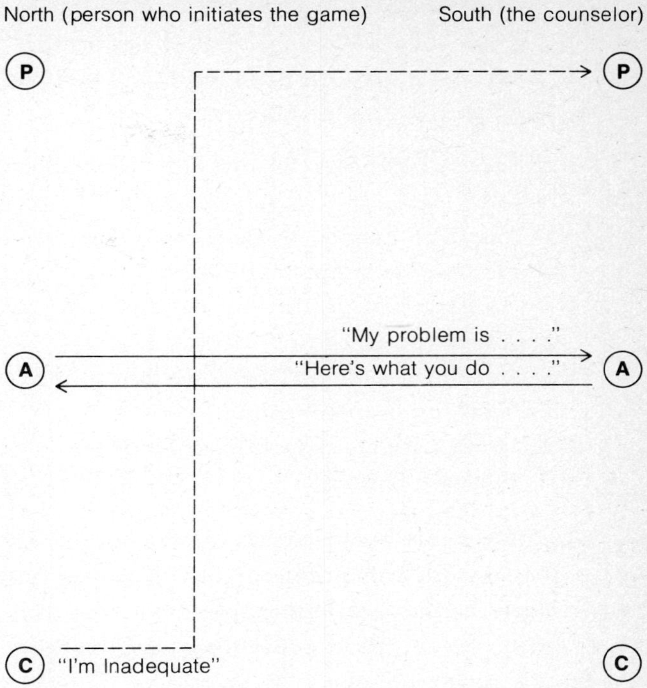

North (person who initiates the game)   South (the counselor)

FIG. 9-4   *"Why don't you — Yes but"*

game? Doesn't she or he want to solve the problem? On the surface the transaction appears to be going from Adult to Adult, but at a deeper level this is a Child-Parent transaction.

North comes across as a Child who is inadequate to meet the situation. This brings out the Parent in the counselor, who immediately proceeds to dispense parental wisdom. North then comes back to the Adult position with "Yes, but (your idea is full of holes)." In diagram form the whole transaction looks somewhat as shown in figure 9-4.

So the transaction has an ulterior motive. North doesn't just want information. He or she wants to hook the Parent of the counselor and get reassurance that the problem cannot be solved. The counselor who offers advice may be falling into a trap.

In the fussy eater we can observe an interesting one-handed version of "Why don't you — Yes but."

She opens as North did by stating that "I have a problem." She describes how embarrassing it is, how bad she feels about hurting others. Then her list of "Why don't I?" is as follows:

> *"Why don't I* repress all my old ideas about food?"
>
> *"Yes, but* I've carried these items around too long for such a simple solution to work."
>
> *"Why don't I* just get up my courage and try some new foods?"
>
> *"Yes, but* the few times I've done that it hasn't changed my problem much."
>
> *"Why don't I* isolate myself from food?"
>
> *"Yes, but* why bother."

That this whole business was really a game and not a real instance of problem solving comes out most clearly in the last paragraph, when she says in essence, "I've tried everything and nothing works. I'll never change." Most games of "Why don't you"—"Yes but" have the same ultimate objective, namely, to gain reassurance that it is OK to go on avoiding any change in the status quo.

If our fussy eater went to a TA therapist, she might very well begin counseling by attempting to involve her counselor in her game of "Why don't you—Yes but." If she did, the counselor would probably recognize it as a game and decline to play. TA counselors are especially trained to recognize games and they know how to intervene in them. The basic counter to the game is to refrain from offering a "Why don't you?" Thus if the opening move is something like "What do you do if . . ." a good response would be "That is a difficult problem. What are you going to do about it?" Or if the opener is "It didn't work out properly," the counter is "That *is* too bad." The counselor may also confront the client directly with a statement such as "I'm only your counselor, not your lifestyle manager."

Rather than playing "Why don't you—Yes but" a TA therapist would be interested in learning about the fussy eater's lifescript. TA therapists be-

lieve that each person describes early in childhood how he or she will live and die. That plan is called one's lifescript. This script contains the outcome for all a person's major life decisions: what kind of a person he or she will marry, how many children they will have, where and how she or he will die, and who will be present at the death scene. Often these decisions revolve around a single major script theme that can be expressed in a word or two:

Building empires
Being miserable
Being helpful
Rescuer
Persecutor
Victim

Exploring lifescripts. Where do lifescripts come from? Often they originate in messages from our parents. These messages are instructions that children may later feel they have to follow:

- "You'll be the world's greatest concert pianist."
- "You'll never amount to anything."
- "What a great nurse you'd make!"

The scripts that often result in a need to seek psychiatric help contain a curse:

- "You're a chip off the old block" (when Father is an alcoholic)
- "You're a wicked child"
- "Go get lost"
- "Drop dead!"

Because scripts tend to originate in such parental messages, a TA therapist might ask our fussy eater to recall the things her parents said to her when she was a child. The therapist might also ask her what she knows about how she got her name. Parents sometimes select nicknames that become an injunction. Thus a father who really wanted a boy gets a daughter. He nicknames her Sam and treats her like a boy. Her lifescript: "Be a man." Some nicknames have obvious script possibilities: "Icky," "Stupid," "Superman," "Crazy," "Skinny."

Another area of inquiry involves finding out what fairy tale or literary dramas may be involved in your lifescript. Children's literature is full of life themes that may be modeled by the child—the frog who became a prince, the ugly duckling who became a swan, the sleeping beauty who waited endlessly for a rescuer, Cinderella (the family martyr who gets even). Sometimes such scripts can be picked up directly by asking the client, "What was your favorite fairy tale?"

The data presented by the fussy eater are of course far too sketchy to enable us to do more than make a few wild guesses about the nature of her lifescript. Nonetheless, the games we play usually have the function of fulfilling the destinies we have written into our scripts. Following are a couple of wild guesses about the sort of lifescripts that might be supported by playing a good game of "Fussy Eater":

Driving People Crazy
Custer's Last Stand or The Battle of the Alamo
    (loser scripts)

Overall, the TA therapist would probably encourage the fussy eater to understand her own unconscious motivation better. This might begin with a few isolated bits of behavior such as fussy eating. But the more basic goal of TA is to come to see the motivation that is directing your entire lifestyle.

"Only by becoming fully aware can you be free": A Humanistic (Gestalt) Approach

Psychologists who represent the third force of humanistic psychology view the person as a natural grower. "We all have a potential for becoming," says Carl Rogers and other proponents of humanistic psychology. To find this potential we must free ourselves of social controls and contraints that limit growth. To grow I must develop the courage to be fully aware of what I am feeling here and now.

So awareness is the key to growth. But how do we become aware? A variety of third-force therapies have developed, each with its own unique approach for encouraging awareness. And as we will see in chapter ten, eleven, and twelve, this interest has motivated humanistic psychologists to investigate meditation, dreams, and even extrasensory perception. Carl Rogers (*Rogerian therapy*) emphasizes developing awareness by encouraging a free, permissive environment between client and therapist. A nonjudgmental attitude by the counselor allows clients to freely explore their own emotions. Empathy is conveyed by reflecting back the clients' deepest feelings. Unconditional positive regard for clients leaves them free to be themselves fully without fear of retribution.

Existential therapy focuses on the "I-Thou" relationship between client and counselor. In this form of therapy the emphasis is on the counselor being a real human being (rather than playing a professional role). Proponents of this style feel that genuine awareness only comes when the therapist stops using techniques as gimmicks.

There are many such awareness-oriented therapies within humanistic psychology. To do them all justice would require another book. So again we choose to be selective. We will explore one of these in depth. The therapy chosen is gestalt (Perls 1965).

Gestalt is a German word that means the forming of an organized, meaningful whole. Gestalt psychology originated with the study of the perceptual principal that we tend to organize our perception. Figure 9-5, for example, is almost invariably seen as a square rather than a series of four separate lines.

Perls felt that we are often aware of only parts of ourselves. We lack a personal gestalt. This leads to behaving and feeling in an abstract, lifeless sort of way. Only by being reunited with these disowned fragments of our personalities can we function as whole people. The goal of gestalt therapy is to help the client become aware of, admit to, reclaim, and reintegrate these disowned fragments.

FIG. 9-5 *How do you see this figure?*

Into the hot seat. Let's see what gestalt might be like in action. Picture a gestalt therapy group. There is a circle of chairs occupied by group members. In the middle sits Fritz Perls, the founder of gestalt therapy, his omnipresent half-smoked cigarette dangling from his finger. In front of him are two chairs. One of them will soon be occupied by whoever decides to work with him today. It is called the "hot seat." A second chair faces the client who will work. It is there for the client to project his or her many selves on to.

If our fussy eater is in the group she will get no attention from Fritz until she declares, "I want to work," and comes and sits down in the hot seat. This is because a gestalt group emphasizes developing inner supports. Being responsible for making your own decisions is the goal of treatment. So you start by deciding for yourself whether or not you want to work with Fritz.

Suppose the fussy eater were to come forward saying she wanted to work. She begins to tell her story. What would Perls do?

For one thing, the fussy eater wouldn't get much of a chance to tell her story to Fritz. As a matter of fact before she got to "I'm a nineteen-year-old sophomore who plans to go on for a business degree" (her first sentence) he would already be at work. As she sat down he would already have noticed her posture and commented on it: "I see a person whose eyes are looking to the group. What are you looking for?" he might ask. If she replies, "I feel nervous" or "I want support," he might get her to try to find the nervousness: "I see your hand is trembling. See if you can exaggerate the shaking. Make it really shake!"

This approach is called symptom exaggeration. Its purpose is to get the client to "own up" to her own behavior, to realize that she and she alone creates her own behavior. "The group doesn't make you nervous. Fritz doesn't make you nervous. You make you nervous," he might say.

If she looks the group over for support he might ask her to read everyone's mind: "What are they thinking about you?" Then she might have to imagine a group member in the chair in front of her and talk to him. The reason for putting her imagined group member there rather than the real person is to get her to own her own projections. It is her projection that makes her feel supported or rejected, not the group member. Hence she can best get acquainted with this aspect of herself by having a conversation with whatever part of her she is projecting on the group.

Likewise she would be encouraged to become aware of her body posture and mannerisms by exaggerating them. Then she might be asked to hold a conversation with a nervous symptom such as a nervous blink or a tapping toe. The purpose of such conversations is to get her to reclaim her own behavior, to know that it is hers.

The same principle holds when she talks about her problem of fussy eating. For example, she says, "I have a thing about food. For instance, I have never in my life eaten such common foods as tomatoes, onions, or peaches. It becomes very embarrassing."

At this point Perls would probably interrupt our fussy eater to try to get her to own this mysterious "it" that embarrasses her so. He might have her put her "thing" in the opposite chair and have a talk with it. The conversation might go something like this:

Fussy: Hi, "thing." What are you doing in me?
Fritz: OK. Now switch to the other chair and be your thing.
Fussy eater (being the thing): I'm here because I like to embarrass you. Leave me alone!

Here we get a hint that topdog vs. underdog polarity may be involved in her problem. In TA terms the "thing" is a bulky, obstinate Child. The topdog may be a demanding Parent. To help her become more aware of this split, Fritz might structure the dialogue a bit more at this point:

Fritz: That sounded like your underdog talking. Let's see if we can get in touch with topdog too. Let's see you get into your topdog for a minute.
Fussy eater (coming on as her topdog): You had better stop embarrassing me or I'll *make you* clear up that plate, underdog.
Fritz: Now be underdog again.
Fussy eater (back in the underdog chair): (in a weak whining voice) Try and make me.
Fritz: You sound unsure. Say it again.
Fussy eater: I said try and make me . . .
Fritz: Say it again.
Fussy: (voice becomes stronger and louder) I said try and make me.
Fritz: Again.
Fussy: (at the top of her lungs) I said: *try and make me*!!
Fritz: (smiling broadly) Now I'm convinced. Go ahead.
Fussy: While I was yelling just now I had a funny feeling. It was just like I was a little girl again. I used to want to fight back like

that when my parents dictated to me. But I was always afraid they would strike me. They seemed so angry and I felt so little.

Fritz: I think you got the message. Your "thing" has been trying to tell you you don't have to be afraid of them now . . .

The major thing the gestalt therapist would try to do with the fussy eater would be to get her to become fully aware of her present feelings. In gestalt therapy, awareness is the key to growth. Techniques such as symptom exaggeration, the hot seat, and the topdog/underdog game are used to accomplish this goal. With awareness comes a feeling of gestalt or closure. Once full awareness of one's feeling is achieved it becomes possible to drop outdated Child feelings and defenses and to become a fully functioning person.

Where to Go for Help: the Helper's Credentials

The important step in selecting a counselor is to examine the helper's credentials. This involves the nature and quality of his or her education, the range of professional experience, and the degree to which the titles the counselor is using accurately reflect education and professional experience.

PSYCHIATRIST

A psychiatrist is a medical doctor specializing in the diagnosis, treatment, and prevention of mental problems. Anyone calling himself a psychiatrist should have completed medical school, a one-year hospital internship, and one or more years of internship in a mental health agency. Psychiatrists are licensed by the state in which they practice. To be certified, a psychiatrist should have an additional two years' experience and must pass a board exam by the American Board of Psychiatry and Neurology.

CLINICAL PSYCHOLOGIST

A clinical psychologist is educated in the science of psychology. Clinical psychologists are trained to do diagnosis and psychotherapy with disturbed individuals. Those who call themselves clinical psychologists should have Ph.D. degrees from a graduate school approved by the American Psychological Association as well as one year of internship in a mental health agency. To get a diploma in clinical psychology requires passing a set of national exams.

COUNSELING PSYCHOLOGIST

A counseling psychologist, like the clinical psychologist, is educated in the science of psychology. Counseling psychologists are trained to work in a wide variety of mental health settings in the community, in industry, or on the college campus. The skills of the counseling psychologist include individual and group counseling for emotional problems, marriage counseling, testing, and other appraisal techniques. To call oneself a psychologist in most states requires a license or certificate. In more and more states both clinical and counseling psychologists are licensed.

PSYCHOTHERAPIST

This term is commonly interpreted to mean a psychiatrist or psychologist who is qualified to do psychotherapy. Legally, however, the term has no status. Thus anyone who cares to do so may use the title.

SOURCES OF INFORMATION

Where do you find out about available therapists? Local sources of information are physicians, social welfare and mental health agencies, the student counseling service at your local university, and the local affiliates of the National Association of Social Workers, the American Psychiatric Association, and the American Psychological Association.

If you have difficulty finding help at the local level, one of the following national associations may be helpful: the National Association for Mental

Health, 1800 N. Kent St., Arlington, Virginia 22209; the American Psychological Association, 1200 17th St., N.W., Washington, D.C. 20036; the Association of Humanistic Psychology, 416 Hoffman St., San Francisco, California 94114; the American Psychiatric Association, 1700 18th St. N.W., Washington, D.C., 20009.

The National Institute for Mental Health publishes a directory of mental health facilities throughout the country. To obtain a copy of Mental Health Directory 1973 (HEW publication HSM 73-9028) contact the Superintendent of Documents, U.S. Government Printing Office, Washington, D.C. 20402.

A therapist's credentials may be checked by contacting one of the professional associations or by using reference material at your local library. The *American Psychological Association Biographical Directory* and the *Biographical Directory of the American Psychiatric Association* are two good sources of information.

OTHER HELPERS

Besides the psychiatrist and psychologist, there are many others who work as professional helpers. Ministers and social workers do much of the marriage counseling in this country and are often turned to for help. Likewise medical doctors often spend some of their time in counseling their patients.

Also there is a growing culture of helpers whose work is in no way regulated or controlled by a recognized profession with a clearly articulated code of ethics. Examples are the numerologist, the astrologer, and many encounter or awareness group leaders. Here there is no legal regulation and seeking help is very much a "let the buyer beware" situation.

Finally there is a growing movement called radical therapy (see Anderson 1973), which views society as the cause of many problems of the individual. This movement tends to view much existing professional help as a form of social oppression. The goal of radical therapy is to free the individual by working towards social change or by encouraging the individual to fight back. Women's Lib, Gay Lib, Insane Lib, and the Radical Psychiatry Center at Berkeley are examples of groups that seek to defend areas our society labels as deviant.

Chapter Nine Summary

In selecting a therapist three questions are of primary importance: 1) Why does this helper think that people seek his or her help? 2) What is the nature of the help he or she offers? 3) What kind of a relationship is this helper willing to have with those who are clients?

Although there are endless varieties of therapy, most of them fall into one of four basic categories: medical, behavioral, dynamic, or humanistic.

1. *The medical view* describes problems as symptoms of an underlying illness. Careful diagnosis of the patient's mental and physical condition is followed by a treatment plan that may include medication as well as psychotherapy.

2. *The behavioral counselor* views emotional problems as a learning malfunction. Somehow the wrong contingencies are controlling our behavior. The goal is to change the behavior. The basic techniques are to change those environmental contingencies that are reinforcing the maladaptive behavior.

3. *The dynamic psychologist* is primarily interested in helping clients to gain more insight into their own motivation or dynamics. One modern dynamic psychology is transactional analysis. The TA therapist helps clients to recognize the games they play and to analyze the broader patterns of their motivations as they are reflected in their lifescripts.

4. *The gestalt view* is that problems arise when we disown or push out of our awareness important aspects of our personality. The gestalt therapist's greatest tool is his or her own awareness of what the client is saying with body movements and other nonverbal clues.

Behavior therapy or counseling A form of professional help in which the focus is on developing an awareness of the environmental contingencies that control the client's behaviors. Problems are solved by changing those reinforcers that are controlling the person's behavior.

Counseling A form of professional help for personal and emotional problems. Counseling may be helpful in planning the kind of lifestyle, career, and marriage relationship you desire in the future, or in dealing with crises in your present life situation. Although in practice counseling is often very much like psychotherapy, the term *counseling* is used to refer to short-term help, crisis intervention, and normal developmental problem solving. *Psychotherapy* refers to help that is longer-term, oriented to producing deep personality change, and concerned with problems of a more severe nature that may even require hospitalization and inpatient treatment.

Dynamic psychology Forms of counseling and therapy that emphasize developing an understanding of one's inner, deeper personality conflicts. Problems are solved by learning what motivates you to behave as you do and discovering the early childhood experiences related to these motives. Some examples are psychoanalysis and transactional analysis.

Generalization The tendency for a response learned to one stimulus to be applied to other similar situations. Many fear responses tend to generalize. For example, a young child bitten by a collie may show a fear response not only to collies but also to Saint Bernards and German shepherds.

Gestalt therapy A form of therapy in which the goal is to become as aware as possible of how one reacts here and now. Problems are largely viewed as resulting from lack of awareness and denial of important parts of our personalities.

Mental illness Although the term *mental illness* is sometimes used in a very general sense to cover every conceivable human emotional problem, we prefer the following more limiting definition: those instances of extreme and prolonged emotional discomfort or gross distortion of reality in which there is likely a clear organic cause such as a brain lesion, a tumor, a germ, or a chemical imbalance.

Projection Attributing one's own needs or emotions to someone else. Examples include the person on a diet who hasn't eaten all day walking up to a friend and saying, "Gee, you look hungry." Another example is the horny young male who *knows* that "a girl is giving me the eye."

Reinforcing event Any external contingency that increases the probability of a particular behavior occurring. Examples: the attention the fussy eater got from her parents for her picky eating; the piece of meat you used to reward your dog with for a trick. Last but not least is my monthly paycheck.

Self-control training A therapy procedure in which the behavior therapist teaches clients the principles of behavior modification. Clients then apply the concepts they have learned to change their own behavior.

Stimulus control A technique for changing behavior by carefully arranging for environmental stimuli that support, encourage, or reinforce a desired behavior. Some common examples are: choosing a place for study that is free of interruptions; taking someone you are sexually interested in to a romantic place with soft music and candlelight.

Symptom exaggeration A gestalt therapy technique in which the client is asked to exaggerate a behavior or symptom such as stuttering, a nervously tapping foot, and so forth.

Exercises   *(for individual and class use)*

You can do the following exercises at your leisure. Perhaps some of these would be more enjoyable with a friend. Those with an asterisk should be done in consultation with your teacher or in class.

1. Try being a behaviorist for a week or two. Choose some area of your behavior that you find puzzling and see if you can discover the contingencies that control it. Smoking, study, and eating habits particularly lend themselves to this kind of analysis.

Recording behavior. Develop a simple, objective way of recording the frequency of the behavior you choose. How many times a day do you smoke? How long do you concentrate on an assignment before your attention drifts? What foods do you eat? How much and when do you eat them? If possible, record your data (see the fussy eater's chart on page 225). This technique is simple, convenient, and supplies dramatic visual feedback about your progress.

Base rate. If you have a good objective measurement system, you should be able to determine from your chart how frequently you normally or naturally behave in this manner. This is your base rate.

Contingencies. Keep a log of what situations you were in whenever the behavior occurred. What events followed the behavior in question? This log, when kept over a period of several weeks or months, will reveal stimulus situations that control your behavior. It will also reveal possible reinforcing contingencies.

Analysis. After a period of observing and carefully recording your behavior, examine your data carefully for stimulus situations and reinforcing contingencies. Develop two or three hypotheses about what controls your behavior.

*Change. You might want to try out a hypothesis by changing the stimulus situations or reinforcing conditions in some way. If you have identified the proper contingencies, this should result in a change in the frequency of the behavior you are measuring. That is, the behavior will now occur less often or more often than the base rate you established.

2. *Becoming aware of games.* Review briefly the game described in this chapter: "Why don't you—Yes but." See if you can think of one instance where you or someone you know were playing a game. Then answer the following questions.

- What do you feel were the psychological advantages that this game provides for you?
- How do these advantages match those outlined in the text for this particular game?
- See if you can remember the specific things that were said. Which came from the Parent? Which from the Adult? And which from the Child? Then see if you can construct a transaction diagram similar to that in figure 9-4, page 227.
- What are some ways you might have intervened with the progress of the game? What consequences would each such intervention have had?

3. Think of a friend of yours who you feel could profit from professional help. In what ways might medical therapy be helpful in dealing with this problem? Behavior therapy? Transactional analysis? Gestalt therapy? From what you know of your friend, which therapy do you think would be most helpful? Why?

Bibliography

Anderson, W. 1973. Breaking out of the therapy vise. *Human Behavior* (December):11.

Bandura, A. 1969. *Principles of behavior modification*. New York: Holt, Rinehart & Winston.

Belliveau, F. and Richter, L. 1970. *Understanding human sexuality*. New York: Bantam.

Berne, E. 1964. *Games people play*. New York: Grove.

————. 1972. *What do you say after you say hello?* New York: Grove.

Frank, J. 1972. The bewildering world of psychotherapy. *Journal of Social Issues* 28:4.

Goldiamond, I. 1973. A diary of self-modification. *Psychology Today* (July): 95.

Harris, T. 1969. *I'm OK, you're OK*. New York: Harper.

Perls, F., Hefferline, R., Goodman, P. 1965. *Gestalt therapy*. New York: Dell.

In a dream we have a clear existential message of what's missing in our lives, what we avoid doing and living, and of material to reassimilate and reown the alienated parts of ourselves.

FRITZ PERLS, *Gestalt Therapy Verbatim*

A Personal Search Through Dreams

I'm a nondreamer, or to be more accurate, a nonrecaller. I dreamed frequently and very vividly as a child, and then I stopped. Recently I've tried to write down my dreams, but often when I awaken I remember only momentarily and then feel the dream slip away from me before I can write it down.

Until about a year ago I had relatively little interest in dreams. Then I encountered the dreams of the Sioux medicine man Black Elk in John Neihardt's book *Black Elk Speaks*. Black Elk's greatest dream occurred when he was approximately nine years old. In it he dreamed of being taken to the Grandfathers (ancestors of his tribe) and was shown the spirit world and many magic symbols and secret powers. The dream also prophesied many of the events that would befall the Sioux in the following fifty years. Black Elk informed Neihardt that the dream occurred while he was in a trance-like coma for twelve days. Witnesses were able to verify that Black Elk had actually been ill at this age and that he had gone into deep coma.

The following brief excerpt may convey some sense of Black Elk's dream. In this part of the dream he was allowed to ride into the future to see the events that would occur in the next four generations. Each part of the dream represented one generation. The first part began in 1863 and ended about the time of the Little Bighorn. This was a time of peace and prosperity for the Sioux. The second through the fourth ascents depict the coming of the white soldiers and the disgrace and rape of the Sioux by the white settlers, as well as the coming of the world war.

And when I looked down, the people were all changed back to human, and they were thin, their faces sharp, for they were starving. Their ponies were only hide and bones, and the holy tree was gone.

And as I looked and wept, I saw that there stood on the north side of the starving camp a

sacred man who was painted red all over his body, and he held a spear as he walked into the center of the people, and there he lay down and rolled. And when he got up, it was a fat bison standing there, and where the bison stood a sacred herb sprang up right where the tree had been in the center of the nation's hoop. The herb grew and bore four blossoms on a single stem while I was looking—a blue, a white, a scarlet, and a yellow—and the bright rays of these flashed to the heavens.

I know now what this meant, that the bison were the gift of a good spirit and were our strength but we should lose them, and from the same good spirit we must find another strength.

The clarity and intensity of this dream fascinated me. Compared to my own dull unimaginative productions, such a dream with its great complexity and symbolism suggested a kind of transcendent capacity for experiencing. I have since discovered that such intense dreams have occurred in others and are well documented (for several excellent examples, see Gardner Murphy's *Challenge of Parapsychology*.)

A second thing that struck me was the way the dream influenced Black Elk. In his society dreaming was viewed as a very respectable and valuable state of consciousness. His dream was acted out very realistically in a tribal ceremony. This ceremony, like a modern gestalt dream workshop (see Perls 1969), was especially designed to integrate the dream into the waking consciousness of the dreamer. The dream became a part of Black Elk's self-image and influenced his identity very significantly.

I decided to begin a serious study of the role of dreams in personality development. I began reading about the psychology of dreaming. I also began trying to remember my own dreams and to study them. My personal dream study has yielded a number of dream interpretations that I regard as significant growing experiences for me. In one of these, a senior professor in my department told me in clear terms what my inadequacies as a psychologist were. As you might imagine, everything he said was simply what I had felt about myself before the dream. But in the dream I could neither deny nor rationalize my failings. It contained some important clues as to what I wanted to do with my professional life. I frequently recall it when I'm feeling a lack of direction.

The second dream had to do with my relationships with others. The essential message that I got had to do with the importance of staying in touch with the feelings of those I care deeply about. It encouraged me to slow down and follow through more with other people.

The third dream is one that I regard as a possible case of clairvoyance. It will be described in chapter twelve.

So much for my dreams. Have you ever wondered what other people dream about? Why we dream? Why some dreams are forgotten? How dreams can be interpreted? The answers to these questions are the subject of this chapter.

What We Dream About: Dream Explorers

Surprisingly enough, there is a wealth of data available on what people (all kinds of people) dream about. Recently this work has been summarized in a very readable book by Edwin Diamond called *The Science of Dreams*. Much of this chapter is based on Diamond's discussion.

Sigmund Freud's *The Interpretation of Dreams* remains the classic in the field. Freud first saw the significance of dreams when he noticed the similarity between the free-flowing neurotic waking thoughts of one of his patients and his own dream life. By a fortunate coincidence, he was working with this woman at the same time that he was forced to exchange his usual bed for a new and very uncomfortable one in which he found it impossible to sleep soundly. Each morning Freud remembered all his dreams of the night and painstakingly wrote them down. Using these dreams as material, he began his own self-analysis. *The Interpretation of Dreams* is generally considered to be Freud's greatest contribution to psychology. In it he analyzes nearly two hundred dreams.

Dream research in the United States began in 1892 when Mary Whiton Calkins, a student of William James, kept a pencil by her night candle and used an alarm clock to awaken herself throughout the night (Diamond 1962). Her analysis of 375 dreams led her to conclude that many (seventy-five percent) of the night's dreams are unpleasant, and most (ninety percent) reflect the activities of the day.

American psychologists really picked up on this "objective-empirical" approach to dream study. In the early part of the nineteenth century dreams were collected from the blind and deaf, from children, from subjects who were fasting, and from just about every other conceivable group. Anthropologists also got interested in dream research and began collecting dreams from people in other cultures.

ELEMENTS OF DREAMS

Calvin Hall, a distinguished dream investigator, felt that the dreams the psychoanalysts were collecting were not typical of what normal people dreamed. So, in the mid-1940s he began asking his psychology students to write down their dreams and what they thought they meant. With the aid of his students he soon collected over 10,000 dreams—the world's largest dream collection.

Hall (1966) found that one very useful way of thinking about dreams was to consider that dreams are plays and each individual is one's own playwright. Thus in Hall's system a dream becomes a clue to our lifescript. Using this analogy, he considered the content of each dream as to its setting, cast of characters, plot (in terms of action and interaction), emotions, and color.

1. *Setting.* Most dreams occur in places with which we are very familiar: thirty-three percent occur in rooms of a house; fifteen percent in cars, buses, or other means of travel; ten percent in settings related to travel such as a bus station. In only five percent of our dreams are we totally unaware of the setting.

2. *Characters.* Hall found that in almost all dreams the dreamer is himself part of the cast. Usually there are two or three others in the cast as well. Family members are very prevalent in our dreams. Children and parents dream of each other; husbands and wives do also. "People who enter our dreams," Hall concludes, "are those with whom we are emotionally involved." It is fairly unusual to have a dream in which you are the sole participant. Hall found only fifteen percent of the dreams in his sample involved only the dreamer. Recent work by Dement is interesting in this regard. Comparing the dreams of normals and schizophrenics, Dement found the dreams of the schizophrenics to be almost totally lacking in content. Often their dreams had no people in them at all but were of simple objects.

Diamond (1962, pp. 106–7) reports several dream records of Dement's schizophrenic subjects verbatim. In one of these dreams the subject saw only a trunk and some curtain rods. In another there was only a shelf hanging in midair. There was no room, no identifiable setting. Most remarkable of all was the total absence of people. Even the subject was absent.

Thus the dream world of the schizophrenic is very much in keeping with his waking experiences. There is very little evidence of deep intra- or interpersonal relationships in either.

3. *Action.* Hall found that certain dreams that Freud regarded as "universal," such as dreams of flying, floating, and falling, occurred very infrequently. Everyday actions such as running, jumping, and riding did occur frequently. These dreams, which he described as "active," accounted for about thirty-three percent of dream actions. Passive activities such as sitting, watching, or talking occurred twenty-five percent of the time.

4. *Emotions.* Hall confirmed Mary Calkins' finding that unpleasant dreams are more prevalent than pleasant ones. Fear was more common than anger. Sadness prevailed over happiness. About half of the dreams had erotic or sexual elements. A number of other significant studies have focused on the aggressive and sexual aspects of dreams. In terms of dream frequency far more dreams are aggressive in nature than are sexual. The ratio of aggressive dreams to sexual dreams is as high as twenty to one in some cultures.

The overall significance of Hall's study of the dream is the discovery that our dreams are merely extensions of our everyday experiences. The setting is likely to be our own home, the characters are family and friends, and the plot is our own lifestyle.

Perhaps the most extensive study of the sexual dream was made by Kinsey (1948, 1953). Eighty-three percent of the males in Kinsey's sample reported having had a wet dream at some time in their lives. There was a wide range of experience reported. Some males reported experiencing orgasm and awakening two or three times in one night, while others reported only a few such dreams in their entire lives. Men in their teens and twenties averaged one such dream a month.

Kinsey discovered that wet dreams also frequently occurred among women, although somewhat less frequently than among men. By the age of forty-five, thirty-seven percent of the women in his sample had had one or more wet dreams. The average was three or four wet dreams per year. When men had these dreams they were usually accompanied by evidence of orgasm. Women were more likely than men to remember the psychological aspect of the experience, that is, the accompanying dream.

5. *Color*. Hall found two kinds of dreams occurring: color dreams and black-and-white dreams. Black-and-white dreams outnumbered color dreams by two to one. He found no evidence that color was related to any other variable. Color, he concluded, does not signify anything by itself.

The Purpose of Dreams

Although much is known about the content of our dreams, why we have them at all remains somewhat of a mystery. Explanations of why we dream range from Freud's concept of the dream as a vehicle for fulfilling unconscious wishes to those who view its function as purely physiological. Despite such differences of opinion, there has been a general consensus that at least some of our dreams have a purpose and may even be therapeutic.

NIGHTMARE THERAPY

Ramon Greenberg recently completed a study (1972) that suggests that one function of dreaming is to help us to adapt to disturbing events in our everyday lives. Subjects in Greenberg's laboratory were shown a very gory film of a cadaver being slit open at the stomach and spine and its skull being sawed open and chiseled away. While viewing this spectacle, measures of stress such as heart rate, skin electrical potential, and amount of perspiration were taken. After the film was over the students were asked to complete a psychological moods test. Most subjects recorded high levels of stress during the film and reactions of "disgust-shock" on the moods test.

That evening all subjects reported to Dr. Greenberg's sleep laboratory and were again wired up. This time the apparatus was designed to detect a dream state by measuring muscle tension, rapid eye movements, and brain waves. One group of volunteers was allowed to sleep through the night undisturbed. A second group was deprived of dreams by being awakened whenever the apparatus registered a dream state. A third group was awakened an equal number of times throughout the night but only at times when the subjects were not dreaming.

Next morning all subjects had to view the gory film again. Although it still seemed far from pleasant, subjects who had been allowed to dream reported less disgust-shock on the moods test. The stress measures showed a fifty percent reduction from the levels the film had generated the previous day. But for those who were deprived of their dreams the levels of stress were almost as high as those recorded on the previous day. Thus dreaming appears to play a role in adjusting to stress.

Analysis of the subjects' dream contents showed that they ranged from simple repetition of the events in the gory film to elements in the subjects' pasts that the film had aroused. It would appear that as these past events were integrated into the dream, the dreamer learned to cope with the trauma. One function of some of our nightmares, then, is to help us deal with the horrors of our waking existence.

SCHIZOPHRENIA AS A FORM OF NIGHTMARE THERAPY

Somewhat the same kind of process may occur in certain forms of schizophrenia. One view of acute schizophrenic reactions is that they are not evils in and of themselves but rather are problem-solving efforts. For one subgroup of patients such acute episodes may lead to recovery and personal growth; for others it may result in complete breakdown.

Those who improve are typically people who have functioned reasonably well until the episode. Usually they have experienced a major failure or very strong feeling of guilt. Such schizophrenics may then withdraw to the point where they think they are dead. Ancient myths of redemption appear in their consciousness, or they may go into a fetal position and rock back and forth for days at a time.

At such times the schizophrenic seems to be searching his or her inner consciousness and fantasies for a new, more acceptable reality, much as the rest of us solve our everyday problems in our nightmares. When the patient finds it he or she often emerges a stronger and better integrated human being than before.

Dreams We Don't Remember

For a very long time there was a myth that some of us dream and others do not. This myth was exploded in the late 1950s by a nocturnal explorer named Kleitman (1960).

The deep silence that prevailed in Kleitman's midnight laboratory in Abbott Hall at the University of Chicago was interrupted only by the perpetual scratching of the pen on the slowly turning EEG record. Then a sharp rise and fall of the pen would be accompanied by the subject's eyes moving back

and forth under his eyelids (such rapid eye movement or REM is an almost sure sign that a dream is occurring). The experimenter would then ring a bell and the subject would struggle awake.

"Were you dreaming?" the experimenter would ask.

"Yes." Then the subject would describe his dream. When finished, he would replace the microphone and settle back to sleep.

A long series of sleepless nights for Kleitman and a lot of interrupted dreams for his subjects yielded the finding that we all dream whether we remember or not. The average is five dreams per night.

If we all dream so much, why are so few dreams remembered? The writer Robert Louis Stevenson once offered a rather fanciful explanation that has since received some support in the laboratory. Stevenson was an excellent dream recaller. Many of his novels and stories were based on his vivid recollections of his dreams. He attributed the role of dreams in his writing to "brownies" who wrote stories for him while he slept.

But even Stevenson sometimes had dreams that were unintelligible and very difficult to remember. His description of his brownies on such nights provides an important insight about the process of forgetting dreams. On occasions such as those Stevenson said of his brownies "They have been too asleep . . . drowsiness has gained his little people, they have gone stumbling . . . and the play to the awakened mind is seen as a mess of absurdities."

This "sleeping brownie" theory corresponds very well to Kleitman's theory of dream forgetting, except that Kleitman uses the language of the biologist. For Kleitman the higher centers of the brain (those that control thinking and memory) are taking it easy during sleep. Dream activity is under less control than waking thinking, and this may lead to a kind of mental activity that the cortex cannot understand or decode.

Diamond (1962) suggests that some persons develop a built-in alarm clock that awakens them briefly during the course of the night. Changes in sleeping environment may also facilitate remembering. Freud reported remembering a series of his dreams at a time when he was sleeping on an unusually hard bed. Sleeping on a mat without a pillow is a regular part of Zen training in which the goal is to learn to witness one's sleeping consciousness while continuing to meditate.

THE NONRECALLER

Some of us seem to have brownies who always fall asleep. We never remember our dreams. This raises the question of how we keep ourselves from remembering. How, in other words, do we go about forgetting to set what Dement calls our "inner alarm clock?"

Freud's answer to this question was contained in his concept of repression. Most writers on the subject tend to agree that some kind of avoidance of experiencing is involved. The only exception appears to be Adler, who once stated that "as a rule people who are courageous seldom dream; they use the daytime for working out their problems." We know of course that Freud had a great ability to recall dreams. It would be interesting (and perhaps amusing) to know whether Adler was a nonrecaller.

Such subjective matter aside, existing research seems to lean more in Freud's direction than in Adler's on this question. Schonbar (1961) has studied the recall of dreams in a group of education students over a four-week period. She divided her subjects into good and poor recallers. The first group reported 213 dreams during the four-week period, the second group only forty-eight. There was a definite difference in the pattern of recalled dreams for the two groups. Good recallers claimed to have remembered dreams from all times of the night. Their dreams were likely to be emotionally charged and unpleasant. Poor recallers tended to remember only dreams that occurred just before they awakened early in the morning. Most of their dreams were emotionally neutral or mildly pleasant. This finding suggests the possibility that nonrecallers tend to suppress unpleasant dreams.

If Freud is correct that dream forgetting is a process of repression, then it could be hypothesized that anxiety dreams would be forgotten more often than pleasant dreams. Herman Witkin (1969) used emotionally charged films to increase the level of anxiety in reported dreams. These films did in fact tend to raise the level of anxiety in the dreams' content. Furthermore, there was a significant increase in the frequency of reports that "I was dreaming, but can't remember what" when his subjects were awakened during the night. Thus Witkin's study, like Schonbar's, supports Freud's contention that forgetting dreams is a way of avoiding anxiety.

HOW TO REMEMBER DREAMS

If (like your author) you thought you seldom dreamed and were surprised to discover from this

to his therapy patients. Shulman's advice is to keep a pencil and paper beside your bed to write down any dream fragments that occur. This technique is almost always successful if you are highly motivated and really try to remember. It is very important to do this immediately on awakening before you do or think of anything else. Herman Rorschach, author of the famous "ink blot" test, carried this even further. Believing that dreams were essentially kinesthetic productions that would be forgotten should the dreamer move too rapidly, open the eyes quickly, or jump out of bed, he advised the dreamer to lie perfectly still with closed eyes until the dream is fully grasped. Perhaps one of these techniques will work for you.

Interpreting Dreams

The interpretation of dreams has been the subject of many books and theories over the years. Many popular books are gross oversimplifications of Freud's ideas about dreams as wish fulfillment and of Jung's dream symbols. Psychoanalytic dream interpretation is far too complex a subject to go into here. Interested readers will find a good introduction to psychoanalytic dream interpretation in Ann Faraday's *Dream Power*.

Some alternative ways to approach dreams are suggested by Hall's system of dealing with the content of dreams as a play (Hall 1966). A second approach that fits well with that of Hall is the gestalt technique of role-playing our dreams. Some examples of dream interpretation along both lines are presented below as models of this form of dream interpretation.

USING OUR DREAMS FOR SELF-UNDERSTANDING

This is in essence the advice of Rosslund Cartwright, a well-known dream researcher at the University of Chicago. In our society the influence of Freud and the psychoanalysts has led us to expect to find "forbidding and dangerous" material

chapter that you actually do dream from three to five dreams a night, perhaps you will become interested in trying to recall more of your dreams. Often merely finding out that we all do dream is enough to significantly increase dream recall. Edwin Diamond reports in his book that at a meeting of psychoanalysts in the late 1950s one participant mentioned that until one week before the meeting she had been unaware of the Kleitman and Dement findings. Upon reading their paper and discovering that she was really a "nonrecaller" rather than a "nondreamer" she suddenly began to remember her dreams: "Since Monday," she reported with a nervous smile, "I have had four dreams that I can remember."

Learning to remember dreams is not always this easy, however. If you wish to remember your dreams you may want to try the suggestion that Adlerian therapist Bernard Shulman (1969) makes

in our dreams. Other societies, such as the Sioux culture of Black Elk, make dream interpretation a natural part of growing up. In a recent book on the psychology of dreaming, Cartwright (1969) suggests that our everyday dream lives can be as enriched as psychedelic drug trips if we can learn to integrate our dreams with our everyday experiences. To this end she suggests that instead of saying to children, "It's only a dream," parents should try to help them understand their dreams. A good way to do this is to explain the dream to the child as "a story you made up in your sleep." The idea that the child has the power to make up such vivid and compelling stories should be described as a wonderful ability rather than something frightening or foreign.

HALL AND ADLER: THE DREAMER AS PLAYWRIGHT
Adlerian psychologists advise us to look at our dreams in terms of 1) the narrative or action that we have written into our dreams, 2) the people in the cast—who they are and what special significance they have for us, 3) the setting—where have we chosen to have our dream enacted, and 4) the mood of the dream and how it reflects our feelings.

These interpretive points are clearly illustrated in a case reported by Bernard Shulman (1969). Shulman had a patient who dreamed he was invited to dinner by a married couple. The dreamer saw himself caressing the hostess at the table in full view of her husband. The patient told Shulman that in the dream he felt guilty for taking advantage of his trusting host. Later, while giving his associations to the dream he revealed that he was engaged in an affair with his landlady while carrying on a friendship with her husband.

The narrative action of this dream exactly parallels a real-life situation that was causing anxiety. In the dream, however, the dreamer relives his anxiety by doing the thing openly. But even in the dream the openness is not complete. This is apparent in the fact that he disguised identities.

A GESTALT APPROACH: ROLE-PLAYING THE DREAM
Fritz Perls, the originator of gestalt therapy, stresses that our dreams are maximally useful to us only after we manage to fully assimilate them into our present awareness. We can all facilitate this process by "being" the various components of our dreams.

Role-playing as Perls used it involves only one person: the dreamer (Perls 1969). Like Hall and Adler, Perls viewed the dreamer as a playwright and his technique places full responsibility for each dream with its dreamer. Thus if I dream of a flowing river it is *my river* and according to Perls I put it in *my dream* for a purpose.

Perls also feels that we construct our dreams in ways that reflect the holes in our personalities:

In a dream we have a clear existential message of what's missing in our lives, what we avoid doing and living, and of material to reassimilate and reown the alienated parts of ourselves.

To help the dreamer reown these parts, a gestalt therapist does several things. First the dreamer must role-play each part of the dream, acknowledging his or her ownership of it by using the first person, e.g., "I am a flowing river." Second, the therapist looks for nonverbal clues that reveal conflict between the parts of the dream. Faraday (1973) reports a gestalt dream session in which the dreamer entered his office and took the elevator. At this point the therapist noticed the dreamer's eyes flushed rapidly to the left and then back again. The therapist asked the man if there was something he failed to mention. The dreamer tried to brush this aside saying he had simply glanced at a room beside the elevator that was unimportant since all it contained was rotten garbage. At this point the therapist asked the dreamer to role-play being the rotten garbage. This quickly led to the dreamer's becoming aware of some parts of his life that he was trying to ignore because he considered them "rotten."

Although a skilled therapist can be very helpful in noticing and focusing on such areas of conflict, the gestalt approach can also be used by an individual who wishes to work with his own dreams. Recently René Rebillot*, a student in one of my courses, decided to experiment with gestalt techniques by getting a friend of hers to take on the role of therapist. After some experimentation she discovered that a tape recorder could substitute for the friend and she began to do her own gestalt interpretation of her dreams. We include here two of her dreams. In the first her friend plays the therapist:

R: I am in a strange land. It turns out that I look just like a girl in this land. People keep mistaking me for her. I meet a guy who

---

*While it has been our practice elsewhere in this text to use fictitious names when dealing with the personal life experiences of others, René has asked that her real name be used. At the time of this dream work she was a senior in liberal arts.

likes me but I run because I think he is mistaking me for the other girl. As I run he chases me. I pass people sitting on the benches between the psychology building and the modern languages building and I see a girl I know. I say, "Hi, Ann" and then realize that I should not have said that, for her name would be different in this world. I keep running.

F: Have a dialogue between you and the guy.

R: (as herself) I don't want to talk to you because I'm afraid that if I talk to you you'll realize that I am not who you think I am. I am not really the girl you're running after.

R: (as the guy) Yes, you are. You look exactly like her. You are the girl I am running after.

R: No I'm not. Don't you understand? I am not the girl you think I am.

F: Say that again.

R: I am not the girl you think I am.
I am not the girl you think I am.
I am not the girl you think I am.
He thinks I am the girl that he knows in this world but I don't know what she is like. I do know that she can't be like me.

F: What are you like?

R: I am a good person. I am basically happy and I am secure. I can be sensitive at times but I reason things out well.

F: Have an encounter with the girl.

R: Hello, you look exactly like me but I don't know what you are like.

R: (as the girl) I am exactly what you are. I'm the same as you.

F: Let's try something else. Try to really become the guy.

R: (as the guy) Why are you running away from me? You know I love you. I don't understand.

F: What do you feel?

R: (as the guy) I am confused. I don't understand why you won't accept me. What do

you fear about me? I can't figure it out. I want to get close to you but you won't stop running.

F: How do you experience yourself?

R: (as the guy) I am a man. I am very masculine and self-assured. I am male.

F: Rene, talk to him.

R: I can't be near you, for you frighten me. I don't know how to act and what to say.

F: What is your right hand doing to your left hand?

R: Stroking it.

F: Say "I."

R: I am stroking my left hand.

F: Have an encounter between your hands.

R: I am glad you're stroking me. I like to be stroked.

R: I like to stroke you.

F: What is your left hand doing?

R: It, or rather I, am coming alive. I am wringing my right hand. I feel like my left hand has come alive. I feel alive. I feel that my right hand is him and my left hand is me. I am passive and he is active and I will not accept him.

F: How do you experience being male?

R: I feel active and self-confident and very, very, competent.

F: Talk about how you experience female.

R: I am passive, less confident, and I don't feel very competent.

F: Try to alternate between male and female.

R: I feel female, I feel calm and quiet.
I am male, I feel that I want to be active and do things.
I want to get up and walk around.

(René gets up and walks around.)

R: I feel active and yet sensitive. I feel competent and secure. I am all these things. I am male as well as female.

When I started to walk around and act active I began to feel more sure of myself and more at home. I felt confident and also calm. I think that the male part, or what I experience as the male part is in me but I have trouble really believing that I am competent all the time.

In this example René (who, like her right hand, is usually a very quiet person) began to experience another side of herself that was more active and felt very competent. She was surprised to learn of this other side of her personality.

Later René began to record her dreams. By listening carefully to her own voice as she described the dream and as she role-played each component she found that she could do a good job of getting herself to focus on conflicts revealed by the dream. Following is an example of how she accomplished this.

R: (on the tape recorder) There are a lot of monks walking along the beach. On the beach there is a man dying. The monks can only see after they have walked twenty-five feet along. The man is before the twenty-five-foot place so the monks cannot see him. He is crying for help. The head monk moves the fence back two feet to where the man is so he can see him. The monks push a fence along and at the twenty-five-foot place they put it down and can see. The monk helped the man.

R: (as therapist) Be the monk.

R: (on the tape recorder) I walk along and I know that I can only see every so many feet. I am closed off except every twenty-five feet I can open up and see. But I see a man and I know that he is dying. I move the fence back so that I can see him and help him.

R: (as therapist) How do you experience not being able to see?

R: (on tape recorder) I experience darkness, total darkness, and then I see sudden light, and then darkness again, then light, and darkness. But this time the darkness is

not complete. I see a man. It is very hazy but I do see him. I know he needs help and I feel that I can see if I want to. I can fix it so I move the fence back and pretend that this is the twenty-five-foot line. Then all is light. I see him clearly. I feel that the light is not going to go away. I do not think I am going to be dark again.

R: (as therapist) Say, "I am not going to be dark again."

R: (on tape recorder) I am not going to be dark again. I am not going to be dark again. I am not going to be dark again.

R: (as therapist) How do you feel now?

R: (on tape recorder) I feel very open and bright and free. I just feel very open. I am light and open and free. I am happy. I see all the time there is no darkness.

When I started to go over this dream I did not expect to discover that I blind myself.

Dreams and Creativity

If dreams provide us with clues to the solution of our personal problems, it follows that they might also provide clues to new ideas as well. Some dreamers routinely use their dreams as a source of creative thoughts. Many writers and scientists report ideas that come to them in their sleep. It was just this technique that won Otto Loewi the Nobel Peace Prize in 1939:

During this discussion [with a fellow scientist in 1903], the idea occurred to me that the terminals of those nerves might contain chemicals . . . and that these chemicals might in turn transmit the nervous impulse to their respective effective organs. At that time, I did not see a way to prove the correctness of this hunch and it entirely slipped my conscious memory until it emerged again in 1920. The night before Easter Sunday of that year, I awoke, turned on the light, and jotted down a few notes on a tiny slip of thin paper. Then I fell asleep again. It occurred to me at six o'clock in the morning that during the night I had written down something most important, but I was unable to decipher the scrawl. The next night at three o'clock, the idea returned. It was the design of an experiment to determine whether or not the hypothesis of chemical transmission that I had uttered seventeen years ago was correct. I got up, immediately went to the laboratory, and performed a simple experiment on a frog's heart according to the nocturnal design . . . its results became the foundation of the theory of chemical transmission of the nervous impulse (Loewi 1960).

Dreams such as Loewi's have sometimes been interpreted as coming from a spiritualistic or supernatural force. Such an explanation is appealing because of the apparently large leap from existing scientific knowledge that Loewi's dream represents. How can such a leap occur? One answer comes from an analysis of scientific thinking. Loewi was in all likelihood working on the problem for seventeen years. Most discussions of creative problem solving suggest the following five steps: 1) Define the question (this was in essence what Loewi did in the conversation in 1903 with a fellow scientist). 2) Gather facts (between 1903 and 1920 came a long career in physiology, which entailed concentration on a wealth of data and playing with ideas and techniques. All of this was crucial input. Without it the ingenious idea would very likely have gone by in his dream without being recognized as such). 3) Wait. 4) A solution pops out spontaneously. 5) Assess the solution. Is it worthwhile or not?

The dream state may be especially helpful for steps three and four, which are largely intuitive processes. Loewi himself acknowledged that he would have probably rejected the experiment he performed as having a low chance of success if he had had the idea in the daytime. Such an interpretation is consistent with one physiological theory of the nature of dreaming. (Diamond 1962, pp. 252–53)

This theory suggests that while we are awake inhibitory impulses are continually sent to the cortex so that only the strong excitory impulses of external sensory perceptions can cause the neurons to fire. At night the process is reversed; there is less inhibition of the cortex so that the weaker impulses of ideas and thoughts stored in the memory can now cause the firing of the neurons. This increased amount of internal stimulation leads at first to dreams and eventually to activity too unpatterned to sustain even dream thoughts. This freerer firing is of course analogous to step four of the creative process outlined earlier.

Robert Louis Stevenson claimed that he actually created many of his best plots while he dreamed. Following is Stevenson's own explanation, which appeared in his *Across the Plains*, of how he used a dream as the basis for *Dr. Jekyll and Mr. Hyde*:

> I can give but an instance or so of what part is done sleeping and what part awake . . . *The Strange Case of Dr. Jekyll and Mr. Hyde* . . . . For two days I sat wracking my brain for a plot of any sort; then on the second night I dreamed the scene at the window, and a scene after, split in two, in which Hyde, pursued for some crime, took the powder and underwent the change in the presence of his pursuers. All the rest was made awake, and consciously, although I think I can trace in much of it the manner of my brownies.

Stevenson's account is remarkable in its suggestion that he could direct his brownies (or, if you prefer, his unconscious) to write him a play. However, there is evidence in laboratory dream research that all of us have to some extent this same ability but seldom use it. Most normal subjects (nonrecallers included) can recall their dreams with the same vivid detail as did Stevenson when they are awakened in the laboratory. The difference seems to be that most of us lack the poet's ability to leap out of bed at the dream's conclusion and write it down.

Chapter Ten Summary

1. *Dream content* is very closely related to our everyday experience. The setting of most dreams is our own home and the characters usually include those with whom we have strong emotional ties. The content of many of our dreams often reflects our daily activities.

2. *The function of dreaming.* A fair proportion of our dreams appears to have a therapeutic function. Sometimes we work through our feelings about a traumatic event by dreaming. Scientists, writers, and other creative individuals often find new and novel ideas in their dreams.

3. *Forgetting dreams.* Everyone dreams four or five times each night. There are several theories of why some dreams are remembered and others are not. Freud explained nonrecall in terms of repression of an unconscious need to avoid anxiety. Biological explanations focus on differences in the quantity and nature of cortical activity. Committing yourself to recalling dreams, keeping a pencil and paper handy, recording dreams the moment you awaken, and interrupting your sleep by a soft alarm clock have all been shown to be very effective ways of increasing recall.

4. *Interpreting dreams.* In Hall's method the dreamer is considered a playwright who has definite reasons for constructing his dream the way she or he does. Interpretation involves taking careful note of the plot, the people you put in your dream, the setting you place them in, and the feelings you have each character portray.

   Gestalt dream interpretation carries this process one step further in that the dreamer is asked to do a repeat performance of the dream, taking the role of each person and piece of scenery.

Glossary

Acute schizophrenia A form of personality disorder characterized by extreme, very exaggerated loss of contact with external reality. The onset is very sudden and can often be related to a recent traumatic life event such as the death of a loved one. Recovery is likewise often fairly rapid.

Cortex The outer layer of the brain; that portion of the brain that enables us to think, analyze, and organize our perceptions.

EEG(electroencephalogram) The pattern of electrical activity in the brain as measured on an electroencephalograph machine. One such pattern is associated with dreaming.

REM Rapid eye movement, characteristic of the dreaming state.

Exercises *(For individual and class use)*

You can do the following exercises at your leisure. Perhaps some of these would be more enjoyable with a friend. Those with an asterisk should be done in consultation with your teacher or in class.

1. *Keeping a dream journal.* Try writing down as many of your dreams as you can recall for a period of one month. See how many you can catch.

- Be sure to keep pencil and paper or a tape recorder and a flashlight beside your bed.
- Urge yourself to recall dreams by saying, "Tonight I will remember my dreams" over and over again until you fall asleep.
- Sit up slowly or try to record your dreams without sitting up at all to avoid "jarring" the dream out of your consciousness.
- If dreams are hard to recall, use an alarm clock (or a devoted roommate) to wake yourself at some unexpected time.
- Write down all dreams in as much detail as you can. Remember that the detail you think is unimportant is likely to be the key to the dream.

2. Try interpreting some of your dreams by Hall's technique. Then if the meaning still eludes you, try gestalt role playing.

3. Try using your dreams to solve a difficult math problem. Work on the problem just before turning in; will yourself to seek a solution in your dreams. Keep a pencil and paper handy and write yourself a reminder to ask yourself for the solution the moment you awaken. Remember, it is crucial to ask yourself for the solution before you move about, sit up, or become fully awake.

Bibliography

Cartwright, R. 1969. In Kramer, M., ed. *Dream psychology and the new biology of dreaming*. Springfield, Ill.: Thomas.

Diamond, E. 1962. *The science of dreams*. New York: Doubleday.

Faraday, A. 1973. *Dream power*. New York: Berkeley.

Freud, S. 1900. *The interpretation of dreams*. London: Hogarth.

Greenberg, R., Pillard, R. and Pearlman, C. 1972. The effect of dream (stage rear) deprivation on adoption to stress. *Psychosomatic Medicine* 34 (3):257–62.

Hall, C. 1966. *The meaning of dreams*. New York: McGraw-Hill.

Kinsey, A., Pomeroy, W. and Martin, C. 1948. *Sexual behavior in the human male*. Philadelphia: W. B. Saunders.

———. 1953. *Sexual behavior in the human female*. Philadelphia: W. B. Saunders.

Kleitman, N. 1960. Patterns of dreaming. *Scientific American*.

Loewi, O. 1960. An autobiographic sketch. *Perspectives in Biology and Medicine* (Autumn).

Murphy, G. 1961. *The challenge of physical research: a primer of parapsychology*. New Yorker: Harper.

Neihardt, J. 1961. *Black Elk speaks*. Lincoln, Nebraska: University of Nebraska Press.

Perls, F. 1969. *Gestalt therapy verbatim*. Layfayette, Calif.: Real People Press.

Schonbar, R. 1961. Temporal and emotional factors in the selective recall of dreams. *Journal of Consulting Psychology* 25:67–73.

Schulman, B. 1969. An Adlerian view. In Kramer, M., ed. *Dream psychology and the new biology of dreaming*. Springfield, Ill.: Thomas, 117–37.

Witkin, H. 1969. Influencing dream content. In Kramer, M., ed. *Dream psychology and the new biology of dreaming*. Springfield, Ill.: Thomas. 285–359.

Chapter Eleven: The Inner Eye (Anxiety, Hypnosis, Meditation and Biofeedback)

A man saw Nasrudin searching for something on the ground.

"What have you lost, Mulla?" he asked.

"My key," said the Mulla. So they both went down on their knees and looked for it.

After a time the other man asked "Where exactly did you drop it?"

"In my own house."

"Then why are you looking here?"

"There is more light here than inside my own house."

IDRIES SHAH, *The Exploits of the Incomparable Mulla Nasrudin*

The Age of Anxiety: Learning Emotional Control

When we are troubled and anxious we usually go hunting for an answer. This search for the key to happiness may lead us to many places. Some of us may turn to activities or hobbies in which we find a sense of satisfaction. Many turn to other people such as friends, family, or a social partner for support and comfort.

All too seldom do we discover the sources of strength that lie within us. Although we may devote years to a career or a marriage in the hope of finding happiness, most of us have devoted almost none of our energy to learning to relax and control our inner emotions.

This is a chapter about learning emotional control. We will discuss anxiety and specific techniques that we may use to turn inward and discover our own resources for handling it. The techniques we have chosen to discuss are 1) self-hypnosis, 2) meditation, and 3) biofeedback. Because it is difficult to understand these techniques without having had some personal experience with them, we will describe several exercises in the text rather than waiting for the exercise section at the end of the chapter. You will be able to understand this chapter better if you allow time to try each exercise as you read.

We live with high speeds, heavy demands, and considerable conflicts. Everything appears to be in a constant state of change and uncertainty. Whole fields of endeavor are made obsolete by rapidly developing technology. Family roles are uncertain and changing; travel is the rule rather than the exception. It is fairly common to have lunch in New York, land in Los Angeles and drive to Anaheim, over seventy miles of freeway, for supper. Little wonder that such a world is full of anxiety.

THE MANY FACES OF ANXIETY

Anxiety is a very complicated state of awareness. It may combine subjective feelings of vague uneasiness or impending difficulties, physiological re-

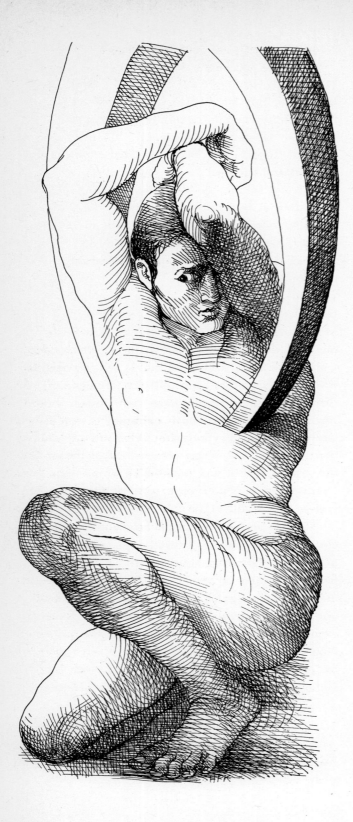

sponses such as a pounding heart and shallow breathing, and many other complicated behaviors. For the purposes of this chapter we will consider three basic aspects of anxiety. For each of these there is a key technique that may be used to calm yourself. In the remainder of this chapter we will discuss those techniques, such as hypnosis and meditation, which are helpful in coping with anxiety.

Doublethink. Anxiety is often characterized by a racing mind that shifts quickly from one thought to another. Our thoughts often shift from an argument with a superior to planning the next day's work to worrying about getting a job to concerns about our mate's feelings for us. Such constant shifting leads to confusion and feelings of helplessness (none of the thinking leads to a decision or plan of action), and our worries spread into more and more areas until our problems are blown way out of proportion. The obvious technique for coping with such a state is to learn to focus your attention. As you will see later in this chapter, the basic procedure used in hypnosis and meditation is to encourage the subject to focus more and more attention on a single stimulus. In hypnosis this concentration is helped by a series of hypnotic suggestions. In meditation, special words (*mantras*), gestures (*mudras*), and postures (*asanas*) are used to provide a means for concentration.

Regret and rehearsal. Anxiety is a state in which our thinking is largely taken up by feelings of regret for what has occurred in the past—such as our attempts to relive past arguments. Anxiety states frequently involve "rehearsing" the bad feelings you expect to occur during future impending disasters—like "What will I do if I fail?" Both regret and rehearsal are often rather futile. It is one thing to be goal-oriented. It is quite another to constantly expect and anticipate failure. Regret and rehearsal only enhance our feelings of helplessness. For this reason techniques such as meditation encourage us to focus our attention and energy on the present.

The ultimate goal of meditation is full, complete living in the here and now.

Repression and tension. The feelings of vague uneasiness that we experience when we are anxious may be due in part to repressing (pushing out of awareness) disturbing thoughts or ideas. These attempts often result in corresponding subconscious efforts to control our breathing and bodily movements. Such hidden conflicts sometimes reveal themselves in the form of dreams, breathing problems such as asthma, excess muscle tension, and physical illness. The concept that anxiety is a physical phenomenon is so basic that it has generated at least three new schools of psychotherapy (bioenergetics, Rolfing, and biofeedback.)

COPING WITH ANXIETY

Anxious people often seem to have forgotten how to breathe. Their breathing is frequently shallow, or irregular, or too rapid. I once had a client who feared he was having heart problems. A trip to a specialist failed to reveal any organic problem, so he came to see me. Listening to his high, thin, almost inaudible speech and shallow breathing suggested the key to his anxiety was to be found in his breathing. Some reassurance from me and a program of breathing exercises, similar to those that will be described in the section on meditation, combined with some talking out of his problems were all that were needed to alleviate his "heart discomfort."

It is no accident that we speak of the anxious person as "tense." Our muscles tend to tighten up when we are worried. Sometimes the tension is somewhat symbolic. I recently worked with an individual who had enormous difficulty relaxing his right arm. It turned out that he experienced a good deal of resentment toward his friends who he felt put him down. He contained his anger in the muscles of his arm. Relaxing our muscles can reduce feelings of anxiety. Later in this chapter we will present brief exercises in yoga and self-hypnosis

Anxiety Symptom	Coping Technique
Doublethink	Concentration Training Hypnosis Meditation
Regret and Rehearsal	Training in staying focused on the here and now Meditation
Repression and Tension	Training in relaxing and in deep breathing Meditation Hypnosis

FIG. 11-1 *A model for coping with anxiety*

for the reader who wishes to learn to relax deeply.

The model shown in figure 11-1 summarizes briefly what has been said so far about coping with anxiety.

In the remainder of this chapter we will discuss a variety of self-hypnosis, meditation, and biofeedback techniques. Each section is designed to give you only a basic introduction. Those who use these methods would do well to consult the more complete discussions in the chapter bibliography. Working with a professional is also recommended.

Methods of Dealing with Anxiety: 1. Hypnosis*

Many common hypnotic induction procedures use suggestions that encourage deep muscle relaxation, feelings of warmth, and visual images that are strong conditioned stimuli for feeling calm, peaceful, and relaxed. For this reason self-hypnosis is a very effective tool for coping with anxiety.

---

*Some of the hypnosis ideas in this chapter are from a forthcoming book on hypnosis and relaxation by Dr. Harley D. Christiansen. We appreciate Dr. Christiansen's permission in allowing us to use some of his manuscript materials in producing this chapter.

Read the following exercise to yourself very slowly, breathing full, deep breaths as you do so. Try to vividly imagine yourself in this scene being lightly hypnotized. If you have been hypnotized before or if you are a very good potential subject for hypnosis, you may find that just reading this will tend to calm you and put you in a state of relaxed attention that will greatly facilitate your concentrating on this chapter. This experiment will be most beneficial if you read slowly and take time to visualize doing the things suggested. Some of my own most relaxing experiences have occurred when I closed my eyes for a while between each suggestion.

Exercise: Self-Hypnosis

I was sitting in a very large, comfortable chair listening intently, because I knew in a moment I was going to be hypnotized. . . . I wondered if it would work, and really wanted to cooperate. "And now we are going to do something that will allow you to relax yourself far more deeply than you normally do." The voice was very soothing. There was something fascinating about the way it resonated the words *deeply* and *relaxed* . . . "Allow yourself to breathe in and out slowly and deeply." I did so and noticed a gradual slowing down of everything: my breathing . . . my thoughts . . . my muscles . . . my body rhythms. Everything seemed to slow down . . . "And nooow," the voice continued, "I want you to think of the word *flowing* as you breathe in." This was said just as I was starting to breathe in, and I found myself slow-in down my breathing still more in order to stay with the words "*flowing, flowing, flowing* . . ." Then as I was breathing out, it continued very slowly, "and now, . . . as you breathe out, think the words *deeply relaxed*." I felt a calmness creeping slowly over me, a feeling of peacefulness and tranquility. I felt the muscles

in the back of my neck relaxing and . . . and then my head began to nod . . .

You may have felt yourself slowing down, relaxing, feeling calmer as you read this. Possibly you noticed your muscles beginning to relax or a slight deepening of your attention on the words: "flowing," "deeply relaxed," "soothingly," "slowly," "peacefulness," "tranquility." If you did, you were entering what hypnotists regard as a light trance.

HYPNOSIS AND EVERYDAY LIFE

A hypnotic trance is in reality an experience that is fairly prevalent in our everyday lives. When we watch a movie and become oblivious to everything except the action on the screen we are in a light trance in which the scope of our awareness has narrowed but its intensity has increased.

Often "trance" experiences occur at dawn when we are conscious of drifting in a light sleep yet are too drowsy to get up. At such times it is often difficult to say whether we are awake or dreaming. Likewise, while trying to drive down a highway late at night I sometimes find my attention narrowing more and more to that single white line while my eyelids feel heavier and heavier . . . there is a feeling of inevitability that those lids will close, whether I want them to or not, that is very trance-like. . . .

There is also the "classroom trance." The instructor in your 3:30 Monday class continues to go over . . . and over . . . and over a point that you are disinterested in. You try harder and harder to listen, but the harder you try, the more your thoughts keep returning to the fact that you had very little sleep last night. Your eyelids may start to flutter at this point and your head begins to nod . . . Voilà! A successful hypnosis session!

If you know what to look for, you will begin to discover hypnotized people all around you. I was working in the public library one day when I was suddenly interrupted by a strange sort of humming sound coming from my right. I looked over to see what was causing it. Over in the corner a young chap was rocking in his chair with closed eyes and rolling head. Some people stared and some laughed, but he continued his rocking totally oblivious to us all. When I looked closer the nature of his "trance" suddenly became apparent. He had on a set of earphones and was listening to jazz. With the earphones shutting off all outer sounds and his eyes closed, the music had become his entire reality. And so my happy jazz buff continued his trip completely alone in his musical space.

CHARACTERISTICS OF THE HYPNOTIC STATE

Ernest Hilgard, an eminent experimental psychologist who has spent years investigating hypnosis in the laboratory, suggests the following character-

istics as a means of identifying what sort of behaviors are to be expected of one who is hypnotized (Hilgard and Atkinson 1967).

The planning function subsides. We can see an example of this point at the beginning of this section in the subject's fascination with the words of the hypnotist. There is a deep trust in a hypnotic relationship, in which the subjects releases his ego-controlling functions to another person. It is like being a baby again and depending solely on your mother for food and nourishment.

Attention is redistributed. As in meditation, hypnotic technique aims at a total concentration of your attention on a single source of stimulation. This may be the hypnotist's voice or, particularly in self-hypnosis, it may involve focusing on a relaxing scene or a physiological response such as the warmth of your hands. Hypnosis usually provides a suggestion about how you should respond to the stimulus, like "The peaceful scene makes you feel calmer," "Your hand is feeling warmer," and so forth.

Reality testing is reduced and reality distortion is accepted. In our ordinary waking state most of us are highly critical and tend to check out and reject experiences that fail to correspond to our preconceived notions of what reality should be like. For example, if I thought I saw a rosebud slowly unfolding in space before me I would probably reach out and try to touch it. If I couldn't feel it I would know it was not really there. Under hypnosis such reality-checking functions tend to diminish. Sensory experiences are taken at face value and accepted for what they are. In other words, inner reality is accepted as more valid than external reality.

Suggestibility is increased. This is, of course, the major characteristic of hypnosis. The technique has been used to suggest to tense persons that they can relax deeply. Pain—such as that experienced in the dentist's office, during childbirth, or during major surgery—can be alleviated by skillful suggestion. In one recent case thirty-one warts were successfully removed from the hand of a nine-year-old fourth grader by the suggestion that the warts on the left side of her hand would tingle and that they would begin to disappear after a week. The warts began to fall off after the first session. Less spectacular but possibly more important is the technique of hypnotic ego strengthening, in which suggestions are made that the subject will experience greater and greater feelings of self-worth, less and less anxiety, and more self-confidence (Hartland 1966). For example, a suggestion such as the following may be used: "Every day . . . you will become emotionally much calmer . . . much more settled . . . much less easily disturbed . . . and every day . . . you will feel a greater feeling of personal well-being . . . a greater feeling of personal safety and security . . . than you have felt for a long time. As you become . . . and remain . . . more relaxed . . . and less tense . . . you will develop more confidence in yourself . . . you will become much more confident in your ability to do what you have to do each day . . . without fear of failure . . . without anxiety . . . without uneasiness. Because of this . . . every day . . . you will feel more and more independent . . . more able to stick up for yourself . . . to stand on your own feet . . . and because all these things will happen . . . you are going to feel much happier . . . much more contented . . . much more cheerful . . . much more optimistic . . . much less easily discouraged . . . much less easily depressed."

The hypnotized person readily enacts acceptable roles. The best subjects for hypnosis are those who can readily adopt new roles. They can readily be someone other than themselves and may behave like that person. This feature of hypnosis is of course what makes the ego-strengthening technique described in the last paragraph so effective. Under hypnosis the conditioning that has led the

subject to feel unsure of himself or herself is weakened. It becomes easier to assume the role of someone who is calm and self-confident because the mental blocks to feeling that way are circumvented by suggestion.

AN OBJECTIVIST LOOKS AT HYPNOSIS

Although there is a wealth of evidence to support the contention that hypnosis is a powerful and useful procedure for changing behavior, there is a considerable amount of controversy over *why* it works. This argument is too complicated to go into in full detail here; however, the basic disagreement centers over whether the behaviors that change do so because the subject is in an altered state of consciousness. This disagreement hinges on the fact that unlike other altered states, such as dreams and meditation, there are no reliable physiological factors that indicate a hypnotic trance. Furthermore, one investigator, Ted Xenophon Barber, in a series of over sixty experimental studies (1970) has consistently found that if subjects are motivated, if they believe that they can be hypnotized, and if the situation is structured to insure that they try hard to cooperate, most of the behaviors such as relaxation, feelings of drowsiness, and responses to test suggestions can be produced without actually hypnotizing the subjects at all.

An interesting case in point relates to the common question, "If I were hypnotized, could the hypnotist get me to do things I normally would view as dangerous, immoral, or wicked?" After a careful review of all the literature in this area, Barber found only two fully documented cases of the alleged use of hypnosis to suggest such acts. In both of these instances there was considerable evidence that hypnosis hadn't really been used.

Furthermore, Barber proposes that suggestions to commit criminal or illegal acts felt to be wrong are often effective *without the subject's undergoing any hypnotic induction* at all. Stanley Milgram's obedience experiment (Milgram 1973—see chapter three for a complete description) is an excellent example. As you recall, Milgram got his subjects to administer over 400 volts to a victim simply by making repeated suggestions to do so in a setting that had some apparent validity. Many of Milgram's subjects were extremely upset and anxious about what they were doing. Some almost broke down under the strain of the experiment—but most obeyed. Clearly, if the situation is right, most of us will go along with authority. Barber argues that it is the *situation* that makes people compliant under hypnosis rather than the "trance."

To test this idea, he compared two methods of influencing his subjects to make slanderous and potentially destructive statements about another person. Method one was hypnosis; method two was a forceful suggestion or sales pitch made while the subject was fully awake. Individuals in both groups tended to make statements that might have resulted in a person being fired. Hypnotic induction was no more effective than forceful waking suggestions in eliciting such behavior. It would appear that those who are terrified about the prospect of mind control have at least as much to fear from their realtor as from their hypnotist.

By now it is probably apparent that in many respects hypnosis is a very normal everyday kind of experience. Most of us have experienced the moments of deep relaxation and/or heavy concentration that are characteristic of light trance without applying the label *hypnosis*. And there are many times in our lives when we are highly suggestible. The concept of hypnotic suggestion may be helpful in understanding many important life experiences such as falling in love or being fascinated by a painting, psychosomatic illness, or the charisma of a political figure—all of which have all or most of the behavioral characteristics that Hilgard proposes pertain to a hypnotized subject. Also, the experience many of us call an "anxiety attack" is in large part a delusion brought about by our own suggestions.

Several years ago I experienced a very frightening personal demonstration of the degree to which my body is susceptible to powerful suggestion from my mind. I was completing my graduate work when I was told by my committee that they felt I should take a more difficult course in statistics than the one I had audited for credit. I felt overwhelmed by the amount of work required and the fear that I would fail the course. The next morning I had arrived for class and begun taking notes when suddenly I found myself perspiring heavily and unable to breathe. My heart began to pound wildly. I recalled a magazine article I had read the night before about heart disease and concluded I was having a heart attack. I was taken over to the health clinic. The doctor examined me and informed me that I had just experienced an anxiety attack. I went home to rest and think out what had happened. The first aspect of the situation involved my own suggestibility in this area. Having had a childhood background of rheumatic fever, I was particularly vulnerable to any suggestion that there was something wrong with my heart. I had read a vivid description of a heart attack in a magazine article just the previous night. The article attributed the cause of heart trouble in young men to overwork and over-achievement. And there I was, a young man of twenty-eight with a background of heart murmur who was taking a course load that already required (or so I thought) studying until midnight or 1 A.M. almost nightly and who had just been ordered by his committee to add another very difficult course to the load. It was a very powerful suggestion.

The second aspect of the situation was purely physical. Any good hypnotist arranges to incorporate suggestions of physical sensations that he or she knows will be occurring. The hypnotist may, for example, tell you to place your hand on your thigh and then a few moments later suggest that "you may begin to notice that your hand is beginning to feel warmer." Your hand will of course be warmer because of the heat of the thigh. Thus you come to see the hypnotist as somewhat psychic.

In my case the class was at 7:30 A.M. on the third floor of an old building with no elevator. I always got up late, rode my bicycle at full tilt to the building, and ran up the stairs to avoid being late. That my heart would beat wildly at such a time is hardly surprising. My interpretation that the symptoms were those of a heart attack were all it took to bring on the adrenalin flush, perspiring, and difficulty in breathing characteristic of strong anxiety.

I returned to class the next day realizing that I might experience more anxiety but determined to face the situation as best I could and try not to be so overconcerned about my grade. The moment the lecturer began to speak I felt the symptoms returning. But this time I discovered that I could control them simply by reassuring myself that I was not ill. All I had to do was to say to myself that it was my fear of the class that was producing the symptoms and that I could relax and the frighteningly strong feelings would disappear as if by magic. The symptoms disappeared after that day and have never recurred.

Anxiety is very often just such a hypnotic illusion as was my experience in the statistics class. It is as though the anxious person had been programmed to generate his or her own anxiety. Just as warts can be cured by means of hypnosis and major surgery performed without an anesthetic, so can symptoms of anxiety be generated as a substitute for coping with our problems. To "cure" such attacks we have to overcome our own conditioning. This sometimes (as in my case) can be done simply by insight and determination. When more help is needed, forms of hypnotic induction procedures such as the one in the following section may be helpful.

Exercise: Self-hypnosis

With this method you can learn to overcome your own conditioning and relax. It is adapted from the self-hypnosis technique of Leslie Lecron (1964). The only thing you will need is an object to fixate on. Once you know the technique almost any object will do. A spot on the ceiling, a door knob, or a small pin are all possible objects. Or use the illustration on the next page. One object that works particularly well is a lighted candle placed so that you can gaze at it comfortably. The flickering flame has a fascinating, hypnotic effect.

Object. To hypnotize yourself you should first get into a comfortable position where you can view the candle. As you watch it, focus all of your attention on its flickering flame.

Take three or four deep breaths to help you relax. Continue breathing slowly and deeply.

Heavy eyes. One suggestion that usually works is to say silently to yourself, "My eyelids will become heavier and heavier." Keep repeating this suggestion in your mind slowly over and over again. As you feel your eyes getting heavier allow them to close whenever you want to.

Hypnotic words. As your eyes close, think words such as "relax now," "deeply relax," and so forth. This will function as a signal to go into hypnosis.

Relaxation. Begin to relax all of your muscles. Start with the toes. Tense them as tight as you can, then let go and allow them to become limp and relaxed. Then do the same with each of your other muscle groups: your legs, your abdomen, your back, and your chest and breathing muscles.

As you relax your chest, you will probably notice a gradual slowing down of your breathing. Sometimes a speeding up occurs as you first enter hypnosis, followed by a slowing down later on.

Now let your neck relax. The neck is a center of tension for many of us. As you relax the neck you may be surprised at how much effort you have been expending just to hold your head erect. Your head may begin to feel very heavy.

As you go still deeper into hypnosis your facial muscles will also relax. One of the signs of hypnosis is the smoothing out of the facial muscles—a kind of woodenness.

Deepening the trance. You will now want to

Methods of Dealing with Anxiety: 2. Meditation

The basic thing that all meditation practices have in common is that they offer a technique for quieting the mind. Our world is often a chaotic one characterized by conflicting demands from others and conflicting rules—an environment that is unduly threatening because of our needs for status, love, and success. Many people need a tranquilizer from time to time. For others in our society, religious faith has provided an alternative to tranquilizers. When we turn to God in prayer it takes an act of faith. Many report the feelings of peace and bliss and oneness that may occur when all of their attention is turned towards God.

Today many others are reporting somewhat analogous feelings resulting from various sorts of meditative techniques derived from Eastern religions. The psychological essense of all these techniques is to clear the mind to concentrate on an unchanging source of stimulation. The desired result is a mind that is quiet, calm, and receptive.

USING CONCENTRATION

Concentration, as it is used here, means focusing more and more attention on a single stimulus object. Useful stimulus objects vary widely with different forms of meditation. They may be a word, a thought, a bodily function (one's own breathing), a koan, rosary beads, or almost anything. Some examples follow:

Numbers. Try to count backwards from ten to one. Focus all of your attention on each number. Whenever your mind wanders return to ten and start over again. Can you focus your *entire* concentration of counting? Or do you find your mind is determined to wander?

Mantra and prayer. In this technique attention is focused on a word or a thought. Unlike many of the other techniques discussed here, the mantra has often been used in the West as well as the East. Perhaps the most widely used mantra in Eastern cultures is *Om* (with the "o" sound held during a long breathing out and the "mmm" tacked on when

relax into a still deeper state of hypnosis. To do this you might visualize an escalator going down. Or if you don't like escalators, try a staircase. Visualize as clearly as you can the steps moving down in front of you. Start counting backwards from ten to zero in your mind imagining yourself stepping onto the escalator and standing with your hands on the rails while the escalator brings you down deeper and deeper.

When you come to zero, imagine yourself stepping off the escalator at the bottom. Then proceed to the next flight and begin counting again as you sink deeper into hypnosis. Lecron suggests doing several such flights of stairs your first session. Once you are proficient, a single flight of steps should be enough to bring you into a state of deep relaxation.

By now you are almost certain to have achieved a state of light hypnosis. Some individuals will gone into a fairly deep hypnotic state. Most will have experienced the narrowed attention and deep relaxation of hypnosis.

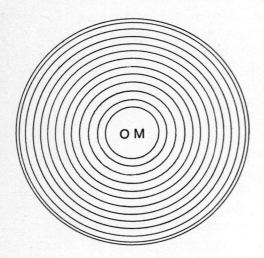

all the breath has been forced from the lungs). This "Om" has great significance in the East. It is a symbol of the fullness and completeness of the total universe.

In the earlier days of the Christian church, it was common for the religious person to spend an entire day contemplating or chanting scripture. Prayer can be enhanced greatly by employing some of the meditative, mental and postural techniques discussed here. Many passages of scripture make excellent mantras.

Though prayer was once used as a centering or calming technique in Western religion, in our pragmatic society prayer often loses its meditative value in the service of our need for efficiency. When I was a child our mother, who was quite devout, used to insist that grace be said before meals. We children always had to say the prayer, a task we did reluctantly. I recall how we used to make it a race to always choose the shortest possible prayer, which frequently spilled out in crescendo, like a flood breaking through a broken dike. My best time was about a second and a half. Eventually Dad got into the spirit of the thing and began to follow our quick prayers with a "Pass the potatoes." All this irreverence was far from welcomed by Mom, who was truly in the minority.

Teaching stories. Much of the anxiety we experience we have created for ourselves. At times there is within us a kind of rigid assurance that the world is exactly the way we view it. For example, my graduate school anxiety attack resulted from my rigid view that I had to receive an A in every course. I believed I had to get all A's to make it through school. These were, of course, my criteria, not those of my graduate committee. Many others received Ph.D.'s who had less than perfect grades. Such rigidity is a psychological defense to avoid experiencing and dealing with the real, more basic source of our feelings of conflict. In my case getting A's allowed me to avoid the more basic issue of coming to accept myself.

To combat rigidity, the Sufis employ especially constructed "teaching stories." The Mulla Nasrudin story that you encountered at the beginning of this chapter is an example. Each story, if read properly, demonstrates the fallacy of assuming that the reality we construct is the "real world." Every story has several different meanings. Only the most superficial of these are attainable by logic. The key to their mysteries is intuition. The Mulla represents our consciousness in all its varied aspects. So in each story we get a glimpse of ourself in one state of awareness. Idries Shah (1973) describes the invulnerable Mulla this way:

"How can one name a fool who is no fool?"
"How can one punish a man who is a multitude?"
"How can one strike a man who is ourself?"

The story that introduced this chapter is an especially good illustration of the way these stories can undercut our rigid ways of looking for the answers to our problems. Let us return to it for a moment.

A man saw Nasrudin searching for something on the ground.

"What have you lost, Mulla?" he asked.

"My key," said the Mulla.

So they both went down on their knees and looked for it.

After a time the other man asked, "Where exactly did you drop it?"

"In my own house."

"Then why are you looking here?"

"There is more light here than inside my own house."

While this story has an obvious superficial moral, it also has a variety of other, deeper meanings. The key to some of these is to treat the story as you would a personal dream. Put yourself in the place of the Mulla.

Relating this story to my anxiety in graduate school, I can readily identify with the Mulla's dogged search for his key. Like him, I worked and worked to find some affirmation that I was competent and intelligent. But in relying only on my grades for feedback I too was looking in the wrong place. Where is the right place? The following exercise may suggest an answer.

Exercise: Concentration

Visualize yourself down on your hands and knees looking for something. What are you searching for?

- Where are you looking?
- What is *your* personal key?
- Try saying, "I have lost my key," and see where your thoughts wander.
- Finally think about the phrase, "My key is in my own house." Where does that take you?

Typically the more superficial meanings of the stories yield themselves immediately. More profound insights occur only after a very long time. The Sufis (who have lots of time) frequantly contemplate such stories for several years without exhausting their richness.

ANXIETY AND OUR BODIES

It is customary in our society to view what we think about as somehow separate from our body functions. This tendency is carried over into the ways people who are clients in psychotherapy describe their anxieties. Many seem to be searching for the root of their feelings of vague uneasiness and tension in external events—"She really made me uptight when she wouldn't talk to me," or "Studying for this course makes me tense." Fritz Perls suggests that such a search is like looking for a needle in the wrong haystack (Perls et al. 1951). Perls explains that the feeling of anxiety is simply the experience of breathing difficulty during any blocked excitement. "Excitement" refers to the heightened energy of arousal whenever there is strong concern whether it be erotic, aggressive, creative, and so forth. When we are excited there is always an upsurge in the metabolic process of oxidation and hence a need for more air. So when you are excited, scared, angry, or sexually turned on, the most natural thing to do is to breathe faster and deeper.

"Feeling anxious" tends to occur when we try to block the excitement. The neurotic person, in Perls' view, is someone who "tries to create the illusion for himself and others of being unmoved, of remaining calm and collected, self-controlled." The technique that many of us use in such an instance is to hold our breath. By so doing we deprive ourselves of the extra air we need when we are excited. And, as a direct result of this self-deception, we suffer from oxygen deprivation and thus "feel anxious."

Furthermore, the process frequently doesn't stop with controlling breathing. Some individuals constrict their chest muscles; others sit perpetually hunched over (Perls calls this the closed position). Others clench their fists. Thus we may come to distort our posture unconsciously in a vain attempt to control showing our excitement. Perls' view that much of what we refer to as anxiety is physical rather than mental has led him to attack anxiety at a purely physical level. This view is also fundamental to bioenergetics, a form of therapy in which individuals utilize purely physical exercises to get at their anxieties (Keen 1973). The following exercise, if carried out properly, will demonstrate the way that anxiety can be attacked at a physical level. It is adopted from Rahula (1973).

Exercise: Awareness of Breathing

Because breathing is such a constant bodily process, most of us have lost all awareness of how we breathe. Concentration on your breathing is an excellent way to introduce yourself to meditation in that it will give you immediate results. You will be able to see an immediate change in your level of energy. It is also an excellent way to calm yourself. Even when you feel tense and excited, you can feel an immediate sense of calm and quietness simply by tuning in to your breathing. Afterwards you will feel as though you just awakened from a good night's rest. Rahula (1973) suggests that posture is extremely important in developing awareness of breathing. He suggests sitting cross-legged with the body erect and alert. An alternative that Westerners may find more comfortable is simply to sit on a chair with the body relaxed but erect.

Close your eyes comfortably. Breathe in and out as you normally would. Gradually allow more and more of your attention to focus on your breathing in and breathing out. You will sometimes notice that your breathing is deep while at other times it may be very shallow. This does not matter. The important thing is that when you take a deep breath you are fully aware that you are doing so.

In other words, your mind is to concentrate fully on your breathing so that you are aware of its movements and changes. Let your awareness of other things such as your surroundings, noises, and so forth, fade more and more into the background. Do not look at anything; do not hear anything; do not think of anything. Notice *only* your in-and-out breathing. Continue doing this for five or ten minutes.

Andrew Weil: LSD to Yoga

Andrew Weil is a drug expert by almost anyone's definition. He has been a physician at Haight-Ashbury Clinic, a journalist who covered Timothy Leary's early experiments with LSD, and a drug researcher who has talked to hundreds of people about their drug experiences. Last, but probably not least, he is a long-time drug user who first became fascinated with feeling high (without the use of drugs) at the tender age of two. How does one become dedicated to the exploration of altered states of consciousness? The following excerpts from his book *The Natural Mind* suggests that Weil's interest, like that of many other psychological explorers, began with a natural childhood curiosity about his own personal experience:

> I was an avid whirler and could spend hours collapsed on the ground with the world spinning around. This despite the obvious unpleasant side-effects of nausea, dizziness, and sheer exhaustion (the only aspects of the experience visible to adults). From my point of view these effects were more interesting than any other state except the one I entered at the verge of sleep. I soon found out that my spinning made grownups upset; I learned to do it with other neighborhood children in out-of-the way locations.

Weil also reports a fairly extensive series of childhood experiments with chemical substances, fascination with anesthesia when his tonsils were removed, and use of alcohol in high school and early in college. He eventually gave up alcohol because he found the physical side-effects and hangovers very unpleasant.

Then his curiosity led him to seek out Timothy Leary.

> I first talked with Leary in his tiny office in the Center for Personality Research on Divinity Avenue. He spoke with sincerity, conviction, and enthusiasm about the potential of drugs like LSD, psilocybin, and mescaline. He envisioned a graduate seminar based on regular consumption of hallucinogens alternating with intensive periods of analysis to identify and apply the insights gained while high. He predicted that within ten years everyone would be using the drugs "from kindergarten children on up." And he did not anticipate strong opposition by society.

Thus encouraged by Leary, Weil soon got together a supply of mescaline and a group of other students interested in drug experimentation. He reports:

> A dozen experiences I had with the drug in 1961 were highly varied. Most were nothing more than intensifications of pre-existing moods with prominent periods of euphoria. Only a small percentage of the time did the sensory changes (such as constant motion of boundary lines and surfaces or vivid imagery seen with the eyes closed) seem worth paying attention to. In a few instances great intellectual clarity developed at the peak of the experience, and insights were gained that had lasting importance. After a dozen trips I was able to see that much of the mescaline experience was not really so wonderful: the prolonged wakefulness and the strong stimulation of the sympathetic nervous system with resultant dilated eyes, cold extremities, and stomach butterflies. Yet its potential for showing one good way of interpreting one's own mind seemed enormous. Why was that potential realized so irregularly?

Where has Weil's search taken him? His current ideas about consciousness are implicit in many later sections of this chapter. Gradually he has shifted his interest towards altered states of consciousness such as hypnosis, yoga, meditation, daydreaming, and other states of consciousness that are not chemically induced. This shift in interest reflects a growing conviction on his part that the pharmacological (chemical) effects of many drugs are far less impressive than the effects of the user's expectations about what will happen. (Weil 1972).

PHYSIOLOGICAL CHANGES DURING MEDITATION

Rahula describes the end product of the breathing method of meditation as "very high mystic attainments and deep intuitive understandings of the nature of things." But, he adds, the immediate results are also very beneficial. The immediate gains, he claims, include inner peace and even better health.

These claims, if true, suggest exciting possibilities for the use of meditation techniques in our anxiety-ridden society. Persons such as Rahula are convinced of the usefulness of meditation by the evidence of their own personal experience and intuition. So are many practitioners of meditation techniques. Others find it impossible to believe that anything as deceptively simple and apparently unscientific as meditation could have such positive effects on individual personalities.

Quite a number of investigations were performed during the 1950s and 1960s on the observable effects of meditation practices. The results of many of these studies are difficult to evaluate because they often employed only one or two subjects. Thus when positive results occurred it was impossible to be sure whether the results were due to the unique abilities of one subject, to the method of meditation used, or to other unidentified variables.

Recently, however, the form of yoga known as transcendental meditation (TM) has become so popular in the United States as to make available a larger number of subjects. This technique also has the advantage of being easily learned. After five training sessions an average person can be considered an "expert."

Wallace and Benson (1972) studied physiological changes in thirty-six practitioners before, during, and after transcendental meditation. Their findings strongly support the contention that TM does in fact produce a very deep state of physical relaxation. Their results show a dramatic picture of a person who is slowing down body metabolism while remaining fully awake. During TM oxygen

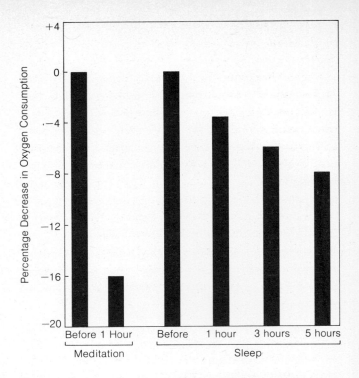

FIG. 11-2 *Oxygen consumption during meditation*

consumption drops sharply and *immediately* to a rate that is only half that of a person deeply asleep (see figure 11-2). Carbon dioxide production also drops. Heartbeat slows and indications of stress such as the concentration of blood lactate and galvanic skin resistance show changes indicative of emotional calming. All in all, transcendental meditation produces an integrated set of physiological responses that characterize deep relaxation. This state is not sleep nor is it very similar to sleep. Most of the physiological changes in transcendental meditation occur much more rapidly and are of considerably greater magnitude than those that occur while we are asleep. This is apparent in figure 11-2. Notice that after five hours of sleep oxygen consumption has been reduced by about eight percent. Twice this decrease is obtained by meditators within the first few minutes of meditation.

Another aspect of the Wallace and Bensen

study was the brainwave patterns observed during meditation. They found that as meditation began there was a characteristic change in their subjects' brainwave activity. This pattern, the alpha rhythm, is essentially the same EEG activity that occurs when one is resting quietly with the eyes closed. A fairly similar pattern has been observed in a study of forty-eight Zen priests and disciples. (Kasamatsu and Hirai 1973). Thus the general kind of brain activity elicited by different meditation practices appears to be fairly similar.

As we will see in the next section, finding a clear brainwave pattern and discovering other consistent physiological changes associated with meditation paved the way for a new and typically Western form of meditation called biofeedback or electronic yoga.

Methods of Dealing with Anxiety: 3. Biofeedback

It is perhaps inevitable that when the Western world discovered the benefits of meditation, its first reaction was to try to speed up the process and make it more practical. In 1958, about the time the early data on the physiological effects of meditation were just becoming known, Joseph Kamiya (1968) was engaged in a different aspect of mind exploration. His interest was inspired by the apparent ability of meditators to be in control of their internal states of consciousness. He decided to see whether a subject could be taught awareness of an internal state.

ALPHA RHYTHM

Kamiya's initial method was very much like Skinner's operant conditioning. Knowing that alpha rhythm often occurs spontaneously, Kamiya decided to try to train subjects to be aware of this rhythm. His subjects were seated in an experimental cubicle and wired to an EEG machine. Whenever the machine registered an alpha rhythm a light went on. After a number of such feedback trials the subjects were instructed to close their eyes and guess whether they were in an alpha or nonalpha state. Most subjects learned the task easily. They went from fifty percent (chance) accuracy the first day to one hundred percent accuracy four sessions later.

Kamiya's study suggested the rather exciting idea that we are capable of far greater awareness of our internal processes than had previously been realized in Western culture. Furthermore, the alpha state he had studied showed the same brainwave pattern that others were finding in skillful meditators. The obvious next question was "Can people learn to 'turn on' the alpha state at will?" If so, could scientists develop a form of "electronic yoga" that could be learned by anyone in a few hourly sessions?

Considerable success is being reported in training subjects to increase the occurrence of alpha. Knowlis and Kamiya (1973) report data from ten subjects who were able to stay on alpha an average of sixty-four percent of the time on the second training trial. Furthermore, given a third (and final) trial on which they were told to "keep alpha off" they were able to do do eighty-seven percent of the time.

How did these subjects generate alpha? Many reported that they simply "relaxed" themselves. Others used techniques similar to the meditation techniques discussed earlier in this chapter, such as focusing their attention on their breathing or on some visual stimulus.

Such rapid training is sometimes touted by advocates as evidence that electronic yoga is already in existence, but there is still much research to be done. It seems unlikely that alpha training alone will produce the complex physiological patterns that Wallace and Benson find characteristic of experienced meditators. It seems more likely that subjects will have to learn to control a wide range of physiological functions simultaneously, such as metabolic functions, heart rate, and so forth. One researcher (Brown 1970) has already developed a very elaborate apparatus for teaching subjects to control several aspects of their physiology simultaneously. If you visit Brown's laboratory as a subject, you see the "music of your mind" in vivid technicolor. On one screen a soothing pastel blue appears as you "turn on" your alpha. On another a warning red light indicates rising stomach activity. Green light patterns appear as metabolism rate increases, and so forth. It's like looking at a giant Christmas tree in which the colored bulbs represent your inner self. As you change yourself the bulbs blink on and off.

BIOFEEDBACK AND MEDICINE

It has long been known that high levels of anxiety and stress can play havoc with your body. Ulcers, colitis, some forms of migraine headaches, and certain heart ailments can all be produced by excessive anxiety and stress. Andrew Weil (1972) goes even further to suggest that illness in general is far more attributable to what occurs in consciousness than it is to a germ or virus. Weil points out that just because certain illnesses tend to occur when a particular germ is injected into the system does not necessarily mean that the illness is caused by the germ.

We live in a world full of germs, some of which are correlated with physical symptoms of infectious disease. But only some of us get infectious diseases, and we get them only one at a time. Why? Because there are factors within that determine the kind of relationship we will have with those germs . . . a relationship of balanced co-existence or one of unbalanced antagonism.

For example, the staphylococci that seem to "cause" boils are normal inhabitants of our skins. . . . the problem is to restore the balance, not to make the staph germ disappear.

Biofeedback techniques constitute a step toward the treatment of illness by psychology rather than by chemicals. Arthur Shapiro (1969) has shown that people can learn to lower their blood pressure. This suggests the possibility of giving such patients compact feedback devices to use in everyday life. By discovering for themselves the physiological consequences of various environments on their own responsiveness, patients could develop insights into the psychology of their particular illnesses and into the means of controlling their symptoms. Many other variations on this basic theme are being contemplated, such as providing feedback about stomach acidity for ulcer patients, giving heart rate feedback to cardiac patients, and so forth.

Chapter Eleven Summary

The major symptoms of anxiety are doublethink, or inability to focus on one thing; regret and rehearsal, or the inability to focus on the here and now; and repression and tension, or the inability to relax physically. The feeling we call anxiety may be thought of as an illusion created by our own suggestible minds and supported by physical symptoms created by these suggestions. Psychological techniques such as self-hypnosis, meditation, and biofeedback may be used to combat the symptoms of anxiety. The essence of all three techniques is to develop more awareness of our inner selves.

1. *Hypnosis.* In hypnosis, awareness of our inner resources is accomplished by means of suggestions. The behaviors to be expected of one who has been hypnotized are: 1) reduced planning, 2) increased suggestability, 3) increased ability to focus attention, and 4) reduced reality testing.

2. *Meditation.* Like hypnosis, meditation teaches us to concentrate on some word, object, or bodily process. The goal is to overcome our own conditioned way of looking at things.

A scientific look at meditation has revealed a fairly clear pattern of physiological correlates such as a decrease in oxygen consumption, carbon dioxide production, and heart rate, as well as changes in blood lactate and galvanic skin resistance. Finally there is a characteristic pattern of electrical activity in the brain called alpha rhythm.

3. *Biofeedback.* In the typical biofeedback experiment some physiological process, such as the alpha rhythm, is monitored electronically. Subjects are told to try to produce the response and are given feedback as to when they are "on alpha" and when they are "off." In addition to learning relaxation, biofeedback may be useful in teaching us to lower our blood pressure, alter faulty heart rhythms, and control stomach ulcers.

Glossary

Alpha rhythm The pattern of electrical activity in the brain that occurs during meditation and other waking states of relaxation. The alpha rhythm is measured by means of an electroencephalogram (EEG).

Anxiety A general feeling of uneasiness, worry, and concern. Some of the symptoms of anxiety are an inability to focus on one thing at a time, a tendency to worry needlessly about the past or the future, and physical tension.

Asana A special posture used in meditation to teach concentration and to incude a particular state of consciousness. The yoga headstand and lotus position (sitting cross-legged) are two such positions that are well known.

Biofeedback training Training a subject to control some autonomic function such as heart rate or galvanic skin response, or some brainwave pattern such as the alpha rhythm by providing the subject with electronic feedback whenever he or she achieves the desired physiological response.

Doublethink A symptom of anxiety characterized by an inability to focus or concentrate on one task at a time.

Ego strengthening A special hypnotic suggestion designed to encourage feelings of calmness, confidence, and inner strength.

Hypnosis A series of suggestion and concentration techniques that may be used to allow an individual to relax, ignore pain, or to produce some other behavior that conditioning has led him or her to believe is impossible.

Mantra A special word that is used as an object of concentration in meditation.

Meditation A series of techniques originally developed in the East to teach the ability to concentrate and to achieve an altered state of consciousness. Although yoga, transcendental meditation, and Zen have received special recognition in the West, there are many other forms of meditation.

Mudra A special gesture used in some approaches to meditation.

Regret and rehearsal The symptom of anxiety that involves an inability to focus on the present and an accompanying tendency to regret past actions and to worry about the future. Examples include preoccupation with thoughts such as, "If only I hadn't . . ." and "What if . . . ?"

"If only I hadn't forgotten that appointment."
"If only I hadn't said that to her."
"If only I hadn't been raised in Nebraska."
"What if . . . I fail to please him?"

"What if . . . she doesn't like me?"
"What if . . . this airplane crashes?"

Repression Repression has been discussed in former chapters as an unconscious tendency to force traumatic thoughts out of our consciousness. In the present chapter we introduced the concept of bodily functions such as breathing and posture as symptomatic of repression. A good example is the catching of one's breath that first occurs in a traumatic situation and then becomes a chronic habit leading to shallow breathing, a weak faltering voice, and so forth.

Transcendental meditation A special Westernized version of meditation that uses a mantra as an object of concentration.

Yoga Although most Westerners tend to associate the term *yoga* with those forms of meditation in which special postures such as the headstand are used, the term is really so broad as to defy definition. Some forms of yoga employ concentration; others use special movements, and still others employ certain postures. A more accurate definition would require going into the religious and philosophic origins of the term.

Exercises *(for individual and class use)*

You can do the following exercises at your leisure. Perhaps some would be more enjoyable with a friend. Those with an asterisk should be done in consultation with your teacher or in class.

1. Throughout this chapter exercises have been introduced to provide an introduction to hypnosis and meditation. You may want to return to those exercises at this point. For hypnosis see pages 266 and 270. Meditation exercises were provided on pages 273 and 274.

2. Because biofeedback requires rather complicated electronic equipment, it was impossible to provide an exercise. For those who would like to experiment with their own ability to control physiological responses the following exercises are suggested. These experiments in controlling your own physiology are best done in a quiet, secluded setting where you will not be interrupted. For those exercises involving control of the circulation a sitting posture is better than reclining.

Breathing. Sit in a relaxed position with your eyes comfortably closed. Allow your attention to center on your own breathing; pay particular attention to the exhaling part of the cycle. Notice how you can let your whole body go at the end of the expiration cycle. After doing this a few times you may begin to notice a heavy feeling in your hands. This heavy feeling is easiest to notice during the little pause at the end of the exhalation. Continue to breathe *slowly*. Continue to *let go* at the end of each expiration cycle.

After a while you may begin to notice a "pleasant" or "peaceful" feeling. These feelings are characteristic of the alpha state.

Sensations of heaviness and warmth. With your eyes still closed, shift your attention to your right arm. Visualize your arm hanging comfortably from the shoulder. Visualize each part of your arm as it hangs there—the upper arm, the curve at the elbow, the forearm, the hand hanging there loosely, and the fingers, heavy and limp. As you exhale and let go at each breath you may notice a feeling of heaviness, a tingling, or even a feeling of warmth in your arm.

Once you notice these sensations of heaviness and warmth, focus more and more of your attention on them. You will find that you can control both these sensations simply by paying attention to them. If you want the arm to feel heavy, notice the heavy feeling; if you want it to feel warm, focus on the warm feeling.

The key to success is to relax. Don't try to make it happen. Don't worry if you don't feel the heaviness or warmth immediately. Just follow the procedure and observe the results. Remember, *heavy* means calm, comfortable, and relaxed.

Bibliography

Barber, T. 1970. *LSD, marihuana, yoga, and hypnosis*. Chicago: Aldine.

Brown, B. 1970. Recognition of aspects of consciousness through association with EEG alpha activity represented by a light signal. *Psychophysiology* 6:442–52.

Hartland, J. 1966. *Medical and dental hypnosis*. London: Bailliere, Tindall, & Cassell. 191–92.

Hilgard, E. and Atkinson, R. 1967. *Introduction to psychology*. 4th ed. New York: Harcourt Brace Jovanovich.

Kamiya, J. 1968. Conscious control of brain waves. *Psychology Today* 1:57–66.

Kasamatsu, A. and Hirai, T. 1973. An electro-encephalographic study of the Zen meditation. In Ornstein, R., *The nature of human consciousness*. San Francisco: Freeman.

Keen, S. 1973. We do not have our bodies: we are our bodies (a conversation with Stanley Keleman about bioenergetics and the language of the body). *Psychology Today* 7(4):65.

Knowlis, P. and Kamiya, J. 1973. The control of electroencephalographic alpha rhythms through auditory feedback and the associated mental activity. In Ornstein, R., *The nature of human consciousness*. San Francisco: Freeman.

Lecron, L. 1964. *Self-hypnotism*. Englewood Cliffs, N.J.: Prentice-Hall.

Milgram, S. 1963. Behavioral study of obedience. *Journal of Abnormal Social Psychology* (March): 371.

Perls, F., Hefferline, R., and Goodman, P. 1951. *Gestalt therapy*. New York: Delta.

Rahula, W. 1973. Meditation or mental culture. In Ornstein, R., *The nature of human consciousness*. San Francisco: Freeman.

Rolf, I. 1963. Structural integration: gravity, an unexplored factor in a more human use of human beings. *Systematics* (June).

Shah, I. 1966. *The exploits of the incomparable Mulla Nasrudin*. New York: Simon & Schuster.

———. 1973. The legend of Nasrudin. In Ornstein, R., *The nature of human consciousness*. San Francisco: Freeman.

Shapiro, D., Tursky, B., Gershon, E. and Stern, M. 1969. Effects of feedback and reinforcement on the control of human systolic blood pressure. *Science* 163:588–90.

Wallace, R. and Benson, H. 1972. The physiology of meditation. *Scientific American*.

Weil, A. 1972. *The natural mind*. Boston: Houghton Mifflin.

Chapter Twelve: ...and Things That Go Bump in the Night
(Frontiers of Awareness and Beyond)

Fishes, asking what water was, went
to a wise fish. He told them it was
all around them, yet they still thought
that they were thirsty.

IDRIES SHAH, *The Sufis*

Frontiers of Awareness

We are accustomed to living in a world that is super-saturated with stimuli. Acid rock, high population density, and demanding time schedules make it imperative that we turn off a certain amount of these stimuli. To a lesser degree this has probably always been necessary in order to deal with our complex external environment. One purpose of the present chapter is to make a case for conserving one of our most valuable resources: our own sensitivity.

I think I got my first glimmering awareness of the need for such a sensitivity conservation program several years ago. I had been reading that many animals are wonderful weather forecasters. Elk, for example, move to shelter two to three days before an impending blizzard. The way they manage this is by using their eardrums like the diaphragm of a built-in barometer. When the barometeric pressure drops rapidly, their eardrums alert them to the impending storm and they seek shelter. I became intrigued with this phenomenon and began to wonder if people had any similar ability that was perhaps weakened by disuse. I began taking notes on the weather. I tried to be sensitive to the pressure of the air on my eardrums. And I attempted to predict whether the weather forecast that evening would indicate a rising or falling barometric reading. Was I successful? In an objective sense I was not. I was right more often than chance, but not often enough to satisfy a statistician. Furthermore, I didn't control for even the most obvious contaminating variables such as seeing that it was about to snow.

One experience that was particularly convincing to me occurred on an evening in early March. It was about to snow. Everything in my environment said it was about to snow. The birds had stopped singing. It was very quiet. The sky was heavily clouded. But for me the strongest cue came from my ears. The air seemed to me to be very heavy. I could feel the pressure difference between my inner ear and the surrounding atmosphere most acutely. I was sure

the pressure outside was dropping very rapidly. I raced home to check my observation. Sure enough, the barometer had fallen dramatically since morning. That night we had one of the heaviest snowfalls of the year.

I include the above example not as an attempt to convince the skeptic but rather to note the role that personal experience plays in our beliefs about such perceptual abilities.

Since my "human barometer" experience I've been very curious about my own sensitivity to my physical environment. Perhaps as we evolved we tended to selectively ignore classes of stimuli that are less essential for survival. Internal stimuli such as those produced by automatic body processes — like breathing and blood pressure cues — may have been forgotten along with reactions to subtle sources of stimulation from the external world.

Recently biological scientists and psychologists have been getting together to study the outer limits of our ability to sense and perceive. And the picture they are producing suggests that we possess almost unlimited potential for sensitivity to an enormously greater range of stimuli than we have imagined in the past. Each day we are unconsciously responding to minute differences in gravity and magnetic pull, sunspots several million miles away, cosmic radiation, and even ion concentrations in the air (Luce 1973). Furthermore, we may possess a built-in biological clock. And finally, there is an increasing amount of data to suggest that we can learn to be consciously aware of these stimuli and to control our responses to them. In the next section we will review some of these discoveries and their implications for our personal growth as well as for our evolution as a species.

As fascinating as these studies on human sensitivity may be, they are merely an introduction to the further frontiers of awareness that we will hypothesize later in this chapter. ESP, ghosts, paranormal abilities, and other "things that go bump in the night" are not usually discussed in a college adjustment text. But in the past few years there has been such a strong resurgence of interest in such matters as to warrant their inclusion. In some regions there has been enough revival in a belief in witchcraft that a few mental health professionals have taken up exorcism as a tool of the trade. And a sudden proliferation of books on the subject of ESP and occult phenomena has increased this trend toward supernaturalism. Our treatment of the occult will largely be limited to a review of parapsychology, that branch of psychology that studies extrasensory capacities in the laboratory. We will look at the implications of some of these studies on an understanding of our basic natures.

So much for a brief preview of some of the frontiers of awareness. We now turn to a closer look at one such frontier — our awareness of gravity.

THE HUMAN BODY AS A PARANORMAL RECEIVER

Thus far, the evolution of our paranormal abilities (in the West) has occurred primarily in the realm of

John Lilly: A Mind Explorer

The material in this chapter represents a kind of search that is excitingly new, yet began with the first introspective thought many millions of years ago. This is the exploration of our minds, our intuition, our awareness. Although the search is old, much of the content of this chapter is very new to Western psychology. In this chapter we will be on the fringes or outer limits of psychology as it is defined in our culture today. John Lilly exemplifies the sort of scientist who becomes interested in the workings of the mind: colorful, intensely curious about his own experiences, and a little bit deviant.

Since early childhood Lilly has devoted himself to discovering the inner secrets of the mind. This led him into bio- and neurophysics as well as the practice of psychoanalysis. In 1954 he became curious about what would happen if a brain were deprived of all external stimuli. He began to immerse himself in the dark world of water. Floating free and weightless, he observed the changes in his own mind. Cherished beliefs, ideas, and concepts seemed to disappear and reappear under the gaze of his objective inner eye. He emerged with a new concept that has guided him ever since: "Every belief is a limit to be examined and transcended."

This sensory deprivation experience generated in turn a curiosity about what happened in the mind of an animal that has a large brain but lives constantly in the water. He decided the only way to find out was literally to ask a dolphin. In 1959 Lilly began a series of ingenious attempts to communicate with dolphins. In *Man and Dolphin* he reports a series of apparently successful attempts.

Lilly found his dolphins had a learning ability that appeared superior to the monkey's and that may even rival ours. When he attached electrodes to a dolphin's brain he discovered a neurological pleasure center. The dolphin responded to stimulation of this center with whistles, exuberant buzzings, and even Bronx-cheering noises. At this point Lilly decided to see what would happen if he wired a switch to the apparatus so that the dolphin could, by pressing the switch with its nose, provide itself with pleasurable electrical stimulation. Lilly noticed the animal watching him intently as he connected this switch to the apparatus. Before he had finished wiring it, the dolphin had already learned how to push it with its nose.

Lilly reports that monkeys learn this same task much more slowly, and tend to learn by trial and error. They fumble around a great deal and usually bump the switch by accident several times before they learn how to use it. Dolphins, on the other, hand appear more purposive. It was almost as though his dolphin were testing out a hunch.

Lilly became convinced of the dolphin's high intelligence. His experiments led him to conclude eventually that the dolphin might even be trying to speak to him. First he managed to train the dolphin to emit a whistle of a particular pitch and intensity for a reward of pleasurable brain stimulation. The dolphin learned this in less than one hour of training. More surprising, however, Lilly discovered when he played back the tape that the dolphin had been mimicking some of the things Lilly said while dictating his report of the hour session onto tape. The words "train repetition rate" and the number "three hundred and twenty-three feet" were imitated, according to Lilly, with great clarity. At other times the dolphin imitated human laughter.

Eventually Lilly's work so convinced him of the high degree of the dolphin's sensibility that he finally decided he had no right to keep such creatures in an experimental concentration camp. This decision occurred after what he describes as a "suicide" by one of the dolphins due to loneliness in captivity.

Lilly has turned his attention to the human potential movement where he is combining the state of sensory deprivation with techniques such as biofeedback and Eastern-style meditation. His goal: to discover and explore as many states of human consciousness as possible, particularly the state of satori (continual bliss) (Lilly 1972).

Overall, John Lilly seems to represent rather well the kind of person who devotes a lifetime to exploring the mind. His interests are broad and far-ranging. His ideas are bold and innovative. He is fascinated by the unknown rather than afraid of it. Most of all, he is intrigued by his own inner experience and is committed to exploring it fully.

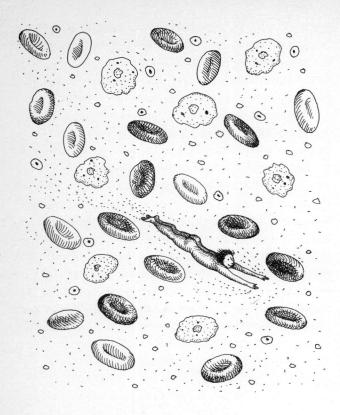

understanding how to control events and processes outside ourselves. But it seems likely that we may be entering a new stage of evolution in which the frontiers will lie within ourselves. As always, science-fiction writers are anticipating such developments. In *Mr. Tomkins Inside Himself* (Gamon and Yeas 1967), for example, the hero can shrink himself to the size of a blood cell and then inject himself into his own body so that he can observe various phenomena inside his heart, cortex, sexual organs, and so on. This theme has also been echoed in several science-fiction movies and in a popular exhibit at Disneyland.

It would appear that with proper training the human body may be a naturally excellent receiver for many kinds of paranormal sense data. One Soviet researcher has pointed out that the phenomena of ESP may be explained by the very structure of the human body, which he feels is a natural transmitter and receiver for long radio waves (Schmeidler 1969).

Frank Brown of Northwestern University has recently discovered that we may have in common with a worm called planaria considerable sensitivity to the Earth's magnetic field (Luce 1973). Worms and snails tend to veer in given compass directions at certain times of the day, the month, and the year. Reasoning that such behavior must reflect a sensitivity to the earth's magnetic field, Brown attempted to manipulate it by simply rotating a bar magnet on the experimental grid where his worms resided. As predicted, the worms changed their tendency to turn in a particular direction whenever the magnet was rotated.

People also seem to respond to magnetic fields. A number of studies by Giirgen Aschoff (Luce 1973) have established that some biological processes can be altered by manipulating the electromagnetic field in our immediate surroundings. This finding parallels the well-known disorientation phenomena experienced by east-to-west air travelers. Such travel tends to be highly disruptive and uncomfortable to passengers—so much so that some businesses are beginning to take special steps to insure that their executives have time to readapt physically before they have to conduct important business.

Some individuals are also capable of discriminating very small differences in magnetic field strength. The French physicist Rocard at the Université de Paris has made similar observations with humans (Luce 1973). In an attempt to understand the mysterious ability of the "dowser" (a person who can "sense" underground water), Rocard followed several dowsers about with a magnetometer (an instrument for sensing differences in electromagnetic pull). He found the successful dowser was responding to tiny changes (3–5 milligauss) in the Earth's magnetic field strength.

Recent studies with animals and pilot work with mental patients have suggested the possibility that we may even be sensitive to and effected by cosmic radiation (Luce 1973). Rats respond to X rays in a way that suggests such stimulation is aversive to them. For years inexplicable outbursts have occurred in mental hospitals. Patients *en masse* become hostile, excitable, even violent. It is like an epidemic of mental anguish. Douglas Hospital in Montreal plotted these epidemics carefully over a period of several months. These data were then juxtaposed against a wealth of other data about ward environments. The outbursts neither correlated with aggression by the staff, changes in medication, and visiting days nor with most environmental variables such as barometric pressure, humidity, and temperature. However, one factor did appear to be predictive of excitement in the wards. Solar flare activity (sunspots) regularly coincided with excitement. This shred of evidence raises the intriguing possibility that we are capable of sensing and responding to minute energy sources formerly thought to be detectable only by very precise scientific instruments.

We already have some crude technologies for bringing such phenomena into our awareness if we choose to. Perhaps the clearest example is the biofeedback technique discussed in chapter eleven. This technique can presumably be applied to any physiological response that can be monitored. We foresee a time in the future when a woman will be able not only to be aware of the precise moment of her ovulation but also to control it consciously. Likewise, it may be possible by means of feedback to get people into given mental states and hence to facilitate and control telepathic responses. Some work is already being done that suggests, very tentatively, that the alpha brain wave state may facilitate ESP, and one very successful demonstration of precognition (Fahler and Osis 1969) has employed hypnosis.

Finally, if we think of the body as a natural receiver, it stands to reason that manipulating it by means of posture and/or structural integration techniques may be useful in increasing its effi-

ciency as a transmitter. Such a conception is suggested by "Rolfing," a form of therapy that attempts to change personality by realigning the body (Rolf 1963). How Rolfing may improve awareness has been discussed by David Sobel (1973).

Sobel postulates that all consciousness is directly related to movement. As the child learns to control its movements it may learn inefficient patterns of muscular response. As it grows and develops, some of these muscular attitudes become fixed. Sensitivity and accurate awareness depend on a balanced, efficient muscular system. Here an imbalance may result in reduced sensitivity to stimuli. It may also result in a chronic emotional attitude that is conditioned by body posture rather than by external events. Our posture and the way we breathe are good examples of what Sobel is talking about. As we saw in chapter eleven, breathing im-

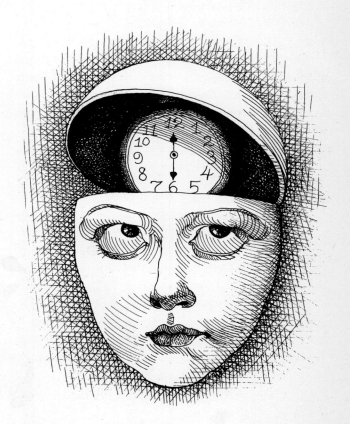

properly can cause chronic feelings of apprehension or anxiety.

The work with dowsers we discussed earlier provides a second modern example of the way posture and body structure may be used to heighten awareness. Returning to that case, once Rocard had established that dowsers were in fact responding to very small amounts of electromagnetic stimulation, he began to study how they did it. He noticed that they held their arms straight out and taut, balancing before them a heavy hickory stick. Since they did this with a fair amount of tension, he thought that perhaps the small changes in electromagnetic stimulation affected bioelectric transmission in their arms. Rocard then created artificial changes in magnetic strength by planting electric coils underground. By giving people feedback as they walked over the test ground, he was able to teach normal persons to detect differences of .3 to 1.0 milligrams in magnetic energy.

Finally, it may be pointed out that this idea of teaching heightened awareness by modifying posture and body structure is actually very, very old. For several thousand years the system of hatha yoga has used mudras (specific gestures) and asanas (postures) to induce different states of consciousness.

BEYOND AWARENESS

The realization that we are capable of responding to a stimulus such as gravity immediately opens the door for two pretty intriguing possibilities. First of all, if we can respond to gravity, do we also respond to many other stimuli we are not normally aware of? Gay Luce has recently reviewed the available research on this topic (1973). As we have seen, he reports evidence that our moods may be subtly influenced by such factors as our body temperature, the concentration of negative ions in the air, and even the time of day.

A second implication of the expanded view of

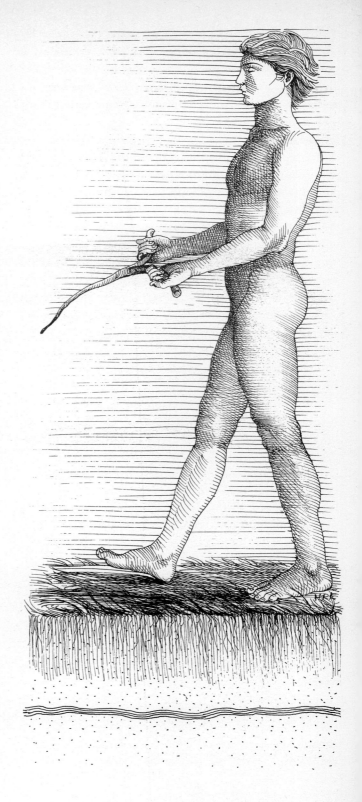

human sensitivity offered in Luce's paper is the possibility that we can respond to a variety of stimuli that have yet to be discovered. Rocard's work with gravity could not have been done until he had at his disposal a concept of "gravity" and an instrument to measure it. For a century before him the claims of dowsers were considered to lack any scientific basis. Might it be, for example, that another person's thought could be detectable by someone who has unusual sensitivity? We now turn with some feelings of uneasiness to the subject of:

"Things That go Bump in the Night"

A student of the famous parapsychologist J. B. Rhine once described an incident that happened to her in which she had awakened during the night hearing her grandmother calling her name (Rhine 1953). She felt strongly that there was something wrong at home and wanted to call her family. Someone talked her out of the idea, however, and she decided to wait until morning. When she did call, she found that her father had suffered a heart attack the previous night. Her grandmother had become upset, and, forgetting the girl was in college, had called for her by name.

Experiences such as the above are difficult to explain in scientific terms. What established means of communication could have made the girl know that her grandmother was calling? Putting aside for the moment reservations that we might have about the accuracy of the reporting or the honesty and motivation of the reporter (she reported it in the office of her professor, the world's most eminent parapsychologist), the incident is very difficult to make sense of. Such psychic experiences have excited the curiosity of many brilliant scholars: Albert Einstein, Sigmund Freud, Madam Curie, William James, and Aldous Huxley, to name a few.

Curiously enough, there are many physicists in the ranks of parapsychology. Part of the fascina-tion of these phenomena for a physicist such as Einstein is the challenge they present to our existing assumptions about the nature of energy, space, and time. Gertrude Schmeidler (1969) describes an experiment in which ESP subjects could detect targets 5000 miles distant as well as targets only three inches away. This experiment suggests the possibility that psychic energy is quite distinct from other forms of energy. All other known types of energy show weakened effects as the distance between the energy source and the target increases.

Spontaneous instances of "prophecy" and certain laboratory experiments of precognition where the subject predicts the order in which a deck of cards will be shuffled imply the existence of a world with nonlinear time. How can one experience the future and the present simultaneously if time flows from point to point in a straight line? Such findings suggest the possibility that the study of psychic phenomena may ultimately lead to radical changes in the way we view both ourselves and our physical world. The energy of the mind may be far more potent than many known physical forms of energy. Our minds may be capable of searching far beyond their own confines for solutions to our problems. And we may discover tremendous sources of power in our own thoughts. Perhaps Jesus' admonition that "faith can move mountains" will one day be verified in the laboratory. And perhaps the study of prophecy will lead us into a new view of time as more like a rubber band than a ruler, and more like a merry-go-round than an express train.

TYPES OF PSYCHIC EXPERIENCES

There are two kinds of psychic phenomena (psi phenomena) that the parapsychologist seeks to study: 1) extrasensory perception (ESP), the process of obtaining information through means other than normal sensory transmission and 2) Psychokinesis (PK), in which observable changes are produced in the physical world by means other than known natural forces.

CASES OF ESP

Parapsychologists classify ESP experiences into three major classes: *clairvoyance* (extrasensory perception of an objective physical element); *telepathy* (reading the thoughts of another person by extrasensory perception); and *precognition* (predicting an event before it occurs by means of ESP).

Clairvoyance. J. B. Rhine (1953) describes an incident in which the mother of an old friend of his had gone away for a weekend visit. This left the father at home feeling slightly indisposed. Suddenly, in the middle of her visit, the mother felt a strong impulse to return home. She could give no rational reason for this impulse; moreover, it occurred in the middle of the night. She only had a general feeling that she should go home. When she got there, she found that the house was on fire. The father was asleep and apparently unaware that anything was wrong.

Parapsychologists would consider the possibility that such an experience is an example of ESP because the lady in question had seemingly perceived a dangerous fire at a distance that ruled out the possibility of having detected the fire by normal sensory mechanisms. Since her husband was asleep and apparently undisturbed, it seems unlikely that what she "received" was a telepathic message from him. Therefore the perception is assumed to be of the fire (an objective event) and constitutes an instance of clairvoyance.

Such hunches seem to be fairly common experiences. Only very seldom are incidents like the following reported in which there are vivid life-like extrasensory perceptions while the person is fully awake:

This incident occurred during World War I. A three-and-a-half-year-old child was playing at his home. Suddenly he stopped and screamed, "My daddy is choking. He's down a hole and he can't see." The data was November 7, 1918. Later, when the father returned from the service, he was able to verify his son's experience. On that same day he had been gassed in a cellar. He was blinded and couldn't see for three weeks (Rhine 1953).

This case might be an example of clairvoyance or telepathy, or both. It is, of course, impossible to know *where* the ESP message came from. If it came from the father's mind it would be called telepathy. If it were a direct perception of what happened in the cellar, it would be called clairvoyance.

CASES OF PSYCHOKINESIS

The second kind of experience that parapsychologists have studied involves producing observable effects in the outer world by psychic means rather than via known sources of physical energy. Examples of such phenomena are levitation (lifting physical objects without using any known physical force or energy); poltergeist phenomena (such as glasses leaping off a table and breaking, windows shaking, windows rattling, presumably due to the presence of a spirit or ghost); and astral projection (the ability to leave one's own body and travel about). Unlike ESP phenomena, there is nothing paranormal about the perceptual aspects of most of these events. Anyone can see a chair rise, hear a glass break, and so forth. Rather, they seem to imply a kind of psychic energy that allows the mind to exert a force on a table, to break a glass, to cause a plant to grow, or even to travel about without the help of the body or of any known physical force.

Psychologically many psychokinetic effects often seem to center on our strong wish for immortality. The following instance of a poltergeist phenomena is fairly representative:

The neighbor of a professor had just died. Because their two families were intrigued by the possibility of spirit survival they had made a mutual pact to provide each other with some evidence of their continued existence if they should die. The night after the neighbor's death, the professor and his wife were aroused by a flashlight that switched on. It was 1 A.M. The professor turned it off. He

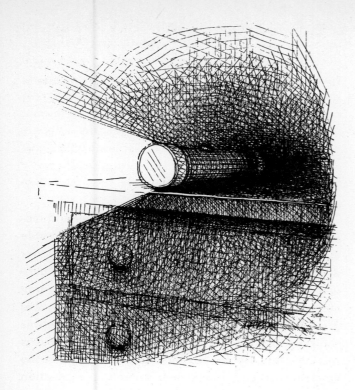

then tried to turn it back on but was unsuccessful. The following morning he tested it again. Again it failed to work. At 1 A.M. that night they were again awakened by the same flashlight spontaneously lighting up in their bedroom. They felt sure their dead friend was responsible (Rhine 1953).

PSYCHIC DETECTIVES

Such spontaneous experiences formed the original subject matter of parapsychology. Early attempts to study ESP and PK focused on documentation and verification. Three questions were common to most such psychic investigations (Murphy 1961): 1) Did the psychic experience (i.e., the dream, or trance, or poltergeist phenomena) occur exactly as the subject said it did? 2) Did the objective (real-world) event that was predicted, dreamed, or visualized occur exactly as the subject said it did? 3) Could it be established that the psychic experience

had been reported to or witnessed by an independent observer prior to the occurrence of the objective (real-world) event? 4) To what extent did it seem probable that the psychic experience and the corresponding real-world event could have been a coincidence?

Taking the example of the World War I child whose father was gassed, the psychic investigator would begin by establishing the validity of the psychic event. Was the mother actually present? Were their other witnesses? What external evidence was available to check the date? Then in step two (establishing the objective event) the psychic researcher might wish to consult existing military medical records and newspaper accounts, as well as to interview any living witnesses. Having established that both events did occur, the established dates would be examined carefully. It frequently turns out that the psychic experiences occur after the objective event and hence may be a result rather than a prediction of the event.

A recent experience of my own may elucidate both the difficulty and importance of checking such dates carefully. For some time now I have been writing a special diary in which I record my dreams as well as any other sensory experiences that interest me. The other night as I reread some of this material I discovered a dream that I had forgotten about that involves my uncle. The dream hadn't seemed particularly remarkable at the time I had it, so I just dutifully recorded it and forgot it. In the interim my uncle died very unexpectedly of cancer. What made the dream interesting now was that from the other events recorded immediately after it I judge that it must have occurred at approximately the time my parents learned of my uncle's illness, but at least a week prior to the time they notified me. I also discovered a notation to the effect that just before having the dream I had had another one from which I had awakened somewhat troubled but couldn't recall what it was about. I returned to sleep and immediately had this rather uninterpretable dream. "I awoke," the notes continue, "thinking about my grandmother's funeral."

Was the dream a clairvoyant message warning me of my uncle's ill health and impending death? The case is convincing to me except for one very crucial point. I failed to record the date of the dream; hence, the only way I have of dating it is by means of a quotation that immediately follows it. I mistrust my memory in this instance. It could be that it occurred somehow *after* my father and mother called to tell me he was dying and that I unconsciously distorted it. Thus although at an intuitive level the dream convinces me of the validity of ESP more than any other experience I have had to date, I cannot as a scientist accept it as proving anything. However, since its occurrence I have taken to recording the dates of my dreams very compulsively.

Finally, there is the matter of coincidence. In the case of the wife who had a hunch and returned home, coincidence might be examined by checking to see how often she had such "hunches" in the past. Someone who constantly anticipates trouble is likely to be correct once in a while.

Also, estimating the probability of the event occurring just by chance is very important. I live in Arizona where (according to the local Chamber of Commerce) the sun shines almost every day. A prophetic dream by an Arizona resident that "tomorrow the sun will shine" would hardly make the headlines.

Hundreds of reported incidents of extrasensory perception have been investigated in the manner outlined above. Most of these are available in the *Journal of Psychic Research*. Some of the most intriguing of these investigations are summarized by Gardner Murphy in *Challenges of Psychic Research* (1961).

Studying ESP in the Laboratory

Although the studies of spontaneous ESP and PK cases are interesting, it is unlikely that such evidence will satisfy our more objective readers. Since the cases happened spontaneously there are relatively few instances where the psychic researcher was present. Typically the researcher had to rely on someone else's report. Even when he or she could be present, as in some of the studies of mediums, the researcher had little control over the situation and could neither manipulate variables in which she or he was interested or control the situation in ways that would convincingly eliminate the possibility of trickery.

In the early 1930s Joseph B. Rhine and his wife Louisa began a series of ingenious card-guessing experiments to provide laboratory evidence about the ESP hypothesis. Their ESP task was to guess which of several possible cards was contained in a sealed opaque envelope. This task provided a test of clairvoyance (that is, sensing the presence of objects). It could also be adapted as a test of telepathy by having a person in one room concentrate on a card while a subject in another room attempted to guess which one he was looking at. It became a test of precognition if the subject were asked to predict the order of the cards *before* they were shuffled. Since there were a specified number of cards in the deck, it was possible to estimate the odds of getting a particular score by chance. For example, in a deck in which the face cards are removed there are ten hearts, ten clubs, ten spaces and ten diamonds. If a subject is given forty trials and is asked to guess the suit of each card as it is presented he or she should get ten (one-fourth of forty) correct by chance. If the subject is just guessing we would expect that most of the scores would be about ten. Likewise we would expect that scores such as five or fifteen would occur somewhat less often. Finally if a subject is just guessing, we would expect scores that are very high or very low only occasionally, if at all. A score of zero or twenty could *almost never* occur. Overall, the distribution of responses that would occur if someone were just guessing would resemble that

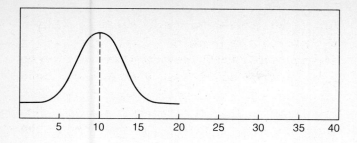

FIG. 12-1 *The expected distribution of ESP scores when subject is "just guessing".*

in figure 12-1. Scores above ten would occur about half the time and scores below ten would occur about half the time. Thus the odds of getting a score of ten by simply guessing are about fifty-fifty.

Rhine and others have sometimes found subjects whose scores consistently far exceed chance. A few have obtained scores that would occur by chance less than one time in a thousand. If you would like to try your hand at Rhine's test of ESP, you will find a modified version in exercise four at the end of this chapter.

MODERN EXPERIMENTAL STUDIES—
PSI PHENOMENA AND THE UNCONSCIOUS

Present research on ESP is moving beyond the question of whether ESP exists. Most parapsychologists feel that its existence has been well established. Current research is focusing more on the process of what is going on. What variables make a difference? What kind of people get high ESP scores? And what factors affect ESP scores? One area of interest is the possible role the unconscious mind may play in producing ESP phenomena. The role of unconscious factors was first suggested in experimental studies in which some subjects scored consistently *below* the range to be expected by chance. It was almost as if the subject were uncon-

sciously trying to make errors. Furthermore, attitudes of disbelief in ESP were found to be correlated with such mistakes. If, as this *psi-missing phenomenon* assumes, there are unconscious processes operating in ESP, then one would further assume that evidence of distortion of ESP responses might have meanings similar to those of the familiar Freudian slips of the tongue or to the distortion of waking events so prevalent in dreams.

CRITICS OF ESP RESEARCH

How do explorers first know they have found a new world? Like Columbus, they themselves may be uncertain. So they go to their friends and describe their experiences to them. When their friends say, "Impossible. There is no such place," they know at least that what they have found is new and novel. If they can survive the scorn and disbelief of these friends and persist in exploration and finally make a case with some who are wise, they may begin to breathe easier and feel that their new world is also real.

In the late 1930s, just a few years after Rhine's early studies became widely known, two separate surveys were conducted to see to what extent psychologists were accepting Rhine's findings (Warner and Clark 1938; Crumbaugh 1938). These surveys found ninety-one and ninety-seven percent respectively of the psychologists in their samples were skeptical of ESP research. Fourteen years later Warner (1952) found the skeptic rate had fallen somewhat, but eighty-three percent were still unconvinced of the validity of ESP research.

In the most recent critical review of parapsychology James Crumbaugh (1969) has found that criticisms of parapsychology have tended to focus on one of the following issues:

1. Statistics
2. Experimental controls for sensory clues, recording errors, experimenter influence, and so forth.
3. Experimenter dishonesty

Recent and vivid demonstrations of the way ESP may be influenced by such unconscious processes occurred in the dream laboratory of Montague Uhlman at the Menninger Foundation (Uhlman et al. 1969). Uhlman wanted to see how much the content of a subject's dreams could be influenced by a telepathic message of a target picture. He and his associates, Stanley Krippner and Sol Feldstein, began their work by selecting twelve subjects who appeared promising in that they claimed to be able to fall asleep easily, dream frequently, remember their dreams, and have positive attitudes towards the possibility of telepathy. After a screening experiment the most successful subject (a male psychologist) was asked to pack his toothbrush and security blanket and report to the dream laboratory for seven nights of intensive sleeping. Our hero was not due for uninterrupted sleep, however. Rather, he was connected to a Model D Medcraft EEG machine. Whenever the machine registered REM's (rapid eye movements), he was awakened and asked to describe his dream. Since he was an "average" dreamer, this meant being awakened from four to seven times every night. He was also asked to provide his memories and associations to the night's dreams when he awoke in the morning.

While he dreamed, an experimenter in a room at the other end of the building randomly selected one of several eight-by-five-inch prints of famous paintings. The experimenter spent about a half hour associating to the target and writing down his associations. This procedure was repeated several times during the night. Copies of the seven potential targets were sent to three judges along with the transcripts of the subject's dreams. From the recorded content of the dreams alone they were asked to rank the target pictures from those they were most sure were used as telepathy targets for the evening to those they felt least sure

were targets. Both the judges and the subject himself were able to sort the target pictures with a significant degree of accuracy, suggesting that somehow ESP messages were transmitted from a soundproof room forty feet away to a dreaming subject. They felt the messages entered his consciousness in the form of a dream. Some of the processes involved are suggested in the following examples.

Searching. On the first experimental night, "Bedtime," by Walter Keane, was selected as a target picture. It shows a girl with long dark hair. Her eyes seem to stare out at the viewer. This staring quality became the theme in several of the subject's dreams during the night. He had three dreams in which he was looking for something. When asked to give his associations to the dream the following morning he finally found what he was looking for.

> It is interesting that in each of these dreams I was looking for something. . . . One thing I can remember or recall was of this . . . woman that had long hair, *long black hair* [our italics].

Distorting. One of the basic tenets of psychoanalytic dream theory is that distortions of material will occur to keep the target picture from being represented in the dreamer's consciousness. Perhaps the most striking demonstration of such unconscious phenomena occurred on the night when the Last Supper by Dali was the target. It shows Christ at the center of a table surrounded by his twelve disciples. A glass of wine and a loaf of bread are on the table, while a body of water and a fishing boat can be seen in the distance.

Excerpts from S's first dream. "There was one scene of an ocean. . . . It had a strange beauty about it and a strange formation."

Excerpts from S's second dream. "I haven't any reason

to say this but somehow boats come to mind. Fishing boats. Small-size fishing boats . . . There was a picture in the Sea Fare restaurant that came to mind as I was describing it. It's a very large painting. Enormous. It shows, oh, I'd say about a dozen or so men pulling a fishing boat ashore after having returned from a catch." [Several aspects of the painting seem to be present here: the fishing boats, a large painting, the dozen men, possibly the twelve disciples, and finally the restaurant, which relates to the eating aspects of the painting.]

Excerpts from S's third dream. "I was looking at a catalog . . . a Christmas catalog. Christmas season." [This association of Christ and Christmas comes out more clearly in his associations the following morning.]

Excerpts from S's fourth dream. "I had some sort of a brief dream about an M.D. . . . I was talking to someone and . . . the discussion had to do with why . . . a doctor becomes a doctor because he's supposed to be an M.D., or something of that nature." [Why doctors? Christ is often known as a physician or healer.]

Excerpts from S's fifth dream. "It had to do with doctors again . . . The picture that I'm thinking of now is the doctor sitting beside a child that is ill . . . it's one of those classical ones . . . it's called 'The Physician'."

Excerpts from S's sixth dream. "I was in this office—a doctor's office again. . . . We were talking about Preston. . . . He's a psychiatrist. A supervisor I had. Before he became a psychiatrist, he was a pathologist."

Excerpts from S's associations: "The fisherman dream makes me think of the Mediterranean area, perhaps even some sort of Biblical time. Right now my associations are

of the fish and the loaf, or even the feeding of the multitudes. . . . Once again I think of Christmas. . . . Having to do with the ocean—water, fishermen, something in this area. . . ." [Recall that Christmas had also emerged in the third dream.]

The progression of associations in this material would be fascinating to a psychoanalyst. First come the elements of the picture; in the first dream there is the ocean; in the second we get the fishing boat, the disciples, and the idea of eating; in the third we finally get a rather disguised reference to Christ. Dreams four, five, and six develop a chain of associations possibly relating to the healing aspect of Christ; finally, in seven and eight we get a development of associations to the "supper" or "eating" theme. The associations the next morning get very close to an actual description of the painting with its Mediterranean setting. The notion of Christ feeding the multitudes is interesting in that there was a loaf of bread in the painting. It's almost as though the subject were on the verge of seeing the Last Supper scene but was distracted by the loaf of bread into a different Bible story.

4. Irreproducibility of ESP results
5. Lack of an adequate theory of ESP and incompatability of ESP results with existing scientific theory (paradigm clash)

Statistics and experimental control. Of these criticisms the first two (poor statistics and experimental control) apply largely to early studies in the field. Reviews by Price (1955), Hansel (1966), and Crumbaugh (1969) find little fault with the experimental technique of ESP researchers. Some writers (Schmeidler 1969) have suggested that the technical aspects of ESP research are even more rigorous than in other established fields in psychology.

Dishonesty. Criticisms on the basis of possible trickery or outright faking of results are fairly recent (Price 1955; Hansel 1966). Hansel presents a history of the psychic frauds perpetrated in the nineteenth century and alludes to deceptions by scientists in other fields. For example, the Piltdown skull found in 1912 turned out to be a hoax. Hansel then analyzes several classic studies to show that a possibility of fraud existed. Such analysis could, of course, be applied to almost any study in any field of science. There is always a chance of dishonesty. Both Crumbaugh and Schmeidler answer this charge by noting that it is improbable that so many studies, in so many labs, by so many different investigators could have been faked. Interested readers will find Hansel's critique of one of the studies and Rhine's rebuttals in Schmeidler's *Extrasensory Perception,* chapters one and two.

Replication. ESP experiments are difficult to replicate, or perform again under the same circumstances. Typically, a subject's ESP score drops when he or she is tested on subsequent occasions. No one seems to know what variables produce these drops or how to avoid them. Moreover, since the variables that produce ESP are unknown, experiments that fail may be said to have lacked these conditions and successful experiments to have hit upon them. This explanation is, of course, circular. The variable that is "sometimes present and sometimes absent" might as well be experimental error as ESP factors.

On the other side of the coin, the argument that ESP studies sometimes fail to replicate, like the argument about possible fraud, could be applied to most other fields of endeavor in psychology. As a matter of fact, it has been.

Paradigm clash. So we get to the final argument. This one is the least rational and yet at the same time the most convincing of all four. It has in a sense already been presented in our earlier discussion of the radically new version of reality that parapsychology studies tend to support. Such a view seems to clash strongly with the prevailing scientific view that we are made up of "flesh, bone, and nerve."

In a sense, the same question was posed long before by Coleridge when he said: "What if you slept? And what if in your sleep, you dreamed? And what if in your dream you went to heaven and there plucked a strange and beautiful flower? And what if, when you woke, you had the flower in your hand? Ah! What then?"

Should we accept the evidence of parapsychology at face value, even though it contradicts both the paradigms of science and those of common sense? It has been many years since Warner found eighty-three percent of the psychologists in his sample skeptical of ESP. What do psychologists think today? As always, there is an objective and a subjective point of view. Some psychologists, such as Donald Hebb, are still skeptical despite the empirical evidence:

> Why do we not accept ESP as a psychological fact? Rhine has offered enough evidence to have convinced us on almost any other issue where one could make some guess as to the mechanics of the disputed process. . . . Personally, I do not accept ESP for a moment, because it does not make sense. My external criteria, both of physics and physiology, say that ESP is not a fact despite the behavioral evidence that has been reported. I cannot see what other basis my colleagues have for rejecting it; and if they are using my basis, they and I are allowing psychological evidence to be passed on by physical and psychological censors. Rhine may still turn out to be right, improbable as I think that is, and my own rejection of his views is—in a literal sense—prejudice (Hebb 1951).

Others, like Lawrence LeShan, have argued from the same data base and with equal feeling that we should welcome such data.

> The human race has dreamed. We have dreamed of men like angels, and have awakened with the long, gold-tipped fingers of angel wings in our hands. The impossible facts of ESP are these feathers. They tell us of a part of man, long hidden in the mists of legend, wit, dream, myth, and mysticism, which our explor-

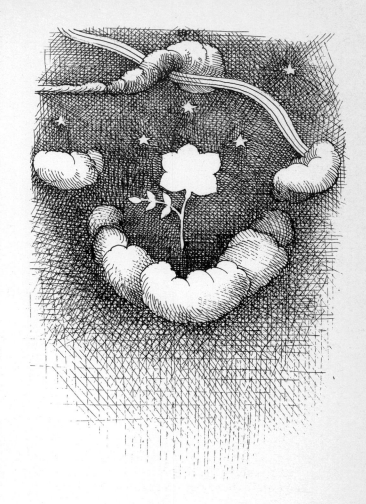

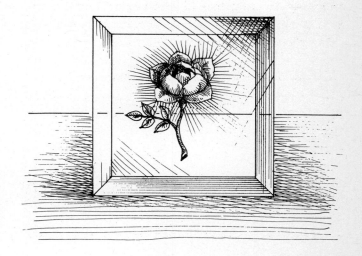

ers of reality in the last ninety years have demonstrated to be scientifically valid, to be real. At the least, we have learned that man is far more than he seems to be, more than the materialist philosopher has ever conceived of, that he can and does touch others and the universe in a way we do not yet understand, but in a way obeying quite different laws than do his senses, that his separation from others and his loneliness in the world are, at least partly, illusion (LeShan 1973).

So it appears that even the objective scientist has a subjective side to his or her personality. And perhaps that is just as well. What do you think about ESP?

Chapter Twelve Summary

The term *frontiers of awareness* is used because we are discussing phenomena that transcend our normal concept of what we are capable of sensing, responding to, or perceiving. One such frontier involves the possibility that we can sense and respond to a far greater variety of stimuli than was formerly considered possible. Such stimuli include our gravitational field, inner biological rhythms, and various forms of radiation.

1.   *Parapsychology* deals with body senses that have yet to be discovered scientifically. Nonetheless, there is a compelling body of anecdotal evidence of what appears to be psychic or psi phenomena. These may be divided roughly into the categories of extrasensory perception (ESP) and psychokinesis (PK).

2.   *Extrasensory perception (ESP)* refers to the process of obtaining information through means other than normal sensory transmission. There are three classes of ESP: 1) clairvoyance, or extrasensory perception of an objective physical event, 2) telepathy, or "mind reading," and 3) precognition, or the ability to predict events before they occur.

3.   *Psychokinesis (PK)* refers to the production of observable changes in the physical world by means other than known energetic influences.

4.   *Psychic detection.* ESP and PK were first studied by a "detective" model of investigation. The essence of this method is to: 1) check the psychic event to see if it actually occurred, 2) check the real-world event to see if it actually occurred in the manner that was reported, 3) search for reliable witnesses, and 4) examine the possibility of coincidence. The major difficulty with such work is that it fails to control important variables and we can never rule out the possibility of coincidence.

5. *Laboratory research.* Early attempts to study ESP in the laboratory focused on the problem of ruling out the possibility of coincidence. Current research tends toward a study of the process itself and factors such as unconscious motivation that influence this process.

6. *Criticisms of psi phenomena.* The concepts of ESP and psychokinesis have yet to receive full acceptance in the scientific community. Most reviews have been highly skeptical. Early criticisms of the statistics and experimental controls in these studies have been answered satisfactorily. More recently, criticisms have tended to focus on the difficulty ESP researchers have in replicating their findings and the possibility of outright dishonesty.

7. *Paradigm clash.* The argument that psi phenomena must be invalid because they conflict with our prevailing assumptions about the nature of reality is referred to here as paradigm clash. This argument cannot be answered by research. It appears that even the objective scientist has a subjective side to his or her personality. And perhaps that is just as well.

Glossary

Astral projection The ability to leave one's body and to travel about, presumably in some spiritual or dematerialized form.

Clairvoyance The perception of an objective external event or object by means of extrasensory perception. The woman who sensed that her house was on fire was used as an example.

Dowser Historically, someone who locates underground water by means of extrasensory perception. However, the studies presented in this chapter suggest that dowsing is not necessarily done by means of ESP but possibly by sensitivity to the earth's gravitational field.

Extrasensory perception (ESP) The process of obtaining information through means other than normal sensory transmission. Clairvoyance, telepathy, and precognition are all forms of extrasensory perception.

Levitation The ability to raise physical objects by means of psychokinesis. The magic carpet is a well-known albeit poorly documented example.

Parapsychology That branch of psychology that studies extrasensory perception, psychokinesis, and occult phenomena in the laboratory.

Poltergeist phenomena Table tapping and other mysterious noisy disturbances. Historically such manifestations have often been explained as actions of a ghost or spirit. An alternative explanation is that such phenomena are dematerialized objects or some new form of energy.

Precognition Extrasensory perception of some objective event before it occurs. The prediction of President Kennedy's assassination by Jeanne Dixon is one well-known example of precognition.

Psi (short for psychic ability) In the laboratory psi refers to a subject's performance in an ESP card-guessing experiment.

Psi-missing phenomenon Referring to instances in which a subject in an ESP experiment performs below chance. Since such a performance cannot be attributed to chance, it may indicate psi ability that is being repressed.

Psychokinesis (PK) The production of observable changes in the physical world by means other than known influences. Levitation, astral projection, and poltergeist phenomena are considered to be the common garden varieties of PK.

Replicate Psychological jargon for the process of doing an experiment over again to see if you can get the same result.

Sensory deprivation experience A situation in which all or most sources of external stimulation are eliminated or greatly reduced. In the laboratory this may be accomplished by techniques such as suspending a subject in a special suit in water to reduce tactile stimulation, using opaque goggles to reduce visual inputs, and using soundproof or padded rooms to reduce auditory inputs.

Structural integration Those therapies and meditation practices that are designed to correct the muscular habits or body defenses that limit our ability to be fully aware. Rolfing and yoga are both structural integration techniques.

Telepathy The ability to read the thoughts of another person by means of extrasensory perception.

You can do the following exercises at your leisure. Perhaps some would be more enjoyable with a friend. Those with an asterisk should be done in consultation with your teacher or in class.

1.   What are your personal beliefs concerning ESP? Poltergeists? Psychokinesis?

2.   How did you develop your beliefs in this area? Did you read about such things? What personal experiences have you had that you feel support your beliefs?

3.   Now consider some other possible origins of your beliefs about psychic experience:

- What did your mother think of psychic experiences?
- What did your father think of them?
- What childhood stories can you recall that involved psychic experience? How did you react to these stories? How did your parents react?
- Overall, what would you say has influenced your beliefs about psychic phenomena the most? Your parents? Personal experience with ESP? Childhood experiences? Scientific studies you have read about?

4.   *ESP — a self-test.* If you are curious about parapsychological phenomena, you may want to try this test for clairvoyance. This is a very simple laboratory procedure similar to the tests Rhine uses in his laboratory. Card-guessing (or ESP) is just one of many possible abilities we might have picked. R. A. McConnell's *ESP Curriculum Guide* outlines other objective procedures for studying abilities in different areas such as ESP picture drawing and psychokinesis.

People who are successful in this experiment are not necessarily mystics. As a matter of fact, repeated successes very often occur in people who have had no previous indication of psychic or paranormal capabilities. Card-guessing is one specific ability and is not necessarily predictive of having spontaneous psychic experiences.

Directions. The experiment requires at least two participants, one of whom will take the role of experimenter and one (or more) to assume the role of subject. When two people do the experiment and both wish to test their abilities, they simply repeat the experiment but reverse the roles so that the experimenter in the first test becomes the subject in the second test.

The experimenter (that's you) begins by taking an ordinary deck of playing cards and removing all the kings, queens, and jacks, leaving a forty-card deck. Shuffle the cards (preferably in another room) and place each in an opaque envelope with the flaps either tucked in or sealed to prevent accidental identification. After the envelopes are filled they should also be shuffled. Since envelopes may have visible differences that could provide visual clues, it is desirable when possible to have this portion of the experiment done by a third party in your absence.

Directions to Subject. Your subject(s) should be informed that successful results are often obtained in this procedure by people who have not previously exhibited evidence of psychic abilities. Best results are obtained when subjects are relaxed, motivated, highly interested in the task, and believe in the possibility of ESP.

Procedure. Show the forty target envelopes to your subject one at a time. Ask the subject to guess whether the card is a club, a diamond, a spade, or a heart. Use a recording form such as that shown in figure 12-2 to record each guess. Place each used envelope in a second pile in a box that will prevent them from sliding out of order. In order to keep your subject's attention, it is advisable to rest after every ten trials. At the end of forty trials, open the envelopes and record the actual suit for each trial. Circle the squares where the subject's checkmark is in the same square as the colored check; total these circled squares (hits) to yield a raw ESP score as shown in figure 12-2.

Interpretation. To give you an indication of how well your subject did, .05 (five chances out of a hundred) is the figure of significance that most experimental psychologists require of their data. Thus an experimental psychologist would be impressed by scores above fourteen hits (or below six) and skeptical of scores between six and fourteen.

Should you become interested in ESP testing and want to learn about alternative tests and ways of increasing the precision of your testing procedures, we recommend the appendixes of R. A. McConnell's *ESP Curriculum Guide* or Rhine and Pratt's *Parapsychology: Frontier Science of the Mind.* Some possible interpretations of your subject's scores are described in table 12.1.

TABLE 12.1

ESP Scores and Some Possible Interpretations

ESP Score	Interpretation
19 or above	*Very high.* Scores above nineteen could be obtained by guessing less than once in a thousand experiments. So something else must have occurred. Did your subject cheat? Did you help him or her beat the odds? Was your envelope really opaque? Or do you have a mystic on your hands?
14 to 18	*High.* Scores in this range occur less than five times out of a hundred experiments. Probably your subject did something besides just guessing. Was it ESP?
7 to 13	*Chance.* Scores in this area are fairly easy to get simply by guessing. It is unlikely that ESP is occurring.
3 to 6	*Low.* Since scores in this area are just as unlikely to occur by chance as are those from fourteen to eighteen, something was probably happening other than just guessing. Perhaps you have a psi-missing effect. Again the possibility of your subject's cheating or your providing hints must be considered.
2 or below	*Very Low.* Such scores only occur once in a thousand experiments. You may have a medium who wants to hide his or her light under a bushel. (Check the subject's name. It may be Clark Kent. If so, you win a year's paid vacation on the planet Krypton. At Bob Wrenn's expense, naturally.)

Trial	Actual Suit	Guess	Trial	Actual Suit	Guess
1	H (Heart)	S	21	C	C
2	H	S	22	S	S
3	C (Club)	C	23	C	D
4	S (Spade)	H	24	D	H
5	H	H	25	C	H
6	D (Diamond)	S	26	D	C
7	S	D	27	S	H
8	D	S	28	D	C
9	H	H	29	C	D
10	H	H	30	D	H
11	D	H	31	H	H
12	D	D	32	S	C
13	C	D	33	S	C
14	S	H	34	H	D
15	D	H	35	D	H
16	S	H	36	H	S
17	H	S	37	H	D
18	S	D	38	C	C
19	S	H	39	C	C
20	C	S	40	C	C

Raw ESP score (Total hits) = 11

FIG. 12-2 *Sample ESP score sheet*

Bibliography

Crumbaugh, J. 1938. A questionnaire designed to determine the attitudes of psychologists toward the field of extrasensory perception. *Journal of Parapsychology* 2:302–07.

———. 1969. A scientific critique of parapsychology. In Schmeidler, G., *Extrasensory perception*. New York: Atherton 58–72.

Fahler, J. and Osis, K. 1969. Checking for awareness in a precognition experiment with hypnotized subjects. In Schmeidler, G., *Extrasensory perception*. New York: Atherton.

Gamon, G. and Yeas, M. 1967. *Mr. Tompkins inside himself: adventures in the new biology*. New York: Viking.

Hansel, C. 1966. *ESP: A scientific evaluation*. New York: Scribners.

Hebb, D. 1951. The role of neurological ideas in psychology. *Journal of Personality* 20:39–50.

LeShan, L. 1973. What is important about the paranormal? In Ornstein, R., *The nature of human consciousness*. San Francisco: Freeman.

Lilly, J. 1969. *Man and dolphin*. New York: Pyramid.

———. 1972. *The center of the cyclone*. New York: Julian Press.

Luce, G. 1973. Biological rhythms. In Ornstein, R., *The nature of human consciousness*. San Francisco: Freeman.

McConnell, R. 1970 *ESP curriculum guide*. New York: Simon & Schuster.

Murphy, G. 1961. *Challenge of psychical research*. New York: Harper.

Uhlman, M., Krippner, S. and Feldman, S. 1969. Experimentally-induced telepathy dreams: Two studies using EEG-REM monitoring techniques. In Schmeidler, G., *Extrasensory perception*. New York: Atherton. 137–61.

Price, G. 1955. Science and the supernatural. *Science* 122:359–67.

Rhine, J. 1953. *New world of the mind*. New York: William Sloan Associates.

———, and Pratt, J. 1957. *Parapsychology: frontier science of the mind*. Springfield, Ill.: Thomas.

Rolf, I. 1963. Structural integration: gravity, an unexplored factor in a more human use of human beings. *Systematics* (June).

Schmeidler, G. 1969. *Extrasensory perception*. New York: Atherton.

Shah, I. 1964. *The Sufis*. New York: Doubleday.

Sobel, D. 1973. Gravity and structural integration. In Ornstein, R., *The nature of human consciousness*. San Francisco: Freeman.

Warner, L. 1952. A second survey of psychological opinion on ESP. *Journal of Parapsychology* 16:284–95.

——— and Clark, C. 1938. A survey of psychological opinion on ESP. *Journal of Parapsychology* 16:284–95.

Glossary

Acid trip A state usually involving hallucinations that occurs after taking a consciousness-expanding drug such as LSD.

Active listening Behaviors that convey to another person that he or she has one's undivided attention.

Acute schizophrenia A form of personality disorder characterized by an extreme, very exaggerated loss of contact with reality. The onset is very sudden and is usually associated with a traumatic event. Recovery is likewise often fairly rapid.

Adaptation An adjustment to the conditions of one's environment.

Adapted child That part of the natural Child ego state that has been altered by parental demands and expectations.

Adult The ego state with which one reasons, evaluates situations, and reaches decisions based on present sense data.

Affiliate To depend on others; to form friendships.

Aggression Hostile behavior caused by fear or anger.

Alpha rhythm A pattern of electrical activity in the brain that occurs during meditation and other relaxed waking states.

Altruism Regard for the interests of others.

Ambivalence Simultaneous liking and disliking of an object, idea, or person.

Amnesia Loss of memory.

Anal stage According to Freud, the second stage of personality development, when a child's erotic feelings are focused on elimination.

Anima The feminine personality aspect in men.

Animism Attributing life to inanimate objects or forces.

Animus The masculine personality aspect in women.

Anthropomorphizing Reading human motivations into the actions of nonhumans.

Anxiety A generalized feeling of uneasiness, worry, and concern. Anxiety symptoms include the inability to focus on one thing at a time, the tendency to worry needlessly about the past or future, and physical tension.

Apparition A ghostly figure or unusual sight.

A priori Referring to conclusions drawn from principles regarded as self-evident and assumed to be true.

Archeology The study of material evidence remaining from life and culture in past ages.

Archetype According to Jung, a form carried in the collective unconscious of the human race.

Asana A special posture used in meditation to teach concentration and to induce a particular state of consciousness.

Astrology The study of the positions and aspects of heavenly bodies in order to predict their influence on the course of human affairs.

Astral projection The ability to leave one's body and to travel about, presumably in some spiritual or dematerialized form.

Atheist One who does not believe in God.

Attitude A belief or feeling that causes a certain response to a given object, event, or situation.

Autonomy A feeling of confidence in one's own powers; independence.

Base line A procedure in which the frequency of one's activities is plotted for a period of time as a reference to compare with whatever changes in behavior one plans to undergo.

Behaviorism The school of psychology that limits itself to the study of observable activities or behaviors.

Behavior modification The applied therapies that derive from behaviorism.

Behavior therapy or counseling A form of professional help in which the focus is on developing an awareness of the environmental contingencies that control the client's behavior. Problems are solved by changing the reinforcers that are controlling the behavior.

Belief An inner conviction of the truth of something.

Biofeedback training Training a subject to control some autonomic function such as heart rate, or alpha rhythm by providing electronic feedback whenever the subject achieves the desired response.

Brainwashing A series of procedures designed to restructure a person's system of beliefs.

Child The ego state that contains recordings of all the internal events (feelings, concepts, etc.) that one experienced as a child.

Clairvoyance The perception of an objective external event or object by means of extrasensory perception.

Claustrophobia Fear of enclosed spaces.

Clinical psychology The branch of psychology concerned with therapy and research in the areas of psychological problems.

Cognitive Referring to the process by which one becomes aware or obtains knowledge of an object, event, or situation.

Cognitive dissonance The disagreement of one's beliefs with each other or with one's behavioral tendencies.

Competence The ability to do something well.

Compulsion An irresistible impulse to commit a repetitive act.

Conditioning Learning a specific response to a stimulus.

Conflict The state caused by two simultaneous incompatible desires.

Conformity Behaving in accordance with a set of standards.

Contingencies Events that may occur but are not necessarily expected.

Control group A group of subjects under the same conditions as the experimental group except for one variable.

Correlation The degree of relationships between two variables.

Cortex The outer layer of the brain that handles functions such as thinking, analyzing, and organizing perception.

Counseling A form of short-term psychological help for personal and emotional problems such as career planning, marital problems, or life crises.

Cryogeny The practice of body freezing soon after death.

Cynicism The tendency to react skeptically to whatever occurs.

Defense An adjustment made, often unconsciously, to escape recognitions that would lower self-esteem or heighten anxiety.

Delusion A belief that is not shared by most people.

Denial Self-deception about true motives or the real state of affairs.

Dependent variable The behavior or effect one is looking for in an experiment; the variable that changes when the independent variable changes.

Depression A sad, pessimistic, futile state.

Deviant Someone who is different from others in a socially significant manner.

Displacement A defense mechanism in which one redirects his emotions or actions toward another target.

Developmental psychology The branch of psychology that is concerned with changes in a person that take place over time.

DNA (Deoxyribonucleic acid) A chemical found in the genes that probably contains instructions for the development of the organism.

Doublethink A symptom of anxiety characterized by an inability to focus or concentrate on one task at a time.

Dowser Historically, someone who locates underground water by means of extrasensory perception. A more modern interpretation suggests that the dowser utilizes an extreme sensitivity to the earth's magnetic field rather than ESP.

Drive An instinctual physiological need, such as thirst.

Dyad A two-person group.

Dynamic psychology Those forms of counseling and psychotherapy that emphasize the importance of developing an understanding of one's inner, deeper personality conflicts. Motivation and early childhood experiences are important units of analysis in such approaches.

Ego In Freud's theory, the part of the personality that corresponds most closely to the perceived self and that has direct access to external reality; that part of the mind that is in contact with the world by means of perception, thinking, and logic. The ego must mediate between the demands of the id and the prohibitions of the superego.

Ego strengthening A special hypnotic suggestion technique designed to encourage feelings of calmness, confidence, and inner strength.

Electroencephalogram (EEG) The recorded pattern of electrical activity in the brain.

Encounter group A special group led by a professional that emphasizes interpersonal communication and awareness.

Empathy Understanding another's feelings.

Empirical Relying upon observation or experiment.

Ethnology The study of biology as it relates to behavior, particularly in relation to how humans and animals evolve and survive.

Eugenics The study of ways we can improve the hereditary qualities of the human race through genetics.

Euthanasia Inducing the death of a person for reasons assumed to be merciful.

Existentialist Referring to the belief that the meaning of the universe is contained within one's own existence and experience.

Experimental psychology The branch of psychology that studies behavior by means of experiments.

Explosive stage According to Perls, the final stage of change. It is an explosion into awareness accompanied by a greater sense of power over one's own life.

Extended family A group of people who live together even though they may not be related.

Extrasensory perception (ESP) The process of obtaining information by means other than normal sensory transmission.

Factor analysis A statistical method for computing the minimum number of factors required to account for the intercorrelations among test scores.

Faith Belief in something that can not be proven empirically.

Feedback External information that tells us how others see our actions or perceptions.

Functionalism A school of psychological thought that emphasizes the usefulness of mental activities and studies the purposes of behavior.

Generalization Applying responses learned to one stimulus to other similar situations.

Gestalt therapy A form of therapy in which the goal is to become as aware as possible of how one is feeling at any given moment. Personal problems are assumed to stem from a lack of awareness.

Group therapy A form of therapy in which the actions of a group cause self-awareness or changes in behavior among its members.

Guilt A feeling of responsibilty or remorse for some offense.

Hallucination A visual experience that has no appropriate external stimulus.

Hallucinogenic Able to produce hallucinations.

Help The ability to convey a feeling of being deeply understood and accepted while simultaneously challenging another person to grow to his or her fullest capacity.

Hot seat The special chair reserved for the member of a gestalt group who volunteers to work with the therapist.

Humanistic psychology A school of psychology that regards people as basically "good" and attempts to deal with the whole person, not just with one's symptoms.

Hypnagogic state The trance-like state between being awake and being asleep.

Hypnosis A series of suggestion and concentration techniques that may be used to allow an individual to relax, ignore pain, or to produce some other behavior that conditioning has led the subject to believe is impossible.

Id According to Freud, our deepest instinctual impulses that are out of contact with the conscious mind and the external world.

Identification Becoming so allied with someone (or something) else that one is unaware that he or she is like the other person (or thing).

Identity A sense of harmony between one's self, one's significant others, and one's social roles.

Identity shock The temporary loss of a sense of who one is caused by some dramatic change in one's interpersonal environment.

Identity type One of three orientations towards personal growth: psychic foreclosure, situational foreclosure, and moratorium.

Illusion A misinterpretation of the relations among stimuli so that what is perceived does not correspond to physical reality.

Implosive stage The second stage of growth in Perls' system. At this stage, one becomes consciously aware of being dissatisfied with some aspect of one's life but still feels powerless to change it. The feelings that commonly occur at this stage are anxiety and depression.

Independent variable The treatment or manipulation made by the experimenter in an experiment.

Internalization Making an external attitude or belief part of one's own set of attitudes and beliefs.

Insight The sudden intuitive grasp of a situation.

Intellectualization A mechanism in which thinking is used as a way of avoiding feelings.

Intuitive Referring to immediate knowing without the use of rational processes.

Koan A special kind of riddle that is used as an object of meditation in Zen. Koans are absolutely insolvable by logic and can be penetrated only by intuition.

Letting be A state of consciousness related to creative thinking and characterized by physical relaxation and giving up logical or conscious problem solving.

Levitation The ability to raise physical objects by means of psychokinesis.

Loser script The kind of unconscious life plan that leads to continued failure.

Love That human condition that exists when the satisfaction or security of another person becomes as significant to one as one's own satisfaction or security.

LSD Lyseric acid diethylamide, a synthetic hallucenogenic drug.

Male chauvinist A man who believes men are superior to women.

Mandala A circular symbol of the universe; often used as an object of concentration.

Mantra A special word that is used as an object of concentration in meditation.

Meditation A group of procedures that helps one turn off the external world and focus on some one of a number of inner experiences; a series of techniques originally developed in Eastern psychology to teach the ability to concentrate and to achieve an altered state of consciousness.

Megalomania An exaggerated notion of how important one is.

Mental illness Those instances of extreme and prolonged emotional discomfort or gross distortion of reality where there is a likely organic cause such as a brain lesion, tumor, infection, or chemical imbalance.

M.M.P.I. The Minnesota Multiphasic Personality Inventory, a diagnostic test of personality disorders.

Model A person whom one copies, consciously or unconsciously.

Moratorium student One who has an orientation that emphasizes personal growth and self-exploration.

Motive A need or desire that causes a person to act.

Mudra A special gesture used in some types of meditation.

Natural child That part of the Child ego state that is the affectionate, curious, self-centered, expressive infant in each of us.

Negative reinforcement The practice of reducing an unpleasant stimulus as one learns.

Neurosis The psychiatric label for those psychological disorders in which one becomes overly defensive to the point that he or she makes poor adaptations to the environment.

Neurotic A form of maladjustment in which one is so self-preoccupied that he or she cannot cope with anxieties and conflicts and develops abnormal symptoms and defenses.

Norm The standard by which a variable is measured.

Nurturant Parent ego state Those Parent tapes that convey support, concern, or overprotectiveness to others.

Oedipal The Freudian term for the phallic stage in which a child is attracted to the parent of the opposite sex.

Opinion A judgment involving an expectation or prediction about behavior or events.

Paradigm The set of assumptions and theories of a body of knowledge at any one point in history.

Paradox A seemingly contradictory statement that may be nonetheless true.

Paradoxical sleep Deep sleep; also known as REM sleep.

Parapsychology The branch of psychology that studies extrasensory perception, psychokinesis, and occult phenomena in the laboratory.

Parent ego state The set of recorded messages sent to us by our parents or parent figures.

Peer group Those who one feels an equal with; one's friends and acquaintances.

Penis envy According to Freud, the female's desire to have a penis.

Perception Awareness of one's inner and outer environments through the interpretation of sensory data.

Personality The individual characteristics that account for an individual behaving and believing as he or she does.

Personologist Someone who studies human personality.

Phenomenon Anything that can be sensed.

Phenomenologist Someone who believes that behavior is determined by the world-as-we-see-it, not the world-as-it-is.

Poltergeist phenomenon Table tapping and other mysterious noisey disturbances. Historically such manifestations have often been explained as actions of a ghost or spirit. An alternative explanation is that such phenomena are the effects of some undiscovered form of energy.

Polygamy The practice of having more than one wife or husband at a time.

Positive reinforcement Rewarding a correct action or response.

Precognition Extrasensory perception of some objective event before it occurs.

Prejudice An attitude or belief based on stereotypes and a lack of real experience.

Prejudiced Parent ego state Those Parent tapes containing value judgments that were introjected from others and have no basis in one's own direct experiences.

Prelogical reasoning Piaget's term for the irrational associations in conceptual thought that are observed in children.

Preparation The aspect of transcendent experiencing in which one gets ready to transcend by mastering relevant basic skills.

Projection Attributing one's own needs or emotions to someone else.

Proxemics The study of space and its effect on behavior.

Psi Short for psychic ability. In laboratory work psi refers specifically to the subject's performance on an **ESP** card-guessing experiment.

Psi-missing phenomenon Referring to instances in which a subject in an **ESP** experiment consistently performs below chance.

Psychically foreclosed The identity type of an individual whose personal dynamics center around avoiding new challenges and hence avoiding change.

Psychiatrist An M.D. with specialized training in mental disturbances.

Psychoanalysis The method developed by Freud for treating neuroses based on determining unconscious motives.

Psychokinesis The production of observable changes in the physical world by means other than known influences.

Psychology The science of behavior.

Psychological defense A series of mechanisms one uses to avoid being unduly threatened and overwhelmed by life experiences.

Psychological game A transaction with an ulterior motive.

Psychosis A severe mental disorder.

Psychosocial stages According to Erikson, the eight stages of personality development from basic trust or distrust (infancy) to integrity or despair (old age).

Quadraplegic A person whose arms and legs are paralyzed.

Rationalization A defense mechanism in which behavior is explained by giving reasons for it.

Reaction formation A defense mechanism in which one acts in a way opposite to his unconscious desire.

Realism Making judgments on the basis of what most people feel to be true.

Reflex An involuntary response to a stimulus.

Regret and rehearsal The symptom of anxiety that involves an inability to focus on the present, to regret the past, and to worry excessively about the future.

Reincarnation To be reborn in another body.

Reinforcing event (reinforcer) Any external contingency that increases the probability of a particular behavior.

REM Rapid eye movement, characteristic of the dreaming state.

Replicate Psychological jargon for the process of doing an experiment over again to see if one gets the same result.

Repression A defense mechanism in which traumatic thoughts are forced out of one's consciousness.

Reticular system A structure in the brainstem that monitors what a person notices or pays attention to.

RNA Ribonucleic acid, a chemical that probably contains instructions for the development of the organism.

Role A pattern of behavior that is expected by ourselves and others in our interpersonal environment.

Rorschach test A personality test that uses abstract inkblots as stimuli for free association.

Sample A representative subgroup chosen from a larger group.

Scapegoat Someone who is a target for hostility unwarranted by his or her behavior.

Schizoid Referring to someone

who relates in an ineffective way to other people and therefore appears strange.

Schizophrenia Any of a group of psychotic reactions characterized by withdrawal from reality.

Script The life play or drama that one "writes" (often at an unconscious level) and lives out.

Secondary reinforcement Rewards or punishments that mediate behavior but do not depend on a physiological response.

Semantics The study of the meanings of words and language.

Sensorimotor Any hook-up between your senses and another functioning part of your body.

Self-actualization Living creatively in such a way that one uses all of one's own unique potentials.

Self-control training A procedure in which the behavior therapist teaches a client the principles of behavior modification and the client then applies them to control his or her own behavior.

Sensory deprivation experiment A situation in which all or most sources of external stimulation are eliminated or greatly reduced. In the laboratory this may be accomplished by suspending the subject in a tank of water or putting the subject in a sound-absorbing room.

Shaping The process of maintaining a certain type of behavior by rewarding behaviors that resemble it.

Situationally foreclosed The identity type of the individual who is unable to fully respond to new situations because of a lack of relevant experiences.

Social psychologist A psychologist who studies how individuals may be influenced by the groups they belong to.

Sterotype A preconceived idea based on a generalization.

Stimulus control A technique for changing behavior by carefully arranging environmental stimuli that support or reinforce a desired behavior.

Stooge In social psychology, someone who agrees to help the experimenter by pretending to be or feel something that he or she is not.

Structural integration Rolf's term for those therapies and meditation practices designed to correct the muscular habits or body defenses that limit one's ability to be fully aware.

Superego The set of attitudes, values, and morals that we have incorporated from our parents and society; in Freud's theory, that part of the personality that most nearly corresponds to the conscience.

Symptom exaggeration A gestalt technique in which the client is asked to exaggerate a behavior or symptom such as stuttering, nervously tapping a foot, and so forth.

T.A.T. The Thematic Apperception Test, a projective test of personality developed by Henry Murray.

Taxonomy A system for classifying objects or events.

Teleology Referring to the belief that one's thoughts, plans, and expectations can influence one's future behavior, regardless of what sort of history one has achieved.

Telepathy The ability to read the thoughts of another person by means of extrasensory perception.

Territorial niche The physical area one believes is one's own.

Thanatology The study of death.

Topdog-underdog In gestalt terms, the polarity in one's personality between the bully and the weakling.

Transactional analysis A system of psychotherapy that helps one understand one's personality by analyzing and interpreting the transactions between oneself and others.

Transcendental meditation A special westernized version of meditation that uses a mantra as an object of concentration.

Transcendent behavior Experiences in which people go beyond their own conception of what they are capable of.

Winner script The kind of life plan (outlook) that results in frequent success and an ability to bounce back after failure.

Yoga A discipline or system of exercises aimed at training the person for spiritual insight and at promoting control of body and mind. While most westerners tend to associate the term *yoga* with those forms of meditation where special postures such as the headstand are used, the term is really so broad as to defy definition.

Zen An Eastern school of thought that asserts that enlightenment can be attained through meditation, self-contemplation, and intuition.

Index

Human potential movement, 18
Hunter, E., 62
Huxley, A., 293
Hypnosis, 11, 265–70, 279, 281;
  exercises for, 266, 270

Ianni, F., 142, 165
Id, 12, 34, 49
Identification, 12 (*See also* Defenses,
  mechanisms of)
Identity, 39–45; shock, 39
Identity types, 41–43; moratorium,
  43; psychically foreclosed, 41,
  42, 50; situationally foreclosed,
  42, 43, 50
Ik, 167
Illusions, 6, 7, 8
Impasse, 96
Impunitive, 188
Independent variable, 162
Indians: Hopi, 123; Sioux, 243, 251;
Inferiority, 13
Input, 5, 6
Insight, 14
Internalization, 60
Intro-punitive, 188
Introspection, 14
Isolation, 114

Jackson, D., 128, 139
James, M., 34, 53, 58, 60, 61, 72, 81
James, W., 14, 85, 150, 165, 245, 293
Johnson, R., 167
Jongeward, D., 34, 53
Jourard, S., 18, 27, 86, 91, 92, 105
Journal, personal, 52
Jung, C., 11, 13, 196, 217, 226, 250

Kagan, J., 20, 21, 27, 186, 208
Kamiya, J., 277, 285
Kasamatsu, A., 277, 285
Kastenbaum, R., 203, 208
Kaufmann, W., 156, 165
Kavanaugh, R., 118, 139
Keen, S., 274, 285
Kempe, C., 188, 208
Kessler study, 131
Kiester study, 57
Kinkade, K., 16, 27, 176, 183
Kinsey, A., 186, 246, 261
Klein, D., 147, 165
Kleitman, N., 248–50, 261
Knowlis, P., 277, 285
Koan, 101

Koch, H., 190, 208
Koestler, A., 96, 105
Koffka, K., 10
Kohler, W., 10
Kookiness, 65, 66
Krapelin, E., 217
Krupp, G., 201, 208

Labeling, 56, 58
La Rochefoucauld, 111
Lassen, C., 170, 183
Latency stage, 12
Leakey, L., 169, 183
Leary, T., 275
Lecron, L., 270, 285
LeShan, L., 299, 302, 311
Levitation, 305
Lewis, H., 18, 27
Life Change Units Scale, 125, 126
Life styles, alternative, 199, 200
Life, to extend, 134
Lifton, R., 125, 126, 139
Lilly, J., 289, 311
Lincoln, A., 85, 97
Lindzey, G., 10
Lipe, D., 172, 183
Listening, active, 73, 77
Loewi, O., 254, 255
London, P., 16, 27
Longfellow, H. W., 85
Loneliness, 196–98
Lorenz, K., 169
Love, 12, 92, 167, 168, 185, 193
LSD therapy, 132, 133, 136 (*See
  also* Drugs)
Luce, G., 288, 290–292, 311

MacPherson, H., 150, 165
Maddi, S., 18, 27
Madison, P., 37, 38, 53
Mahl, G., 157, 165
Male, growing up, 175
Maltz, M., 86, 105
Mantras, 264, 271, 281
Markson, E., 131, 139
Marquis, D., 141
Marriage, 71, 198–202; open and
  closed, 191
Masculine, 8, 14
Maslow, A., 11, 17, 27, 84, 85, 88, 90,
  96, 97, 105, 177, 183, 185, 191, 208
Masters-Johnson, 186
Masturbation, 12

May, R., 11, 213, 217
McConnell, R., 311
McCormick, P., 35, 53
McDaniel study, 59
Meaning, 5
Meditation, 271–76, 279, 281 (*See
  also* Transcendental meditation)
Meehl, P., 146, 165
Melendy, M., 11
Mencke, R., 19
Mencken, H., 203
Mental illness, 56, 57, 59, 237
Milgram, S., 56, 67, 81, 173, 183,
  189, 200, 268, 269, 285
Milne, A. A., 5, 27, 187
Modeling, 60, 160, 188
Mondale, W., 189
Morris, J., 145, 165
Motives, 39, 40
Moyer, K. E., 169, 183
Mudras, 164, 281
Muir, J., 85
Muchison, C., 10, 27
Murphy, G., 9, 27, 244, 261, 295,
  296, 311
Murray, H., 10, 27

Nadelson, C., 177
Nagel, S., 176, 183
Nagy, M., 123, 139
Nature, 8
Need hierarchy, 17
Neihardt, J., 243, 261
Neugarten, B., 131, 139, 204, 208
Neurosis, 11, 24, 101
Newton, N., 176, 183
Nightmares, 247, 248
Normative, descriptive, 10, 18,
  23, 186
Noyes, R., 127

Obedience, 67
Objectivity, 8, 9, 15, 19, 56, 268, 269
Oedipal stage, 12, 24
Old age, 130, 131, 203, 204
O'Neill, N., 191, 198, 208
Openness, 41–43
Opinion, 141
Oral stage, 12
Orgler, H., 13, 27

Pain, 55
Paradigm clash, 298, 304

Bob Wrenn and Reed Mencke's *Being* was
designed by James Stockton. The cover and
part openers were done by Pat Maloney.
Sheila Sullivan illustrated chapters 1, 2, 3, 4,
and 6; chapters 5, 7, 8, 10, 11, and 12 were
illustrated by Heather Preston Kortebein.
Barbara Hack executed the technical
illustrations. The book was set in Linofilm
by Applied Typographic Systems of
Mountain View, California. The text itself is
composed of a mixture of typefaces:
Bookman, an antique style with strong serifs,
forms the body of the text; Plantin, a revival
of a sixteenth-century type face, and
Palatino, a modern calligraphy-based face,
compose the heads. Case studies are
displayed in Helvetica, a modern sans serif
face. *Being* was printed and bound by
The George Banta Company, Menasha, Wisconsin.
Sponsoring editor: Karl Schmidt
Project editor: Kay Nerode